AF605902

CARTOGRAPHIES OF DISAPPEARANCE: VESTIGES OF EVERYDAY LIFE IN LITERATURE

ENRIC BOU

Cartographies of Disappearance

Vestiges of Everyday Life in Literature

UNIVERSITY OF TORONTO PRESS
Toronto Buffalo London

Toronto Buffalo London
utorontopress.com

ISBN 978-1-4875-5467-5 (cloth) ISBN 978-1-4875-5469-9 (EPUB)
ISBN 978-1-4875-5468-2 (PDF)

Toronto Iberic

Library and Archives Canada Cataloguing in Publication

Title: Cartographies of disappearance : vestiges of everyday life in literature / Enric Bou.
Names: Bou, Enric, author.
Series: Toronto Iberic.
Description: Series statement: Toronto Iberic | Includes bibliographical references and index.
Identifiers: Canadiana (print) 20240365925 | Canadiana (ebook) 2024036600X | ISBN 9781487554675 (cloth) | ISBN 9781487554682 (PDF) | ISBN 9781487554699 (EPUB)
Subjects: LCSH: Spanish literature – 20th century – History and criticism. | LCSH: Realism in literature. | LCSH: Spain – In literature. | LCSH: Spain – In art. | LCSH: Spain – Social life and customs.
Classification: LCC PQ6073.R4 B68 2024 | DDC 860.9/006–dc23

Cover design: Gareth Lind
Cover images: iStock.com/GaudiLab; courtesy of the author

An earlier version of this book was published by Edicions de la Universitat de Barcelona in 2023.

We wish to acknowledge the land on which the University of Toronto Press operates. This land is the traditional territory of the Wendat, the Anishnaabeg, the Haudenosaunee, the Métis, and the Mississaugas of the Credit First Nation.

University of Toronto Press acknowledges the financial support of the Government of Canada, the Canada Council for the Arts, and the Ontario Arts Council, an agency of the Government of Ontario, for its publishing activities.

Conseil des Arts
du Canada

Funded by the Government of Canada | Financé par le gouvernement du Canada | Canada

E o esplendor dos mapas, caminho abstracto para a imaginação concreta,
Letras e riscos irregulares abrindo para a maravilha.

Alvaro de Campos

Reality? It is the toothbrush waiting at home for you in its glass, a bus ticket, a pay-check and the grave.

Orson Welles, *F for Fake*

Au théâtre du quotidien les stars sont: le pain, le lait, la quincaille, la viande, le linge blanc, l'heure juste, le cheveu court et toujours l'accordéon.

Agnès Varda, *Daguerréotypes*

Ce qui se passe chaque jour et qui revient chaque jour, le banal, le quotidien, l'évident, le commun, l'ordinaire, l'infra-ordinaire, le bruit de fond, l'habituel, comment en rendre compte, comment l'interroger, comment le décrire?

Georges Perec

Contents

Illustrations

Preface: Uncovering the Potential of Banality

According to the *Cambridge Dictionary*, *banality* is "the quality of being boring, ordinary, and not original." Gregory Seigworth would add that banality "is temporal succession tipped on its side: making way for the simultaneous and the subjacent." Similarly, "banality is spatiality arranged (perhaps deranged) in a manner that allows for a plurality of spaces to inhabit any single space" (234). This book addresses the representation of everyday life from a very different perspective than that of the Spanish authors quoted at the beginning. The focus is on literary texts and artistic forms that help uncover the potential of banality, one of the key aspects of the everyday. Lefebvre proposed in 1987:

> In modern life, the repetitive gestures tend to mask and crush the cycles. The everyday imposes its monotony. It is the invariable constant of the variations it envelops. The days follow one after another and resemble one another, and yet – here lies the contradiction at the heart of everydayness – everything changes. But the change is programmed: obsolescence is planned. Production anticipates reproduction; production produces change in such a way as to superimpose the impression of speed onto that monotony. Some people cry out against the acceleration of time, others cry out against stagnation. They're both right. ("The Everyday and Everydayness" 10)

The everyday is a matter of study and observation, particularly from a social sciences perspective, but much less so from the humanities perspective. Other observers have expressed complementary definitions as expressed in the epigraphs of this book. Orson Welles said that reality is "the toothbrush waiting at home for you in its glass, a bus ticket, a paycheck and the grave" (Welles). Agnès Varda in *Daguerréotypes* spoke of the everyday as a theatre: "Au théâtre du quotidien les stars sont:

le pain, le lait, la quincaille, la viande, le linge blanc, l'heure juste, le cheveu court et toujours l'accordéon" (In the theatre of everyday life, the stars are: bread, milk, hardware, meat, white linen, the right hour, short hair and always the accordion).[1] And Georges Perec was puzzled about how to find words to explain what we see: "Ce qui se passe chaque jour et qui revient chaque jour, le banal, le quotidien, l'évident, le commun, l'ordinaire, l'infra-ordinaire, le bruit de fond, l'habituel, comment en rendre compte, comment l'interroger, comment le décrire?" (*L'infra-ordinaire* 7; What happens every day and what comes back every day, the banal, the everyday, the obvious, the common, the ordinary, the infra-ordinary, the background noise, the habitual, how do we account for it, how do we question it, how do we describe it?) The novelty of my approach is to explore four major instances of representing the everyday in literature and the arts: routines and disappearances (chapters 1 and 2), observations of the nearby (chapters 3 and 4), the uses of public transportation (chapters 5 and 6), thanatourism (chapter 7), and food (chapters 8 and 9). Thus, the chapters in the book address instances of banality and its potential for generating alternative meaning.

In the first chapter, "Defying or Defining the Everyday: Poetics of Everyday Life," I start with an overview about the search for happiness and its centrality in everyday life. This is followed by a thorough examination of different views into the study of the everyday. Drawing on the work of theorists such as Ben Highmore and Michael Sheringham, which in turn explored the work of Henri Lefebvre, Michel de Certeau, Marc Augé, and Siegfried Kracauer, among others, I discuss the studies and concepts that have been useful to construct the study of the everyday mostly from a sociological perspective. I also introduce the notion of alternative cartography. Maps have a significant political, social, and historical value. Digital mapping allows for interaction and rewriting and goes beyond the flaws of Google maps and other such initiatives and helps us – users, readers – to look at the world from a different perspective.

Chapter 2, "Singing the Everyday, Signing or Signalling the World: On Catalogic Poems," starts with an examination of the presence of lists in our everyday, inspired by Umberto Eco's distinction between the "poetics of everything included" and the "poetics of the etcetera" (7). Similar to Proust's use of enumeration to establish relationships and divisions that also have a therapeutic function, this chapter focuses on, among other examples, three poems: Jacques Prévert's "Tentative de description d'un dîner de têtes à Paris-France" (1931; Attempt to describe a dinner of heads in Paris, France); Bob Dylan's "Desolation Row" (1965); and Jaume Sisa's "Qualsevol nit pot sortir el sol" (1975;

Any night the sun may rise). They are interrelated examples based on the list concept and loosely interconnected as all of them elaborate lists of people who can be found in or are related to specific places. The three poems are written against the grain, opposing the mainstream thinking of the day, and are based on enumeration and chaotic cataloguing and with perceptional attention to the everyday: class differences and the monotony and beauty of working (Prévert); claiming a place in which to live (Dylan); and enjoying friendship, celebration, and happiness as post-hippie values based on a magical childlike world (Sisa). The everyday is filled with the unorganized accumulation of objects and beings, and humans feel the unbearable inclination to make sense of it all. These are long catalogic poems that sing the everyday, signalling alternatives to the world and helping us reassess it.

Chapter 3, "Autopsies of Everyday Life," draws on a definition by Paul Virilio in *The Aesthetics of Disappearance*. He defined *picnolepsy* as the condition of brief lapses in time, momentary absences of consciousness, or, as he puts it, fleeting instances of life escaping. This is a key concept connected to disappearance that I use to analyse three instances of exploration of the everyday, by Josep Carner, Marta Rojals, and Joan Todó, paying special attention to matters of disappearance, particularly of what we may call invisible traditions as recorded in early twentieth- and twenty-first-century literary texts. The three authors combine newspaper articles (in the style of the German *feuilleton* from the 1920s) with their poetry and/or fiction writing. Carner was an ethnographer of the near past. Rojals and Todó can be read as ethnographers of the near present, and the three of them are able to perform an autopsy of the everyday through picnolepsy. These writers look at reality from a very different perspective, as a special kind of mortuary investigation. They assemble the materials of an autopsy, treating reality almost as if it were a cadaver or the contents of a special kind of forensic inquisition.

Chapter 4, "Vicent Andrés Estellés's *Trencadís*, or Attention to the Infra-ordinary," analyses a crucial aspect in Vicent Andrés Estellés's poetry, the fact that it is inhabited by an elementary materiality made of objects and sex, food and smells, death and pain. His attention to smallness produces a very characteristic presence of everyday life. Estellés's poetry has been linked to a kind of social realism, as it was called in the 1960s, and this established a limitation in the way his poetry has been read. Despite the poet's social commitment, the reading perspective adopted by most critics is limited in scope. In this chapter I propose to read, or reread, Estellés's poetry not from the limiting eyes of an extremely ideological perspective but rather by emphasizing the poet's attention to everyday reality. I am especially interested in paying attention to the smallest aspects of reality that populate Estellés's poetry, particularly death and life, pleasures and pain, and self-reflective writing. This chapter is inspired by considerations of Nuccio Ordine in *L'utilità dell'inutile* (The usefulness of the useless) and Josep M. Esquirol in *La resistència íntima: Assaig d'una filosofia de la proximitat* (Intimate resistance: An essay of a philosophy of proximity), two essays that are extremely useful in discussing the uses of collage and the approach to the everyday experience in the poetry of Estellés.

More than half of the world's population live in urban areas. For human beings living in such an environment, public transportation is a major need, as I discuss in chapters 5 and 6, where I propose a review of two different urban means of transportation: trams and metros that are obsessively present in an urban everyday. Chapter 5, "Churches and Trams," discusses how artists and writers have tried to express the experience of the modern city, its spaces, the clash of simultaneity, and the anonymity provided by public spaces. I argue in some detail the issues represented in a series of texts: the use of trams as a way of travel and trams as objects with a symbolic meaning, based on the juxtaposition of the old and the new; trams as metaphors of the problems and situations that arise in modernity; the sensations and experiences provoked in this modern world, ranging from fear of dizziness, negative attitudes, visceral rejection, or the innocent and candid acceptance of the urban experience; and the tram as an element that synthesizes the contradiction between the random and the systemic that is characteristic of life in the city.

Chapter 6, "Thresholds in Barcelona's Metro," proposes an analysis of Barcelona's metro system following David Pike's threshold concept, key to the topography of the "vertical city." This is done through reading maps and literary texts that illustrate three closely related issues: an interpretation of Barcelona's metro network and its meanings; the disappearance of some metro stations and underground spaces, such as hidden connecting corridors, which create a shallow presence of the past in the present and are examples of urban spaces that are buried and forgotten; and subway life as portrayed in some literary texts with particular emphasis on the use of mythology.

We are what we eat. And eating is a central activity in the everyday. In the final chapters I address issues related to food and death, issues that belong to the field of environmental humanities. Chapter 7, "Forms of Thanatourism: José Pla and Josep M. Espinàs," uses a reflection on a special version of *Fernweh*, the one that brings you to nearby realities which are observed as if they were distant ones. Starting with a discussion of Xavier de Maistre's book *Voyage autour de ma chambre* (1794) and Almeida Garrett's *Viagens na minha terra* (1846), I propose a way of reading contemporary books of that nature following the approach of Georges Perec's *L'infraordinaire* and Jean-Didier Urbain's *Ethnologue mais pas trop* (Ethnologue but not too much). I analyse the works of two authors that are representative of exploring nearby territories: *Viaje en autobús* (1941) by Josep Pla and the many examples of "viatge a peu" (travel on foot) by Josep M. Espinàs, focusing on his *Seguint tot l'Ebre amb un primitiu Velosolex* (1961; Following the entire Ebro river with a primitive Velosolex). Both authors agree on a rejection of faster, more modern means of transportation and in their texts amplify a manifesto in favour of slowness. Pla's book expresses a rejection of postwar situations, manifest in a blurred and indirect way against autarky, but at the same time denies progress and speaks out against the dangers of modernity. In doing so, Espinàs and Pla develop an interest in thanatourism and a fixation on food.

Chapter 8, "Beggars Can't Be Choosers: From Autarky to Globalized Gastronomy in Spain," addresses five different ways in which food speaks to us: Pardo Bazán's post-colonial criticism expressed through food; a surrealist approach in Buñuel's cinema; table manners as discussed by Larra; the shortage of food and the hunger that were an obsessive and persistent reality during the Spanish Civil War and postwar period of the twentieth century; and the recent sophistication and cosmopolitanism of Spanish cuisine due to the transformation of the country by the presence of immigrants. I am interested in highlighting the passage from a culture of survival during the civil war and the Franco regime to one of greater abundance and sophistication with the arrival of democracy. The current recognition of Spain as one of the gastronomic destinations in the world modifies part of a historical and cultural past, which includes the ethnic transformation experienced by Spanish society. From the perspective of food studies, one can examine the relationships of the individual with food and analyse how this connection produces a large amount of information about a society.

The final chapter, "Food and the Everyday in Spain: Immigration and Culinary Renovation," offers a reflection on two interrelated topics: the modification of eating habits in Spain, a key aspect of everyday life, through the presence of an enormous migration movement that started in the 1990s; and the intervention of migrant workers in the food chain, particularly in rural areas with heavy agriculture development such as Lleida and surrounding towns. It bestows a reading of two recent texts (a film and a book) that deal with immigration and food issues. Both *El próximo Oriente* (The Near East) by Fernando Colomo and *La pell de la frontera* (The border's skin) by Francesc Serés offer evidence about the transformation of contemporary Spain through food. In these texts food is a powerful device of social and physical control and encapsulates some of the many adjustments that have occurred in Spanish society. The kitchen, at home or at the restaurant, as a private or as a public space, becomes a setting to display the fine line between the familiar and the uncanny, between a domestic and thus safe environment and a hostile environment.

Some sections of this book appeared in a different version as articles or book chapters. I thank the editors and publishers for permission to use this material: "Singing the Everyday, Sign(al)ing the World: On Catalogic Poems," *Arizona Journal of Hispanic Cultural Studies*, vol. 19, 2015, pp. 265–83; "Autopsies of Everyday Life: From Josep Carner to Marta Rojals (and Joan Todó)," in *Catalan Narrative, 1875–2015*, edited by Jordi Làrios and Montserrat Lunati, Studies in Hispanic and Lusophone Cultures 16 (Cambridge: Legenda, 2020), pp. 15–31; "Vicent Andrés Estellés, o l'atenció a l'infraordinari," *Reduccions: Revista de poesia*, nos. 98–9, April 2011, pp. 128–48; "Churches and Streetcars in Barcelona: Ways to Modernity," *Romance Quarterly*, vol. 46, no. 4, fall 1999, pp. 204–15; "*54045*: Atzar i tramvies en la modernitat," *Rassegna Iberistica*, no. 97, October 2012, pp. 7–25; "Cartographies of Disappearance: Thresholds in Barcelona's Metro," *Journal of Urban Cultural Studies*, vol. 3, no. 3, 2016, pp. 347–71; "*Viaje en autobús* de José Pla: Formes del tanaturisme," in *Funcions del passat en la cultura catalana contemporània: Institucionalització, representacions i identitat*, edited by Josep-Anton Fernàndez and Jaume Subirana, UOC (Lleida: Punctum, 2015), pp. 179–96; "Food and the Everyday in Spain: Immigration and Culinary Renovation," *Transhispanic Food Cultural Studies*, special issue of *Bulletin of Spanish Studies*, vol. 96, no. 1, 2020, pp. 1–20; and "Hambre y pan duro: De los años de la autarquía a la gastronomía globalizada en ámbito español," in *Repensar los estudios ibéricos desde la periferia*, edited by José Colmeiro and Alfredo Martínez-Expósito, Biblioteca di Rassegna iberistica 13 (Venice, Italy: Edizioni Ca Foscari, 2018), pp. 115–30.

I would like to express my appreciation to all who made this volume possible. To Enric Balaguer (Universitat d'Alacant), Elide Pittarello (Università Ca' Foscari Venezia), and Maria Fernanda de Abreu (Universidade Nova de Lisboa), among many others, for the opportunity to present early versions of this work to inquiring audiences. Other people with whom I had the opportunity to discuss the ideas in this book are Chiara Bertola, Tom Cushman, Joan de Déu Domènech, the late Jonathan Knudsen, José Joaquín Parra Bañon, Neus Penalba, Marilyn Sides, and Rosi Song. I would like to thank all of them – and particularly Sarah and Alexandre who patiently supported and endured years of research and writing.

CARTOGRAPHIES OF DISAPPEARANCE

Introduction

And life, some think, is worthy of the Muse.

George Meredith

It was at the turn of the last century that my good friend (and excellent writer) Marilyn Sides pointed to an unexplained sentence in an article I was writing about travels to nearby places. I kept referring to "the intricacies of everyday life" without really explaining what I meant by "intricacies." I did not know then what I meant, but with this book I am getting much closer to that goal. A few years later, in 2009, while I was participating in a seminar at the Universitat d'Alacant on "Escriptures del jo," a presentation by Xavier Pla – another good friend –on Josep Pla and the study of the everyday from a theoretical perspective caught my attention. This book, in a way, is a derivation from those two unrelated moments, and I am most grateful to those two friends for their *a loro insaputa* (without their knowledge) provocative thoughts and encouragement. The opening statement by George Meredith comes from sonnet XXV in his book *Modern Love*, a sequence of fifty sixteen-line sonnets about the failure of a marriage and that stresses the ability of literature to portray modern everyday life. It was used by Mercè Rodoreda as an epigraph in her novel *La plaça del Diamant* (*In Diamond Square*).

In December 2012 I organized at the Università Ca' Foscari Venezia (UCF) a *giornata di studio* (one-day workshop) on "Explorations of Everyday Life." It brought together a group of scholars from Europe and the Americas who were interested in addressing everyday life from a variety of perspectives. How is the everyday experienced within a Catalan/Spanish context? Are there particular experiences that achieve a specific and unique representation or theoretical response in art, film, or literature? Other research questions included: How and to what extent have issues of identity, space, historical memory, and immigration affected everyday life in Spain? And how have those issues been represented in literature and film? The focus was on Catalan/Spanish culture, but the long-range goal was the applicability of our findings to other European countries. The driving force behind the workshop was the paucity of these kinds of examinations in an Iberian context.

Rafael Abella's *La vida cotidiana bajo el régimen de Franco* (1985; Everyday life in Spain under the Franco regime) and Sánchez Vidal's *Sol y sombra: De cómo los españoles se apearon de las mayúsculas de la historia dotándose de vida cotidiana* (1990; Sun and shadow: How Spaniards got out of history with a capital H and endowed themselves with daily life) are two of the few examples available, though none of them proves to be a consistent approach to defining from a theoretical perspective what everyday life is.[1] Both books tackle the issue in very different ways. From the perspective of a historian, Abella follows "el hilván del acontecer de los hechos" (the basting of the happening of the facts) and studies "una sucesión monográfica de los diversos aspectos de la cotidianeidad, desconectados de la realidad por el fluir de los acontecimientos" (a monographic succession of the various aspects of everyday life, disconnected from reality by the flow of events). He is interested rather in "aquellos fenómenos que marcaron más decisivamente la pauta de nuestra existencia national" (11–12; those phenomena that most decisively marked the pattern of our national existence). In twenty chapters he covers, among other topics, fashion, the black market, marriage, church, and tourism.

Sánchez Vidal tries to solve, in ten sections written as short essays, the riddle of several coincidences such as the simultaneous arrival in Spain of the Beatles' record *Sgt. Pepper's Lonely Hearts Club Band* and the use of credit cards. He is willing to emphasize the consequences brought about by these and other minor events (the most seemingly nondescript facts), always giving them preference over great historical episodes, with the aim of reaching a convincing interpretive synthesis of the past. In the end, his book is a list of events that chronicles Spain's late arrival into modernity and postmodernity.

Another take is the contribution by sociologist Amando de Miguel, who in *Cien años de urbanidad: Crítica de costumbres de la vida española* (1991; One hundred years of urbanity: Critique of customs of Spanish life) explored a sheaf of texts or manuals of courtesy, civility, and good manners, which had been published throughout the nineteenth century in Spain as a way to describe a society from the list of prevalent manners, fashions that prevailed, values that were imposed, and forms that were respected. The book is made up of sixteen chapters among which we can find the norms of civility; old manuals and new customs; gallantry without gallants; personal and social relationships; composure, fashion, and appearance; the use of the telephone; and smoking and drinking (*Cien años de urbanidad* 14, 19). In yet another volume by Amando de Miguel, *La vida cotidiana de los españoles en el siglo XX* (2001; The daily life of the Spanish in the twentieth century), he studied the great transformation of Spain during the twentieth century, focusing on "minimal events of daily life." Organized in ten chapters, the book included the mental and ideological attitudes that cause transformation, the civil war and its aftermath being crucial events. He also covered personal interests: love, sex, and affections; the sense of time and the organization of a day; body care; the art of aging; entertainment; outfit and fashion; life outdoors; the company of everyday objects (from packaging to gifts); and consumption (*La vida cotidiana*).

Interestingly enough, there have been more scholarly inquiries devoted to the study of the everyday in the early modern period, such as *Escritura y vida cotidiana de las mujeres de los siglos XVI y XVII (Contexto mediterráneo)* (Medina Arjona and Gómez Moreno). "Post Scriptum: A Digital Archive of Ordinary Writings (Early Modern Portugal and Spain)" is a project by Maria Rita Braga Marquilhas that aims to collect and publish Portuguese and Spanish private letters written during the seventeenth to early nineteenth century.[2] These are unpublished epistolaries written by authors from different social backgrounds that survived by chance because the Inquisition and the civil courts used them as criminal evidence. These textual resources treat everyday issues related to past centuries. Everyday life has also been addressed from a philosophical point of view. Agís Villaverde, for instance, proposes to build a hermeneutic of everyday life in three different ways: using a theoretical model based on the philosopher's own experience of facing the world, or simply from his speculations; studying the possibility of approaching the realm of everyday life using literary texts, fiction above all, to the extent that the writer constructs a plot culled from daily life; and trying to reconstruct the keys of meaning that work in everyday life by searching for their signs in philosophical texts, through whose intricacies life slips (15).

Historians such as Díaz Barrado have paid attention to the renewal in everyday life after Franco's dictatorship. This last author's point is that culture and daily life were radically altered in the last quarter of the twentieth century by the combined effect of technological change and the impact of mass media. Díaz Barrado pays attention to what has been razed and the new habits that set the course into the twenty-first century. Another remarkable approach, from a historical perspective, is the one in a volume edited by Mónica Ghirardi that deals with the everyday during the colonial period in Argentina, covering elite families, women, blood, and patrimony; war, powers, institutions, and politics; slaves, Indigenous peoples, and the sick of the popular sectors in the colonial everyday life; society, population, family strategies, and mobility practices; the cultural and the symbolic in the practices and spaces of everyday life; militancy, politics, and sexuality; and the social and political aspects of the colonial period.

Similarly, Montoya Ramírez and Aguilar Escobar have edited a volume that addresses aspects of everyday life in Andalusia from a linguistic perspective. The book highlights the work carried out on the basis of the collections of notarial records that allow insights into various aspects of daily life as a substantial part of society. A more recent contribution by Manuel Espín, *Vida cotidiana en la España de la posguerra* (2022; Everyday life in postwar Spain), focuses on specific historical events from the perspective of everyday life such as the first days after the war, the Nazi presence in Spain, the Hendaye Franco-Hitler meeting, the daily hardships of the autarky, the Blue Division, the role of women, the United Nations boycott, the years of hunger, Eva Perón's trip in 1947, the return of the Americans, and the Concordat or the pacts with the United States in 1953. In this book Espín portrays an exhaustive picture of the life of a generation that tried to survive in the Spain of autarky, the long period from 1939 to the beginning of the 1950s, when the rationing cards came to an end. The autarky is, without a doubt, an indisputable protagonist of the book, conceived as a consequence of the Second World War and the subsequent isolation suffered by the Franco regime due to its commitment to Nazism and fascism. Most events are presented from the perspective of radio shows, cinema, or popular songs that are witness to the harsh realities of that time. Again, as in other books, it is a historical overview, without any critical perspective on the representations of the everyday. My book clearly departs from this kind of approach.

Meta-cartographies of the Everyday: A Genealogy

Critical examination of everyday life began between the last decade of the eighteenth century and the first decade of the nineteenth century. It was during the twentieth century that this attention became more focused on the social sciences, first by authors such as Lefebvre and then by Certeau, and previous findings by Benjamin and Simmel were included in their conceptualizations. The social sciences reflect an interest developed in philosophical approaches (from Kant onwards), or literary products (such as Poe's invention of the detective novel and Baudelaire's street poems or innovative prose poems), or artistic avant-garde (cubism, futurism, Dadaism, surrealism), and include the advent of psychoanalysis, particularly Freud's investigations. By the end of the nineteenth century many thinkers in psychological studies had begun to question the idea of society as an organic whole, governed by general, shared principles. Nowadays social scientists tend to focus on ways in which human beings develop their intuitive knowledge of particular social processes and how they use this knowledge in order to act in a creative way. This includes symbolic and intersubjective meanings that are used by human beings in a conscious way to communicate among themselves and make sense of the world in which they live.

The study of everyday life implies a twofold strategy, taking into account contextual aspects of everyday life and the subjective experience of each social actor. As explained in social psychology, the everyday consists of what emerges as recurrent and very close (intimate) in a human being's life. Much research has been done in the social sciences about transformations of the family environment, but very little research has been identified as specifically relating to the impact that literature has on the construction (or reflection) of the everyday. During the last few decades, growing lines of inquiry from cultural studies, feminism, and media studies have developed an increasing interest in the sphere of everyday life. This interest draws from a surge in critical consideration of everyday life, what Henri Lefebvre called the "connective tissue" of all conceivable human thoughts and activities. To date there have been several studies on daily life, Highmore's work being of particular interest as he follows the steps of Freud (1901), Lefebvre (1971), Vaneigem (1967), Certeau (1980), Bargh (1997), the Situationist International, Gardiner (2000), and Sheringham (2006). Vaneigem, for example, equates modern city life with some of the social troubles that plague our societies: isolation, humiliation, miscommunication, and troubles, which he relates to the embarrassment of being but a "thing." Bargh points to the fact that "much of everyday life – thinking, feeling, and doing – is automatic in that it is driven by current features of the environment (i.e., people, objects, behaviours of others, settings, roles, norms, etc.)" (2). This is mediated by automatic cognitive processing of those features, without any mediation by conscious choice or reflection.

In his book *Everyday Life and Cultural Theory: An Introduction* (2002), Ben Highmore uncovers an impressive range of theories of everyday life that are linked to developments and experiences of the late nineteenth and twentieth centuries. He focuses on authors such as Georg Simmel, the surrealists, Walter Benjamin, Henri Lefebvre, and Michel de Certeau, who have considered the everyday to be an important subject of cultural, social, and philosophical analysis. This book was complemented with a wide-ranging anthology of critical texts that drew on the tradition of everydayness, *The Everyday Life Reader* (Highmore 2002). In the introduction to the first book Highmore declares: "It is to the everyday that we consign that which no longer holds our attention. Things become 'everyday' by becoming invisible, unnoticed, part of the furniture. And if familiarity does not always breed contempt, it does encourage neglect" (*Everyday Life and Cultural Theory* 21). A book by Michael Sheringham, *Everyday Life: Theories and Practices from Surrealism to the Present* (2006), summarizes approaches to studying the everyday by adding to these authors the work of philosophers and writers including Maurice Blanchot, Martin Heidegger, Georges Perec, and Roland Barthes. The everyday is what we never see for a first time but only see again (Blanchot 14).

Highmore starts his discussion by linking the everyday to cultural theory, using a curious metaphor that he does not explore further: "This book is a route-map of one particular path through the many varied possibilities that are suggested by connecting the terms 'everyday life' and 'cultural theory'" (*Everyday Life and Cultural Theory* vii). He is surprised that *theory* "could be the name we reserve for the most insistent puzzling about aspects of life that are taken as problematic" (vii). When trying to define *the everyday*, Highmore falls for a paradox: "its special quality might be its lack of qualities. It might be, precisely, the unnoticed, the inconspicuous, the unobtrusive" (1). Commenting on Sherlock Holmes's attraction to the everyday, he writes: "While the particular mix of *boredom, mystery* and *rationalism* that he puts in play is central to figuring everyday life, we need to look elsewhere to see how this mix is related to everyday modernity. We need to disentangle this contrary mixture of forces to see how their entanglement figures the everyday as both known and unknown, comfortable and uncomfortable" (4; emphasis added). It is remarkable that Highmore never developed this metaphor of the route-map any further. I will return to this metaphor in the next section.

Highmore pinpoints work as an essential component of routines, systems, and regulatory techniques that create boredom: "The repetition-of-the-same characterizes an everyday temporality experienced as a debilitating boredom" (*Everyday Life and Cultural Theory* 8). A perfect example is the situation of Gustave Flaubert's Madame Bovary: by ceaselessly reading romantic novels, she discovers a way to live the illusions of aristocratic sensual romance and thus escape the banality of bourgeois everyday life (*Everyday Life and Cultural Theory* 11). Together with work, one has to take into account the home, where people dwell, as the most significant factor in the everyday landscape. How to get from one place to the other is a matter of concern for most human beings; thus transportation gets into the picture.

The daily life of modernity is saturated with commodities, and some of the most vivid aspects of the phantasmagoria are found in shop-window displays and exhibitions. Highmore concludes in his introductory chapter: "The everyday offers itself up as a problem, a contradiction, a paradox: both ordinary and extraordinary, self-evident and opaque, known and unknown, obvious and enigmatic" (*Everyday Life and Cultural Theory* 16). The author's point is that a "significant concern for theorizing the everyday is the problem of generating a suitable form for registering everyday modernity," and he thus detects a significant gap: "the everyday has suffered from inattention, but the kinds of attention that are available are severely out of step with the actuality of the everyday" (22). He is well aware that his approach has some limitations. In fact, everydayness remains opaque and it escapes attention: "If everyday life, for the most part, goes by unnoticed (even as it is being revolutionized), then the first task for attending to it will be to make it noticeable. The artistic avant-garde's strategy of 'making strange,' of rendering what is most familiar unfamiliar, can provide an essential ingredient for fashioning a sociological aesthetic (to use Simmel's term)" (23).

Everyday life can be represented as something utterly routinized, static, and unresponsive, but at the same time it can provide pungent insight, startling dynamism, and ceaseless creativity. Everyday life integrates a form of "depth" reflexivity, which is related to the ability of human beings to adapt to new situations and survive life challenges. At the same time, daily life implies mammoth cross-cultural and historical situations of unpredictability. As observed by sociological approaches, which pay particularly attention to ethnographic, empiricist issues, everyday life is construed as a perpetual and distinctive feature of the social world, and as such it remains an essentially non-problematic component of social existence (Gouldner). By contrast, other theorists who apply more of a humanities approach ponder whether everyday life has a history intimately related to the dynamics of modernity. It is plagued by abundant contradictions and marked by a considerable degree of internal complexity (Crook et al.). The everyday is "poly-dimensional" (Maffesoli, "Sociology of Everyday Life"): fluid, ambivalent, and labile but also unpredictable and full of surprises: "La vie quotidienne dans toute sa grisaille et dans son aspect le plus banal est (toujours) riche d'imprévu et ouverte à de multiples potentialités" (Maffesoli, *La conquête du présent* 31; Everyday life in all its dullness and in its most banal aspect is (always) rich with the unexpected and open to multiple potentialities).

One of the chief goals of this book is to start a scrutiny of everyday life, to expose its contradictions and tease out its hidden potentialities, and to advance the study of the prosaic to the level of critical knowledge. Incidentally this is what some Spanish and Catalan writers have tried to do, particularly Larra and Emili Vilanova, practising a minor literary genre such as *costumbrismo* (literature of local customs and manners). In that kind of literature – following Baquero Goyanes – we can attest that there are two determining elements, apparently opposed: the normal and the extraordinary, the everyday and the surprise. Or, in other words, triviality and emphasis. The good *costumbrista* writer is the one who teaches to look and to discover, the one who is capable of giving literary grace to the small anecdote of every day, the daily triviality of the characters and environments that surround us. *Costumbrista* articles usually use a perspectival effect, thus offering what is known to all under a new and revealing light (Baquero Goyanes 26–8).

Everyday life includes the ways in which people typically act, think, and feel on a daily basis. Everyday life can be described as mundane, routine, natural, habitual, or normal. Besides sleeping one third of the day, several activities are regularly performed: eating, traditionally three times a day; working; and commuting, hours spent going and returning from the workplace. Generally evenings are devoted to leisure time. Class, age, and gender, however, lead to differences in the way we spend our day.

Hegel (quoted by Lefebvre) once wrote: "Was ist bekannt ist nicht erkant" (Lefebvre, *Everyday Life* 132; The familiar is not necessarily the known). It is crucial to study familiarity in apparently well-known spaces and situations. Georges Perec coined in 1973 the term *l'infra-ordinaire* (the infra-ordinary). He used it to describe those minimal aspects of reality on which he wanted to focus his investigation. He noticed our eyes are conditioned to scan the horizon of our habitat only for the unusual, leading us to pay more attention to the exceptional and to forget about the anonymous *endotic,* a term that Perec used in opposition to *exotic*. To begin investigating the infra-ordinary, Perec invites us to ask what may seem, at first, to be trivial and futile questions, in order to provoke the necessary discontinuity between signs and habits of observation. The aim is to reveal underlying trends within the common, almost ignored realities: "What happens every day, the banal, the quotidian, the evident, the common, the ordinary, the infra-ordinary, the background noise, the habitual; how can one account for it, how can one question it, how can one describe it?" (*L'Infra-ordinaire* 11). As noted by Perec, defamiliarization is a technique of inquiry, which requires both perseverance and inventiveness and which must also resist systematization. By using this technique, Perec was recalling an old Walter Benjamin idea about the interpretation of history: the conception of the historian not as a genealogist but as a collector looking for traces of lost systems. It was Walter Benjamin, in "Surrealism: The Last Snapshot of the European Intelligentsia," who described the process by which, beyond the aid of dreams or hashish, an individual perceives the most ordinary, overlooked objects of everyday reality – from obsolete train stations to out-of-place arcades – as uncanny, supernatural, and irrational. Benjamin would call it a "profane illumination." As he put it, "this profane illumination did not always find the surrealists equal to it, or to themselves, and the very writings that proclaim it most powerfully, Aragon's incomparable *Paysan de Paris* and Breton's *Nadja*, show very disturbing symptoms of deficiency" (209).

Maurice Blanchot recognized that it is extremely difficult to define the everyday: "Whatever its other aspects, the everyday has this essential trait: it allows no hold. It escapes. It belongs to insignificance, and the insignificant is without truth, without reality, without secret, but perhaps also the site of all possible signification" (14). Because the everyday escapes, it makes "its strangeness – the familiar showing itself (but already dispersing) in the guise of the astonishing" (14). It is difficult to perceive because one has always looked past it; it is difficult to introduce into a whole or "review it," enclosed as it is within a panoramic vision. Besides being difficult to grasp, the everyday is ubiquitous. Michael Sheringham has summarized the problem in the following terms:

> The everyday is a zone of opposition, intersection, or interconnection – of the accidental and the permanent, imagination and affect, the personal and the social. It is constituted by sequences of individual actions (dressing, eating, shopping, walking), but within a context of relations and interactions where the individual is actor as well as agent. The *quotidien*

> involves continuity but also change, repetition but also variation and evolution. It is made up of routines, but major events (often long anticipated or long remembered) are also part of its fabric, as are festive moments, "mini-fêtes." It is universal (through its link to the human condition in general) but also variable, inflected by climate, class, and gender. It is both independent of and marked by history. (300)

Several books, from different venues, play with the idea of associating (and mixing) the ordinary with the extraordinary. Charles Panati's inventive title *Extraordinary Origins of Everyday Things* (1987) is an encyclopedia of sorts. One reviewer noted, "It is 480 pages of fact piled upon fact without any synthesis whatsoever" (*Los Angeles Times*). Another one is Amato's *Everyday Life: How the Ordinary Became Extraordinary* (2016).[3] He starts with a chronological development and seeks to examine "the making of everyday life across a trajectory from the material and social to the mental and cultural, reaching to modern times with the accelerating move from the industrial and democratic to the primacy of abundance, consumption, design and invention, and individual choice, consciousness and imagination" (8). His inner explorations of daily life lead him to literature and poetry (8). Amato considers the everyday as a founding force: "The everyday – a mix of things and people, thought and actions, memory and imagination, work and habits – runs in and out of the heart and becomes the hearth of our meaning. And the everyday creates our sense of place" (10). He stresses the link to materiality: "Things, bodies and habit tie the knot of everyday behaviour. Everyday life, even in its wishes, conjectures and dreams, grows out of and through ordinary, common, typical and repeating ways of body and things" (13).

When one is dealing with the everyday, two things come immediately to mind: tedium and repetition. Dailiness is boring and reflects the subject's placement in the senseless replication and endless monotony of activities that they (or we) do without much awareness. The boredom of everyday life can be related to that of the assembly line: the more it changes, the more it remains the same. Maurice Blanchot stated that the dullness of the everyday comes from its consideration as "the inexhaustible, irrecusable, always unfinished daily" (13). Lefebvre too argued that "the everyday imposes its monotony" through its unremitting succession: "The quotidian is what is humble and solid, what is taken for granted and that of which all the parts follow each other in such a regular, unvarying succession that those concerned have no call to question their sequence" (*Everyday Life* 24). What characterizes the everyday's tedium is its *seriality*. It is a word that has been used to refer to the banal, the quotidian, the average, the inconspicuous, and the invisible. Marcel Duchamp, when inventing the ready-made, claimed to have chosen everyday objects "based on a reaction of visual indifference, with at the same time a total absence of good or bad taste ... In fact a complete anesthesia" (171).

Henri Lefebvre argued a Marxist interpretation of everydayness (*quotidienneté, Altäglichkeit*) or banality as a soul-destroying feature of modernity, while extending Marx's analysis by discovering new forms of alienation and arguing that capitalism organizes relations of production in an exploitive manner, which produces several forms of alienation in workers. In Lefebvre's opinion, rather than resolving alienation, consumption is part of the mis-recognition of their alienated state by modern consumers, in a cycle which he referred to as the "mystification" of consciousness. This is concentrated in a metonymy for the everyday routine of a Parisian, or more generally urban, worker: "metro, boulot, dodo" (metro, work, sleep), roughly same old same old or rat race. He was inspired by a Pierre Béarn poem in *Couleurs d'usine* (1951):

> Au déboulé garçon pointe ton numéro
> Pour gagner ainsi le salaire
> D'un morne jour utilitaire
> Métro, boulot, bistro, mégots, dodo, zéro
>
> (Rush in boy punch your number
> Thus to earn the salary
> Of a dreary utilitarian day
> Metro, work, bistro, cigs, sleep, zero) (Qtd. in Gooden and Lewis 104–5)

Against "mystification," against the banality of the everyday, Lefebvre proposes the concept of "moments," that is experiences of revelation, déjà vu sensations, and especially love and committed struggle.

Other authors have focused on the political implication of the everyday. For Agnes Heller (1970), daily life is both concrete and abstract, reliant on embodied practices and unthinking assumptions. Studying both socialism and capitalism, she delineated an incisive portrayal of alienation through her attention on transformations in the late 1960s, such as the impact of Che Guevara and the role of the sexual revolution: "Our question, then, is this: accepting all these structural facts as true and basic, is everyday life necessarily alienated, and therefore, is a radical re-structuring of everyday life possible within the continuity of its fundamental structure?" (223).

Observations

Let us go back to Highmore's first attempt at rationalizing the study of everyday. When trying to organize an "archive" of the everyday, he pointed to two problems. The first is linked to the "organization and limits that might be placed on such a necessarily disordered archive" (*Everyday Life and Cultural Theory* 24). How can one organize such a staggering amount of material? The second problem deals with how to organize the archive: "If the archive is made up of a polyphonic everyday, then how is it to be orchestrated into meaningful themes or readable accounts? How can one construct an intelligible articulation from the archive that doesn't submerge the polyphonic beneath the editorial voice at work?" (24). In fact, Highmore is dealing with a problem similar to the one that Umberto Eco encountered when trying to discuss the list,[4] the unmanaged accumulation of singularities, and a constrictive order that transforms the archive into disciplined accounts (24). I will go back to this in a moment.

Highmore perceives a significant part of his book as an outline of some of the elements of an "aesthetics" of the everyday, meaning both the experience of the everyday and the problem of registering it, taking into account the work of Simmel and Benjamin and various forms of surrealism. From this starting point he draws a genealogy of experts and a variety of reflections on the everyday. Simmel's work focuses on the incidental and the meagre, without venturing into elaborate theoretical outlines, the fragment being the trademark of his sociological approach. Walter Benjamin continued Simmel's project of a sociology of modernity, particularly in his unfinished (and unfinishable, argues Highmore) *Arcades Project*, as a way to grasp the emergence of modernity in all its contingencies as it hardened into cultural forms. Surrealism provided two methodological tools for attending to the everyday: the process of montage, seen here as the most crucial representational form for the everyday; and a "reworking of social anthropology that mobilizes it for attending to the domestic everyday" (Highmore, *Everyday Life and Cultural Theory* 30).

Likewise, Highmore portrays surrealism as the arrival of the marvellous into the everyday. He perceives surrealism as a form of social research into everyday life: "collage (or montage) provides a persistent methodology for attending to everyday life in Surrealism. In its juxtaposing of disparate elements (umbrellas, sewing machines, etc.) it generates a defamiliarizing of the everyday" (*Everyday Life and Cultural Theory* 46). Collage is both a way of breaking habits of the mind that would submit the everyday to normalizing impulses and a suitable form for representing the everyday. Surrealism is about an effort, an energy, to find the marvellous in the everyday, to recognize the everyday as a dynamic montage of elements, to make it strange so that its strangeness can be recognized. Faced with the deadly boredom of the everyday, the surrealists take to the street, working to find and create the marvellousness of the everyday (46–7). He also considers Aragon's *Le paysan de Paris* (1924), a book in which one passage presents a "geography" of everyday pleasure, the best antidote to the everyday as mundane. In the sensual realm of the hairdressers Aragon contemplates the teaching of a bodily geography (Highmore, *Everyday Life and Cultural Theory* 56). In the work of Simmel, Benjamin, and surrealism the sphere of everyday life is perceived as quintessentially urban.

The modern metropolis is seen as a realm in which the problem of the everyday is unavoidable. This is due partly to the spectacular technological changes brought about by modernity and partly to a romanticization of the city. From a different yet complementary perspective, around 1937 a group of observers established in the United Kingdom a mass-observation project of daily life. They were seeking answers to basic questions such as, What are the particular experiences and activities that characterize everyday life in the modern world? How do different social groups experience everyday life? How can these experiences and activities be attended to and represented? (Highmore, *Everyday Life and Cultural Theory* 75–7).

A key element in this genealogy of studies is the work of Henry Lefebvre. In both sections of volume 1 of the *Critique of Everyday Life* Lefebvre proposed not only that the study of everyday life was a study of alienation under conditions of modernity but that the transformation of everyday life would be brought about by the de-alienation of human beings and the creation of the total person, and that this could be seen as an "end of history" (120). *La vie quotidienne* suggests the ordinary, the banal, but, more importantly, for Lefebvre it connotes continual recurrence, insistent repetition. It is repetition that is crucial to Lefebvre's meaning of the term *everyday life*: the daily chores as well as those routinized pleasures that are meant to compensate for the drudgery. Even that which is "out of the ordinary," for example a camping trip, is part of everyday life because it is part of the cycle of work and leisure: the yearly holiday, the weekend, the birthday celebration, the office party, and so on. As Lefebvre writes in *Everyday Life in the Modern World*, "everyday life is made of recurrences: gestures of labour and leisure, mechanical movements both human and properly mechanic, hours, days, weeks, months, years, linear and cyclical repetitions, natural and rational time" (18). If Lefebvre stresses the repetition and tempo of everyday life, then he does so because, by emphasizing ideas of recurrences, he can articulate his most fundamental and radical working of the concept of everyday life: everyday life as the interrelationship of all aspects of life (Lefebvre, *Everyday Life* 128). Lefebvre's work is closely connected with the avant-gardist practice of making the familiar strange. His writing evidences a literary inclination that works to defamiliarize the familiar (Highmore, *Everyday Life and Cultural Theory* 142–3).

According to Shields, Lefebvre's perception of the everyday was closely linked to his idea of urban life: "The urban is social centrality, where the many elements and aspects of capitalism intersect in space despite often merely being part of the place for a short time, as is the case with goods or people in transit. 'City-ness' is the simultaneous gathering and dispersing of goods, information and people. Some cities achieve this more fully than others – and hence our own perceptions of some as 'great cities' per se" (*Key Thinkers* 280). As it is well known, Lefebvre explained historical notions of space on three axes. The "perceived space" (*le perçu*) of everyday social life and commonsensical perception blends popular action and outlook but is often ignored in the professional and theoretical "conceived space" (*le conçu*) of cartographers, urban planners, or property speculators. Nonetheless, the person who is fully human (*l'homme totale*) also dwells in a "lived space" (*le vécu*) of the imagination and moments that have been kept alive and accessible by the arts and literature. This "third" space not only transcends but has the power to refigure the balance of popular "perceived space" (*Production of Space*; Shields, *Profiles*).

Lefebvre's critique of everyday life focused on the urban environment as a space for the intensification of the alienation of everyday life, as well as a site for its possible transformation. From a Marxist perspective he saw contemporary everyday life as exploitative, oppressive, and relentlessly controlled (he wrote about the terrorism of advertising; *Everyday Life* 106) and "the bureaucratic society of controlled consumption" (*Everyday Life* 68–109). Lefebvre perceived everyday life as simply lived experience, and that "modernity and everyday life constitute a deep structure" ("The Everyday" 11). But it was difficult to read a structure because everyday life was opaque and it would be defined by "what is left over after all distinct, superior, specialized, structured activities have been singled out by analysis" (*Critique of Everyday Life* 197; Highmore, *Everyday Life and Cultural Theory* 115).

Michel de Certeau's *The Practice of Everyday Life* has been read from a myriad of perspectives. He stresses that "the cultures of everyday life are submerged below the level of a social and textual authority" (qtd. in Highmore *Everyday Life and Cultural Theory* 31). While those cultures tend to remain invisible and unrepresentable, they perform something like a guerrilla war on these authorities. Highmore reduces the discussion to a problematization of "cultural theory as a theoretical architecture based on a division between power and resistance. Certeau's work suggests a productive affinity with the project of psychoanalysis" (31). In a memorable passage from *The Practice of Everyday Life*, Certeau evokes an everyday that is at one and the same time both absent and present in the archive:

> Was it fate? I remember the marvelous Shelburne Museum in Vermont where, in thirty-five houses of a reconstructed village, all the signs, tools and products of nineteenth-century everyday life teem; everything, from cooking utensils and pharmaceutical goods to weaving instruments, toilet articles, and children's toys can be found in profusion. The display includes innumerable familiar objects, polished, deformed, or made more beautiful by long use; everywhere there are as well the marks of the active hands and laboring or patient bodies for which these things composed the daily circuits, the fascinating presence of absences whose traces were everywhere. At least this village full of abandoned and salvaged objects drew one's attention, through them, to the ordered murmurs of a hundred past or possible villages, and by means of these imbricated traces one began to dream of countless combinations of existences. (21)

While the activities of use are missing, the marks they have left are not. These signs ("the presence of absences") are just audible to those who are prepared to "dream of countless combinations of existences." Certeau's everyday life project is not simply mourning the impossibility of ever registering the everyday. Part of its power is that it continually evokes the everyday as a theoretical and practical possibility (Highmore, *Everyday Life and Cultural Theory* 163).

This experience by Certeau (presence of absences) can be linked to an astonishing exhibition, "Die Welt der DDR," that I visited in Dresden in November 2017.[5] It was a good example of *Ostologie*, which can be partially translated as nostalgia for the East, of the German "democratic" republic, a fairly widespread phenomenon in that part of the country that achieved an international resonance thanks to the film *Good bye Lenin!* (2003). The exhibition aimed to reconstruct out of some rubble a world that had disappeared. It is a reality that no longer exists, the disappearance of which some Germans are celebrating, but with a very bizarre point of ambiguity. It has a still-photo effect, like scenes from an old movie never shot, a sensation of freezing. The objects, the magazines (they have survived badly), correspond to a backward world that existed thirty years ago. What would be the effect of trying to present what the Federal Republic of Germany was like thirty years ago (with the Baader-Meinhof and so on)?[6] The layout of the space and the sections they chose for that German exhibition took a microscopic vision of the everyday life that had already gone: particularly small cars but also many aspects of life – typewriters, postal service, women's hairdressing, hospital equipment, pharmacy, medicines, certificates of belonging to the Communist Party, computers at work, electrical appliances. From the school: a classroom, with slogans and awkward benches, full of photographs of the great leader Walter Ulbricht. From housing: mountable furniture, pre-Ikea furniture, very cluttered toys. There was even a kind of Scalextric "Matusser," toys, military uniforms, and the reproduction of the beds in barracks. There were excerpts of leisure: sports and electronics, camping, photography. Also there was a reproduction of a typical shop, Konsum, halfway between the Spanish late nineteenth-century Ultramarinos store and the neighbourhood supermarket. The Konsomol: where they have what they have and there is no need to order very exquisite products. Computer Technik: with the sophisticated "Robotron" computers. The selection reduced everyday life to two areas, public and private, with a focus on technologies that no longer exist. This German exhibition is an excellent example of the will to catalogue, to map, the many disappearances that permeate the everyday.

Likewise, Spanish writer Carmen Martín Gaite wrote *El cuarto de atrás* (1977; The back room) in which she recovered a crucial decade of Spanish history, right after the civil war, through culture, customs, and events, as well as revisiting her own life through her memories. The book is a recovery of those elements of the period that for Martín Gaite were relevant, on both a collective and a personal level. Moreover, they are useful for reconstructing the reality of the Spanish postwar period through a writer who experienced it first-hand through the evocation of dressmakers, hairdressers, songs, dances, novels, customs, language idioms, bars, and cinema. She made a compilation of the elements of everyday life that stood out in the period after the civil war and were common to her generation. The popular elements served, much more than dates, places, and other historical information, to situate the events in time, as they were references that shaped the reality of the moment. Martín Gaite tends in her novel to enumerate certain objects that were typical of everyday life, in an attempt to recover these elements and associate them with the customs of the period she is describing. This is observed in several passages, for example, when she describes the contents of her grandmother's sewing basket or when she recounts the activities carried out by the maids in her house in Madrid:

"De la tapadera de mimbre entreabierta escapan carretes, enchufes, terrones de azúcar, dedales, imperdibles, facturas, un cabo de vela, clichés de fotos, botones, monedas, tubos de medicinas, allá va todo, envuelto en hilos de colores (*El cuarto de atrás* 96; From the half-open wicker lid escape spools, plugs, sugar cubes, thimbles, safety pins, bills, a candle line, photo stencils, buttons, coins, medicine tubes, there goes everything, wrapped in coloured threads). Or in another excerpt: "continuaban desde entonces limpiando, impertérritas, cazuelas, azulejos, picaportes y molduras; ... ropa limpia, planchada y guardada dentro de las cómodas, ajuar de cama y mesa, pañitos bordados, camisas almidonadas, colchas, encajes, vainicas" (157; they continued since then to clean, undaunted, pots, tiles, doorknobs and mouldings; ... clean clothes, ironed and kept inside the chests of drawers, bed and table linen, embroidered cloths, starched shirts, bedspreads, lace, hemstitches), paying attention to the minor activities performed by women working in the household: "aquel arrastrar, frotar y sacudir de escobas, escobillas, plumero, zorros, cogedor, paño de gamuza, bayeta, cepillo para el lustre" (165; that dragging, rubbing and shaking of brooms, brushes, several kinds of dusters, dustpan, chamois cloth, cloth, brush for polishing). Martín Gaite's novel thus becomes an invaluable sociological document, "a novelized social history told, crucially, from a woman's perspective" (Davies 239). She intended to reflect on the relationship that history has with stories. What interested her were precisely those everyday stories shared by a whole generation. In fact, when her classmate Ignacio Aldecoa died in 1969, she reflected:

> Me di cuenta por primera vez de que la Historia con mayúsculas está compuesta por pequeñas historias, y que solo la brusca desaparición de nuestros compañeros de brega con la vida, además de abrirnos los ojos sobre la precariedad de ese don que dábamos por seguro, es capaz de hacernos ver la urgencia de una tarea ineludible, una tarea con la que se inicia la madurez: la de heredar las historias que el muerto compartió con nosotros o nos legó y de enmarcarlas en la Historia, es decir en el espacio cronológico en que sucedieron. (*Pido la palabra* 359)
>
> (I realized for the first time that History with a capital letter is made up of small stories, and that only the sudden disappearance of our companions in the struggle with life, besides opening our eyes to the precariousness of that gift we took for granted, is capable of making us see the urgency of an unavoidable task, a task with which maturity begins: that of inheriting the stories that the dead shared with us or left us and of framing them in History, that is, in the chronological space in which they happened.)

This is why certain insignificant objects (sewing kit) or a forgotten space (the back room) become centres of attention and crucial to performing memories. The disappearance of a companion or friend makes her aware of the fragility of memories and the need to reconstruct them in order to prevent their disappearance.

In his conclusion, commenting on a book by Harry Harootunian, *History's Disquiet: Modernity, Cultural Practice, and the Question of Everyday Life*, Highmore suggests a way to bring together "the global generality of modernization with the specificity of regional and historical cultural continuities and discontinuities." The study of the everyday would provide an appropriate perspective for cross-cultural studies of modernity, particularly to insist "on the uneven experiences of modernity on an international and intranational scale" (*Everyday Life and Cultural Theory* 176–7). This cross-cultural attention to the everyday would provide "an opportunity to re-imagine cultural studies. In other words it might help to re-animate cultural studies in imaginative ways" (178).

A more recent book by Ben Highmore, *Ordinary Lives: Studies in the Everyday* (2011), puts together aesthetics and the everyday by creating a genealogy from the Enlightenment of Baumgarten, Shaftesbury, and Hume, through James and Dewey, to Jacques Rancière. According to Highmore, art is part of a "world of feelings" that must take its place together with "shoes, gardens, rivers, houses, faces, plants and so on" (11). In the book he includes examples such as chairs, popular music, curries, and housework. He examines our relationship to familiar objects (a chair), repetitive work (housework, typing), media (distracted television viewing and radio listening), and food (increasingly varied in multicultural Britain). If previous approaches dealt with the question "What does everyday life mean?" this book provides a vital starting point, examining the meanings of everyday life in a developed society by showing "how the confusions, routines, intricacies and surprises of daily life, that are felt so 'personally,' are always connecting us to a realm of communal (and differentiated) life" (6). Ordinary life is collective even when it is experienced as isolated and desolate. Highmore is interested in giving presence to "the pulsings of affect: the risings and fallings of hope, love, hatred and irritation; the minor and major disturbances of life set against and within a world of day-to-day habits, routines and collective sentiments" (12). The book covers "everyday aesthetics," where he develops philosophical and theoretical inquiries to develop an aesthetics of ordinary life. In one chapter, "Familiar Things," he poses a dialogue with Michel Serres's suggestion that, rather than dividing the world into subjects and objects, we treat many different kinds of objects as "quasi objects" and many kinds of subjects as "quasi subjects." In the chapter "Doing Time: Work Life," Highmore looks into the world of work and how it shapes notions of time, temporality, and temporal experience, including boredom, waiting, anticipating, and routine. "Absentminded Media" is dedicated to the roles of media in everyday life, particularly the concept of "distraction." He sees distraction as crucial for attending to everyday media. His chapter 6, "Senses of the Ordinary," analyses the question of habit and routine in the domestic realm. The final chapter, "Towards a Political Aesthetics of Everyday Life," presents everyday life as a consistent theme of state politics: it is used in a number of forms "but is primarily used as a vehicle of protection against all kinds of real-and-fantastical threats" (20).

Finally, to complete this genealogy, it is worth mentioning the work of French philosopher Bruce Bégout for whom "la vie est … par essence – c'est-à-dire par nécessité – quotidienne non pas ontiquement, sur le mode dégradé (et forcément dégradant) de l'esquive et de la médiocrité, de la déchéance et du nivellement, mais ontologiquement, en tant que traduction immédiate du conflit, au sein de l'exister, entre l'extase et la stance" (Highmore, *Ordinary Lives* 465). (Life is … in essence – that is to say, by necessity – not daily ontically, based on the degraded mode (and inevitably degrading) of dodging and mediocrity of revocation and leveling, but ontologically, as an immediate translation of the conflict within the existing, between ecstasy and stance.) This passage stresses Bégout's approach to the everyday in terms of degradation and mediocrity, and based on its ignorance, our naive adherence to the lies of the everyday. Ecstasy refers to human consciousness as it is always "consciousness of." The human being is a being of experience, always "out of it." The stance means the very need to live, to survive, to be "for himself." Everyday life thus assumes the form of all traditional and usual actions and of the accounts that support a social group or community. The everyday is the stage in which we develop our multiple abilities, as individuals or members of a collectivity, thus becoming integrated in society and capable of interacting humanly with one another.

There have been a few critics who from a strictly literary or cultural studies perspective have set the agenda when studying the everyday. In 2000, Michael Gardiner wrote *Critiques of Everyday Life: An Introduction* about theories of everyday life, "the crucial medium through which we enter into a transformative praxis with nature, learn about comradeship and love, acquire and develop communicative competence, formulate and realize pragmatically normative conceptions, feel myriad desires, pains and exaltations, and eventually expire" (2). He dialogued with a significant number of theorists and approaches, including the surrealists and Henri Lefebvre; the Situationist International and Michel de Certeau; Agnes Heller and the relationship between the everyday, rationality, and ethics; the work of Mikhail Bakhtin, particularly carnival and intersubjectivity; and Dorothy E. Smith's feminist perspective on everyday life. He tried to tease out some of the common threads that link each of the thinkers and traditions. Nevertheless, Highmore's work is the most comprehensive study of the everyday, but besides there being considerable theoretical interest in recent years in the study of the everyday, one must acknowledge that literature and the arts remain largely unexploited areas in contemporary explorations of the everyday.

Representations

It is surprising that Highmore does not include in his scrutiny the monumental work of Italian literary critic Francesco Orlando, *Obsolete Objects in the Literary Imagination: Ruins, Relics, Rarities, Rubbish, Uninhabited Places, and Hidden Treasures*. Orlando's book corroborates Highmore's thesis that literature provides an irreplaceable observatory for mapping the everyday. A project such as Orlando's study on the disappearance of objects is fundamental as a way to map, from a Freudian perspective, the life of objects that surround or did surround us. Orlando explored Western literature's obsession with outmoded and non-functional objects (ruins, obsolete machinery, broken things, trash, etc.). Combining the insights of psychoanalysis and literary political history, Orlando traced this obsession to a turning point in history, at the end of eighteenth-century industrialization, when the functional became the dominant value of Western culture. He managed to reread most of Western literature to identify distinct categories into which obsolete images could be classified, providing an amazing number of examples. His study can be read as the zenith of Orlando's life, the one in which his culture and his ethos come into contact with the theoretical system built in previous volumes, in particular in *Per una teoria freudiana della letteratura* (1973).

Orlando discusses the parallel between obsolete objects and the theory of the return of the repressed that was developed in his essays of more direct Freudian inspiration. He selects the cases of antifunctional repressions on the basis of three constants: a syntactic, which coincides with the form of the list; and two themes, namely the material consistency of the listed elements (things, objects, concrete places, not abstract entities) and the connotation of uselessness, of age, of desuetude precisely. His selection of numerous examples is taken from masterpieces of major literatures as support for a project that is much more than a verbal *Wunderkammer*. The book is stained by traces of structuralism, with its binary oppositions, and concludes with the proposal of twelve categories. The intersection between a formal constant (the list) and two thematic constants (things and their obsolete condition) therefore provides the unitary probe necessary for a potentially unlimited search.

Through a whole series of theoretical passages that lead, decision after decision, to a level of abstraction sufficient to define categories that are useful for a classification, several constants are identified. He speaks first about images of non-functional corporeality, naturally meaning by "functional" (or not) a value relative to that text (and to the culture to which it belongs); that is, they will be objects presented as useless or obsolete in that precise discourse and not as such in the extratextual reality. The result is a semantic tree, whose roots are the lowest common denominator of non-functional corporeality, which is gradually branching from the abstract towards the concrete, and in which each branch is represented by a binary opposition: the crown of this inverted tree with the roots up, made up of twelve categories "not to be distinguished too much," which is the title of the long fifth chapter in the book. The process of identifying the categories progressively fills the space between that general constant which is the theme of the book itself, and the more than one thousand texts consulted (of which the pertinent loci have been carefully filed), constituting the very heart of the work and practically coinciding with the classification itself (Orlando, *Obsolete Objects* 205):

THE SOLEMN-ADMONITORY
THE THREADBARE-GROTESQUE
THE VENERABLE-REGRESSIVE
THE WORN-REALISTIC
THE REMINISCENT-AFFECTIVE
THE DESOLATE-DISCONNECTED

THE MAGIC-SUPERSTITIOUS
THE SINISTER-TERRIFYING
THE PRECIOUS-POTENTIAL
THE STERILE-NOXIOUS
THE PRESTIGIOUS-ORNAMENTAL
THE PRETENTIOUS-FICTITIOUS

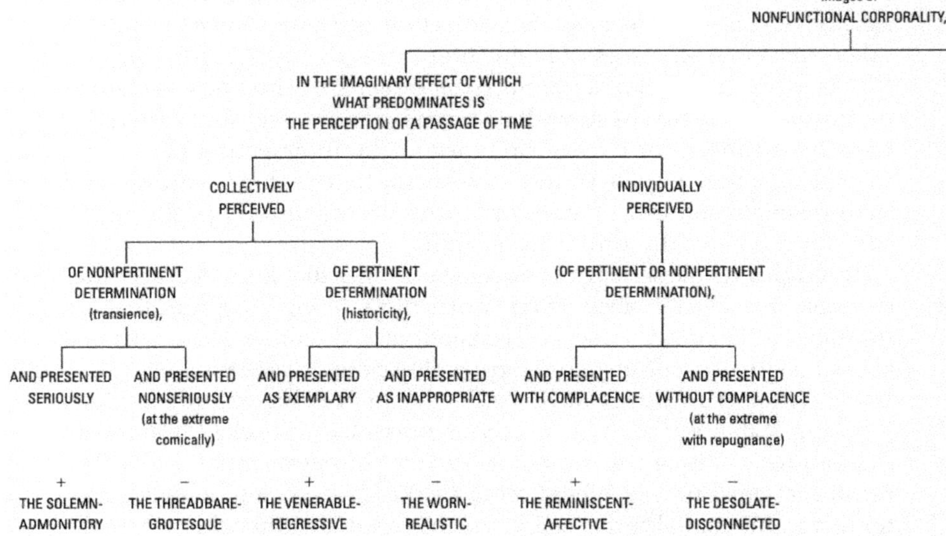

Figure 1. Francesco Orlando's classification in *Obsolete Objects in the Literary Imagination*, p. 205

The first half of the classification ends with categories linked instead to an individual context: objects that awaken memory, often in a sort of sentimental pilgrimage (the centrality of affective recovery is in the definition of mind-affective) or in the opposite of repugnant obsession, present onwards from the nineteenth century and much more so in the twentieth-century (the so-called desolate-disconnected). The second half of the tree focuses entirely on the great impact on the imagination that, in the present, the wrecks of a past time can have: from magical objects to those charged with horror, from treasures buried in the sea depths to the destructiveness of certain aspects of nature. The tree finally ends in the opposition, all cultural, between the object that becomes a prestigious antique and the one that, significantly, must conclude the entire construction, thus assuming a privileged position: *kitsch* (Sapegno 1027).

Orlando's project stresses the centrality of language and its crucial role in the way we conceive and explain reality in our interaction with the world. A British critic and social theorist also wrote about

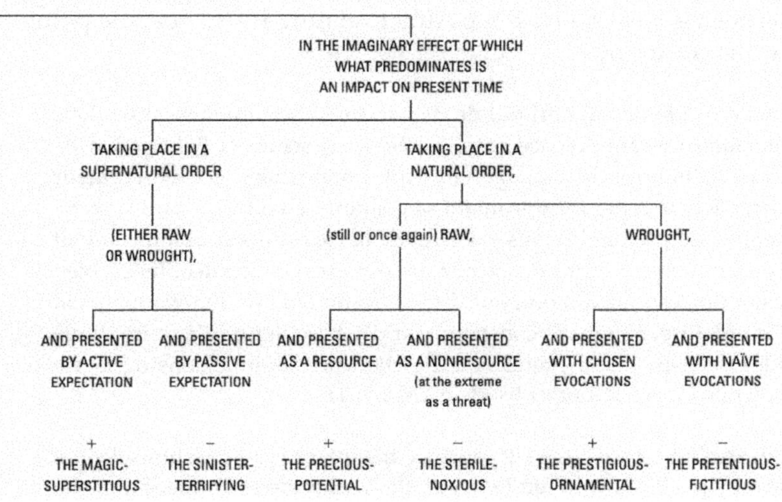

the construction of the world through idioms and epigrams. Richard Hoggart, in *Everyday Language and Everyday Life* (2003), explored the idioms and epigrams used by the English working-class. He examined the very innards of working-class life and its idioms, paying attention to a language that arose in relation to home, with its main characters being wives and mothers, husbands and fathers, and children, and all the main topics related: wars; marriage; food, drink, health, and weather; neighbours, gossip, quarrels; and old age and death. By doing so, Hoggart identified the sayings and special nuances of the English working-class that have made it identifiable as such, from the rude and obscene to the intellectual and imaginative. He also touched on religion, superstition, and time, the beliefs that animate language: "That adages, apophthegms, epigrams and the like are over-used is a tribute both to their handiness – they save time and thought – and their attraction; they almost all use images and we almost all love images. They are often pictorial, colourful, striking in a way we had not ourselves thought of. They yoke what seem like disparate things together in ways we had also not thought of, until it was done for us. They can be neat, alliterative, attractively counterbalanced" (Hoggart 160). Hoggart's research poses an important question: Is there a way of narrating the everyday? This question has been answered by René Audet relating it to a specific point of view, that of the spy:

> L'écrivain qui tente aujourd'hui de dépeindre le quotidien se situe dans une position précaire, coincé entre le réel qu'il scrute et l'obligation de distance qu'impose le langage. Frôlant l'imposture, cet observateur s'apparente à un espion, empruntant sa posture – en retrait, lisant la scène qu'il épie, interprétant les faits et gestes de la vie ordinaire comme autant de signes formant la trame d'une histoire non encore racontée. Tel est bien le karma de l'espion, si l'on peut dire: à la frontière de l'univers de son objet de filature, craignant constamment d'y basculer et d'être impliqué dans les événements, il prend note de chacune des inflexions de la vie quotidienne de la personne observée. (Audet 1)
>
> (The writer who today tries to portray the everyday finds himself in a precarious position, wedged between the reality he scrutinizes and the obligation of distance imposed by language. Bordering on the imposture, this observer resembles a spy, borrowing his posture – withdrawing, reading the scene he watches, interpreting the facts and gestures of ordinary life as so many signs forming the fabric of a story not yet told. Such is the karma of the spy, if we can say so: on the border of the universe of his spinning object, constantly fearing to switch to it and to be involved in events, he takes note of each of the changes in the daily life of the person observed.)

This "récit du quotidien" is performed in a different way than a regular narrative. Constructed from uneventful material, the everyday narrative disintegrates as narrative – in the sense of a teleologically defined text, centred on a plot and actions that overturn a universe:

> Manifestation d'une narrativité débridée, il mobilise des types discursifs comme la description, le lyrisme, l'essai et la digression, qui ont pour conséquence sinon de maintenir le discours en deçà du récit, à tout le moins de la visée du discours narratif, qui est généralement de témoigner d'une expérience tout en supportant la mise en place d'une fiction. (Audet 21)
>
> (Manifestation of an unbridled narrativity, it mobilizes discursive types such as description, lyricism, essay and digression, which have the consequence, if not of keeping the discourse below the narrative, at

the very least of the aim of the narrative discourse, which is generally to bear witness to an experience while supporting the setting up of a fiction.)

The everyday narrative is opposed to fiction that acts as a witness to an experience. It is a narration unrestrained that deals with an uneventful topic, focusing on description, lyricism, similar to an essay, and filled with digressions.

1

Defying or Defining the Everyday: Poetics of Everyday Life

Birth and death are the ultimate bookends, and between them a muddied narrative unfolds.
Jan Morris, *Trieste and the Meaning of Nowhere*

A Life Project: Happiness

The everyday can be defined as the routine that happens day after day and becomes our most permanent reality. In the sociological sense, and according to symbolic interactionist authors, "[t]he reality of everyday life further presents itself to me as an intersubjective world, a world that I share with others. This intersubjectivity sharply differentiates everyday life from other realities of which I am conscious" (Berger and Luckman 44). Human activity transforms the world of subjective interpretations into an objective and coherent reality. The everyday is made up of different identifiable areas of life, such as the home, the street, the subway, the park, the workplace, and institutions. It contains the work of urban residents, their ordinary routines such as shopping, eating, moving from one place to another by car, bus, or on foot, working and recreating, among others. Life can be reduced to two bookends as stated by Jan Morris in the epigraph: "Birth and death are the ultimate bookends, and between them a muddied narrative unfolds" (2010).

When we read literary texts focusing on the everyday, our eyes open up to a new reading of our daily environment. For instance, there are two texts by Julio Cortázar, "Autopista del sur" (1994; Southern highway), and *Los Autonautas de la cosmopista* (1983; Cosmopist autonauts), each set on a highway. After reading them, it is no longer possible to travel through the innocuous highway space without rethinking what it means and about its seemingly magical qualities, or how we inadvertently use it. One of the difficulties of cultural studies is its crucial investment in the politics of identity, difference, and otherness (Highmore, *Everyday Life Reader* 2–3), forgetting that texts are also formal constructs that convey a meaning and illuminate our *Weltanschauung*. Another element fundamental to the existence of the everyday is the observer: the writer or reader has an important role as *witness* that allows the everyday to exist. It is this regard that makes what otherwise would be unconscious, inexistent, come to life. It makes sense of Lefebvre's notion that lived, social space is inextricably linked to represented, imagined space, and that both are central to an understanding of everyday life (*Production of Space* 38–9).

The pursuit of happiness may be the most elementary (and hidden) aspect of everyday life. A recently deceased Spanish lawyer used to say about political ambitions, "La vida es lo que pasa cuando te levantas por la mañana, si duermes bien, si duermes mal. La vida no son novelas de miedo." (Life is what happens when you get up in the morning, if you sleep well, if you sleep poorly. Life is not horror novels.)[1] Life is made up of small invisible pleasures and routines that we perform without paying much attention to them. But all these little things constitute our perception of happiness. In his book *Sapiens*, Yurval Harari stresses a significant change that occurred in the late eighteenth century, right at the beginning of modernity. He notices the ways in which, since that time, humanity has addressed happiness and become a centrepiece in our view of the world. When the British colonies declared independence on 4 July 1776, "the most important principle dictated by the American god was somewhat different from the principle dictated by the gods of Babylon. *The American Declaration of Independence* asserts that: 'We hold these truths to be self-evident, that all men are created equal, that they are endowed by their Creator with certain unalienable rights, that among these are life, liberty, and the pursuit of happiness'" (Harari 120). Harari is surprised that historians have paid very little attention to anything but politics, society, economics, gender, diseases, sexuality, food, clothing: "they have seldom stopped to ask how these influence human happiness" (128). We live without devoting much attention to what constitutes happiness, because, although the long-term history of happiness has never been studied as a subject, "almost every scholar and layperson has some vague preconception about it" (422). Human capabilities have increased throughout history, but Harari concludes very sceptically, "Given the proven human propensity for misusing power, it seems naïve to believe that the more clout people have, the happier they will be" (422). That is to say: accept the little you have and live a happy and decent life.

During the long and strange confinement of 2020, I went back to a book I had bought a few years earlier, *Small Pleasures*. In theory this is a book "to guide us to the best of life's small pleasures ... an intriguing, evocative mix of small pleasures that will heighten our senses and return us to the world with new-found excitement and enthusiasm."[2] There are fifty-two chapters that help the reader explore all the tiny pleasures hidden in our lives. Apparently – this is not declared anywhere – Alain de Botton, the bestselling author who has specialized in making high culture available to the masses, wrote it as a self-help book for New Agers trying to find consolation. This book speaks to the need of many human beings to be guided, but, most importantly, it speaks to the need to be helped in discovering a meaning to their lives. It is not a coincidence that this consolation can be found in small invisible things that lie around us. In the book he includes being up late at night, pleasant exhaustion after a productive day, whispering in bed in the dark, midnight walks, flirtation – all belonging to the ideology of small pleasures. It becomes a how-to for grown-ups. It makes me think of those people who claim that happiness is not just an emotion but above all a skill that can be formed and trained. For them it means that happiness is a social technology that is necessary for each person's potential to blossom through a happiness training plan.

Botton's musings are superficial. In 2011 the UN started a more significant and thorough approach, pursuant to the Bhutanese resolution passed by the General Assembly in June 2011. They invited national governments to "give more importance to happiness and well-being in determining how to achieve and measure social and economic development." One of the remarkable conclusions is the proposition: "institutionally, building a government that is trustworthy and functions well, and culturally, building a sense of community and unity among the citizens are the most crucial steps towards a society where people are happy" (*World Happiness Report, 2020*).

Against this corporate vision of happiness Alain Badiou gives the word *bonheur* a definition that cannot be found in any dictionary: "Le bonheur, c'est lorsque l'on découvre que l'on est capable de quelque chose dont on ne se savait pas capable" (48; a possible definition of happiness might be to discover in oneself an active capacity of what we unknowingly possess). But it is the anthropologist Marc Augé who, in his latest book, gives us a definition based on real-life experience. According to him, today happiness is expressed in different ways: the happiness of meeting a face, a landscape, a book, a film, a song, an otherness received and reinvented; the happiness of remembrance and fidelity; happiness that is sometimes instantaneous and, often, quickly vanishes but remains in the memory; happiness that returns or is fresh. All these different ways of experiencing happiness exist only for those who have desired them to the point of having invented them, in spite of time, doubt, and fear. They are ways of knowing happiness that are granted to everyone, regardless of origin, culture, or sex: a happiness of resistance, the idea of which will always remain new, despite today's mediocrity – moments of happiness "despite everything" (Augé, *Bonheurs du jour* 141).

My tour of happiness linked to small things can be completed with a personal remembrance. In the mid-1980s I spent a couple of months in Paris doing research at the Bibliothèque Nationale. I was staying at friend's apartment that had a print on the back of her front door, a sonnet by Plantin (see figure 2). Every morning when leaving the apartment to catch the metro at Porte d'Orléans, I would read a few lines and think about it during the day.

Christophe Plantin's sonnet is a down-to-earth theory of life: it is the duty of every human being to make the best of life. He enumerates basic needs to fulfil the will for happiness. First and foremost, he pays attention to possessions: house and garden and good wine, to which he adds an affable family life and a good relationship with friends and acquaintances. Following Aristotle's and Horatio's "aurea mediocritas," he emphasizes the need for restraint because happiness can be achieved by being honest, sticking to your beliefs, and living a devout life.

The preoccupation with happiness has a long tradition, particularly with discussion of the difficulties in attaining it. A very well-known excerpt by Seneca from his *Moral Letters to Lucilius* explains many things about human beings' natural inability to attain happiness because we carry, as Pierre Bourdieu put it, a *habitus* that hinders any opportunity. In particular it is worth remembering the letter "On Travel as a Cure for Discontent," in which Seneca stresses the impossibilities of finding a new life by travelling far away: "Are you surprised, as if it were a novelty, that after such long travel and so many changes of scene you have not been able to shake off the gloom and heaviness of your mind? You need a change of soul rather than a change of climate. Though you may cross vast spaces of sea, and though … your faults will follow you whithersoever you travel." He even mentions a remark by Socrates: "Why do you wonder that globe-trotting does not help you, seeing that you always take yourself with you? The reason which set you wandering is ever at your heels." Then he asks the ultimate question: "What pleasure is there in seeing new lands? Or in surveying cities and spots of interest? All your bustle is useless. Do you ask why such flight does not help you? It is because you flee along with yourself. You must lay aside the burdens of the mind; until you do this, no place will satisfy you … Anything you do tells against you, and you hurt yourself by your very unrest; for you are shaking up a sick man."

These words are echoed by the Greek poet Cavafy, who reflected on this limitation from a different perspective in his poem "The City":

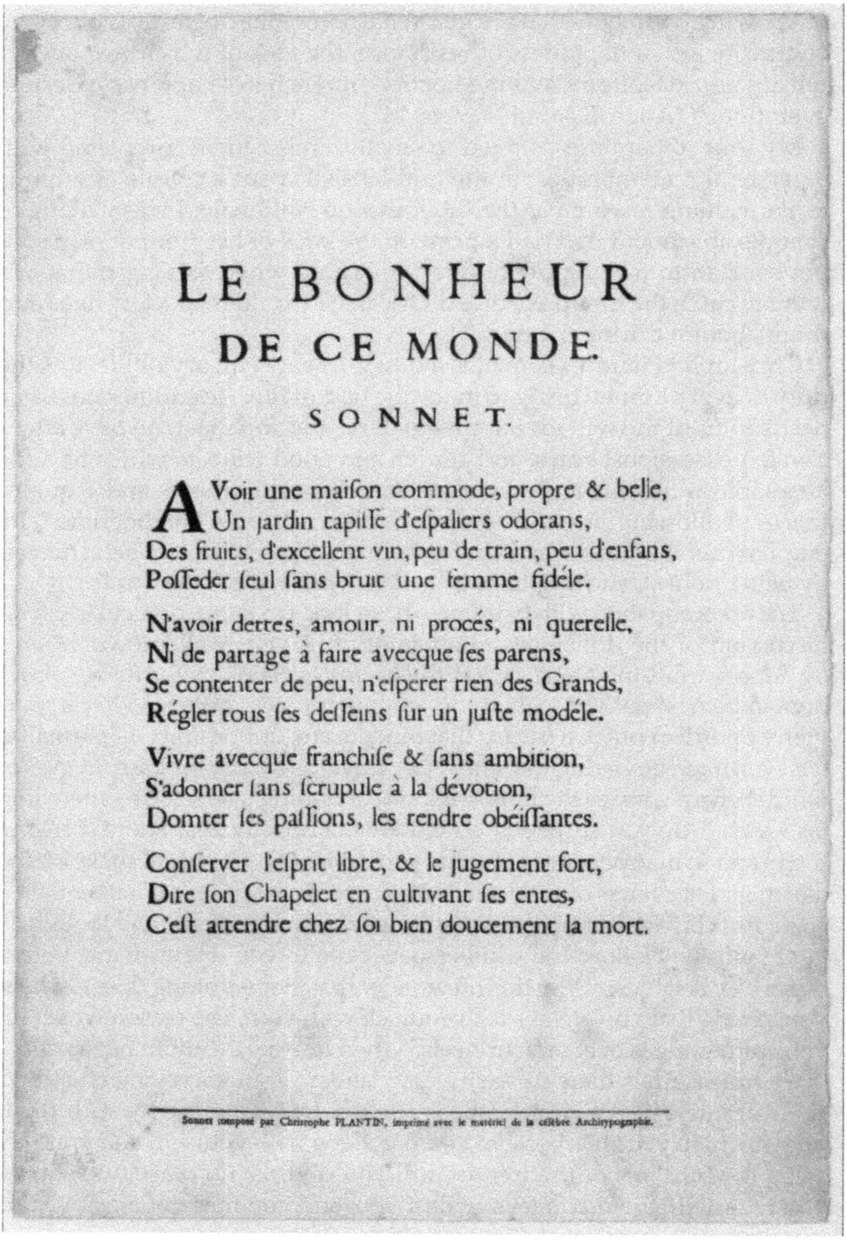

LE BONHEUR

DE CE MONDE.

SONNET.

AVoir une maiſon commode, propre & belle,
Un jardin tapiſſé d'eſpaliers odorans,
Des fruits, d'excellent vin, peu de train, peu d'enfans,
Poſſeder ſeul ſans bruit une femme fidéle.

N'avoir dettes, amour, ni procés, ni querelle,
Ni de partage à faire avecque ſes parens,
Se contenter de peu, n'eſperer rien des Grands,
Régler tous ſes deſſeins ſur un juſte modéle.

Vivre avecque franchiſe & ſans ambition,
S'adonner ſans ſcrupule à la dévotion,
Domter ſes paſſions, les rendre obéiſſantes.

Conſerver l'eſprit libre, & le jugement fort,
Dire ſon Chapelet en cultivant ſes entes,
C'eſt attendre chez ſoi bien doucement la mort.

Sonnet composé par Christophe PLANTIN, imprimé avec le matériel de la célèbre Architypographie.

Figure 2. Christophe Plantin, "Le Bonheur de ce monde" (Happiness in this world), National Library of Australia

the poet wanted to find another city, a better one, but he knows it is impossible because he only sees the black ruins of his life. In the second stanza he recognizes that he will not find another country because he has destroyed his life not only in his own city but also everywhere in the world. Cavafy constructs an asyndetic list that gives the illusion that his is an endless list, and in the second stanza he directly responds to the concerns of the first, stating, "This city will always pursue you." Cavafy suggests that the voice in the poem must take accountability for its own actions. The final two lines of Cavafy's "The City" summarize his response to the speaker: now that you have wasted your life here, you have destroyed it everywhere. Changing your city does not change the fact that you are unhappy. You must first realize why you are unhappy, seeking personal growth from within, then maybe you can think about changing your "city."

Happiness is also founded in material aspects. Japanese author Soetsu Yanagi has defended the importance of *mingei*, which means "crafts of the people." He explains: "It is meant to stand in contrast to aristocratic fine arts, and refers to objects used by ordinary people in their daily lives. These objects include household effects such as clothing, furniture, eating utensils, and stationery. In common parlance they are referred to as 'ordinary things' (*getemono*), 'the roughly made' (*sobutsu*), and 'sundry implements' (*zatsugu*). All of these are counted as mingei or folk craft" (7–8). A few pages later he confirms the linkage between good design and a comfortable life: "In recent times a shadow has fallen on our sense of beauty, on our aesthetic sensibility. There are undoubtedly many reasons for this, but one is certainly the fact that our everyday utilitarian utensils and implements have become so ugly. It is these ugly things that surround us throughout the day, from morning to night – the clothing we wear, the utensils we eat from, the furniture we make use of. Without our realizing it, these unattractive objects have had an enormous impact on our sensitivity to beauty" (12).

Beauty and happiness are elementary constituents of the everyday. We have seen so far that the presence of the everyday in literary texts may have a wakening effect as their presence acts like a mirror, allowing readers to compare what they read with their own life experience. But very little has been done to study the everyday in literature.

Ways of Reading the Everyday

A crucial text in the scrutiny of everyday life is Roland Barthes's *Mythologies* (1957), in which he offers examples of readings that deal with the status of technocratic icons within contemporary society (the Citroën DS, the Eiffel Tower), together with articles on the importance of advertising, or an analysis of the front cover of a *Paris-Match* magazine showing a young black soldier saluting the French flag. Barthes is fundamental to contemporary cultural studies because he was among the first to take mass culture seriously and to apply to it methods of analysis that were formerly the preserve of high culture. Thus, he manages to make the myth "a type of speech," arguing that "the universe is infinitely fertile in suggestions. Every object in the world can pass from a closed, silent existence to an oral state, open to appropriation by society" (*Oeuvres* 109). His are virtuoso readings of phenomena that "are always brimming over with meanings, a potent vehicle for hidden messages and half-formulated desires" (Moran, *Reading the Everyday* 22). Barthes provided us with a rhetoric, a model reading tool.

Inspired by Roland Barthes, Joe Moran's *Reading the Everyday* focuses on work and office spaces, such as the call centre, notes the commute as a distinctive form of workspace, and investigates the rules, technologies, architecture, and politics of the London Underground. Another chapter explores the often-fraught politics of traffic circulation and urban space. Moran also discusses the cultural associations surrounding another archetypal non-place, the highway service station. Finally, he examines how ideas and representations of the house have both mirrored and obscured the housing market. His aim is "to show how the cultural materials that have been representing our everyday lives over the last few decades have often served to deny or obscure this potential for change." His is a political approach with the goal "to transform our everyday lives for the better … to see the everyday not as the eternally tedious or pathetically comic residue of contemporary life, or simply as a sphere of overlooked ordinariness, but as the real space in which we lead our actual lives" (169). His is a good example of an ethnology of the nearby that, following the example of Roland Barthes and Georges Perec, has become very popular.

In this vein, Richard Sennett's trilogy *Homo Faber* is a remarkable project that addresses a significant issue in everyday life. He draws "on the ancient idea of Man as his or her own maker – a maker of life through concrete practices." His quest is "to relate how people shape personal effort, social relations and the physical environment" (*Together* x). He is keen on emphasizing skill and competency because in his view "modern society is de-skilling people in the conduct of everyday life." He points to the overwhelming number of machines, which are many more than humans can handle; while it is possible to communicate between people in more and sophisticated ways, there is less awareness of how to communicate well. To conclude: "Practical skill is a tool rather than a salvation, but, lacking it, issues of Meaning and Value remain abstractions" (x). Sennett calls our attention to how we do things, the practical (manual) aspect inherent to the everyday.

From a semiotic perspective Jurij Lotman provided other interesting insights in his essay "The Poetics of Everyday Behavior in Eighteenth-Century Russian Culture." According to him, only an observer who perceives everyday behaviour as a semiotic phenomenon can experience it aesthetically: "[a] foreigner, for whom the everyday life of another culture is an exotic experience, can perceive that life as an aesthetic fact" (68). One of the problems in analysing the everyday is its invisibility, particularly for those who are too close: "The direct participant in a culture, as a rule, is simply unaware of its distinguishing qualities. In the eighteenth century, however, the everyday behavior of the Russian nobility underwent such an elemental transformation that it acquired uncharacteristic features." Thus, Lotman writes: "In every group with a relatively developed culture, human behavior is organized according to the following basic opposition: (1) The ordinary, everyday, customary social behavior which members of the group consider 'natural'; the only possible, normal behavior; (2) All types of ceremonial, ritual, nonpragmatic behavior. This category includes state ceremonies, religious cults and rites, and all those activities that 'native speakers' of a culture perceive as having an independent meaning" (68). People in a specific social or cultural group learn the first type of conduct as they do their native language: "No one would think of providing such an audience with a grammar of the language of social behavior, a metatext describing its 'correct' norms" (68). Instead, the second type of conduct is learned as if it were a foreign language, with rules and grammar books: "At first its norms are assimilated and then, on their foundation, 'texts of behavior' are constructed. The first type of behavior is acquired naturally, unconsciously. The second is acquired consciously, with the aid of a teacher, and its mastery is usually celebrated in a special rite of initiation" (68). The distinction established by Lotman is useful to distinguish between the private and the public sphere. Although in contemporary social life there is significant overlap and interaction between the two spheres, they were once separate. Information and communications technologies have led to the collapse of the public-private divide.

Another suitable example is provided by the very successful book series by Swedish author Karl Ove Knausgaard, *My Struggle*. The author was inspired by some big events that mark a life: achieving love, the death of one's parents, the birth of a child, writing a book. Knausgaard's opus is able to direct our attention to minor events: in a long drive to see his grandparents; in a swimming lesson; in grocery shopping; in playing a guitar; in making tea; in cleaning a bathroom. A reviewer noticed that after reading the first volume he was looking at his own life with more attention: "Making coffee in the morning, working out at the gym, shaving afterward, reading a book, thinking deep thoughts, writing an essay, visiting a museum, browsing in a bookstore, my desk, calling my mother. Over and over, it's the same pattern: envision, fantasize, plan, execute, and then succeed or fail, gloat or mourn, survive to fight another day, summon up, or discover, your will again" (Rothman).

Reading about everyday experiences most certainly has a mirror effect (as mentioned earlier): we are trapped by the intricacies of somebody's life that are warily similar to those in ours. Sigmund Freud, in *The Psychopathology of Everyday Life* (1901), discussed everyday life as a way to explain wrong actions with the help of psychoanalysis. Freud was interested in deviations from the stereotypes of everyday demeanour, such as seemingly unintended reservation, gaps in memory, verbal errors, and random movements and actions. Those were a manifestation of unconscious thoughts and impulses. With this enumeration he delineated an initial series of activities linked to the everyday. For Freud, what appears to be coincidental or unexplained might in fact be a clue to some deep hidden truth. We clearly see that affects and the everyday are closely related. What we need is a map to navigate through that relationship.

Everyday Affects

The study of the everyday intersects with affect theory, a theory that is founded in Spinoza's and Deleuze's writings: beings and bodies are not independent but rather are affected by and affect other bodies as a condition of being in the world (Massumi; Ahern). Massumi noted that "the body, when impinged upon, is described by Spinoza as being in a state of passional suspension in which it exists more outside of itself, more in the abstracted action of the impinging thing and the abstracted context of that action, than within itself" (92). There is a double effect provoked by the awareness of affects: "In Spinoza, it is only when the idea of the affection is doubled by an idea of the idea of the affection that it attains the level of conscious reflection. Conscious reflection is a doubling over of the idea on itself, a self-recursion of the idea that enwraps the affection or impingement, at two removes" (92). Some concepts proposed by Deleuze and Guattari are also instrumental as they do not define an organized and mapped field but, as stated in *A Thousand Plateaus* (1987), advocate a kind of knowledge based upon the rhizomatic, not the arborescent, and in terms of scale the molecular, not the molar.

This cartographical approach is rather significant when addressing the everyday. The cultural geographer Nigel Thrift, who is interested in the non-representational, explores in *Non-representational Theory: Space/Politics/Affect* (2008) ways of analysing everyday life in terms of what he calls "the geography of what happens" (2). He acknowledges the eternal difficulty of defining an ever-changing experience: "the human sensorium is constantly being re-invented," and "what is experienced as experience is itself variable" (2). Furthermore, theorists and practitioners of affect theory stress an idea very dear to me, how the act of reading creates a sort of mirror effect and interacts with our own lives: "a phenomenon that the common reader regularly encounters: If we venture close enough, literature has the potential to transform us by opening our bodies to hitherto inaccessible experiences, expanding our sense of how the life of others might *feel*. This feature of literary engagement, though, is seldom highlighted and explored in contemporary literary criticism" (Skiveren 219). Reading texts through an everyday life perspective changes dramatically how we perceive the intricacies of it. And in some texts it is more evident than in others.

From the perspective of studying the everyday, Kathleen Stewart's *Ordinary Affects* is a book that establishes a series of observations on present-day North America, not from the point of view of a scholarly ethnographer but from her own experience. Writing in the third person helped her create the critical distance that rigorous academic scholarship requires. At the same time, however, the chosen narrative format makes readers "affective ethnographers," encountering the extraordinary out of ordinary situations. Observation allows Stewart to uncover a nearby, unobserved world formed by the association of intensities, superficial sensations, perceptions, and expressions. The subject is "a thing composed of encounters and the spaces and events it traverses and inhabits" (79). As defined by Stewart: "Ordinary affects … are an animate circuit that conducts force and maps connections, routes, and disjunctures. They are a kind of contact zone where the overdeterminations of circulations, events, conditions, technologies, and flows of power literally take place. To attend to ordinary affects is to trace how the potency of forces lies in their immanence to things that are both flighty and hardwired, shifty and unsteady but palpable too. At once abstract and concrete, ordinary affects are more directly compelling than ideologies, as well as more fractious, multiplicitous, and unpredictable than symbolic meanings" (3). This remark points to the invisibilities of the everyday – something obsessive, ever present but at the same time unnoticeable. Her observation could be linked to a 1970 essay by Roland Barthes published in *Les Cahiers du cinema* entitled "Le troisième sens: Notes de recherche sur quelques photogrammes de S.M. Eisenstein." Barthes focused on studying the effects of a strange sense, a different sense from that of connotation or symbolic meaning and also from that of denotation. This third level of meaning, what he also called an obtuse sense, stubborn, escaping description, stood where language had ceased, and linguistics would be of no help in grasping it. Stewart adds something more on "ordinary affects": they are "public feelings … but they're also the stuff that seemingly intimate lives are made of" (2). It is a way of organizing life.

Ben Highmore, reviewing *Ordinary Affects*, linked the book to what Raymond Williams identified in 1958, that "culture is ordinary." He signalled a commitment to the messy, provisional, and deeply corporeal "whole ways of life" of a community, a culture. "Ordinary" is the world pulsing with life in its very singularity, existing across and in the interstices of the arbitrary and unhelpful distinctions we cannot help making between "labour" and "love," "private" and "public," "text" and "context," "art" and "economics" ("Something Ordinary" 4). Ordinary affects could also be linked to *habitus*, the concept defined by Pierre Bourdieu that refers to the physical embodiment of cultural capital, to the deeply ingrained habits, skills, and dispositions that we possess due to our life experiences (Bourdieu 82–3).

Kathleen Stewart, in the afterword to *The Affect Theory Reader*, proposes a definition for affect and its many connections to the everyday. To her, affect is "the commonplace, labor-intensive process of sensing modes of living as they come into being." It is what links everything: "[t]he lived spaces and temporalities of home, work, school, blame, adventure, illness, rumination, pleasure, downtime, and release are the rhythms of the present as a compositional event – one already weighted with the buzz of atmospheric fill" ("Worlding Refrains" 340). I will move now to a discussion of the most significant theories and ways of approaching the everyday.

Explorations

Interest in the everyday has been developed in many fashions. Some books explore what is changing or disappearing. Others examine overlooked aspects of the everyday. A significant number of fairly recent books provide excellent examples of an ongoing interest in picturing (observing, analysing) the everyday. Orvar Löfgren's *On Holiday: A History of Vacationing* (1999) looks at some of the ways in which vacationing has evolved as an important part of modem life, searching for new experiences and understandings. The author sees vacationing as a cultural laboratory in which people are able to experiment with new aspects of their identities, their social relations, their interactions with nature, and daydreaming and mind travelling. (7) Lofgren argues that vacations and holidays are searches for utopia. It is a book about the ways in which the tourist industry has marketed dreams and taught the affluent traveller how to see and experience "vacationscapes."

Joe Moran has published *Queuing for Beginners: The Story of Daily Life from Breakfast to Bedtime* (2007), which is a history of postwar British daily habits, such as queuing, commuting, and office life.[3] He unravels an alternative history of postwar Britain, paying attention not to political, social, or lifestyle changes but to habits and routines. In particular, he describes how the United States has had an impact on British life: "The smallest details of mundane life can tell us stories about much larger national and global changes." The book is organized around one pattern, a single day, "in order to explore the hidden meanings and histories of daily life." Each one of the sixteen chapters covers a routine activity, roughly one for each hour of the day from getting up to going to bed: having breakfast, commuting, and queuing. More modern habits – checking emails, watching television, eating ready meals – would be almost entirely new and strange to his subjects, but they might detect some residue of older social habits even in these activities. His selection of habits follows two principles: "they are near-universal (my apologies if you do not work in some sort of office, but the majority of workers do and the proportion is rising) and are done without much deliberation, and certainly without giving much thought to their histories" (6–7). Moran focuses on a series of uninteresting events that unfolded across Britain:

> Millions of people woke up and had instant coffee and a cereal bar for breakfast. They all rushed for the train and stood pressed up against each other in a crowded carriage. They all arrived at the office, went to their desks and spent the morning there, occasionally getting up to go to the photocopier or the staff kitchen for a gossip. At lunchtime, they all stood in the queue at the bank, then they all bought a sandwich and came back to eat it at their desks. They all checked their emails, and then nipped outside for a smoke. They all had to attend a boring staff meeting. At half past five, they all walked out of the office, weaving in between the rush-hour traffic. They all had a quick, after-work drink with each other, then they all went home and stuck a ready meal in the microwave. They all ate it on the sofa while zapping through the television channels. After they had all watched the late-night weather forecast, they all went upstairs, tucked

> themselves up in bed and drifted off to sleep. Nothing out of the ordinary happened: nobody became ill, got the sack, married, divorced, gave birth or died. It seems to be a story without a protagonist or a plot – just one thing after another. I think we had better start at the beginning. (7–8)

Moran's book brings to mind Orvar Löfgren and Billy Ehn's *The Secret World of Doing Nothing* (2010). The authors there seek to comprehend what is going on when people feel attracted to or repelled by the prospect of "doing nothing," particularly "waiting patiently or furiously, performing routines absentmindedly, and 'escaping reality' in more or less fanciful daydreams," and to illuminate these "empty" times as full of significance. They are also interested in how these activities may be interconnected and how they have evolved and changed in different cultural contexts. They make a cultural analysis of these three themes, trying to answer Georg Simmel's question: "How is society possible? In what ways do such mundane activities as waiting, following routines, and daydreaming – which are often solitary – organize and support everyday life? How can they tell us something about larger social and existential issues?"(Löfgren and Ehn 6). A year earlier, Elizabeth Shove, Frank Trentmann, and Richard Wilk edited a book, *Time, Consumption and Everyday Life: Practice, Materiality and Culture (Cultures of Consumption)* (2009), that confronts anxieties related to speed being out of control and examines the changing rhythms and temporal organization of everyday life. Running themes of the book include questions of coordination and disruption; cycles and seasons; and the interplay between power and freedom and between material and natural forces. The book has a three-pronged approach that allows us to understand "how multiple temporalities co-evolve and intersect, how patterns of time and space are reproduced in daily life, and how material culture acts as a conduit in the production and consumption of time" (6).

Food has become a world obsession, and a fully fledged scholarly field has grown alongside the increasing prevalence of food studies. A recent volume by Antoine de Baecque, *La France gastronome: Comment le restaurant est entré dans notre histoire* (2019; La France gastronome: How the restaurant became part of our history), shows how the restaurant, a modern and contemporary everyday destination, was an important site in the creation of metropolitan culture and is a place where everything that interests students of culture comes together: production, consumption, exchange, the material, the symbolic, the local, and the global. It is a more down-to-earth version of Rebecca L. Spang's *The Invention of the Restaurant: Paris and Modern Gastronomic Culture* (2001), which provides a critical history of French gastronomic culture.

Svetlana Boym's *Common Places: Mythologies of Everyday Life in Russia* (1995) is an attempt to describe cultural practices in the Soviet Union. She focuses on common places, banality, bad taste, and what is left out in general discussions on Soviet Russia because "the everyday mythologies and rituals of ordinary life that are hidden behind political, ideological, or artistic screens, [are] deemed irrelevant for the heroic conception of the national identity in Russia or for Soviet ideology" and remain inscrutable to Western political scientists and journalists, causing the inner workings of the culture to remain a mystery (2). She studied hidden aspects of Russian culture – "the attitudes toward ordinary life, home, material objects and art, as well as expressions of emotion and ways of communication" – because they differ dramatically from "Western European or American versions of modernity" (2–3). Her book is organized around several Russian cultural "untranslatables" "that reflect common places of everyday life" (4). Her chapter "Writing Common Places" is devoted to the "literary disease of 'graphomania'" (27) and marks the transformation of the common place from a spatial parameter into a rhetorical figure based on major figures of Russian literature such as Pushkin's Lensky, Dostoevsky's Makar Devushkin, Captain Lebiadkin, Chekov's housewives, or Nabokov's Liza Pnin (174). In *The Future of Nostalgia* (2002) she explores the web of memory and mythologizing that underpins the human longing for vanished worlds. "Nostalgia tantalizes us with its fundamental ambivalence; it is about the repetition of the unrepeatable, materialization of the immaterial" (20). Focusing on twentieth-century Eastern and Central European exiles, Boym considers how nostalgia operates in modern culture. She identifies two main tropes of the modern condition: restorative nostalgia and reflective nostalgia. "Restorative nostalgia stresses nostos and attempts a transhistorical reconstruction of the lost home. Reflective nostalgia thrives in algia, the longing itself, and delays the homecoming – wistfully, ironically, desperately. Restorative nostalgia does not think of itself as nostalgia, but rather as truth and tradition" (21). The former "puts emphasis on nostos and proposes to rebuild the lost home and patch up the memory gaps," while the latter "dwells in algia, in longing and loss, the imperfect process of remembrance." Whether we place emphasis on the first or second parts of the term makes a great difference for Boym because the former usage of *nost*algia provides an intellectual basis for the "antimodern myth-making of history" that operates "by means of a return to national symbols and myth and, occasionally, through swapping conspiracy theories" (41). Reflective nostalgia, meanwhile, can produce an ethics of resistance to paranoid narratives that portray the world as divided between conspiratorial enemies and fellow patriots.

Cartographies and Disappearances

As I have discussed so far, everyday life is a subject that can be approached from many different angles. Take, for example, the case of Ira Glass, the Canadian host of an excellent NPR broadcast that handles many aspects of the everyday, always from an ironic perspective. He has a difficult time trying to define what he does in the show: "We think of the show as journalism … [W]hat we're doing is applying the tools of journalism to everyday lives, personal lives. Which is true. It's also true that the journalism we do tends to use a lot of the techniques of fiction: scenes and characters and narrative threads" ("This American Life"). Narrative (fiction or even autobiography) becomes a powerful tool to explore the everyday.

There is a rather amazing fact in modern life: it is organized around a series of generational milestones. We measure our collective identities in accordance with the shared experience of public events, including successful films and popular songs. *Boyhood* (2014), a film by Richard Linklater, pictures in painful detail the most obvious aspects of the life of a boy growing up in the United States in the twenty-first century. It is a film about people who are struggling with everyday problems. *Boyhood* can be related to the impulses that originated with Italian neorealism, when scenes were shot on location, with no professional extras and with a largely non-professional cast. The stories focused on everyday people with an emphasis on the unexceptional routines of everyday life in rural settings or working-class neighbourhoods. Neo-realism asserted that recording everyday life was the biggest show one could capture on film. Whether we like it or not, generational milestones become part of the architecture of our being and a kind of private currency trading with our partners.

We have seen in the case of Orlando's inquiry that disappearances are closely related to the everyday. A good way of looking at disappearances was explained by Siegfried Kracauer in his last book, *History: The Last Things before the Last*, where he indicated that his life's work was reducible to a single purpose: "the rehabilitation of objectives and modes of being which still lack a name and hence are overlooked or misjudged" and which "despite all that has been written about them are still largely *terra incognita*" (4). For Kracauer, the discipline of history is particularly suited to this task, not only because it often deals with disregarded aspects of life but also because it is a necessarily tentative mode of inquiry lying somewhere between the abstractions of philosophy and the "pseudo-scientific methodological strictness" of social science (214). Kracauer also states that chance configurations are fragments and that photography further tends to suggest endlessness. A genuine photograph precludes the notion of completeness. Its frame marks a provisional limit; its content points beyond that frame, referring to a multitude of real-life phenomena that cannot possibly be encompassed in their entirety (57–9). Kracauer compares the examination of historical evidence with the observation of ancient photographs, in the sense that the two have a kind of stubborn reality that must be acknowledged, but they also suggest infinity and that they cannot complete our knowledge of the past.

In this book I propose an alternative way of looking into the everydayness by crafting a cartography of the everyday as detected mostly in literary texts. I need first to address what I understand by cartography. According to J.B. Harley and David Woodward, new formats of maps are "graphic representations that facilitate a spatial understanding of things, concepts, conditions, processes, or events in the human world" (16). These authors have introduced more contemporary forms of mapping, linking geographic knowledge with power and practice. Their view is a stimulating rejection of the authority claimed by analogue maps and suggests an alternative method to portray everyday life. Up until recently, map-making was concerned with picturing the world as a product of physical geography, paying attention to location, scale, and distance. Maps have a significant political, social, and historical value. As opposed to analogue maps, digital mapping allows for interaction and rewriting.

In fact, one precedent worth mentioning is the activity as a mapmaker of Madeleine de Scudéry, whose *Carte du Tendre* appeared as an illustration to her novel *Clélie* (1654–61). In her map (figure 3) the road to love begins at the city of Nouvelle amitié (New Friendship), located at the bottom of the map. There are three tributaries to the River of Love that flows up the map's centre: Respect, Esteem, and Affection. Along the right bank of the Inclination River, we can read the names of various way stations such as Fresh Eyes, Love Letter, Big Heart, and Generosity that invite the traveller to rest and contemplate. On the opposite shore, Complacence, Little Care, Attendance, and Obeisance offer alternatives to virtue, driven by passion.

This is a topographical and allegorical representation of the Land of Love, where the lover must find his way to the heart of his lady (from the city of New Friendship) between many perils and many trials (there is a risk of getting lost in dangerous seas, Enmity, or the Lake

Figure 3. Madeleine de Scudéry. *Carte du Tendre* (The map of Tendre) (1654–61)

of Indifference). On the map the land of Tendre is crossed by three great rivers (Respect, Esteem, Affection), dotted with towns (Tendre-sur-Estime, Tendre-sur-Recognition, Tendre-sur-Inclination) and villages less favourable to the feeling of love: Gossiping (Médisance) and Wickedness (Méschanceté), with the danger of falling into the Sea of Enmity (Mer d'Inmitié). Likewise, if the man ends up in Negligence or Inequality (Negligence, Inegalité) or Oversight (Oubli), he risks falling into the Lake of Indifference (Lac d'Indiference). The *Carte de Tendre* defines, through allegory, an ideal variety of amorous behaviour, perfectly in tune with the gallant aesthetic of the time, made up of attentions and respect, devotion, perseverance, and restraint, as well as ardour.[4]

Some contemporary artists have also played with the idea of a new kind of cartography. Guy Débord and his *situationistes* friends made several night outings through the city of Paris. What is relevant is the visual translation, the graphic montage, and the mapping not

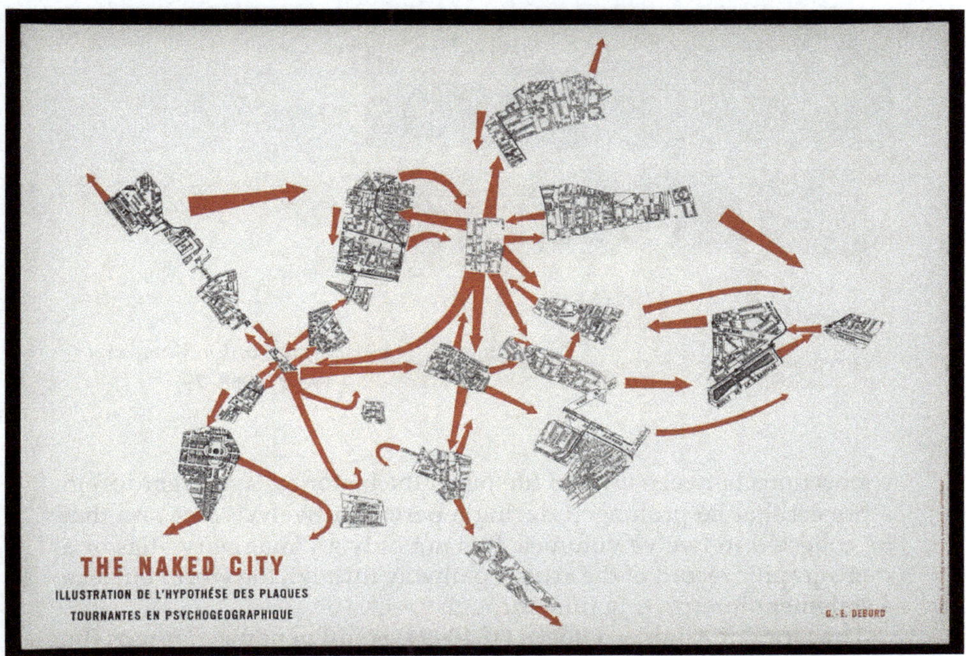

Figure 4. Guy Débord, *The Naked City* (1957)

of the actual path followed but of the conceptual possibilities triggered by these nocturnal adventures. As described in *The Naked City* (1957; see figure 4), Paris looks like a collage of areas separated from each other but united and dominated by red arrows that traverse the groove of emotional currents and bestow a precise psychogeographic relief. The map proposed by Débord represents a city laid bare, broken up and reassembled in a completely subjective way and therefore disconnected from the topographical motif and open to the infinite possibilities offered by the mind. According to the Situationist's project, psychogeography was born from the need to decline the precise exploration of the city while recording psychological states found in different neighbourhoods.[5]

An analogous experiment can be found in the work of Japanese artist On Kawara, particularly in the series *I Went* (1968–79; see figure 5). The series provides a good example of a willingness to preserve the memory of the banality of life through the traces of distances travelled by the artist during a period of his life. A red line is witness to the

Figure 5. On Kawara, *I Went* (1968–79)

connections between art and life (as in the historical avant-gardes) in a project that he prolonged during a period of twelve years and that he collected in twelve volumes. It is not only an imaginary atlas or a mere graphic record of the artist's pathway through the world but also a statement interpreting time through space.

The work of Alighiero Boetti (1940–94) is full of maps. Perhaps the most well-known is the series *Mappe*, map-based works that reflect Boetti's long-term preoccupation with systems and classifications applied to the natural world. (See figure 6.) In his work *City of Turin* (1967) the ordinary everyday life prevails. Boetti re-appropriates his city by reinventing it and giving it a new topography precisely on the basis of his experience: the highlighted areas go beyond the usual tourist routes and entice the user to measure Turin with a different perspective that focuses on the lesser-known areas of the city that will never appear in a tourist map. They create the disappearing cartography of an individual's life with his personal connections to a space. Starting in 1971, for each of his *Mappe*, Boetti traced a world map onto canvas, coloured it according to the national flag of each country, and then gave the canvas to Afghan craftswomen to use as the base for a tapestry. The more than 150 *Mappe* of different colours and sizes form a symbolic portrait of the passage of time and shifting world politics. He grew up in the Arte Povera environment, which was marked by a rediscovery of the primordial, understood in his case as an opportunity to regain possession of "original" attitudes.

Malagasy artist Malala Andrialavidrazana has created some flabbergasting maps that defy our notion of cartography. We see lush

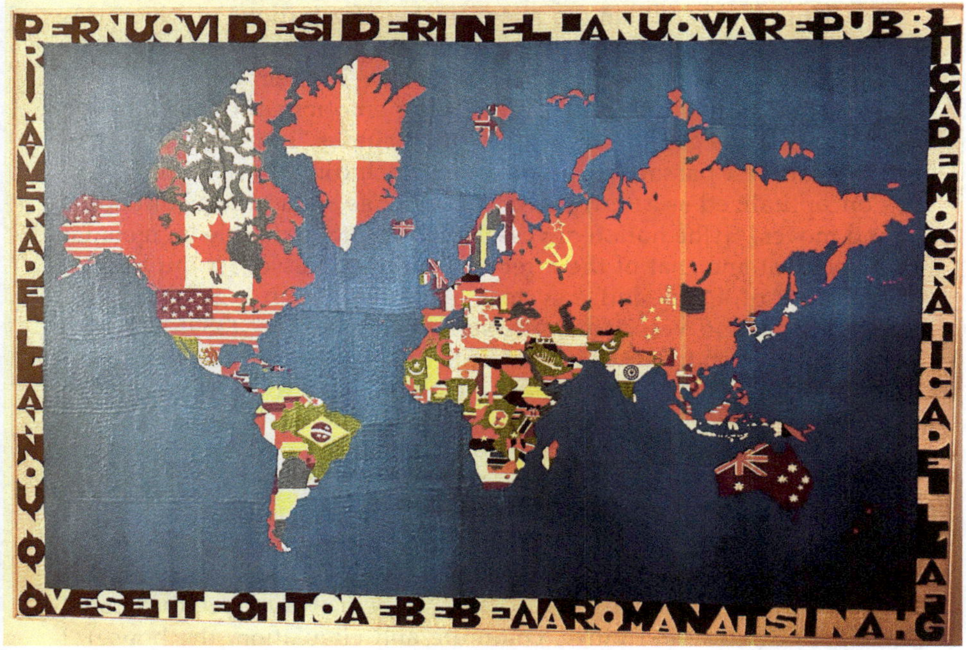

Figure 6. Alighiero Boetti, *Mappa* (1978). Courtesy of Giuglio Alessandri. Photograph: Enric Bou

forests and tigers, lions, fish and dragons, set in brilliantly coloured nineteenth-century maps. They present an exuberant version of the colonial world, taking in beauty and much pain. As an exponent of the African diaspora, her maps tell the tormented history of the South of the world: an intricate tangle of invasions, violence, and abuse that over the centuries has characterized the poorest countries on the planet such as Madagascar. In the *Figures* series she creates a patchwork by combining banknotes (a symbol of economic power), old maps (a mirror image of rich European nations during the colonial era), and the covers of the thirty-three-rpm albums that the artist listened to as a girl. All of these elements are mixed with foliage of tropical trees and exotic animals, together with black heroes and shapes of slaves. The result is a claim against the horror, splendour, and exploitation erected by colonialism.

These examples serve as proof of the ways in which an alternative cartography can be constructed out of an analogic point of departure. Two of them are allegorical configurations of itineraries one can make. The other two encapsulate a personal experience with a series of movements on an urban space. To them one could add Giuliana Bruno's reflection on mapping emotions through cinema. She speaks of a geographical atlas that includes "inhabitants and the forms of their passage through spaces, including the spaces of life." Conceptualized as a "terrain of 'vessels,'" as a place that both holds and moves, "[t]he notion of vessel incorporates a double image: that of the boat and that of the artery (as in blood vessel); it implies the container of a flux and a system of routing. Such a geography of inhabitants and vessels may be subject to charting" (239). She also gets inspiration from Madeleine de Scudéry's *Carte de Tendre* (Map of tenderness). Emotion and affect are always tied to memories, time, history and space, and almost always perceived as disappearances – ruins and relics. Geography expresses the movement of history, understood as a space, as layers of lost experiences.

I want to propose a way of reading the everyday that takes into account previous work by scholars such as Highmore and Gardiner, and their genealogy of theorists, while advancing the discussion a few paces. Partially following Joe Moran's study of everyday in the United Kingdom (work and office, commute and circulation, the house), I have divided my areas of interest into five crucial aspects of the everyday: routines and disappearances; observing the nearby; using public transportation; thanatourism; and food. These activities have been chosen with a mixed-criteria – diachronic and synchronic. Our everyday is filled with traces of the past. As suggested by Lefebvre, memory and the everyday tend to be viewed as opposites. Memory is seen as "a typical process of accumulation and therefore an essential component of mechanisms that materialize and technicalize such a process," whereas the everyday is perceived as not cumulative: "Everyday life, when it changes, evolves according to a rhythm that does not coincide with the time of accumulation ... Thus, an illusion is created of the unbroken continuity of houses, buildings and cities from the oriental town of proto-history down to the present day" (Lefebvre, *Everyday Life* 61). In *Cartographies of Disappearance* I apply many of the findings about analysing the everyday from a sociological and theoretical perspective to a reading of a limited sample of texts that provide nevertheless excellent examples of a different way to read literature and of addressing the everyday.

My objective in this book is to stress the fact that very few scholars have addressed everyday life from a strictly literary perspective. Thus, I propose to focus on the invisibility of the everyday as expressed in examples belonging mostly to Catalan and Spanish literature, in a few crucial areas. The everyday is a matter of study and observation, particularly from a social sciences perspective, but much less so from a humanities perspective. My approach is novel because I set out to explore five major instances representing the everyday in literature and the arts. This approach will provide an alternative cartography of a hidden world, a world that disappears as it is created; we take a glance at it and expose the intricacies that we have failed to see.

2

Singing the Everyday, Signing or Signalling the World: On Catalogic Poems

All the world's a stage,
And all the men and women merely players;
They have their exits and their entrances,
And one man in his time plays many parts,
His acts being seven ages.
[..]
Last scene of all,
That ends this strange eventful history,
Is second childishness and mere oblivion,
Sans teeth, sans eyes, sans taste, sans everything.

William Shakespeare, *As You Like It*

On 11 August 2014 cartoonist Roz Chast published in *The New Yorker* a humorous version of genesis, *Creation: The True Story*. It was a reinterpretation of creation with an interesting variation: on the third day God "created a list," instead of the official version, when God created dry land, seas, plants, and trees. What is remarkable here is not the rewriting of the Old Testament but the monument to procrastination that this cartoon implies.[1] Lists are an excuse to not finish anything, a compromise to avoid accomplishing a task – something that may remind us of Shakespeare's *The Tempest*: "We are such stuff as dreams are made on, and our little life is rounded with a sleep" (4.1.41). In the final pages of Jeffrey Eugenides's novel *The Virgin Suicides* the narrator tries to solve the puzzle of the death of the four Lisbon girls: "In the end we had the pieces of the puzzle, but no matter how we put them together, gaps remained, oddly shaped emptinesses mapped by what surrounded them, like countries we couldn't name ... What lingered after them was not life, which always overcomes natural death, but the most trivial list of mundane facts: a clock ticking on a wall, a room dim at noon, and the outrageousness of a human being thinking only of herself" (246). The sense of emptiness described in the paragraph brings forth both the puzzling mystery of the gaps of everyday life – a sensation compared to an unknown map – and at the same time the urgency of solving microscopic, almost hidden, problems. The disappearance of a group of young women creates this hollow space immersed in the incomprehensible absurd of little details that one can hardly perceive but that are at the same time poignantly full of meaning.

From a similar perspective, Ramón Gómez de la Serna designates the geography of life's leftovers when discussing Madrid's Rastro market as a concept. What is essential about the Rastro, he wrote, is its condition of marginality, as some sort of refuge for discarded objects refuted by civilian life:

> El Rastro es siempre el mismo trecho relamido de la ciudad, planicie, costanilla, gruta de mar o tienda de mar, que es lo mismo, playa cerrada en que la gran ciudad – mejor dicho –, las grandes ciudades y los pueblillos desconocidos mueren, se abaten, se laminan como el mar en la playa, tan delgadamente, dejando tirados en la arena los restos casuales, los descartes impasibles, que allí quedan engolfados y quietos hasta que algunos se vuelven a ir en la resaca. (74–5)
>
> (El Rastro is always the same shimmering stretch of the city, plain, small coast, sea cave or sea tent, which is the same thing, closed beach where the big city – better said – the big cities and the unknown small towns die, are beaten down, are laminated like the sea on the beach, so thinly, leaving on the sand the casual remains, the impassive discards, which remain there engulfed and still until some of them leave again in the undertow.)

Consequently, the Rastro is a sort of beach where leftovers from a worldwide shipwreck surface, which are the "restos casuales, los descartes impasibles." Watching the everyday, with its essential attention to minutiae, calls for an expert eye but also a detective who can picture abnormalities lagging under reality's surface. Both Eugenides and Gómez de la Serna point to the unorganized accumulation of objects and beings and the unbearable inclination to make sense of it all.

Everyday life is filled with lists of things: what to do, what to buy, whom to invite, and where to go and lots of unfulfilled New Year's resolutions. Precisely, lists of people are a way to describe attendees to an event. A tedious casual activity such as making lists can turn into something more complex, thus turning upside down practices and almost forgotten activities. I will discuss three interrelated examples that are based on the list concept and are loosely interconnected as all of them elaborate lists of people who can be found in, or are related to, a specific place: Jacques Prévert's "Tentative de description d'un dîner de têtes à Paris-France" (1931; Attempt to describe a dinner of heads in Paris, France), Bob Dylan's "Desolation Row" (1965), and Jaume Sisa's "Qualsevol nit pot sortir el sol" (1975; Any night the sun may rise).[2] All three poems could be typified with the words that Michael Bishop used to describe Prévert's poem: "The anaphoric cascade of words is irresistible, contagious, witty, full of yet pertinent both general and specific allusions to social mores, punning, satirical, freely flowing" (9). By focusing on such a unique selection of texts, I will be able to reveal underlying trends within the common, almost ignored realities.

The poems I deal with include instances of serialization or enumeration. They deal with regular events immersed in continuity and change, repetition and variation. Prévert's poem "Tentative de description" is a sardonic depiction of a state dinner. Bob Dylan's "Desolation Row" has been described as a sort of Fellini-esque parade of grotesques and oddities featuring a huge cast of iconic characters. Jaume Sisa's song "Qualsevol nit pot sortir el sol" (Any night the sun may rise) is a long poem-song in which Sisa enumerates a list of characters, real or from fictional sources, to recreate the parade of guests arriving at a night party. Before analysing these texts in detail, I need to discuss the issue of everyday life and seriality because it is at the core of my reading of the three texts.

Seriality and the Everyday

The use of the rhetorical device enumeration can be identified as a method of looking around to encompass the wide variety of actions and people that populate the landscape of the everyday. Umberto Eco made some extremely useful remarks in the context of a Louvre exhibition. As he put it, there are remarkable pictorial solutions that artists have used for a visual representation of the list. Eco theorized about the list's fascination. He included verbal lists (from Homer to Pynchon) and visual ones (from a fifth-century Greek shield to Christian Boltanski installations). As a good cataloguer he thrived with subdivisions. Thus the two major types of list are those that correspond to the "poetics of everything included" and those expressing the "poetics of the etcetera" (Eco 7).[3] The first aims to complete and close, albeit temporarily: the old phone book is a list of phone numbers and also a quite exhaustive list of the inhabitants of a city. The second exploits the association ability of the human mind in constant motion, for instance the section of the inventions of Professor Franz de Copenhague in the Spanish postwar magazine *TBO* (Tausiet). These inventions of *TBO* were small follies and pitfalls of imagination and had no physical boundaries. Noteworthy is the case of Marcel Proust, who fell asleep while reading train timetables, and who includes several lists of people's names in the *Recherche*. In a famous chapter Proust combats insomnia with lists of names of towns he would like to visit:

> [M]ais j'avais beau les comparer, comment choisir plus qu'entre des êtres individuels, qui ne sont pas interchangeables, entre Bayeux si haute dans sa noble dentelle rougeâtre et dont le faîte était illuminé par le vieil or de sa dernière syllabe; Vitré dont l'accent aigu losangeait de bois noir le vitrage ancien; le doux Lamballe qui, dans son blanc, va du jaune coquille d'œuf au gris perle; Coutances, cathédrale normande, que sa diphtongue finale, grasse et jaunissante couronne par une tour de beurre; Lannion avec le bruit, dans son silence villageois, du coche suivi de la mouche; Questambert, Pontorson, risibles et naïfs, plumes blanches et becs jaunes éparpillés sur la route de ces lieux fluviatiles et poétiques; Benodet, nom à peine amarré que semble vouloir entraîner la rivière au milieu de ses algues; Pont-Aven, envolée blanche et rose de l'aile d'une coiffe légère qui se reflète en tremblant dans une eau verdie de canal; Quimperlé, lui, mieux attaché et, depuis le moyen âge, entre les ruisseaux dont il gazouille et s'emperle en une grisaille pareille à celle que dessinent, à travers les toiles d'araignées d'une verrière, les rayons de soleil changés en pointes émoussées d'argent bruni? (388–9)
>
> ([B]ut in vain might I compare and contrast them; how was one to choose, any more than between individual people, who are not interchangeable, between Bayeux, so lofty in its noble coronet of rusty lace, whose highest point caught the light of the old gold of its second syllable; Vitré, whose acute accent barred its ancient glass with wooden lozenges; gentle Lamballe, whose whiteness ranged from egg-shell yellow to a pearly grey; Coutances, a Norman cathedral, whose final consonants, rich and yellowing, crowned with a tower of butter; Lannion with the rumble and buzz, in the silence of its village street, of the fly on the wheel of the coach; Questambert, Pontorson, ridiculously silly and simple, white feathers and yellow beaks strewn along the road to those well-watered and poetic spots; Benodet, a name scarcely moored that seemed to be striving to draw the river down into the tangle of its seaweeds; Pont-Aven, the snowy, rosy flight of the wing of a lightly poised coif, tremulously reflected in the greenish waters of a canal; Quimperlé, more firmly attached, this, and since the Middle Ages, among the rivulets with which it babbled, threading their pearls upon a grey background, like the pattern made, through the cobwebs upon a window, by rays of sunlight changed into blunt points of tarnished silver?)

In this case, to say the names, associating them with each other, establishing relationships and divisions, has a therapeutic function. Basically a list is an enumeration. But a list is also a story, what Eco calls the "rhetoric of enumeration"(45), which corresponds to the rhythm of sounds, associations producing a long list of words, as we can perceive in Marcel Proust's example. At another level, "Rumba de Barcelona" by Argentinian singer Gato Pérez has a ritornello that is a series of names, the different neighbourhoods in the city:

Somorrostro, Bon Pastor,
Hostafrancs, la Guineueta,
Sans, Carmelo, Guinardó,
Poble Sec, Barceloneta.
Meridiana, Hospitalet,
Sant Adrià, Verdum, Roquetes,
Valle Hebrón, Les Corts, Sagrera,
Horta, Coll, Trinitat Vella.
Camp de l'Arpa, Montjuïc,
Born, la Mina i Sant Andreu,
el Morrot per allà Can Tunis,
Zona Franca i Poblenou,
Santa Eulàlia, Casc Antic,
Clot, el port i la Verneda.
I Gràcia rei de tots els barris, de la festa i del sabor. (Pérez)

There are other type of lists that may be used to organize the chaos of everyday life, categories, subcategories, annotations, that can go from the banality of a shopping list that we jot down before going to the supermarket, to a list of things that we need to change to improve our life, live more calmly, more consciously, as the never-achieved New Year's resolution. Enumeration has been used since ancient times as a rhetorical device. It was known as *poesia catalogica* or catalogic poetry.[4] They include instances of Talmudic rhetoric or the Dantesque world of medieval compendia (Brochu). Enumeration forces exhaustiveness, but it is not an easy task. As Perec puts it, "Rien ne semble plus simple que de dresser une liste, en fait c'est beaucoup plus compliqué que ça n'en a l'air: on oublie toujours quelque chose, on est tenté d'écrire etc., mais justement, un inventaire, c'est quand on n'écrit pas etc." (*Penser/Classer* 21–2; Nothing seems simpler than making a list; in fact, it is much more complicated than it seems: we always forget something, we are tempted to write *etc.*, but precisely, an inventory is when we do not write *etc*).[5] One can also recall the case of *The Pillow Book* (枕草子, Makura no Sōshi), a book of observations and musings recorded by Sei Shōnagon during her time as court lady during the 990s and early 1000s in Heian Japan. It is a collection of stories, lists, and writings based on the likes and dislikes of the world and what interests her personally.

Seriality is a crucial device for many nineteenth- and twentieth-century poets and artists: Arthur Rimbaud used it in his poem "Bateau Ivre." Other examples include Pablo Neruda, Jacques Prévert, André Breton's boxes, Salvador Dalí's prose poems, Georges Perec, Italo Calvino, Roland Barthes (with, among other glowing examples, his series *J'aime, je n'aime pas* in *Roland Barthes par Roland Barthes*). It is worth mentioning that more contemporary lists share another feature. The lists written by James Joyce or Jorge Luis Borges, to name just a few, are very different from the lists in Homer's epic poems. These lists are constructed because "they wanted to say things out of a love of excess, hubris, and a greed for words, for the joyous (and rarely obsessive) science of the plural and the unlimited" (Eco 137). Thus we get close to the chaotic enumeration. Jaime Alazraki, when dealing with enumeration in Borges's poetry, asked: "But what exactly do enumerations enumerate in poetry?" In his own answer to this rhetorical question he made a distinction between Whitman and other writers. In Whitman, enumerations list the diversity or even chaos "of a country, time, or people, in order to cluster that diversity into a unity: the poem renders that oriental bazaar of our unordered civilization – in the words of Spitzer – into 'the powerful Ego, the 'I' of the poet, who has extricated himself from the chaos'" (Alazraki 152). Alazraki's point is that Borges uses enumeration in his poetry in a very different way than Whitman does. Nevertheless, he recognizes that "Borges … has employed this particular type of enumeration, proper to pantheism, in his fiction, in the description of divine vision or theophanyies in stories like 'The Aleph' … and 'The God's Script'" (152).

Lists are very close to chaotic enumeration, that kind of list that at first glance does not have unifying criteria. They summarize in a sort of expressionist and seemingly little-articulated way the unattainable complexity of the world or describe states of metaphysical suffering. A well-known text by Borges entitled "Epílogo" in *El hacedor* (1960) pictures this mixture:

> Un hombre se propone la tarea de dibujar el mundo. A lo largo de los años puebla un espacio con imágenes de provincias, de reinos, de montañas, de bahías, de naves, de islas, de peces, de habitaciones, de instrumentos, de astros, de caballos y de personas. Poco antes de morir, descubre que ese paciente laberinto de líneas traza la imagen de su cara. (*Obra poética* 158)

(A man sets himself the task of drawing the world. Over the years he populates a space with images of provinces, kingdoms, mountains, bays, ships, islands, fish, rooms, instruments, stars, horses, and people. Shortly before his death, he discovers that this patient labyrinth of lines traces the image of his face.)

Borges's paragraph stresses meta-literary aspects. In this case the totality is the addition of little pieces and arbitrariness: "of provinces, kingdoms, mountains, bays, ships, islands, fish, rooms, instruments, stars, horses, and people." In yet another text, *La biblioteca de Babel*, Borges highlights problems related to his profession as a librarian and to the absurdity and impossibility of any attempt at classification:

> De esas premisas incontrovertibles dedujo que la Biblioteca es total y que sus anaqueles registran todas las posibles combinaciones de los veintitantos símbolos ortográficos (número, aunque vastísimo, no infinito) o sea todo lo que es dable expresar: en todos los idiomas. Todo: la historia minuciosa del porvenir, las autobiografías de los arcángeles, el catálogo fiel de la Biblioteca, miles y miles de catálogos falsos, la demostración de la falacia de esos catálogos, la demostración de la falacia del catálogo verdadero, el evangelio gnóstico de Basilides, el comentario de ese evangelio, el comentario del comentario de ese evangelio, la relación verídica de tu muerte, la versión de cada libro a todas las lenguas, las interpolaciones de cada libro en todos los libros, el tratado que Beda pudo escribir (y no escribió) sobre la mitología de los sajones, los libros perdidos de Tácito. (*Narraciones* 109)
>
> (From these incontrovertible premises he deduced that the Library is total and that its shelves record all the possible combinations of the twenty-something orthographic symbols (a vast number, but not infinite), that is, everything that can be expressed: in all languages. Everything: the meticulous history of the future, the autobiographies of the archangels, the faithful catalogue of the Library, thousands and thousands of false catalogues, the demonstration of the fallacy of those catalogues, the demonstration of the fallacy of the true catalogue, the Gnostic gospel of Basilides, the commentary of that gospel, the commentary of the commentary of that gospel, the true account of your death, the version of every book in every language, the interpolations of every book in every book, the treatise that Bede could have written (and did not write) on the mythology of the Saxons, the lost books of Tacitus.)

Borges, who enjoyed demonstrating the limits of reason, wrote a classification of the animals that were found in an encyclopedia, which defies any logic:

> En sus remotas páginas está escrito que los animales se dividen en (a) pertenecientes al Emperador, (b) embalsamados, (c) amaestrados, (d) lechones, (e) sirenas, (f) fabulosos, (g) perros sueltos, (h) incluidos en esta clasificación, (i) que se agitan como locos, (j) innumerables, (k) dibujados con un pincel finísimo de pelo de camello, (l) etcétera, (m) que acaban de romper el jarrón, (n) que de lejos parecen moscas.[6] (*Prosa completa* 221)
>
> (On those remote pages it is written that animals are divided into (a) those that belong to the Emperor, (b) embalmed ones, (c) those that are trained, (d) suckling pigs, (e) mermaids, (f) fabulous ones, (g) stray dogs, (h) those that are included in the present classification, (i) those that tremble as if they are mad, (j) innumerable ones, (k) those drawn with a very fine camel-hair brush, (l) others, (m) those that have just broken a flower vase, (n) those that look like flies from a long way off.)

One of the absurdities in this list is that it is organized against the most basic principles of logic, and one of the terms is included in the same classification: "(h) incluidos en esta clasificación" (those that are included in the present classification). According to Leo Spitzer's clarification in *La enumeración caótica en la poesía moderna*, chaotic enumeration is a special version of what he called "estilo enumerativo" (enumerative style), which is characterized by a frequent use of anaphor and asyndeton. As he put it, chaotic enumerations are a sort of "catálogos del mundo moderno, deshecho en una polvareda de cosas, que se integran no obstante en una visión grandiosa del Todo-Uno" (13; catalogues of the modern world, shattered into a dust bowl of things, which are nevertheless integrated into a grandiose vision of the All-One). He pointed to Walt Whitman's poetry in which this kind of enumeration was used often:

> [A]cerca violentamente unas a otras las cosas más dispares, lo más exótico y lo más familiar, lo gigantesco y lo minúsculo, la naturaleza y los productos de la civilización humana, como un niño que estuviera hojeando el catálogo de una gran tienda y anotando en desorden los artículos que el azar pusiera bajo su vista; pero un niño que, siendo además sabio y poeta, extrajera poesía y pensamiento de una lista de áridas palabras; un niño genial, con el genio verbal de un Victor Hugo. (Spitzer 13–15)
>
> (He brings the most disparate things, the most exotic and the most familiar, the gigantic and the minuscule, nature and the products of human civilization, violently close to one another, like a child leafing through the catalogue of a great store and noting down in disorder the articles that chance places under his eyes; but a child who, being also a wise man and

a poet, extracts poetry and thought from a list of arid words; a child of genius, with the verbal genius of a Victor Hugo.)

Spitzer, in a curious coincidence with some of the theories put forth by Walter Benjamin (*Selected Writings* 60), thought that the increase of attention to chaotic enumeration was directly linked to the growth of big stores in France and the United States. The poems commented on in this chapter offer to the reader a sort of life's catalogue, bestowing an underlying to life's most obscure aspects and connections. Actually in the three poems selected, this is indeed what happens: the authors succeed in creating an immense catalogue by assembling lists of characters, mixing them up, and establishing an appraisal of the world through a selection of human-invented or real beings. According to a modernist approach, these are not closed catalogues ("the poetics of the everything included") but open ones, because chaotic enumerations are a powerful device to reflect the uneasiness of being in the world, the unlimited things to grasp. The everyday implies a degree of repetition and, potentially, monotony. Gardiner states that although "everyday life can display routinized, static and unreflexive characteristics, it is also capable of a surprising dynamism and moments of penetrating insight and boundless creativity," because the everyday is "'polydimensional': fluid, ambivalent and labile"(6). Here the eye of the artist and writer can help to distinguish between plain monotony and the endotic in everyday life.

Three Poems, Three Views

Returning to the three poems (Prévert's "Tentative de description," Dylan's "Desolation Row," and Sisa's "Qualsevol nit pot sortir el sol"), the most noticeable aspect of these texts is precisely the irresistible "anaphoric cascade of words" (Prévert). But at the same time each one of them has unique characteristics. The poems go from the politic to the overtly satirical, taking harsh political, critical stances and putting together an amalgamation of eccentric people, real and cartoon-like celebrities, through a technique close to what Leo Spitzer, as we have seen, used to define as "chaotic enumeration." Prévert's poetry aims to create a shock effect: the reader has to get off his or her hinges, has to break from habits of thought, from reading automatism, and get rid of old sensitivity. However, it is poetry that is organized according to two main themes clearly defined: symmetry and antagonism. Prévert creates a false sense of security for the reader and then immediately withdraws the intellectual armchair. His images are spectacular at creating conflict and incoherence based upon a well-calculated inventory.

These first lines in his well-known poem "L'Inventaire" offer an excellent example of what Prévert did best:

Une pierre
deux maisons
trois ruines
quatre fossoyeurs
un jardin
des fleurs

un raton laveur (*Œuvres complètes* 131)

(A tripe / two houses / three ruins / four gravediggers / one garden / some flowers / the raccoon)

Prévert never ceased to describe people under their mask, especially those forming the institutional microcosm – aristocrats, politicians, priests, judges, including fathers and teachers – that is, anyone exercising any form of authority. He endeavours to depict the daily life of people in the street, of those who form the base of the social pyramid, and for whom he feels a deep affection. The unemployed, the murderer, and all the outcasts of society become, under his pen, sympathetic beings whom we want to forgive everything. They are people like us, living with open eyes, confronting somehow everyday life: "Il est terrible / Le petit bruit de l'oeuf dur cassé sur un comptoir d'étain / Quand il remue dans la mémoire de l'homme qui a faim" (Darsy 2020; It is terrible / The little noise of the hard egg broken on a tin counter / When it stirs in the memory of the man who is hungry).

As stated by Pierre Weisz, in the poem "Tentative de description" "C'est encore la technique de l'instantané, mais non plus celle du spontané. Les images se juxtaposent, se bousculent, se multiplient, mais nous sommes loin du réflexe viscéral" (36; It is still the technique of the instantaneous, but no longer that of the spontaneous. The images are juxtaposed, jostled, multiplied, but we are far from the visceral reflex). In fact Prévert's poetry has coined an expression that is crucial for my purpose, "inventaire à la Prévert" (inventory à la Prévert). This is a list, an heteroclite enumeration, an inventory that apparently has neither beginning nor ending. This is precisely what the poems I have selected have in common: they create an "énumération burlesque d'éléments sans rapport entre eux, dans un but poétique ou ludique" (*Dictionnaire;* burlesque enumeration of unrelated elements, with a poetic or playful purpose). Even though they are very similar to Spitzer's chaotic enumeration, these examples include a proximity to religious forms such as the litany.

The poem "Tentative de description" pays attention to the everyday. It was published as the opening poem in the book *Paroles* (1949).[7] A comment by the publisher stresses this fact by mentioning that the cover in the first edition was "un graffiti urbain photographié par Brassaï et maculé de lettres capitales écarlates peintes à la hâte. Le signal était puissant, choisi: marginal dans la vie et dans les arts" (Prévert, *Paroles*; an urban graffiti photographed by Brassaï and smeared with scarlet capital letters painted in a hurry. The signal was powerful, chosen: marginal in life and in the art). Other critics emphasized the fact that Prévert was attentive to everyday life. According to Maurice Naudeau, Prévert's popularity was based on his ability to reproduce a down-to-earth "lyrisme de la vie quotidienne" (lyricism of everyday life). He is the only poet of the time who can "sans tomber dans le prosaïsme … exprimer notre univers matériel, le reconstruire sous nos yeux" (Prévert, *Œuvres complètes* 999–1000; without falling into prosaism … expresses our material universe, reconstructs it before our eyes). It is remarkable what Bataille wrote about Prévert's poetry. He derides pure poetry of the time (Valéry and others) and defends that in *Paroles* "l'événement est le thème de la poésie" (the event is the theme of poetry) as opposed to a "poésie poétique" (poetic poetry). He adds:

> Je puis dire aussi de la poésie de Jacques Prévert qu'elle est en même temps la fille et l'amante de l'événement. "Elle change. Elle change tout et tout la change. Pas une parcelle immobile, pas de place accordée au repos, au regard en arrière, au *c'est bien ainsi, j'attends la récompense* …" C'est ce qu'on peut dire de cette poésie, et peut-être aussi est-ce là qu'il faut dire de la poésie entière, qui n'*est* qu'à la condition de changer. (Prévert, *Œuvres complètes* 1007–8)
>
> (I can also say of Jacques Prévert's poetry that it is at the same time the daughter and the lover of the event. "She changes. She changes everything and everything changes her. Not a single immobile parcel, no place given to rest, to look back, to the *it is well so, I wait for the reward* …" This is what can be said of this poetry, and perhaps this is also what must be said of all poetry, which *is* only on the condition of change.)

Another feature of *Paroles* is its political commitment. René Laporte wrote an article titled "Gravé sur les murs de tous les jours – Jacques Prévert: *Paroles*," which pays homage to the front page of the first edition. He sees in *Paroles* "de quoi armer les rêves de toute une génération … une poésie de combat, 'against' la bêtise, contre les préjugés" (with what to arm the dreams of a whole generation … a poetry of fight, "against" the stupidity, against the prejudices), expressing "un état de révolte permanente" (a state of permanent revolt). In his mind the book will have on many readers the effect of an explosion similar to a vengeful and desperate graffiti, as if Prévert had engraved it with a knife on the walls of the night and that it will make "l'épopée d'un temps où ce n'est pas toujours très drôle de vivre … Prévert ne tire pas ses coups de feu au hasard. Il vise avec soin et il connaît ses cibles" (the epic of a time when it is not always very funny to live … Prévert does not fire his shots at random. He aims carefully and he knows his targets) (qtd. in Prévert, *Œuvres complètes* 999–1001). The book belongs in the streets, uses plain language and is extremely provocative, incompatible with pure poetry (i.e., Valéry).

The text of *Paroles* was extremely popular. André Breton included a large excerpt of it in his 1939 *Anthology of Black Humor*. Gaëtan Picon stressed Prévert's "extraordinaire puissance d'invective et de violence vengeresse" (231; extraordinary power of invective and vengeful violence). He even compared his attacks to Daumier's drawings. At the time the volume was published, many critics stressed its commitment to social issues. Jean Rougel, for instance, wrote: "Toute cette vision poétique de l'univers s'encadre … dans une conception très précise des rapports humains. Prévert est solidement révolutionnaire, non par théorie, mais parce qu'il perçoit, avec une sorte d'infaillible instinct, les mouvements divers de la lutte des classes" (Prévert, *Œuvres complètes* 1000). (All this poetic vision of the universe is framed … in a very precise conception of human relations. Prévert is solidly revolutionary, not by theory, but because he perceives, with a kind of infallible instinct, the various movements of the class struggle.) Bataille pointed to "le pouvoir d'exprimer comme nul autre … les drames et les bonheurs du quotidien" (Prévert, *Œuvres complètes* 1000; the power to express like no other … the dramas and joys of everyday life).

The poem "Tentative de description" opens on a litany with a list of participants and the proceedings of their actions. From the incipit, Prévert associates in the same information the bigots, the well-off, and the nationalists. It can be read as an ironic pastiche of society journalism and a pamphlet in which he declares his artistic and social freedom. Every line is filled with political, literary associations. After building his text on appearance–reality antithesis, he may also want to show that we should not rely on the first appearance of the work. He begins by attacking the literature both through writers he loves (Hugo, Baudelaire) and through others he despises (Peguy). Both the litany and the poem end with the evocation of the sadness in the life of workers whose only day off is tempered by the prospect of boring days of work ahead, something with which one experiments when there is little time to rest and most of the time is devoted to work.

In the poem there is a clear distinction between those who have been invited and those who have not. Prévert takes sides in favour of the have-nots as some sort of vendetta against "Ceux qui pieusement … / Ceux qui copieusement …" (François 74; Those who devoutly … / Those who copiously …). Prévert denounces "des profiteurs de 1930, de ceux qui vivent de la patrie, de ceux qui s'engraissent aux dépens du peuple, des heureux du jour" (*Œuvres complètes* 1010; the profiteers of 1930, of those who live off the country, of those who get fat at the expense of the people, of the happy few). In his long enumeration of the invited and non-invited people to the state dinner Prévert makes a shrewd distinction between both groups with the use of a capitalized *Ceux* or non-capitalized *ceux* in the last part of the poem. There is also a clear distinction between the speech of the president and that of the poet. The president speaks by associations of ideas, commonplaces, or stale cultural reminiscences. This speech, senseless in its derisory automatism, turns to emptiness and meets only emptiness. Whereas the second speaker uses "une parole foudroyante qi fait peur et qui déplaît" (1011; a lightning word that frightens and displeases).

Prévert's poem can be read in many ways: as an ironic pastiche of *fait divers* (local-news) journalism, a political pamphlet, a declaration of artistic and social conformism, a philosophical poem (*Œuvres complètes* 1013). It is a poem that can be easily divided into seven sections, which correspond to significant moments of the event:

- Enumeration of disguised guests arriving at the Elyseé Palace.
- Description of the comic-looking "têtes" of "grands hommes," with reminiscences of a carnival situation, the big-heads. These are figures that feature an oversized, carton-pierre head. The heads are worn with a matching costume.
- President's speech, in which the president makes fun of himself and stresses the obvious as he wears a "somptueuse tête d'œuf de Colomb" (sumptuous egg head of Columbus) that allows him to declare, "C'était simple, mais il fallait y penser" (It was simple, but you had to think about it).
- Interruption by a little girl: "la musique s'est calmée et la mère à tête de morte en a profité pour pousser sa petite fille à tête d'orpheline du côté du Président" (the music calmed down, and the mother with the head of a dead woman took the opportunity to push her little daughter with the head of an orphan to the side of the President).
- Arrival of a man with "à tête d'homme." In the middle section a poet who has not been invited to the state dinner, and who

interrupts the celebration, creates a situation of terror: "Mais soudain tous de trembler car un homme avec un tête d'homme est entré, un homme que personne n'avait invité et qui pose doucement sur la table la tête de Louis XVI dans un panier" (But suddenly all trembled because a man with a man's head entered, a man whom no one had invited and who gently places on the table the head of Louis XVI in a basket). He makes a long speech that is interrupted by someone who throws a carafe at him and kills him. His speech is a vindication of simple non-duplicitous life.

- A carafe is launched, killing the poet "avec un tête d'homme" (with a man's head).
- Beginning of a new day, as a way of asserting that life goes on, but paying attention to inequalities among citizens: "Le jour se lève, mais le soleil ne brille pour tous" (The day rises, but the sun does not shine for all).

In this last section of the poem we reconnect with the first one. As indicated earlier, Prévert emphasizes social issues of the day, but he also depicts boredom in minute detail, the foundation of the everyday. Both the first and the last section sound as some sort of litany. Life returns to normal, that is to its everyday boredom and routine, with an emphasis on those human beings and the bottom of the social ladder. It is not a coincidence that Prévert in the last section of the poem, consisting of another long enumeration of characters who work (as opposed to the characters in the first section), uses it to assert workers' rights, and he does so with lines such as "ceux qui fabriquent dans les caves les stylos avec lesquels d'autres écriront en plein air que tout va pour le mieux" (those who make pens in cellars with which others will write in the open air that all is well). The everyday work of the poet is consistent with a condemnation of certain ways of life. The days of the week are enumerated in the final verse, a signal to the utmost presence of everydayness. Normal lives are forgotten in the minutiae of not-seen characters and jobs, as opposed to the fake world introduced in the first part of the poem.

In a *Daily Telegraph* review (10 November 1965) of the *Highway 61 Revisited* album, Philip Larkin described "Desolation Row" as a "marathon," with an "enchanting tune and mysterious, possibly half-baked words" (151). However, Dylan's critic and biographer Andy Gill described the song as "an 11-minute epic of entropy (decline, degradation, decomposition, breaking down, collapse; disorder, chaos), which takes the form of a Fellini-esque parade of grotesques and oddities featuring a huge cast of iconic characters" (89). Both critics stress two distinctive characteristics of the song: its chaotic length and the accumulation of marginal and iconic characters in this *row*, a word in the title that can be read in several ways, most particularly as a number of people or things in a more or less straight line or as a street with a continuous line of houses along one or both of its sides. *Desolation* can be understood as a state of complete emptiness or destruction. *Desolation Row* can be a counterculture destination, both a state of mind and a real place. The name could derive from the combination of two titles: Jack Kerouac's *Desolation Angels* and John Steinbeck's *Cannery Row*. A friend of Dylan, musician Al Kooper, who played electric guitar on the first recordings of "Desolation Row," suggested that Desolation Row is in Greenwich Village in New York City, "an area infested with whore houses, sleazy bars and porno supermarkets totally beyond renovation or redemption" (Polizzotti 133). Place, emotion, and people are crucial in my reading of this text.

Bob Dylan released this epic song in August 1965 as the final piece in the album *Highway 61 Revisited*. The controversial winner of the 2016 Nobel Prize in Literature, Bob Dylan is one of the most significant poets and songwriters of the twentieth century, and this piece by itself might be his claim to fame (Gilmour 24). "Desolation Row" is the only acoustic folk song on the record, a strong departure from Dylan's earlier albums. It is a song based on depth of metaphor, with carefully structured depth and allusions to real life and fictitious characters. In his day Bob Dylan challenged conventional values and was perceived as dangerous figure, a leader of the civil rights movement in the United States. Similarly to what T.S. Eliot did in *The Waste Land*, Bob Dylan refers to a world in disorder. It is not a coincidence that Eliot is one of the poets mentioned in the song. Dylan portrays the state of the world through metaphors, reacting against flawed philosophies such as materialism, religion, or science. Above and beyond an immense pessimism, he claims a new enlightenment and responsiveness through the use of a number of unrelated sketchy sections, and each adds depth to his central theme. Dylan describes negatively what he can see, particularly the chaos, corruption, and a general feeling of emptiness. By the end of the song he reveals that he is in great contentment in Desolation Row, witnessing peacefully all of this destruction. The song was written during the Cold War, at a time of great political upheaval, when young people were beginning to declare their opposition to a world view and moral principles that they felt were obsolete. There is a remarkable change: "In 'Desolation Row' Dylan turns his back on drug visions and visionary hopes to face reality as he sees it, and he sees the world in the aspect of a carnival, specifically a freak show, with all the grotesques on prominent display" (Johnson 138). The song can be read as a detailed catalogue of grotesquery and nightmares or as the account of a parade of grotesques that pass before the poet, a stream of images generated by a letter full of gossip that he has just received from an old acquaintance (Johnson 137–8).

The song is organized in ten stanzas, each one dealing with different personalities and situations. It creates "a kaleidoscopic hodgepodge of elements from this muddled up, truth-seeking, topsy-turvy world that we all pass through on our journeys of life" (Wright). It includes historical characters (Einstein, Nero), biblical (Noah, Cain, and Abel), fictional (Ophelia, Romeo, Cinderella), literary (T.S. Eliot and Ezra Pound), and some invented ones such as Dr. Filth (Freud?) and his suspicious nurse. One of the clues to reading the song may lie in the final stanza, where he refers to a letter. The song is essentially his reaction to a letter that he received from someone who we may infer is a woman. Stanza 1 focuses on the postcards being sold, which is a reference to an event that occurred in Minnesota, in which two black men were lynched and hung, and photographs of their hanging were put on postcards. The last two lines indicate the location of the voice (and his Lady): "As Lady and I look out tonight / From Desolation Row." Stanza 2 introduces Cinderella and Romeo, mixing two dramatic characters from fairy tales and Shakespeare. She cleans the place: "Is Cinderella sweeping up / On Desolation Row." Stanza 3 continues the mixing of characters, in this case from the biblical figures Cain and Abel (who have been banished to Desolation Row) and the Hunchback of Notre Dame. The Good Samaritan is visiting: "He's going to the carnival tonight / On Desolation Row." In other stanzas Dylan includes Ophelia (from *Hamlet* or the woman who wrote the letter), and Einstein disguised as Robin Hood: "he was famous long ago / For playing the electric violin / On Desolation Row." Also appear the Phantom of the Opera and Casanova: "And the Phantom's shouting to skinny girls / Get Outa Here If You Don't Know / Casanova is just being punished for going / To Desolation Row." Stanza 9 includes the Titanic and real-life writers T.S. Eliot and Ezra Pound: "Titanic where lovely mermaids flow / And nobody has to think too much / About Desolation Row." The final is the most important stanza, and it is separated from the rest of the song by a long harmonica solo. Here the voice reveals that he received the letter in which the sender discusses her life, friends, and various circumstances of trivial nature. The voice cannot relate to her because they have come apart and the voice does not recognize people from the past any more ("All these people that you mention / Yes, I know them, they're quite lame / I had to rearrange their faces /And give them all another name"), thus concluding: "Don't send me no more letters, no / Not unless you mail them / From Desolation Row." This final declaration seems to make very clear that Desolation Row is a metaphorical place, not a physical location. The song is a powerful mixing of cultural figures, politicians, and literary characters, but in the end it all comes down to the idea of entropy (decline, degradation, decomposition, breaking down, collapse; disorder, chaos). The final letter has been considered a reference to the "Open Letter to Bob Dylan" written by Irwin Silber in *Singout Magazine,* condemning Dylan for betraying the left-wing cause (Tuffley). While this reading may be close to the truth, the final stanza is a significant departure from the tone in the rest of the poem. Instead of a mixture of characters and times and situations, here there is a reference to time past, to not recognizing or not being close any more to the sender of that letter. In fact he begs the sender, who belongs to a past with faces he does not recognize any more, to become a part of Desolation Row, thus making it a very positive place:

Yes, I received your letter yesterday
(About the time the doorknob broke)
When you asked how I was doing
Was that some kind of joke?
All these people that you mention
Yes, I know them, they're quite lame
I had to rearrange their faces
And give them all another name
Right now I can't read too good
Don't send me no more letters, no
Not unless you mail them
From Desolation Row (Dylan)

Any listener to the song quickly recognizes the repetition of words from the title in the last verse of every stanza: From/On/Into/To/About Desolation Row. The song makes one think of the Shanghai back alleys that connected lines of depressed two-storey houses. It is a space in the present without a future, an island, and a sort of echo from a long time gone past. In Dylan's text he takes us a step further in Augé's non-places, constituted by imaginary collage-assembled places, in which a confluence of people from different lineages and of entities occur.

In the song the chaotic enumeration creates a surreal atmosphere related to this unappealing Desolation Row. Dylan claimed that the song was "a minstrel song through and through. I saw some ragtag minstrel show in blackface at the carnivals when I was growing up, and it had an effect on me, just as much as seeing the lady with four legs" (Gunderson). The everyday is introduced by the reading of a letter. It makes the surreal collapse and takes us back to reality. By contrast with the bizarre, which is the core of the song, it makes everyday life more present. The list of characters that inhabit Desolation Row – that can also be linked to "death row" – may represent an alternate way of looking at the world. They are substitutes for the faces that he does not recognize any more: "I had to rearrange their faces / And give them all another name."

Singer and composer Jaume Sisa struck a gold mine with his 1975 song "Qualsevol nit pot sortir el sol" (Any night the sun may rise). It became extremely popular and was instantly perceived as a sort of hymn that encapsulated a moment of profound transformation in Catalonia and Spain. Although some music critics underscored its naive aspects, others were delighted with the political reading it offered. An early reading of this song stressed one of its main features, the fact that it mixes objects and characters, styles and referents, that do not allow a stable identity to be configured: "amb uns procediments emparentats amb el kitsch, buscant unes formes expressives noves i originals, d'una aparença barroera i fins i tot xarona, gairebé com a resultat de la superació de l'educació sentimental de l'autor mitjançant uns mètodes clarament revulsius, que guanyen en profunditat" (Garcia-Soler 62; with procedures related to kitsch, looking for new and original expressive forms, with a muddled and even garish appearance, almost as a result of overcoming the sentimental education of the author through clearly repulsive methods, which they gain in depth). Mercè Picornell, with a keener eye and some distance, defined the song in perceptive terms: "aprofita bagatges inconnexos per construir representacions que no són més que collages i simulacres" (215; it takes advantage of disjointed baggage to construct representations that are nothing more than collages and simulations). According to Picornell, this mixture should be related to "l'apropiació avantguardista del kitsch que genera una nova sensibilitat moderna: el *camp*" (215; the avant-garde appropriation of kitsch that generates a new modern sensibility: the *camp*). According to Teresa Vilarós, this song is a long, warm, and sad litany. She claims that the party has been organized to celebrate the end of Franco's dictatorship, and therefore she misses names of left-wing characters, authors, or politicians. In her obstinate reading she complains that "los que van llegando no son aquellos que esperaríamos encontrar, nombres y personas más o menos comprometidas políticamente con grupos de izquierda y por tanto dispuestas al final de la dictadura" (206; those who are arriving are not those we would expect to find, names and people more or less politically committed to leftist groups and therefore ready for the end of the dictatorship). She even declares that the house to which people have been invited to party is a metaphorical representation of Spain.[8] Picornell insightfully corrects her because it is not a real house but "la casa imaginària i amb els balcons que apareix recurrentment en les seves cançons" (229; the imaginary house with the balconies that appears recurrently in his songs).

The song provides a message of hope ("de les tristors en farem fum"; we will make smoke out of sorrows) and is a great ode to friendship and to sharing ("només hi faltes tu … tu també pots venir si vols"; only you are missing … you can come too if you want), and thus it could be read as a sort of chant to hippie and communal living. Nothing could be further from the truth. It is a long poem-song in which Sisa enumerates and mixes up a long list of characters from children's short stories, classic children's literature, folk tradition, film, and comics that belong to his childhood memories and shared with listeners of the song. Sisa himself declared: "Mi casa no existe en la Tierra, o dicho de otro modo, la casa que existe en la Tierra no es exactamente mi casa. La mía es la casa de los sueños, la casa de la poesía, la casa de un ideal abstracto de belleza, de emoción, de alegría, de fiesta" (Paisse). (My house does not exist on Earth, or in other words, the house that exists on Earth is not exactly my house. Mine is the house of dreams, the house of poetry, the house of an abstract ideal of beauty, of emotion, of joy, of celebration.) He combines a fantasy world and reality, enticing the listener to participate in his imaginary party.

If we reorganize the apparently chaotic list of names, we come up with five series of spheres from which the characters come:

Children's stories	Blancaneus, Pulgarcito, Els tres porquets, Peter Pan, Patufet, Pinotxo, Guillem Brown, La caputxeta vermella, llop ferotge
Popular literature	Sinbad, Ali-Babà, Gulliver, Barbablava, Frankenstein, Dràcula, Tarzan i Chita, Superman, King Kong, Moby Dick
Cartoons	Tom i Jerry, Bambi, Cocoliso, Popeye
Comic-book characters	Snoopy i el seu ocell, Doña Urraca, Carpanta, Pato Donald, Astèrix, Roberto Alcázar i Pedrín, la família Ulises, Capitán Trueno, Mortadelo i Filemón
Religious and popular figures	Jaimito, Home llop, Marieta de l'ull viu, Reis Mags d'Orient i el Pare Noel, l'home del sac,[1] la dona que ven globus, la bruixa Calixta, Charlot (Charles Chaplin), La Monyos, emperadriu Sissi, Guillem Tell, El caganer,[2] Pepa Maca,[3] En Pasqual.[4]

Notes:
1 The boogeyman, literally "the man with the sack."
2 A scatological Nativity figure.
3 Pepa Maca comes from a sardana, "La Pepa Maca."
4 This character comes from a *cuplet*, "El vestit d'en Pasqual," and from a comic-book character Pascual criado ideal.

The song is witness to Sisa's pseudo-surreal approach to reality. He started his career experimenting with rock music and folk groups. Grup de folk imitated singers such as Pete Seeger, Arlo Guthrie, and Bob Dylan. Sisa found an original surrealist way to become a singer and composer (Soldevila i Balart 271–2). He defined himself as a "transcantautor galàctic" (Muñoz i Lloret 22).

It is very obvious that the song is built around a list. When Sisa wrote the song, he started writing a list of characters reminiscent of his childhood readings, but he did not know what to do with all of them. He declared on a televsion special devoted to the song, "It seemed a phone book" (Gràcia). Consequently, he decided to invite them to a party and to make groups with the characters. Here we have the two ways of reading the song: children listening to it as a collection of characters that belong to their imaginary world; and adults paying more attention to nostalgia, remembering when they were children, and, also in accordance with a hippie mentality, welcoming everybody to the house.

In other similar songs such as "El setè cel" Sisa presents lists of realities. In that song he describes a non-astrological or religious version of the Seven Heavens, the seventh being the ultimate state of bliss, a place that harks back to the days before Copernicus and exists also in Islamic writings. In "El congrés dels solitaris," he establishes lists and categories of lonely people, accumulating chaotic and non-related characters: "La vídua del Baró Rampant, la veu de la senyora Francis, / un latin lover un pèl ranci i una lectora de Cioran" (The widow of the Rampant Baron, the voice of Mrs. Francis, / a Latin lover with stale hair and a reader of Cioran).[9]

Sisa's "Qualsevol nit ..." epitomizes a common everyday situation: making a list of guests to invite to a dinner or party. In compliance with his "transgalàctic" view of the world he introduces an impossible list of guests and helps the listener of the song to recreate a surreal aspect of the everyday where we belong. The song title, and the refrain, "Qualsevol nit pot sortir el sol" (Any night the sun may rise), stresses the unreal situation:

> Oh, benvinguts, passeu passeu, ara ja no hi falta ningú,
> O potser sí, ja me n'adono que tan sols hi faltes tu.
> També pots venir si vols, t'esperem, hi ha lloc per tots.
> El temps no compta, ni l'espai, qualsevol nit pot sortir el sol. (Sisa)

> (Oh, welcome, come in, come in, now there is no one missing, / or maybe yes, I already realize that only you are missing. / You can also come if you want, we are waiting for you, there is room for everyone. / Time does not count, nor space, any night the sun may rise.)

The final stanza announces the sense of inclusion, inviting the listener to be part of the celebration, in a no-time and no-space, where the sun may rise at night.

Singing, Signalling

All three texts are closely related to moments of decadence and crisis. The three authors use some sort of surreal approach to alleviate the situation, and they all make a gifted and obsessive use of enumeration in their compositions. Catalogues are linked to epic rhetorical devices, and they are used to enumerate. Catalogues are a truthful literary form that can be found in different eras. In archaic and classical times we find political texts trying to link two registers always by the same verb: "in the genealogy of gods with the state of affairs in the Theogony or the genealogy of heroines and the actual establishment in the Catalogue of women the verb is 'giving birth.' Cities are linked to the Trojan War in the Homeric catalogue of ships, but we can also find small killing catalogues in the Iliad, or argumentation catalogues in Parmenides' poem 'On Nature' or season catalogues in Thucydides" (Steinrück 6). Anti-epic approaches, however, may be associated with the everyday where perpetual change creates sameness, and within this sameness there is direction, pattern, and constancy.[10] It is a way of stating that in a world of perpetual change there is an essential constancy of being. In these three poems we can recognize a mixture of Eco's distinction between the "poetics of everything included" and the "poetics of the etcetera." Similarly to Proust's use of the enumeration, they establish relationships and divisions, and this has a therapeutic function.

The way in which Prévert, Dylan, and Sisa organize the poems is also significant. They refuse a feature of advanced societies. According to Eco, in advanced cultures that have a more in-depth and sophisticated knowledge of the world, it is mandatory to describe their surroundings in a hierarchical manner, with a specific form; primitive cultures, having only a vague idea of the universe, will favour the informal list, never finished, never closed, aspiring to infinity. In fact, what cannot be counted can be explain or described but never enters into a count.

The three texts discussed here are written against the grain, opposing the mainstream thinking of the day, and based on enumeration that is chaotically cataloguing, with perceptional attention to the everyday: class differences and the monotony and beauty of working (Prévert); a place in which to live (Dylan); and friendship, celebration, and happiness as post-hippie values based on a magical childlike world (Sisa). Prévert and Dylan write poems that are extremely provocative and denounce a political and moral status quo at a time of harsh political realities: the rise of communism and fascism, the Vietnam War. "Tentative de description" opposes the Elysée fake power and also that of the lay people. "Desolation Row" shows a back alley, almost a hidden place, filled with celebrities, and serving as a refuge for outcasts. "Qualsevol nit" legitimizes the party, a special night, mixing a huge collection of characters from comic books and adolescent novels. All three excel with puns and ironic turns. They are not a tedious taxonomy of the everyday but a sort of wake-up call, an invitation to see the everyday from a different perspective. These are long catalogic poems that sing the everyday, signalling alternatives to the world, helping us reassess "le quotidien: ce qu'il y a de plus difficile à découvrir" (Blanchot 14; everyday life: the hardest thing to discover).

3

Autopsies of Everyday Life

Outra vez te revejo,
Cidade da minha infância pavorosamente perdida …
Cidade triste e alegre, outra vez sonho aqui …
Eu? Mas sou eu o mesmo que aqui vivi, e aqui voltei,
E aqui tornei a voltar, e a voltar,
E aqui de novo tornei a voltar?
Ou somos todos os Eu que estive aqui ou estiveram,
Uma série de contas-entes ligadas por um fio-memória,
Uma série de sonhos de mim de alguém de fora de mim?

Álvaro de Campos, "Lisbon Revisited" (1926)

Vanishing

There is a long list of vanished cities: Machu Picchu in Perú, Petra in Jordan, Teotihuacan in Mexico, Timgad in Algeria, Vijayanagara in Southern India, Mesa Verde in Colorado, Babylon in Iraq, Carthage in Tunisia – just a few examples of cities destroyed by war, famine, and climate changes. One of the most compelling is the case of Pompeii. It was once a thriving metropolis, but the eruption of Mount Vesuvius in AD 79 buried the city in volcanic ash. When it was rediscovered by chance in 1749 and excavated, it revealed a time capsule of city life during the Roman Empire. The sheer amount of objects, paintings, and other memorabilia were like a snapshot of everyday life. Another remarkable example of frozen city life is the city of Pripyat in Ukraine, which once had a population of around fifty thousand, many of whom were employed at the Chernobyl nuclear power plant. Its proximity to the plant led to its downfall. In the days following the 1986 Chernobyl nuclear disaster, the entire population had to be evacuated to survive the high radiation levels. When radiation levels decreased, tours were legal in the "Zone of Alienation," and visitors could observe nature reclaiming the leaking buildings.

In the essay *The Aesthetics of Disappearance*, Paul Virilio introduces the key concept of picnolepsy. Inspired by epilepsy – a neurological disorder marked by sudden recurrent episodes of sensory disturbance, loss of consciousness, or convulsions – Virilio defined *picnolepsy* as the condition of brief lapses in time, momentary absences of consciousness, or, as he puts it, fleeting instances of life escaping. Picnolepsy is produced by speed and is a characteristic of the pace at which we live our lives. As Virilio stated, if epilepsy is little death, picnolepsy is tiny death. Our awareness of living is made up of an infinity of little deaths, little accidents, little breaks, little cuts in our life, made of sounds, visual effects, what is remembered. It corresponds to a montage of temporalities, which is closely related to the technologies of organizing time (48).

The picnolept "make[s] equivalents out of what [he] has seen and what he has not been able to see" (*Aesthetics of Disappearance* 10). Virilio presents an example, that of the awkward child bothered by the adults who are in a position of authority over him:

> People want to persuade him of the existence of events that he has not seen, though they effectively happened in his presence; and as he can't be made to believe in them he's considered a half-wit and convicted of lies and dissimulation. Secretly bewildered and tormented by the demands of those near him, in order to find information he needs constantly to stretch the limits of his memory. When we place a bouquet under the eyes of the young picnoleptic and we ask him to draw it, he draws not only the bouquet but also the person who is supposed to have placed it in the vase, and even the field of flowers where it was possibly gathered. (10)

Referring to the kind of absence that occurs not only during particular states such as REM sleep but also in our general experience of space-time relations as a series of fragmented frames, the idea of picnolepsy lies behind Virilio's assertion that "architecture is just a movie" (*Aesthetics of Disappearance* 65), and as an experience it can be likened to that of oblivion caused by disappearance. Even though he thinks of picnolepsy in terms of contemporary society, the concept can also be usefully applied to the problem of space disappearance and transformation. As Walter Benjamin wrote, "articulating the past historically does not mean recognizing it 'the way it really was.' It means appropriating a memory as it flashes up at a moment of danger" (*Selected Writings* 4: 391). My purpose is to analyse three instances of exploration of the everyday, by Josep Carner, Marta Rojals, and Joan Todó, paying special attention to matters of disappearance, and particularly to what we might call the invisible traditions as recorded in literary texts of the early twentieth and twenty-first centuries.

Between *Feuilleton* and *Elzeviro*

I would like to begin with a reflection on the impact of the flâneur's attitude on Josep Carner's prose and the adoption of *feuilleton* techniques or other related forms. Literary prose was pivotal in Josep Carner's career as a writer until the Spanish Civil War. Collaborations with the press were an example of a Noucentista-themed activity – educating and entertaining – in parallel with the way in which Eugeni d'Ors, the Pantarca, wrote in his *Glossari*. Many of Carner's articles in *La Veu de Catalunya* and *La Publicitat* were collected in volumes such as *Les planetes del verdum* (1918), *Les bonhomies* (1925), *Tres estels i un ròssec* (1927) or the posthumous publications *Del Pròxim Orient: 1935–1936* (1973), *En els Tròpics* (1994). All these books are exceptional examples of his dedication.[1] With an undeniable European inspiration, by subject and technique, Carner managed to turn local issues, news stories, neighbourhood gossip, into articles of social, moral, and political opinion, that is into pieces of great literature.

According to Marcel Ortín, a scholar of Carner's prose, it was during the Genoa period that Carner began to write a new form of literary article "que consisteix en la recreació assagística de motius pròxims" (Ortín, *La prosa literària* 275; consisting of the essay recreation of local motives). Ortín considers that there is a clear difference between the articles collected in his book and those that he did not consider publishing. In the latter, "predomina el judici critic sobre fets d'actualitat i la intenció crítica" (284; judgment prevails over current events and critical intent). In the others, the author is present in the elaboration of the themes: "en el tractament característic (admirat, irònic, paròdic) i en les associacions personals que estableix entre motius reals i imaginats" (284; in the characteristic treatment (admired, ironic, parodic) and in the personal associations that he establishes between real and imagined motives). It is a very peculiar, non-journalistic style, one that is distinguished "per un determinat ritme, una tria característica del vocabulari, una originalitat en la invenció de frases que no es troben en escriptors que treballen més amb els llocs comuns, un gran compte a l'hora d'escollir els mots més ajustats, i un gran poder de variar el ritme i l'estructura de l'oració perquè s'avinguin a l'esperit d'allò que s'està dient en aquell moment" (284; by a certain rhythm, a characteristic choice of vocabulary, an originality in the invention of phrases that are not found in writers who work more with commonplaces, being very careful when choosing the most appropriate words, and with a great power to vary the rhythm and structure of the sentence so that they agree with the spirit of what is being said at that moment).

As I indicated in "Noucentisme 2.0" (2018), Josep Carner's unclassifiable prose (and the entire Ors's *Glossari*) can be read from a *feuilleton* perspective. Here I want to delve deeper into this consideration. According to Daniel Spitzer: "Ein Artikel der nicht in der Zeitung gehört aber doch dort steht, ist ein *Feuilleton*" (qtd. in Maierbruger 152; An article that does not belong to the newspaper, but you read it there, is a *feuilleton*). The *feuilleton* reflects the urban culture of the time. It is a genre of writing that allows the writer great freedom in terms of content, composition, and style; the text is hybrid, which implies that use is made of different genre structures, both journalistic and literary (Schorske). The *glosses* by Ors are closer to *feuilleton* than to the outline of any philosophical treatise. Consciously or not, Ors appropriated a journalistic genre and in his own way became a "gasetiller d'eternitats" (gazetteer of eternities), but a gazetteer, after all. The *feuilleton* work is a time palpitation. And it has an obvious correspondence in Carner's prose. In his literary articles the portrait of everyday life and leisure is of great importance. Sunday evenings ("Diumenge a les nou del vespre"; Sunday at nine in the evening), for example, served Carner to introduce comic situations and moralizing reflections. He concluded that free time had three components: self-determination, freedom, and hedonism.

Ortín, with very good judgment, pointed out that Carner's arrival in Genoa changed the way Carner wrote articles (*La prosa literària* 302). The ones he wrote from Genoa were very different from those written earlier. He lived there between March 1921 and September 1924. Every day he would read three or four Italian newspapers, *La Stampa* being his favourite. He later became a fan of the *Manchester Guardian*. But in addition to the possible coincidence with the German *feuilleton*, the closest model was *prosa d'arte*, an Italian literary phenomenon limited to a period of about twenty years after the First World War: "it means to evoke something somewhat vague under an epistemic approach … In fact, the boundaries with other so-called 'minor genres' such as *elzeviro*, chapter, fragment or poetic prose are often not even noticed by the writers who practice them" (Gubert 9–10). *La Ronda* was the magazine promoting this so-called *prosa d'arte*. The essay, the *elzeviro*, and the chapter, halfway between lyrical prose and critical annotation, are some of the most typical forms of *La Ronda* neoclassicism.[2] *Elzeviro*, explains Beppe Benvenuto, was the opinion article, *prosa d'arte*, controversial article, or even a review, which appeared on the third page or in the cultural pages of newspapers. It was a typical genre of the early twentieth century in Italy. Benvenuto's overly nationalist view is that the *elzeviro* did not exist anywhere else in the world. It had been invented on 10 April 1901 by Bergamini, director of the *Giornale d'Italia*, who devoted an entire page (the third) to Eleonora Duse's debut as a performer of D'Annunzio's *Francesca da Rimini*. The golden moment occurred in the period between the two world wars, precisely as a defence against fascism (Benvenuto 27–8).

What Italian critics do not know is how to relate this short article (the *elzeviro*) to the *feuilleton*, a type of writing that had been practised passionately in German culture since the late nineteenth century, especially by journalists and writers of the interwar period. As Jeffrey Eugenides recalled, the best way to define a *feuilleton* was to refer to what it was not: "It isn't news. It isn't the metro report. The opposite of an editorial, a feuilleton is descriptive, philosophical, meandering and poetically inclined" ("Joseph Roth's Movable Café"). Although it is a French word, it was used in this sense in Vienna at the turn of the century. One of its practitioners, Alfred Polgar, said, "Life is too short for extensive literature, too precarious for slow descriptions, too psychopathic for psychology, too fictional for novels" (Eugenides, "Joseph Roth's Movable Cafe"). Joseph Roth had his own definition: "to say things that are true in half a page" (Hoffmann 19). Joseph Roth commented on what he wrote: "The feuilleton is as important as politics is for the newspaper and for the reader it is even more important." And he added with a certain arrogance: "The reason people buy the newspaper is me. Not the parliamentary report. Not the main article. Not foreign news … I don't write 'witty columns.' I draw the portrait of the time" (qtd. in Hoffmann 16).

Josep Carner's articles could also be compared to those of Siegfried Kracauer. As Philippe Despoix proposed, Kracauer has many affinities with another of the great observers of the second half of the twentieth century in France, Roland Barthes in *Mythologies* (1957). According to Despoix, Kracauer inaugurates a way of observing new phenomena from an "existential sociology." Kracauer noted that the disappearance of traditional beliefs and rites facilitates the emergence of new aesthetic cults. Interest in the ephemeral – new musical rhythms, speed – reveals a serious crisis in the relationship between modern man and death (Despoix 8). Kracauer also considers the relationship between mass culture and the economic sphere to be important. In the words of the critic, "[t]he aestheticization of everyday life in the ornament of the masses manifests itself as the mythical symptom of a technique whose functionality remains utopian, as the part of nature unknown to modern economic reason" (Despoix 10). Both Kracauer and Carner make an immediate chronicle, objectified by the almost daily ascertainment of the new rites of the modern city. These are the elements of an anonymous biography of the metropolis: the day-to-day in Kracauer's essays is the Berlin of the 1930s; in Carner's is the longed-for Barcelona or the new cities he discovers.

Carner, one can say, writes some urban miniatures, a type of text that focuses on a small anecdote: an encounter in the street, a gesture, an ephemeral event. All the attention is focused on the form: what is happening and proper writing. In his miniatures, narration is organized in a ritualized form and ends with the event described. It is at the crossroads of literary essay and ethnographic writing, which is why it is so useful in capturing the moment in its aesthetic dimension. Carner had neither the training nor the sociological interest of Kracauer, but he was a phenomenal observer. We could apply to him the same definition articulated by Kracauer when he said that he observed "Unscheinbare Obeifliicheniiusserungen" (Mülder-Bach 10; discrete expressions on the surface).

Josep Carner, Ethnographer of the Everyday

The Jaussely Plan (1907) and the Reforma (1908, later the Via Laietana) were two important urban projects that transformed Barcelona in significant ways at the beginning of the twentieth century. Principally intended to create a direct link between the new neighbourhood of Eixample and the city's harbour, they led to the destruction of 2,199 homes and many medieval palaces and affected 10,000 people. Among the buildings demolished it is worth mentioning the palace of the Marquis of Monistrol, the palace of the Marquis of Sentmenat (from which Jeroni Martorell saved a window that he used to restore the Casa dels Canonges), and the convents of Sant Sebastià and Sant Joan de Jerusalem where Pau Claris's grave was located, to name just a few. Some buildings were saved and some were relocated (or, I should say, reappeared in) the so-called Barri Gòtic (Gothic Quarter).[3] Josep Pijoan recounted the failed effort to build a huge catalogue that would record this important and now-disappeared part of Barcelona's past:

> No sé si fins volíem prendre l'índex antropomètric als aborígens barcelonins, ni si volíem conservar llur vocabulari de recargolats renecs, però sí recordo que comptàvem amb En Josep Carner, qui era aleshores *disponible* i ningú millor que ell per immortalitzar el perfum de les alcoves amb calaixeres,

escaparates i relíquies i quadros de canemàs dels barcelonins del segle passat, amb llurs costums, mitologia, tradicions, tabús, creències d'ultratomba, fórmules màgiques, confraries, oracions, balls, etcètera. (Pijoan 22)

(I do not know if we even wanted to measure the anthropometric index to Barcelona's aborigines, or if we wanted to keep their expletive vocabulary, but I do remember that we were counting on Josep Carner, who was the best available to immortalize the perfume of the alcoves with drawers, and the display cabinets and relics and the canvas paintings of Barcelona in the last century, with their customs, mythology, traditions, taboos, belief in afterlife, magic formulas, guilds, prayers, dances, etcetera.)

But Enric Prat de la Riba, the then president of the Catalan Mancomunitat, decided to forget about that project, and "els records etnogràfics de la gran ciutat s'han dispersat als quatre vents, sense possibles recuperacions" (Pijoan 23; ethnographic memories of the great city have been scattered to the four winds, with no possible recovery). Pijoan also recorded the reaction to this process of destructive renewal of Joan Maragall, who had no fond memories of the disappeared neighbourhood where he grew up, exasperated as he was by the stench of the sewers.

Clearly, reactions to this disappearance of an entire neighbourhood ranged widely, from the totally elegiac to, in Maragall's case, the plainly indifferent. But in particular contrast to the cavalier attitude of Maragall is the attitude of Josep Carner, as portrayed by Pijoan, who undertook the ethnographic task of cataloguing the sensory details of the lost neighbourhood. This was indeed the kind of thing at which Carner excelled in poetry collections such as *Auques i ventalls* (1914; Strip cartoon with rhyming couplets and fans), or in his many contributions to the Barcelona press that were compiled in volumes such as *Les planetes del verdum* (1918; The predictions of the bird) or *Les bonhomies* (1925; Positive attitudes). Josep Pla believed that Carner was a "considerable escriptor en prosa, cosa natural atesa la gran força expressiva de la seva poesia" (*Notes disperses* 278; an excellent prose writer, understandably, given the great expressive power of his poetry). Carles Riba claimed that one could not read Carner's prose without thinking about his poetry (95). Estimates of Carner's achievement vary: Maurici Serrahima held the view that whatever worthwhile comments, jokes, and observations might be incorporated in Carner's acute and often funny texts, the author was in the end successful in neither narrative nor essay, and that the topics he dealt with were always topics of general conversation (818). Alan Yates was unabashedly puzzled when he had to describe Carner's articles: "La dificultat d'assignar-los una denominació exacta ('narracions curtes,' 'articles' – per qualificar-los d'alguna manera) indica un dels trets peculiaríssims de la prosa carneriana" (123–4; The difficulty of assigning them an accurate label ("short stories," "articles," to describe them somehow) indicates the peculiar characteristics of Josep Carner's prose). Joan Fuster, however, thought that Carner's articles had considerable literary value: "Transferits al llibre, ofereixen una unitat i una consistència que semblen premeditades i d'una peça" ("Pròleg" 13; Collated in book form, they exhibit a unity and consistency that seem premeditated and well thought-out). In the end, it was Fuster who unlocked the secret of Carner's prose, emphasizing precisely its ability to document a disappeared past. Fuster pointed out that Carner was writing from Italy, remembering a Catalan society of the 1920s that was fast fading away and populated by characters that were anachronisms in the modern world. Fuster concluded:

> Avui, que tot això queda a penes diluït en l'enyorança dels ancians supervivents, nosaltres comencem a trobar-hi una nova curiositat, com en un àlbum de família. Ens hi sedueix la imatge d'una societat i d'una topografia que han canviat, o que fins i tot han desaparegut per sempre més, i que tanmateix conserven sobre el paper, embalsamades, una entranyable iridescència sentimental. I d'alguna manera *Les bonhomies* són també un document històric. ("Pròleg" 15)
>
> (Today, when all this remains barely diluted in the nostalgia of the elderly survivors, we begin to find a new curiosity, as in a family album. We are seduced by the image of a society and a topography that have changed or even disappeared forever more, and yet retain on paper, embalmed, a charming sentimental iridescence. And somehow *Les bonhomies* is also a historical document.)

In one article from *Les bonhomies*, "Habitants de la nit" (People of the night), Carner portrays with vivid imagination a series of human beings whom he locates in an urban landscape at night:

> Un celibatari misàntrop, que surt a passejar el seu gos. – Un home estrany, de cara lluent, que us demana caritat en francès (¿qui ha demanat mai, de dia, caritat en francès?), aquell home necessita que sigui de nit i *que hi hagi una certa solitud*). – Un vidu que ha passat la cinquantena i s'arriba fins a Canaletes: havia tingut ideals i emocions, i avui no li resta sinó un culte meticulós de la higiene: és per higiene que dóna un miler de passes abans de ficar-se al llit, però com que l'ambient dels vidus és la paradoxa, surt a dar el seu passeig salutífer a l'hora que les porteres piquen les catifes de les escales. – Dos vellets suaus, marit i muller, que ixen cada nit una mica tard a sentir música:

quan fa calor s'asseuen prop d'un teatre de sarsuela o d'opereta i quan fa fred van a un cafè on hi hagi pianista i es permeten el luxe de dues granadines. – El senyor que ha sopat a casa d'uns amics: porta una flor al trau i fuma un *Caruncho*; se sent encarcarat, entresuat i magnífic. – El marit que s'ha barallat amb la dona: heu-vos-el aquí amb el capell mal recolzat damunt la testa, les mans crispades: hom reconstitueix l'escena de la revolada amb què ha tancat la porta del pis per aquest senzill detall: *s'ha oblidat de posar-se la corbata*. Encara no se sap si va a un music-hall, a tirar-se a mar o a esperar el primer tren per la línia de Vilafranca. (Carner, *Les bonhomies* 148)

(A celibate misanthrope, who goes out to walk his dog. – A strange man, with a shiny face, who is begging in French (who has ever begged during the day, in French?), it has to be at night and *there needs to be a certain solitude*). – An over-the hill widower walks to Canaletes: in the past he had ideals and emotions, and today he only has a meticulous worship of hygiene: it is because of hygiene that he walks a thousand steps before going to bed, but since widowers live in paradox, he goes out to perform his constitutional when the doorwomen clean the stairs' carpets. – A gentle old couple, husband and wife, who go out a little late every night to hear music: when it's hot they sit near a zarzuela or operetta theatre, and when it's cold they go to a café where there is a pianist and they allow themselves the luxury of drinking two grenadines. – The gentleman who has dined at some friends' house: he carries a flower on his jacket and smokes a *Caruncho*; he feels stiff, sweaty, and magnificent. – The husband who has had an argument with his wife: here he is with an ill-fitted hat, his hands twitching: one can reconstruct the scene of the slam with which he closed the door of the apartment because of this simple detail: *he has forgotten to put on his tie*. He still does not know if he is going to a music hall, to jump into the sea, or to wait for the first Vilafranca line train.)

What unites these characters is that all of them are out of place: they belong to a world that is disappearing. They include a misanthropic bachelor; a beggar who speaks in French; a widower obsessed with hygiene; an old couple who, after listening to a concert of popular music, indulge in a soft drink; a man with a flower on his jacket who smokes a cheap cigar; a husband without a tie who has just quarrelled with his wife and is hesitant in the middle of the street, not knowing what to do and where to go next. Carner portrays a human landscape of vices and attitudes that belong to the category of *genteta* (the low, despicable people). Gabriel Ferrater defended Carner against those who said that he was an "estilitzador de manies de genteta" ("Pròleg" 7; an analyst of *genteta* obsessions). But in *Les bonhomies* we encounter instances of the *genteta* that Carner liked to criticize, the same type of people he included in many of his poems. In yet another example, we realize how he establishes a catalogue of bad taste that is also a document of the way in which Barcelona apartments were decorated at the time. In "Les coses lletges" (Ugly things), he writes a long list of kitsch objects:

> Un pastoret de color de rosa que aguanta una bombeta elèctrica, una tricromia amb una escena andalusa qualsevol, un gosset de guix per a clavar-hi l'escuradents, limiten cada dia, amb llur banalitat, com unes petites ídoles malèfiques, la imaginació, que és el do dels infants i de llurs padrines les fades. Creix llavors, a poc a poc, en els dolços infants, una cosa lletja i irresistible, com els "desigs" de les dames en certs moments interessants de llur vida: una golafreria de coses que dringuen fals, que lluen fals, que encisen un dia la mirada grollera, i l'endemà degoten fàstic i desesperació. És el Mal Gust, una cosa que esgarrifa més que no el grinyol de l'esmolet. (Carner, *Les bonhomies* 67–8)

> (A pink little pastor who holds an electric bulb, a trichrome with an Andalusian scene, a plaster dog where one can leave used toothpicks, limit each day, with their banality, like little evil idols, the imagination, which is the gift of children and their godmothers the fairies. It grows then, little by little, in those sweet children, an ugly and irresistible thing, like ladies' "desires" at some interesting moments of their life: a gluttony of things that ring falsehood, that shine false, that attract rude looks, and the next day drip revulsion and despair. It's Bad Taste, something that makes your skin crawl more than a knifegrinder's screech.)

Carner here itemizes the most horrifying objects one might find in any Barcelona apartment and abhors their effects during the early stages of life. He also establishes a catalogue of what Pijoan calls "ethnographic memories of the big city" before they disappear without anyone having the chance to recuperate them, and the list is his method for doing so. Such a rhetorical device – enumeration – can be understood as an act of looking around to survey and record the wide variety of actions and people that populate the landscape of the everyday. As I have discussed in the previous chapter, Umberto Eco makes some useful observations in this regard. He points out that artists have resorted to a range of remarkable solutions in the attempt to represent the list, and he goes on to theorize them. As a good cataloguer, Eco relies on subdivisions. He considers the verbal (from Homer to Thomas Pynchon) and the visual (from a fifth-century Greek shield to Christian Boltanski installations) and concludes that the two major types of list are those that correspond to the "poetics of everything included" and those expressing the "poetics of the etcetera" (7). The first aims for comprehensiveness and closure, albeit temporary: the old phone book is at once a list of phone numbers and a comprehensive catalogue of the inhabitants of a city. The second exploits the human mind's capacity for association, as is the case in Carner's enumerations. Carner is also playing a well-known children's game: *Un, dos, tres, pica paret* (a variation of hide-and-seek) in which a player or observer facing the wall tries to catch the other players when they move, which corresponds to picnolepsy as defined by Virilio.

Sometimes Carner performs an autopsy of reality by enumerating what has disappeared. At the beginning of "Un amic íntim" (A close friend), for exemple, he provides an elaborate theory of disappearances in our everyday landscape:

> Per a adornar-nos d'una gràcia necessitem en general adoptar un previ determini pedantesc: "Avui esmerçaré una estona per dar un tomb inútil i sentimental." Les coses, per a impressionar-nos si us plau per força, no tenen més remei que, amb llur desaparició, emportar-se'n una mica de la nostra vida. Tots nosaltres, amb alguna recança, amoixem reminiscències de coses que no veiérem sinó d'esma i que ja no hi són: conservem, talment, la flor emmusteïda que ens donà una noia de la qual no hem sabut ni sabrem mai la color dels ulls. Així, abans de morir, ja ens anem projectant gradualment en l'ombra. (Carner, *Les bonhomies* 165)
>
> (To realize the elegance of something, we generally need to adopt a pedantic attitude: "Today I will be doing some walking in a useless and sentimental way." Things, to impress us, in a forceful way, have to take away a little of our life as they disappear. All of us, with some remorse, love reminiscences of things that we hardly saw but that are not there any more: we keep, perhaps, a withered flower given us by a girl the colour of whose eyes we do not know and will never know. So, before dying, we are gradually throwing ourselves into the shadow.)

Things that surround us cannot but take with them a little bit of our life when they disappear, and these sometimes insignificant, hardly noticed disappearances Carner emphatically links to death. Elsewhere in the text he exhibits his exceptional ability to perceive and give a sense of invisible changes, for instance ending the article with an elegy for the decidedly quotidian object of the umbrella:

> No us convido pas a les reminiscències literàries del paraigua: el paraigua de l'oncle rural de *vaudeville*, el paraigua panxa enlaire de l'estudiant i la

modisteta, el paraigua nerviós i prim de la jove dama, el tendal solidíssim del capellà, el paraigua diminut de la *divette* amb el qual hom assenyala un espectador i amaga la fingida escena del bes, el paraigua oficial del senyor de copa alta que va a una cerimònia a l'aire lliure (dos estris a la vegada! – pensa el bon senyor – una desgràcia mai no ve sola!), el paraigua deformat i bruixenc de la castanyera, el paraigua tort del pagès, el paraigua perforat del fumador, el paraigua del poruc que obrint-lo i tancant-lo espanta els gossos, el paraigua del ric celibatari egoista i prudent, arborat per bé que no hi hagi sinó un cap de núvol a l'horitzó, contrapart elegant – seda, malaca i or – del baròmetre que hi ha en una repiseta, ben acuradament embeinat quan el somriure del cel és equívoc, mai no deixat a ningú, i només temerós d'haver de caure, després d'acompanyar cada vegada amb més freqüència el seu encirat senyor als enterraments, a les mans d'algun nebot inexpert. (Carner, *Les bonhomies* 166)

(I do not invite you to hear the umbrella's literary reminiscences: the vaudevillesque umbrella of a rural uncle, the student's umbrella upside-down while he walks with a young dressmaker, the skinny and nervous umbrella of a young lady, the solid tent of a priest, the small umbrella of a *divette* with which she points to a spectator and behind it fakes a kiss, the official umbrella of a gentleman with high hat on that goes to an open-air event (two objects at the same time! – he muses to himself – misery loves company!), the deformed and witchy umbrella of the chestnut-roasting lady, the peasant's twisted umbrella, the smoker's holed umbrella, the coward's umbrella that he opens and closes to scare away dogs, the rich single's umbrella, selfish and pedantic, opened up even when there is no trace of an upcoming storm, stylish counterpart – silk, malacca cane, and gold – of the barometer that sits at home on a little shelf, always at hand when a threatening sky sticks out, never lent to anybody, and only fearful of becoming the property, after accompanying its uptight owner to increasingly frequent funerals, of an amateurish nephew.)

The passage's keen sense of the relations between umbrellas and the particularities of their owners is remarkable. As Carner concludes, he turns towards the reader: "No: us convido a considerar com el paraigua ha esta íntimament unit a l'evolució de la vostra personalitat" (Carner, *Les bonhomies* 166; No: I invite you to consider an umbrella as something closely linked to the development of your personality).

All these examples might make us think of the rapidity with which contemporary urban space evolves. Fast changes are characteristic of the urban environment and can instigate the unravelling of memory, affecting everyday life and changing imperceptibly how we relate to our environment. As Zoë Thompson puts it, "the aesthetics of disappearance is intrinsically linked to the aesthetics of change as urban spaces evolve" (162). According to Thompson, Siegfried Kracauer stressed in his essay "Straße ohne Erinnerung" (Street without memory; 1932) that "one's memories can be shocked into being, as familiar landmarks disappear, or are erased entirely by the destruction of the space in which they stood." For Kracauer, such erasure was the installation of an eternal now, a constant presentness (Z. Thompson 162). Thompson suggests that this is reminiscent of Baudrillard's fear that "memory itself will be eradicated by the imposition of simulated versions of the past, synthetic histories engendered by a process of 'museification" that produces an officially sanctioned form of cultural memory' (162). Baudrillard writes, in a passage that resonates with Virilio's idea of picnolepsy: "it is no longer buildings which burn or cities which are laid waste; it is the radio relays of our memories you can hear crackling" (qtd. in Z. Thompson 162). Carner's itemizations of unravelling hidden spaces, his records of the physical and emotional network of which they are part, create a map of the city and of its inhabitants in the past, exploring space as a mute witness to changes in everyday life. My contention is that picnolepsy offers an instructive key to this aspect of Carner's work.

Transformation of urban space has long been a preoccupation of writers and artists alike. According to Christoph Asendorf, "circulation finds its concrete expression in *démolitions*" (69). In Charles Baudelaire's poem "Le cygne" (The swan), the poet witnesses the disappearance of a world, an entire Parisian neighbourhood swallowed up by Hausman's reforms:

> A fécondé soudain ma mémoire fertile,
> Comme je traversais le nouveau Carrousel.
> Le vieux Paris n'est plus (la forme d'une ville
> Change plus vite, hélas! que le coeur d'un mortel);
>
> Je ne vois qu'en esprit tout ce camp de baraques,
> Ces tas de chapiteaux ébauchés et de fûts,
> Les herbes, les gros blocs verdis par l'eau des flaques,
> Et, brillant aux carreaux, le bric-à-brac confus.
>
> [..]
>
> Paris change! mais rien dans ma mélancolie
> N'a bougé! palais neufs, échafaudages, blocs,
> Vieux faubourgs, tout pour moi devient allégorie
> Et mes chers souvenirs sont plus lourds que des rocs.
>
> (*Oeuvres complètes* 85–7)

(Suddenly made fruitful my teeming memory,
As I walked across the new Carrousel.
Old Paris is no more (the form of a city
Changes more quickly, alas! than the human heart);

I see only in memory that camp of stalls,
Those piles of shafts, of rough-hewn cornices, the grass,
The huge stone blocks stained green in puddles of water,
And in the windows shine the jumbled bric-a-brac.

[...]

Paris changes! But naught in my melancholy
Has stirred! New palaces, scaffolding, blocks of stone,
Old quarters, all become for me an allegory,
And my dear memories are heavier than rocks.)

The poet voices how the past, the "spirit" of the place, where now he finds new bridges and boulevards, lingers on in his mind.[4] The city of modernity is used as a kind of clock or metre that measures variations accurately. Disappearances and transformations and the cityscape are read as indicators of the transience of life. The metaphor used to convey remembrance – rocks – is also noteworthy.

Many of Gaziel's works elegize past times and missing spaces in a similar way. In his memoir, *Tots els camins duen a Roma* (1958; All roads lead to Rome), Gaziel provides a rich and eloquent chronicle of Barcelona at the turn of the nineteenth to the twentieth century. He remembers that it was a city

> molt comprimida, força allunyada encara de Montjuïc i, sobretot, de Collserola; s'alçava enmig de l'ample aiguamoll de la maresma, tota voltada d'un bosc de xemeneies. Aquest bosc fabril – del qual només queden ara restes, que aviat desapareixeran del tot – era llavors un espectacle imponent, la materialització mateixa de l'esperit de la centúria extraordinària que havia creat la màquina de vapor, la indústria moderna, la democràcia, el liberalisme i la grandesa de la capital de Catalunya. Contemplada de lluny estant i des d'una certa alçària, la ciutat, guarnida amb el seu cenyidor de xemeneies que anaven traient glopades de fum – blanques, negres, grises i groguenques –, semblava un pastís d'aniversari, fet de pinyó i ametlla, on havien clavat tantes candeles enceses com dies feiners té l'any. (30)

> (compact, still far from Montjuïc and, above all, Collserola; it stood in the middle of the wide wetland of the marsh, surrounded by a forest – of

> chimneys. This factory forest, of which nowadays very little remains and what remains will soon disappear completely – was then an imposing spectacle, the very materialization of the century's extraordinary spirit that had created the steam engine, modern industry, democracy, liberalism, and the greatness of Catalonia's capital city. Contemplated from afar and from a certain height, the city, decorated with its belt of chimneys that were expelling gulps of smoke – whitewashed, black, grey, and yellowish – looked like a birthday cake, made of pine nuts and almonds, in which they had stuck as many candles as there were working days in a year.)

It was a city without any trace of

> tramvies elèctrics, automòbils ni tampoc bicicletes, perquè encara no era inventat el pneumàtic. Només circulaven carruatges particulars, generalment luxosos, o cotxes públics, també anomenats "pesseters," perquè des que arrencava el cavall fins que el passatger arribava a lloc, mentre pel camí no fes parada, el trajecte valia una pesseta; tartanes, molts carros, uns tramvies rudimentaris, també de tracció exclusivament animal, i uns ripperts de dues empreses en competència: *La Nueva Condal* i *La Catalana*. Tots els vehicles eren tirats per cavalls, eugues, mules o rucs. (32)

> (electric trams, cars or bicycles, because the tire was not yet invented. Only private carriages, usually luxurious, or public cars, also called *pesseters*, because from the moment the horse started walking towards the passenger's destination, if it did not stop anywhere, the journey cost a *peseta;* traps, many carts, rudimentary trams, also exclusively drawn by animals, and *ripperts* of two rival companies: La Nueva Condal and La Catalana. All the vehicles were drawn by horses, mares, mules, or donkeys.)

The picture of Barcelona presented in Gaziel's memoir has an excellent counterpoint in newspaper articles he published in *La Vanguardia*. Assiduously avoiding the picturesque or superficial detail, there he manages to capture the poetry of living in the city as he raises questions and talks about the frustrations of the educated citizen.

In a memorable article entitled "Pequeña elegía urbana" (Little urban elegy), Gaziel evokes the transformation of mechanical life in the city through an account of his forty-year personal relationship with the Sarrià train line. He writes as the tunnel under Balmes Street is to be inaugurated, with the result that the train will move underground and cease to travel along the surface of the city. The article ends thus:

> ¿Es un sueño? No; es algo parecido: cuarenta años de vida … Al constatar sus extraordinarias mudanzas es forzoso sentir que, en nuestra brevedad,

todo lo que fuimos en el seno de esa vida municipal gigantesca, se borra paulatinamente, y nuestra propia vida se va convirtiendo poco a poco en estampas del tiempo pasado.

(Is it a dream? No. It is something similar: forty years of life … When acknowledging its extraordinary changes we must feel that, in our brevity, everything that we witnessed within that giant municipal life, is gradually erased, and our life is gradually becoming a series of engravings from the past.)

As the subterranean world swallows a former surface train, Gaziel detects an important transformation in city life, and in his account of it there is an overlap between elegy for a time past, anxiety over the speed of change, and an awareness of transience: we are destined to be swallowed and disappear. One cannot but recall Gilloch's reflection on disappearance: "For it is paradoxically the act of obliteration, the present absence of the former cafés which brings them so vividly to mind. Demolition and erasure bring with them a sudden appreciation of what is no longer there" (300).[5] *Picnolepsy* is a way of labelling this phenomenon of the sudden disappearance of objects, parts of the city, attitudes, and ways of living. We could thus define it as the unremitting alternation between tiny moments of consciousness and diminutive "deaths" of unconsciousness.

Disappearance and Crisis

The 2008 financial crisis hit Southern European countries hard, leaving large groups of young graduates without any significant prospects of finding a job. Thus, a narrative of the crisis has flourished. Consequently, we are in front of a new exceptional economic, cultural, and social paradigm, which in its essence is not only multidimensional but also multidirectional. It is having an impact on Europe, and contemporary narrative is expressing the new social structure and the many transformations in human relationships. According to Manuel Castells, "the crisis of global capitalism that has unfolded since 2008 is not merely economic. It is structural and multidimensional. The events that took place in the immediate aftermath show that we are entering a world with very different social and economic conditions from those that characterized the rise of global, informational capitalism in the preceding three decades" (Castells et al. 2). Individuals and communities have articulated cultural representations and intellectual responses to such an unprecedented situation whose far-reaching effects transcend national borders. In Southern European countries, including Spain,

Portugal, Italy, and Greece,[6] the crisis has prompted a complete rethinking of democratic, social, and cultural values. The economic and cultural repercussions of this new development have triggered transformations and changes that literature is just beginning to register and document.

Like Carner, many contemporary Catalan writers have engaged in chronicling disappearance and transformation in the everyday. However, they do so from a slightly different perspective. Some pay attention to the modern city. Others, hit hard by the financial crisis, return to the small rural communities where they grew up, viewing their hometowns from new urban perspectives and realizing how much (and how fast) the world around them has changed. I propose to analyse these upheavals and their depiction in two recent fictional or autofictional texts. The characters/narrators in these texts, without jobs, and in some instances without a love life, go back to their hometown for sentimental reasons. In *Primavera, estiu, etcètera* (2011; Spring, summer, etcetera), Marta Rojals has her protagonist Èlia return to a small town that resembles Rojal's own hometown, La Palma d'Ebre. In *L'horitzó primer* (2013; First horizon), Joan Todó revisits La Cènia.

Rojals writes a generational novel that centres on characters in the mid-thirties demographic, paying special attention to their everyday lives in Ribera d'Ebre. One of the main issues is the dichotomy between city and village: the protagonist struggles constantly with the idea of returning to her hometown, and her struggles mingle with episodes and images from her childhood and adolescence (her first love and so on). Attention is also paid to the problems, disappointments, and frustrations involved in migrating to Barcelona, where she now lives. Having left her hometown to study and work there, Èlia is puzzled by her new condition as a migrant. A friend tells her:

> – Ei, que per ser emigrant no cal anar a viure a l'altra punta del planeta, es pot ser emigrant de moltes coses, de realitats, de sentiments, de la llengua, també. Perquè cadascú té la pàtria que té, i se'n pot sentir allunyat encara que et trobis a deu quilòmetres, i la pot enyorar encara que siguis a tres hores de tren. (Rojals 112)
>
> (Hey, to become an emigrant it is not necessary to move to the other side of the planet. You can be an emigrant of many things, realities, feelings, language, too. Because everybody has a hometown, and you may feel far from it even though you are only ten kilometres away, and you may long for your hometown even if you are somewhere at a three-hour distance by train.)

To this, Èlia answers that she has felt very lonely and foreign in a place such as Barcelona. She does not know anybody in the apartment building where she has been living for ten years. She is extremely concerned that a new neighbour is surprised that she can speak Catalan: "Va i em diu '*Ay, hablas catalàn?, però ¿tú eres de aquí?*' T'ho pots creure, la tia?, d'on vol que sigui, de Singapur?" (Rojals 112–13; And she tells me in Spanish, "*But do you speak Catalan? Are you a local?*" Can you believe this? From where does she want me to be, Singapore?). At the end of the novel, Èlia flies to Lisbon to visit her sister who is expecting a baby. Through the plane's window she observes her hometown with a panoptic perspective that allows her to make unexpected connections:

> Recolzo el front a la finestreta de policarbonat i, en el moment precís, el Google Earth ja és un sotabosc de fulles de roure. Entre el trencaclosques de peces verdes i terrosses, localitzo la serp negra de l'Ebre i li segueixo els capricis fins on gairebé es fa un nus: el Meandre. I ara he de mirar, i una mica cap a la dreta, i ja hi tinc ubicada la crosta verda del Montsant … Però les coses que no es veuen, pel fet de no veure's, no tenen per què no existir. I *allí*, tot i que ara no ho veig, existeix un *patchwork* de teulades secretes, i sé que n'hi ha una amb una antena que sembla un penja-robes, i que dos pisos més avall hi té un telèfon inalàmbric que ningú no pensarà de carregar; sé que hi ha una altra teulada que, un pis més avall, hi té un sofà reclinable massa modern, i que al vespre hi jaurà un home que encendrà un Winston amb el cendrer al pit. (Rojals 362–3)

> (I lean my forehead against the polycarbonate window and, at the right time, Google Earth becomes a vegetation of oak leaves. Among the earthy green puzzle pieces, I locate the black serpent of the Ebre river and I follow its whims until it almost becomes a knot: the Meander. And now I look a little to the right, and there I have located the green scab of Montsant mountain … But things unseen do not cease to exist simply because they are not seen. And *there*, even though now I cannot see it, there is a patchwork of secret roofs, and I know that there is one with an antenna that looks like a clothes line, and two floors below there is a cordless phone that nobody will remember to charge; I know that there is another roof, a floor below, under which there is a recliner sofa that is too modern and in the evening a man will light up a Winston cigarette with an ashtray on his chest.)

This very detailed description of what she sees, and what she does not see, from the plane's window is a reconstruction of spaces she knows too well, spaces that are the remnants of a world to which she no longer belongs. At the same time, without naming them, she summarizes the main characters and repetitive actions they have performed in the novel, as if this passage were a perfect abstract of the narrative. The rather unusual perspective, her intimate world seen from the air with a Google maps perspective, gives the narrator a sense of security, but it also introduces a vanishing point, the point at which something that has been decreasing disappears altogether. She is daydreaming about what she sees and remembering what the distant landscape seen from the air hides, and in the end she is awakened by a stewardess who asks her, "¿Café, señora?" (Coffee, madam?). She reacts forcefully: "*Señora*? *Señora* tu!, no et fot?" (Rojals 362–3; Mrs., Mrs. you! My foot!). The stewardess's use of *señora*, rather than *señorita* (miss), brings home for Èlia the passage of time, and from a panoptic perspective she now zooms in on a few houses she knows well, a move that encapsulates both the events in the novel and a human geography only made visible by virtue of a piercing look at reality.

Joan Todó's *L'horitzó primer* likewise deals with the experience of being a foreigner at home. The narrator regards this situation as being of the kind that Victor Turner defined as liminal: individuals or entities are "neither here nor there; they are betwixt and between the positions assigned and arrayed by law, custom, convention, and ceremony" (Turner 95). The narrator perceives slight changes in his own behaviour and has many doubts about how to interact with his neighbours: "Aquesta sensació de foranitat. Fa gairebé tres mesos que ets aquí, i tot ha canviat subtilment. Ja s'han adonat que has tornat per quedar-te … Ja no saps, per exemple, quan saludar" (Todó 87). (This feeling of being foreign. It has been almost three months since you arrived here, and everything has changed. They have already noticed that you're back to stay … You do not know, for example, when you should say hello.) Also: "No ha sabut endevinar quan és que la gent d'aquí va al bar, quan cal trucar-los, com funcionen les coses" (88; He has not been able to guess when people here go to the bar, when to call them, how things work). He makes a long list of typical activities performed by families during the local festivities (57–9), but it does little good, and his isolation also reminds him of the passage of time (he is nearly forty). As a result of all this, he comes to a pessimistic conclusion regarding the book he intends to write: "Seria una novel la sense protagonista únic, o potser l'únic protagonista seria el temps, o el mateix poble, la comunitat, una espiral de llenguatge, una novel la sense argument que tu i jo no escriurem. ¿Qui la llegiria?" (59). (It would be a novel without a main character, or perhaps the only protagonist would be the time or the village, the community, a spiral of language, a plotless novel that neither I nor you will write. Who would read it?) The quotidian pervades his memory:

> T'adones que, idèntics a si mateixos, aquests dies s'han perdut en un sospir. Aixecar-se, esmorzar, comprovar mails, llegir, passejar, comprovar mails,

dinar, prendre notes per a una possible versió llarga del pregó de festes, comprovar mails: una rutina només trencada pels dies que has anat a ajudar el teu pare a carregar llenya a la finca, que després guardàveu al garatge, vora la caldera de la calefacció. La resta són hores que pareixen engolides per un forat negre, menys pesants que no marca el calendari, dies que semblen perduts. Ja és, però, el que vas aprendre aquells estius que anaves a treballar a la fàbrica: que les hores s'allarguen com un turment si estàs atent a elles, que es cremen com la palla si en lloc d'estar comptant quantes peces falten per polir et concentres en la perfecció singular de cadascuna; al cap i a la fi, acabar la pila no volia dir res perquè, igual que la roca de Sísif, quan l'acabaves ja n'esperava una altra. Però després s'encongeixen en el record: en una situació de monotonia semblant Hans Castorp va descobrir que quan un dia és com tots, tots els dies són com un qualsevol, i el temps s'accelera. Les últimes setmanes mateix, les que has passat aquí navegant entre ofertes de feina, llegint, sense fer gaire res, atuït per la manca de sortides, aixecant projectes com estels que l'endemà deixaven d'interessar-te, ara semblen un sol minut angoixós; mentre que les Festes d'agost, quan vas fer el pregó, pareixen un any sencer. (Todó 154–5)

(You realize that, identical to each other, these days have been wasted doing nothing. Getting up, breakfast, checking mails, reading, walking, checking mails, lunch, taking notes for a possible long version of the speech at the *festes*, checking mails: a routine only interrupted by those days when you helped your father to load firewood at the farm, to store it in the garage, near the heating boiler. The rest are hours that seem swallowed up by a black hole, lighter than the calendar indicates, days that seem lost. It is, however, what you learned during those summers you worked at the factory: hours are excruciatingly long if you watch them; they go very quickly if instead of counting how many pieces are left to be cleaned, you concentrate on polishing each of them to perfection; in the end, finishing the stack did not mean anything because, like the rock of Sisyphus, as soon as one was finished, another one was there. But afterwards they shrink in your memory: in a similar repetitive situation, Hans Castorp discovered that when one day is like any other, every day is like any other, and time accelerates. Take these last weeks you have spent here considering job offers, reading, doing nothing much, devastated by the lack of opportunities, raising projects as if they were flying kites only to forget about them the next day, these weeks seem now a single anguished minute; while the festivities of August, when you made the speech, feel like a whole year.)

Todó appears to be gesturing here towards *l'infra-ordinaire* (the infra-ordinary), the term coined by Georges Perec in 1973 to denote those unglamorous elements of reality on which he hoped to zero in: "[w]hat happens every day, the banal, the quotidian, the evident, the common, the ordinary, the infra-ordinary, the background noise, the habitual" (*L'Infra-ordinaire* 210). Perec reminds us that our eyes are conditioned to scan the horizon of our habitat only for the unusual; therefore, we tend to neglect the anonymous endotic (another of his coinages, an antonym of *exotic*). And it was Walter Benjamin who described the process by which, without the aid of dreams or hashish, an individual perceives the most ordinary, overlooked objects of everyday reality – from obsolete train stations to out-of-place arcades – as uncanny, supernatural, and irrational, a process he called "profane illumination" (*Arcades Project* 209). These concepts, as well as that of picnolepsy, are useful to understand the texts examined here – by Carner, Gaziel, Rojals, and Todó – all of which detect major transformations in apparently insignificant changes to the everyday.

Autopsies

Milan Kundera once mentioned Herman Broch's reflection on the purpose of the novel: to discover what only a novel can discover is the raison d'être of the genre (Kundera 5). The sharpest writers have managed to condense narrative into a few topics. These topics are not mere plots (myth or elegy) but the inner filter that forces the writers to investigate large abstractions and to give a reactive response, to express their ideas in a personal way, interleaved in the time in which they live. The texts examined here include names and places and temporal changes and react to the absurdity of everyday life in a big impersonal city through elegy or by evoking mythical spaces and ways of life that have disappeared.

In a section of *The Arcades Project* that mocks the claustrophobic and chaotic mess of the bourgeois living room, Benjamin writes:

> Living in these plush compartments was nothing more than leaving traces made by habits. Even the rage expressed when the least little thing broke was perhaps merely the reaction of a person who felt that someone had obliterated "the traces of his days on earth." The traces that he had left in cushions and armchairs, that his relatives had left in photos, and that his possessions had left in lining and etuis and that sometimes made these rooms look as overcrowded as halls full of funerary urns. This is what has now been achieved by the new architects, with their glass and steel: they have created rooms in which it is hard to leave traces. (701–2)

Likewise J.G. Ballard was fascinated by reality as a depository of quotidian objects with magic and poetic effects: "I'm always struck by the enormous sort of magic and poetry one feels when looking at a junkyard filled with old washing machines, or wrecked cars, or old ships rotting in some disused harbor. An enormous mystery and magic surrounds these objects" (qtd. in Revell). What is the relevance of this for us as we conclude? Carner was an ethnographer of the near past, and Rojals and Todó of the near present, but all three perform what I have called autopsies of the everyday, and all three can be better understood by considering them in terms of picnolepsy. These writers look at reality from a very different perspective, as a special kind of autopsy. They assemble the materials of their mortuary investigation, treating reality almost as if it were a cadaver or the contents of a special kind of forensic inquisition.

4

Vicent Andrés Estellés's *Trencadís*, or Attention to the Infra-ordinary

Montage and Collage

In a letter to Roberto Fernández Retamar, Julio Cortázar defined art as a mode of cognition, made up of "experiencias tangibles de contactos directos que no tiene nada que ver con la información o la erudición, pero que es su equivalente vital, la sangre misma de Europa" ("Acerca" 276; tangible experiences of direct contacts that has nothing to do with information or scholarship, but which is its vital equivalent, the very lifeblood of Europe).[1] In some of his novels he promoted a fragmented delivery that encouraged the reader to become distracted, and took into account the many connections between what was presented to the reader and their everyday life experience. As Jean Franco put it, Cortázar felt the need to supply the materials that he had excluded from the text and to explain the interruptions that he had experienced during the writing of a novel:

> [L]as interacciones de la vida y de la lectura son apenas tenidas en cuenta por el novelista, un poco como si solamente él y sus criaturas estuvieran metidos en el continuo espacio-tiempo y su lector fuese en cambio una entidad abstracta que sostendrá en algún momento un paquete de doscientas páginas entre los dedos de la mano izquierda y dispondrá de un tiempo corrido para agotarlas. (Qtd. in Franco 111)
>
> (The interactions of life and reading are barely taken into account by the novelist, a bit as if only he and his creatures were embedded in the space-time continuum and his reader were instead an abstract entity who would at some point hold a packet of two hundred pages between the fingers of his left hand and have a running time to exhaust them.)

A clear example of this procedure can be seen in Cortázar's essay "La muñeca rota" (The broken wrist) in *Último Round* (Last round), in which he also remarks that the reader seldom reads a novel continuously. Reading, then, is always a process made of pauses during which everyday life intervenes.[2] Moreover, in Cortázar's novel *Rayuela*, Morelli – a writer and important character in the book – introduces the notion of collage, conceiving it as a series of photographs:

> [N]o es cine sino fotografía, es decir que no podemos aprehender la acción sino tan solo sus fragmentos eleáticamente recortados. No hay más que los momentos en que estamos con ese otro cuya vida creemos entender, o cuando nos hablan de él, o cuando él nos cuenta lo que le ha pasado o proyecta ante nosotros lo que tiene intención de hacer. Al final queda un álbum de fotos, de instantes fijos: jamás la vida realizándose ante nosotros, el paso de ayer al hoy, la primera aguja del olvido en el recuerdo. (Qtd. in Franco 115)
>
> (It is not cinema but photography, that is to say that we cannot apprehend the action but only its Eleatically cut fragments. There are only the moments when we are with that other whose life we think we understand, or when they speak to us about them, or when they tell us what has happened to them, or when they project before us what they intend to do. In the end we are left with an album of photos, of fixed moments: never life unfolding before us, the passage from yesterday to today, the first needle of oblivion in the memory.)

Thus, Morelli defends collage as a more accurate form of mimesis. In another excerpt Cortázar adds that the continuity between different images is provided by a relentless effort to establish connections. They acquire a cinematic continuity because they help to "rellenar con literatura, presunciones, hipótesis e invenciones los hiatos entre una y otra foto" (qtd. in Franco 115; fill in the gaps between one photo and the other with literature, assumptions, hypotheses, and inventions). These reflections by Julio Cortázar point to the usefulness of collage in representing certain aspects of reality, a continuity that is otherwise difficult to grasp and which constitutes a starting point in this discussion of nearby experiences and attention to minimal aspects of reality in Iberian settings.

This approach brings us close to Walter Benjamin's use of montage and collage. Benjamin aimed at developing collage and montage as constructive principles for a progressive form of writing. He states that the *Passagenwerk* "must develop to the highest point the art of citing without citation marks. Its theory connects most closely with that of montage" (*Arcades Project* 860).

Benjamin describes the method of literary montage as a mode of historiography: "I needn't say anything. Merely show. I shall purloin no valuables, appropriate no ingenious formulations. But the rags, the refuse – these I will not inventory but allow, in the only way possible, to come into their own: by making use of them" (*Arcades Project* 460). His goal is "not [to] inventory but [to] allow," not to curate but to permit, to open the content and make it available to the artist. For Benjamin, the idea of literary montage was (literally, in light of his anti-fascist, pro-historical materialist context) a revolutionary philosophy aimed at rethinking history itself. Benjamin did not understand history as a smooth, streamlined process or a perfect chronology, but as something that he refers to as the moment of "danger," the "flash," "interference," and "catastrophe." It is the "constellation of dangers," Benjamin argues, that the materialist presentation of history "comes to engage" (*Arcades Project* 475).

Following some considerations by Nuccio Ordine in *L'utilità dell'inutile* (2013; The usefulness of the useless) and Josep M. Esquirol in *La resistència íntima: Assaig d'una filosofia de la proximitat* (2015; Intimate resistance: Essay on a philosophy of proximity) related to everyday life, I will address the poetry of Valencian author Vicent Andrés Estellés. I will use the metaphor of collage, in which different elements retain their discreteness and their fragmentary quality, to explore his works. I will focus on how he depicts the everyday, following the example of French writer Georges Perec, who became a master of the *infra-ordinaire*. In *Je me souviens* (I remember) Perec established an extensive collection of little disappearances that draw a map of forgotten collective insignificant memories. They are not "des souvenirs, et surtout pas des souvenirs personnels, mais des petits morceaux de quotidien, des choses que, telle ou telle année, tous les gens d'un même âge ont vues, ont vécues, ont partagées, et qui ensuite ont disparu, ont été oubliées" (4; memories, and especially not personal memories, but little pieces of daily life, things that, such or such year, all people of the same age have seen, have lived, have shared, and then they have disappeared, have been forgotten).[3] According to Perec, they were not worth remembering; they were so minuscule that they did not deserve to be part of history or to be included in the memoirs of statesmen or celebrities.

Philosophical Perspectives on Uselessness

Attention to apparently irrelevant things in life has been developed recently from complimentary perspectives by the Catalan philosopher Josep Maria Esquirol and the Italian literary critic Nuccio Ordine. Both propose a rethinking of life's priorities, stating the need to go back to more basic elements in life. Esquirol, for instance, elaborates a "Cartografia del no-res" (Cartography of nothingness). He proposes a series of substitutions: resistance instead of will to power, proximity instead of the superman, doubts instead of confidence, memory instead of future. As he puts it, "[e]n lloc de la voluntat de poder, la resistència; en lloc del superhome, la proximitat; en lloc de l'afirmació, problematicitat; en lloc del futur, la memòria" (27; instead of the will to power, resistance; instead of superman, proximity; instead of affirmation, problematization; instead of the future, the memory). He considers everyday life to be constituted by repetition, contrast, joy, and difficulty, but overall by proximity, "el punt més decisiu de tots: la proximitat" (57; the most decisive point of all: proximity). In his view, the everyday is based upon a paradox because everyday repetition becomes a long-lasting event: "res dura més que la repetició quotidiana" (63; nothing lasts longer than daily repetition). It is an apparent emptiness filled with sense: "Allò que omple el dia a dia, i el pas dels mesos i dels anys, es pot considerar com poca cosa, com una mena de vida de poca alçada, mediocre, que no excel leix ni sobresurt en res, com una vida muda 'materialista,' de vol ras" (65). (Nothing lasts longer than repetition. That which fills the day to day, and the passage of months and years, can be considered as little, as a kind of life of low height, mediocre, that does not excel or excel in anything, as a dumb life "materialist," flying low.) In spite of appearing meaningless, it is full of sense: "La senzillesa de la quotidianitat beu d'un saber molt especial; d'un saber discret lligat al gest que és realment admirable i que se'ns esmuny en voler sistematitzar-lo ... Mirar bé allò que fem quan fem alguna cosa ens acosta a la forma suprema de coneixement que hi ha en el gest" (67). (The simplicity of everyday life drinks from a very special knowledge; of a discreet knowledge linked to the gesture that is truly admirable and that we are ashamed of when we want to systematize it … Looking carefully at what we do when we do something brings us closer to the supreme form of knowledge that is in the gesture.)

There are other sentences worth noticing because they provide a program of sorts: "Apropiar-se de la quotidianitat i de la senzillesa de la vida d'alguna manera ens 'salva'" (Esquirol 54; Appropriating the everyday and the simplicity of life somehow "saves" us). Esquirol's point is very similar to a sociological view of the everyday summarized by authors such as Ben Highmore and Michael Sheringham. It might be useful at this point to remember what the latter has written about the contradictions that are easily encountered when studying the everyday:

> [T]he everyday is a zone of opposition, intersection, or interconnection – of the accidental and the permanent, imagination and affect, the personal and the social. It is constituted by sequences of individual actions

> (dressing, eating, shopping, walking), but within a context of relations and interactions where the individual is actor as well as agent. The *quotidien* involves continuity but also change, repetition but also variation and evolution. It is made up of routines, but major events (often long anticipated or long remembered) are also part of its fabric, as are festive moments, "mini-fêtes." It is universal (through its link to the human condition in general) but also variable, inflected by climate, class, and gender. It is both independent of and marked by history.[4] (Sheringham 300)

Everyday life implies a paradoxical process of repeatedly constructing each day anew on a routine basis. It is not static but rather a means for articulating changes in communities and ways of life, while further reflecting ongoing changes in attitudes, politics, and identity. The everyday effectively erodes traditional spatial categories to create and reveal new and less stable versions of the ordinary. One could argue that it amplifies Marc Augé's notion of non-place, where places lose their real and symbolic sway and become indeterminate spaces in which meaning is uncertain, in flux, or non-existent.

Indeed, the way in which Sheringham addresses the everyday is very similar to Esquirol's because they both stress the importance of repetition and variation: "La característica de la quotidianitat és més aviat la repetició i la rutina; però no exactament la repetició del que és idèntic (finalment sinistre i insuportable), la repetició del que és similar, en una mena de síntesi entre allò que ja és conegut i allò que és una mica nou" (Esquirol 55; The characteristic of everyday life is rather repetition and routine; but not exactly the repetition of what is identical (ultimately sinister and unbearable), the repetition of what is similar, in a kind of synthesis between what is already known and what is somewhat new). Esquirol even claims the need to abhor superficiality, which is linked to the boasting of appearances but leads to the disappearance of the everyday: "En la societat de l'aparença, ens quedem en la vanaglòria del petit poder jeràrquic o en la verborrea associada a l'aparició mediàtica, i la vida corrent continua quedant arraconada" (57; In the society of appearance, we remain in the vainglory of the small hierarchical power or in the verbiage associated with the media appearance, and ordinary life continues to be cornered). Thus, with Esquirol we can vindicate the intimacy of the places in which we live and work, of the ancient ways of living, or of what in Catalan used to be summarized in the petit bourgeois expression "la caseta i l'hortet," or "casa e bottega" in Italian, or "live only for one's family and one's work" in English, which represents the soundtrack of our lives.

By contrast, Nuccio Ordine focuses on the centrality of non-useful things, such as culture. He starts his book with a declaration of intentions:

> [H]o voluto mettere al centro delle mie riflessioni l'idea di utilità di quei saperi il cui valore essenziale è completamente libero da qualsiasi finalità utilitaristica. Esistono saperi fine a sè stessi che – proprio per la loro natura gratuita e disinteressata, lontana da ogni vincolo pratico e commerciale – possono avere un ruolo fondamentale nella coltivazione dello spirito e nella crescita civile e culturale dell'umanità. All'interno di questo contesto, considero utile tutto ciò che ci aiuta a diventare migliori. (Ordine 7)

> (I wanted to place at the centre of my reflections the idea of utility of those pieces of knowledge whose essential value is completely free from any utilitarian purpose. There are knowledges for their own sake that – precisely because of their gratuitous and disinterested nature, far from any practical and commercial constraints – can play a fundamental role in the cultivation of the spirit and the civil and cultural growth of humanity. Within this context, I consider anything that helps us become more useful.)

He criticizes the will to succeed in a materialistic society and expresses his sadness at the lack of priorities in our society. Specifically, he attacks materialism and the imposition of a culture of fast growth. It hurts to see men and women engaged in a mad gallop to the promised land of earnings, where everything around them – nature, objects, other human beings – loses its interest. Against this, he insists on the need to return to the discovery of life's small things and pleasures:

> Lo sguardo puntato sull'obiettivo da raggiungere non permette più di cogliere la gioia dei piccoli gesti quotidiani e di scoprire la bellezza che pulsa nelle nostre vite: in un tramonto, in un cielo stellato, nella tenerezza di un bacio, in un fiore che sboccia, in una farfalla che vola, nel sorriso di un bambino. Perché, spesso, la grandezza si percepisce meglio proprio nelle cose più semplici. (Ordine 18)

> (A gaze focused on the goal to be achieved no longer allows us to grasp the joy of small, everyday gestures and to discover the beauty that pulsates in our lives: in a sunset, in a starry sky, in the tenderness of a kiss, in a blossoming flower, in a butterfly that flies, in the smile of a child. Because, often, greatness is best perceived in the simplest things.)

This last sentence is indeed an important statement: "often, greatness is best perceived in the simplest things." In fact, it is an inversion of priorities, a confirmation that size does not matter. In this way he can also praise the need to embrace uselessness as a way of life, and thus proposes it as a central goal in life:

> Se non si comprende l'utilità dell'inutile, l'inutilità dell'utile, non si comprende l'arte ha osservato giustamente Eugène Ionesco. E non a caso, molti anni prima, Kakuzo Okakura, nel descrivere il rituale del tè, aveva individuato nel piacere di raccogliere un fiore per regalarlo alla propria compagna il momento preciso in cui la specie umana si era elevata al di sopra degli animali: "Quando intuì l'uso che si poteva fare dell'inutile – spiega lo scrittore giapponese ne *Lo Zen e la cerimonia del tè* – l'uomo fece il suo ingresso nel regno dell'arte." In un solo colpo, un doppio lusso: il fiore (l'oggetto) e l'atto di raccoglierlo (il gesto) rappresentano entrambi l'inutile, mettendo in discussione il necessario e il profitto. (Ordine 18–19)

> (If one does not understand the utility of the useless, the futility of the useful, one does not understand art rightly, observed Eugène Ionesco. And it is no coincidence that, many years earlier, Kakuzo Okakura, in describing the tea ritual, had identified the pleasure of picking a flower to give as a gift to one's mate as the precise moment when the human species had elevated itself above animals: "When he sensed the use that could be made of the useless" – the Japanese writer explains in *Book of Tea* – "man made his entrance into the realm of art." In one fell swoop, a double luxury: the flower (the object) and the act of picking it (the gesture) both represent the useless, questioning the necessary and the profitable.)

Consequently, objects (objectives) and gestures need to be reassessed. Everyday life is the framework for the satisfaction of needs such as feeding or sleeping, and also, in part, the satisfaction of wishes; everyday life is the place for human relations – with work colleagues, with other members of the family, with friends – entailing pleasures, reconnaissance, and conflicts derived from these relations. Everyday life is also the place for language: it is filled with gestures and words.

I would like to assert that the Iberian Peninsula has occupied a peripheral centrality (Bou, "On Rivers and Maps" 3–26) that has pioneered this kind of attitude. The Iberian world has practised a claim to little things and uselessness. The use of collage discussed earlier can be added to the equation because it provides a useful tool that allows us to read in a different way. Collage must be carefully differentiated from montage and metaphor. Cortázar has described it as "the most heterogeneous and permissive of formal principles. Indeed, it is a formal principle only after the fact – it does not require certain kinds of parts or rule any out" (Franco 116). In a collage (unlike montage and metaphor), the different elements retain their discreteness, their fragmentary quality. Furthermore, I suggest that we can adopt collage as a more accurate form of mimesis. It may be the most adequate form to express a singular Iberian position, that of an interest in little things.

Josep M. de Sagarra: Fragments of the Suburban Space

Another powerful example of everyday life comes from Josep M. de Sagarra's poetry. "Cançó de suburbi" (Song from the suburbs) is a poem published in *Cançons d'abril i de novembre* (April and November songs). Written between 1915 and 1917, the poem captures the transformation of society from a suburban, almost rural atmosphere to an industrial one.

[1] M'estimo l'horta escanyolida que de la fàbrica es ressent, i em plau voltar la meva vida d'aquest paisatge indiferent.	[1] I love the little vegetable garden dominated by the factory, and I'm glad to turn around my life of this indifferent landscape.
[2] I em plau l'estona virolada: gent d'amanida i berenar. Una donzella espitregada i una cançó que fa plorar.	[2] And I like the crazy time: salad-and-snack people. A gutted maiden and a song that makes you cry.
[3] I l'home humil que a l'aire ensenya un front valent i un ull esclau, i va amb la gorra i l'espardenya i el farcellet i el vestit blau.	[3] And the humble man who shows in the air a brave brow and a slave eye, and goes with the cap and espadrilles and the bundle and the blue dress.
[4] Aquí jo veig que el món se m'obre fred i terrible com la mort. I és tan mesquina i és tan pobra la campaneta del meu cor!	[4] Here I see that the world opens up to me cold and terrible as death. And she is so mean and she is so poor the bell of my heart!
[5] Dels llagoters fuig la corrua i en el meu rostre no hi ha vel i em puc mirar l'ànima nua sense cap mica de recel.	[5] The corrua flees from the flatterers and there is no veil on my face and I can look at my naked soul without any suspicion.
[6] Estimo l'horta desolada; el presseguer ensopit que es mor, i l'arengada platejada, porró de sang, tomàquet d'or.	[6] I love the desolate garden; the drowsy peach tree that dies, and the silver herring, blood leek, golden tomato.

[7] Jo vaig seguint la vostra dèria, homes estranys de bones dents, que tornareu a la misèria una miqueta més contents!	[7] I keep following your craze, strange men with good teeth, that you will return to misery a little happier!
[8] Durin els mals, durin les penes, llàgrima, rosa, perla i bes. Duri aquest cor i aquestes venes, duri aquest ull que no veu res.	[8] May the evils last, may the sorrows last, tear, rose, pearl, and kiss. Last this heart and these veins, Last this eye that sees nothing.
[9] Vestit encès que el goig estripa, dansa per mi! Home lleial, vine, fumem la nostra pipa damunt de l'herba virginal.	[9] Dressed on fire that joy tears apart, dance for me! Loyal man, come, let's smoke our pipe on top of the virginal grass.
[10] Digue'm les vives meravelles del teu treball, del teu turment. Sota el concert de les estrelles, anem fumant tranquil·lament.	[10] Tell me the living wonders of your work, of your torment. Under the concert of the stars, let's smoke quietly.

(Sagarra 35–6)

This is a masterful, serene, and at the same time devastating poem that offers the vision of a finished yet changing world, of a city that is being transformed and whose suburbs are slowly losing their rural atmosphere. We realize the contrast between two cultures expressed in two conflicting areas: the push of the city that dramatically changes an ancestral way of life, and the struggle for industrialization versus the urbanized countryside as an idealized version of the lost-paradise myth. The poet is fascinated by a world that is strange to him because it is very far from his social origins and not directly linked to his ancestry. He observes and admires it to a certain extent, and he feels embittered when watching these "loyal men" who have no control over their future. It is possible to identify a series of oppositions in almost every stanza. The poem could be divided in two sections (stanzas 1–5 and stanzas 6–10), marked by the parallelism between *M'estimo* and *Estimo*. The first four stanzas introduce this outright conflict: a conflict of spaces, such as *horta-fàbrica* (1) and of feelings and people such as a young woman *virolada, espitregada,* singing a song that *fa plorar* (2). There is also an oxymoron referring to how poor workers behave and dress: "un front valent i un ull esclau" (3), and an observation related to a way of life that is dying, "el món se m'obre / fred i terrible com la mort" (4). The next stanzas introduce a slight change: the flatterers (*llagoters*) leave, and, in a moment of sincerity, the poem's speaker is able to observe himself without any self-pity (5). Next, in the second part of the poem, Sagarra introduces a very sensual view of the world, stressing an envy of food, having only simple things to eat, and clearly establishing a parallelism with stanza 1 (6). He comments on how working-class people will accept their poverty after having a good meal (7). In stanza 8, there is one line, "llàgrima, rosa, perla i bes," which is filled with metaphors that summarize love and sensuality, completed with two powerful metaphorical associations: *cor* and *ull*, meaning "to love" and "to watch." The three appearances of the verb *durar* imply repetition and continuity. In stanza 9, two synecdoches are used to introduce a woman, who is reduced to a *vestit encès*, and a man who is referred to through a pipe (*fumem la nostra pipa*). There are also effective parallelisms with stanza 2 (the young woman) and 3 (*l'home humil*). The pleasure of smoking is reinforced in the following and last stanza. The poet asks for assertions about "vives meravelles / del teu treball, del teu turment." Under the starry night sky, smoking quietly becomes again a metaphor for a life that continues without major upheavals.

Sagarra's point of view is characteristic of his approach to reality. Due to his aristocratic origins, he was always fascinated by small things that he identified with the lower class. This was particularly striking in his major novel *Vida privada* (1932) (X. Pla, "Recepció" 385–409). The remarkable beginning of *Vida privada*, where Frederic de Lloberola wakes up in a strange bed belonging to an old lover, has many more cinematographic references than literary ones. Just like Döblin and Dos Passos, the writing in Sagarra's *Vida privada* has something documentary-like in it. The writer, camera on his shoulder, walks through private chambers and the red-light district in search of material. We are far from the realists' and naturalists' experimental laboratory of the nineteenth century. We are facing not a slow and over-detailed psychological analysis but a fragmentary construction, without a single centre, offering a sum of impressions, with loosely knitted details.

Realism and Journalism

Vicent Andrés Estellés's poetry is inhabited by an elementary materiality made up of things and sex, food and smells, death and pain. His interest in smallness provokes a characteristic presence of everyday life. Estellés's work is marked by, in addition to autobiographical elements, a certain realism, close to the social or historical, as it was called in the 1960s, and which establishes a clear limitation on the critical interpretations of his poetry. Despite the poet's deep class consciousness, this is not the only perspective from which his poems can be read. Estellés's life and work were infused with a powerful sense of reality that goes beyond the realism of the nineteenth-century aesthetic or the social and historical realism aesthetic school of the 1960s. In this chapter I propose to read, or reread, Estellés's poetry, not from the limiting eyes of an extremely ideological aesthetic but rather by emphasizing the poet's attention to everyday reality. As a complement to the previous chapter I am especially interested in paying attention to the smallest aspects of reality that crowd Estellés's poetry.

I must add, from a more personal point of view, that from my first contacts as a reader with the poet, to listening to him in performances at the Ateneu Barcelonès, to visits to the Plató clinic during the long months of preparation for the interview I did with him for *Serra d'Or* magazine in 1978, I was attracted by Estellés's ability to incorporate and transform any fragment of reality into his poems or even into his relationship with the world. He would conceive of fragments inspired by crude reality, incorporate them into his verses, with colours and smells, and turn it all into literature (Bou, "Vicent Andrés Estellés"). The roasted pepper, the oral narration of the unorthodox anaesthesia that a nurse had administered to him, the morning defecation, were all well anchored in reality but transformed into something poetic and elementary.

Reading Estellés's poetry, it is very obvious to think in terms of everyday reality. In fact, the first, illustrious, readers immediately did so. The presence of everyday life was indicated by Joan Fuster in the prologue to the first volume of the 1972 edition of Estellés's *Obra completa* precisely to refute the qualification of Estellés as a social poet: "En el fons, és una poesia balzaciana, si se'm tolera la fórmula. És una poesia que podria haver estat novel.la: novel.la de Balzac" (Fuster, "Nota" 33). (Basically, it's Balzac poetry, if I'm allowed the formula. It is a poem that could have been a novel: Balzac's novel.) In Fuster's opinion we see a way of relating the incorporation of elements of everyday life with literary genres and rhetorical resources: journalism, nineteenth-century literature, the contrast of real and literary realities. This was underscored by the emphasis on the importance of minuteness and the fundamental differences with the Valencian poets and poetry that was made by literary critics in Catalonia at the time:

> La poesia de Vicent Andrés Estellés respon a febre ambulant, a les esperances conjugals, als sentiments i als ressentiments de la precarietat perdurada. A Barcelona, la poesia, la feien, persones d'una altra mena: individus amb cara de protonotari apostòlic, catedràtics, fills de papà revoltats, oficinistes orgullosos de ser-ne. L'Estellés fa la poesia d'un carrer de València,

del "trenet" de València a Burjassot: un residu humà vigorós, que es debat en l'esperança de continuar vivint. No oblidem, però, el marc del principi: quan tothom fornicava malament, menjava malament, moria malament. (Fuster, "Nota" 32–3)

(The poetry of Vicent Andrés Estellés responds to travelling fever, to conjugal hopes, to the feelings and resentments of enduring precariousness. In Barcelona, poetry was written by people of a different kind: individuals with the face of an apostolic prothonotary, professors, sons of rebel fathers, office workers proud to be one. Estellés makes the poetry of a street in Valencia, from the 'train' from Valencia to Burjassot: a vigorous human residue, which struggles in the hope of continuing to live. Let's not forget, however, the framework of the beginning: when everyone fornicated badly, ate badly, died badly.)

Fuster also linked Estellés's poetry to Spain's poverty and misery after the civil war. As is often the case, the critic only talks about his own delusions and justifies his aesthetic choices, his sense of reality.

In a similar way, Josep Pla expressed an opinion in *Notes del capvesprol* that, half seriously and half ironically, raised the issue by introducing an emphasis on the professional dedication of Vicent Andrés Estellés, with whom the Empordà author could feel many affinities, as they both shared journalism as a profession, and this influenced their work and *Weltanschauung*:

La impressió que m'ha fet el senyor Estellés és que és un gran prosista, un considerable prosista, que escriu en vers ... I com a prosista és un xerraire impressionant, inacabable, frondosíssim. És la característica dels grans prosistes: agafeu Balzac, o Dickens, o Tolstoi ... A mi em sembla que el senyor Estellés ha transportat el periodisme del seu ofici a formes literàries excel·lents, d'un realisme complex i poètic ... Al meu entendre és un prosista de sempre, fascinat per la realitat i per la vida. (J. Pla, *Notes del capvesprol* 183)

(The impression Mr Estellés has given me is that he is a great prose writer, a considerable prose writer, who writes in verse ... And as a prose writer he is an impressive talker, never-ending, prolific. It is characteristic of the great prose writers: take Balzac, or Dickens, or Tolstoy ... It seems to me that Mr Estellés has transported the journalism of his profession to excellent literary forms, of a complex and poetic realism ... In my opinion, he is a long-time prose writer, fascinated by reality and by life.)

Other critics have delved into this approach to everyday life. As Francesc Parcerisas pointed out, it is not necessary to understand everyday life as purely a series of descriptions of the most common elements that are part of our individual and social lives. Rather, he recognizes the turning point of the artistic consciousness in these everyday elements as symbols of a shared world that acquire a value of correlated objectives available to express the emotions that strike the sensitivity of a contemporary poet. Parcerisas mentioned resources such as accumulation – the fact that everyday life is shown not as a *captatio benevolentia* towards the reader but as a direct implication of reading, that is, as an act of consciousness to be able to reach the distance between reality described by the poet and the voice that tells it to us. He also highlighted the fact that the referential world that surrounds the poet is a complete world (59–60). Josep Ballester Roca, however, at the beginning of a "small walk" through the poet's work, highlighted two "vertebrae" of the many that characterize the work of the poet from Burjassot: first, what he called the denial of silence; and second, everyday life (64). In the opinion of Vicent Salvador, agreeing in part with Josep Pla, this attraction to everyday reality could have a basis in the poet's professional activity as a journalist:

> Estellés és molt menys selectiu, menys depurador envers l'anècdota. La seva malla lírica deixa passar tot de detalls descriptius, els personatges típics d'un quadre d'època, molts esdeveniments quotidians. L'elegia esdevé, així, crònica social. I el periodista – el testimoni de la microhistòria – hi treu el cap. Davant l'espectacle de la postguerra, de la misèria i les repressions de tota mena, Estellés palesa el seu tarannà de cronista apassionat, escassament estilitzador, i fa un inventari dels personatges i els esdeveniments que constitueixen aquell món. (Salvador n.p.)

> (Estellés is much less selective, less purifying towards the anecdote. His lyrical mesh allows everything from descriptive details to pass, the typical characters of a period picture, many everyday events. The elegy thus becomes a social chronicle. And the journalist – the witness of the micro-history – sticks his head out. Faced with the spectacle of the post-war period, of misery and repression of all kinds, Estellés reveals his temperament as a passionate chronicler, with little stylization, and makes an inventory of the characters and events that make up that world.)

The fact that Estellés's poetry can be perceived as some kind of inventory can suggest a historical or sociological model: as an elaborated and comprehensive enumeration of reality. The enumeration of reality becomes hidden, immersed, in everyday life. Critic Guillermo Carnero was also interested in this view of Estellés's work. In particular, he linked the long comparisons in Estellés's poetry to a homage to Ausiàs

Marc and a way of including fragments of everyday life in poetry: "le viene a Estellés otra forma de cotidianismo que consiste en el planteamiento de comparaciones cuyo plano comparativo es un vulgarismo, con lo que se consigue mayor viveza en la representación, por lo insólita" (Carnero 33; Estellés comes with another form of everydayness that consists in the use of comparisons whose comparative plane is a vulgarism, with which greater vividness is achieved in the representation, because of its unusualness). In all these approaches the poet's interest in everyday reality is related in terms of an assimilation with the realism of the nineteenth-century aesthetic school; the professional dedication to journalism, which sprinkles poetry; or his rhetorical attitude.

The Infra-ordinary and Magmatic Language

But maybe we are missing the point. It seems to me that, in addition, the everyday element in the poetry of Vicent Andrés Estellés can be related to a whole series of writers who have expressed an interest in smallness, the god of small things, who have depicted intimacy as their closest reality, private life in the real and direct sense. This kind of approach has allowed Estellés to attend to everyday life from an observation of the reality surrounding him – a completely innovative perspective. My approach does not directly renounce those previous readings that view his work with a militant historical realism and that make it a Valencian representative of a politicization of Catalan literature, or that relate it to journalism or realism. All this is obviously present, but what I intend is to take the reading of Estellés's poetry a step further by introducing a skewed perspective.

In fact, when Estellés was looking for material for his verses, his attitude towards reality was very close to that of the anthropological interests of French writer Georges Perec, or the observations of Julio Cortázar in books such as *La vuelta al día en ochenta mundos*, or *Los autonautas de la cosmopista*. As we have seen in my introduction, in 1973 Perec coined the term *infra-ordinaire* to refer to the minimal aspects of reality that he found particularly attractive and deserving of study: "Ce qui se passe vraiment, ce que nous vivons, le reste, tout le reste, où est il? Ce qui se passe chaque jour et qui revient chaque jour, le banal, le quotidien, l'évident, le commun, l'ordinaire, l'infra-ordinaire, le bruit de fond, l'habituel, comment en rendre compte, comment l'interroger, comment le décrire ?" (*L'infra-ordinaire* 7). (What really happens, what we live, the rest, everything else, where is it? What happens every day and comes back every day, the banal, the everyday, the obvious, the common, the ordinary, the infra-ordinary, the background noise, the usual, how do we account for it, how do we interrogate it, how do we describe it?) Perec was interested in the background noise of life, in what seemed invisible but which is an essential everyday substance, that is, the seemingly most banal aspects. He believed that there was a need to talk about those parts of life and proposed a stimulating minimalist observation of reality. The French author claimed the need to interrogate, in the sense of analysing, everyday life:

> Interroger l'habituel. Mais justement, nous y sommes habitués. Nous ne l'interrogeons pas, il ne nous interroge pas, il semble ne pas faire problème, nous le vivons sans y penser, comme s'il ne véhiculait ni question ni réponse, comme s'il n'était porteur d'aucune information. Ce n'est même plus du conditionnement, c'est de l'anesthésie. Nous dormons notre vie d'un sommeil sans rêves. Mais où est-elle, notre vie? Où est notre corps? Où est notre espace? (Perec, *L'infra-ordinaire* 7–8)
>
> (Questioning the usual. But we are used to it. We don't question it, it doesn't question us, it doesn't seem to be a problem, we live it without thinking about it, as if it carried neither question nor answer, as if it carried no information. It is not even conditioning, it is anaesthesia. We sleep our lives away in a dreamless sleep. But where is our life? Where is our body? Where is our space?)

Perec was well aware that our eyes are accustomed to scanning our habitat for only unusual things, paying more attention to the exceptional and forgetting the anonymity of the *endotic*, a term that he opposed to the *exotic*. To begin the investigation of the infra-ordinary, Perec invites us to ask ourselves seemingly innocent, trivial, and almost meaningless questions but questions that provoke the discontinuity between signs and observation habits. Strangeness, according to Perec, is an observation technique that requires perseverance and imagination and is difficult to systematize. Estellés, without having read Georges Perec, is interested in this minimal aspect of reality, and, without the tools of the social researcher, he achieves a very complete approach to the infra-ordinary.

Yves Bonnefoy's definition of language can also be applied to Estellés's poetry. As he wrote in *La longue chaîne de l'ancre*, language is "un ici qui respire et expire l'ailleurs, méduse aux dimensions d'une mer qui serait le monde" (45; a here that breathes and breathes out the elsewhere, medusa with the dimensions of a sea that would be the world). Poetry, then, in a conception that is akin to that of the Valencian author, has an osmotic relationship with the world, with reality, from which it extracts matter and meaning. At the same time, it tells us about the dimensions of Estellés's commitment. As in the case of the map of the emperor in the story by Jorge Luis Borges, the poet's wish is that his review of the infra-ordinary coincide with the world. This desire to cover the whole is what justifies the colossal dimensions of his literary project. The composition of works such as *Coral romput* (1971; Broken coral) or *Mural del País Valencià* (1996; Mural of the Valencian country)[5] would have been a lifelong project for any other poet but Estellés. In his case, they are small episodes of a larger more ambitious project.

These two concepts, the infra-ordinary and the magmatic conception of language, go hand in hand in Estellés's poetry. They give us a measure of his project, conditioned by the dimensions of smallness, of an intimacy at hand, a grandiose conception of the universe, and the impact of the poet. In this context Estellés's poetry has the character of a touch on the ground, of incorporating as an alternative poetic material the most insignificant, the infra-ordinary. As indicated by Parcerisas, accumulation is one of the modes that Estellés uses to introduce daily life, and he manages to establish an authentic catalogue of daily life (Parcerisas 54). This is also related to the poet's will, explicit or not, to become a witness and chronicler of a world that was slowly disappearing. From his attention to everyday life, Estellés elaborates his particular foray into the world of memory.

The places of memory, which have interested scholars such as Maurice Hallbwachs, are immersed in the spaces of everyday life. As the French sociologist states, we are always in space, and only the spatial image, which, due to its stability, gives us the illusion of something that is not changing through time, allows us to rediscover the past in the present. The image of the humankind of old time that has materialized, like a tracing, in the materiality of things and buildings and the strength of the tradition of place comes precisely from how those things existed as an image. In places where memory is most powerfully liberated, the bonds that bind us to those places are revealed, and the connections of an "invisible society" are highlighted:

> C'est l'image seule de l'espace qui, en raison de sa stabilité, nous donne l'illusion de ne point changer à travers le temps et de retrouver le passé dans le présent; mais c'est bien ainsi qu'on peut définir la mémoire; et l'espace seul est assez stable pour pouvoir durer sans vieillir ni perdre aucune de ses parties. (Hallbwachs 201)
>
> (It is the image alone of space that, because of its stability, gives us the illusion of not changing through time and of finding the past in the present; but this is how we can define memory; and space alone is stable enough to be able to last without growing old or losing any of its parts.)

The "places of memory" in Pierre Nora's definition ambiguously combine past and present, sacred and prosaic, individual and collective memory.

Ancient places, in the words of Jan Assman, provide us with matter for our memories because there is an excess of memory that is expressed without words. Perhaps a reading of the appropriation of the Latin classics by Estellés must suffice, beyond the intertextual and parodic dialogue that it provokes. It is closer to a pastiche, considering the classics as mute ruins of the land's past, where the poet lives and writes. History is inscribed in the stones of valleys, in the villages that bear witness to the various generations that have lived there. Sacred objects such as tombstones on church walls are marble signs of devotion; objects of common use, such as a work utensil or antique furniture, become a testament to permanence and stability, and thus to continuity. With the inscription of the self in time, the hot surface of remembrance, memory becomes a spectacle of an increasingly intimate, everyday past (Tarpino 18–21).

This kind of memory is far removed from the narcotizing discourses of politics or even history and is very attentive to small family memories, small epics of places. This type of memory corresponds to the spaces of everyday life that we recognize in the work of Estellés and that have a triple dimension: love and death; attention to food and the smallest acts of life; and self-reflective writing.

Death and Life

Estellés's poetry is filled with an unfathomable vitalism, with attention to subjects like death, love, and friendship, and topics such as *carpe diem* and *aura mediocritas*, meals, motherland (in a localistic sense or in a very broad one), and writing. Estellés shows us in many poems his vision of death so that in appearance it seems very banal, and he is interested in what will happen after death. In poem VII of *Horacianes* he asks himself ironically about his future fame: "que restarà de nosaltres? / ho canviaria tot per un vers romput de safo. / com ens veuran? / potser jo seré un pallasso de roma." (What will be left of us? / I would change everything for a broken verse from Sappho. / how will they see us? / maybe I will be a clown in Rome.) What is remarkable about the poem is how he muses with an undeniable nonchalance, his indifference towards death. Because death is inscribed in the acts of daily life, it is one more step in the life chain. Even the writing of elegies or obituaries cannot solve it:

> mai no he tingut por de la mort.
> És una por que no he sentit.
> He acceptat, en silenci, sense
> escriure elegies ni necrologies,
> la mort dels meus i el meus

amics. Amb la tomba, s'obria significativament
el misteri. (Estellés, Horaciana VII)[6]

(I have never been afraid of death. / It is a fear that I have not felt. / I have accepted, silently, without / writing elegies or obituaries, / the death of mine and mine / friends. With the tomb, it opened up significantly / the mystery.)

In some poems Estellés is also concerned with what we could call death's materiality. The author dignifies his death with simplicity and humility. We can read in Horaciana LVII:

us deixaré, a la meua mort, una àmfora.
Si no pot ser una àmfora serà almenys un perol.
Us pregue que la trenqueu i tragueu comptes,
quantes pedretes blanques i quantes de negres contenia.
Únicament llavors
podreu escriure honestament la meua nota necrològica.
Podreu saber com fou la meua vida
més enllà dels poemes.

(I will leave you, at my death, an amphora. / If it can't be an amphora it will at least be a saucepan. / Please tear it up and take stock, / how many white stones and how many black stones it contained. / Only then / you will be able to honestly write my obituary. / You will be able to know how my life was / beyond the poems.)

He also introduces a perspective on his future fame, the "obituary note," and how the chronicle (the balance) of a life is based on the contrast between black and white stones (real objects) and symbols that summarize positive and negative aspects of an entire life. The diminution of the container, from amphora to pot, indicates an interest in vulgar objects, closer to everyday life.

Horaciana XVII could be considered simply made up of eschatological content. In the poem Estellés reviews all the daily activities that take place in the bathroom. As I pointed out before, beyond eschatology, what is remarkable is how his gestures acquire a highly symbolic meaning. The poem opens with a "good morning" greeting inspired by water – as a cleaning tool – and all the instruments used to get up and be polished:

bon dia, grapat d'aigua,
escarpidor, gillette, sabó, dentífric.
Bon dia, normalitat o hostilitat de l'oratge,

volum de merda que he amollat I mire.
Oh, bon dia, veïna, que tornes del mercat.

(Good morning, handful of water, / razor, gillette, soap, toothpaste. / Good morning, normality or hostility of the weather, / volume of shit I've softened and look. / Oh, good morning, neighbour, you're back from the market.)

Rhetorical devices such as enumeration make us feel the passage of time in a seemingly banal and intimate moment of a purely infra-ordinary quality. The third verse offers a contrast between "normalitat" (normalcy) and "hostilitat de l'oratge" (hostility of the weather), which introduces the "volum de merda" (volume of shit) and at the same time greets a female neighbour returning from the market. In this way he manages to put on the same level the eschatological elements of intimate life and the elements of public life, in which he relates to others. The element that unites them is the "good morning," a greeting that in this way acquires a new meaning. Estellés imposes on us this destabilizing and innovative sense. The mixture of private and public continues in the following three verses:

aquesta bona merda, assaonada i fràgil,
dóna ganes
d'invitar a sucar-hi el veïnat. (Horaciana XVII)

(this good shit, seasoned and brittle, / makes you want / to invite the neighbourhood to soak in it.)

In the last few tristiches the poetic voice is allowed to introduce a level of reflection on the transience of life and thus an approach to the Horacean theme of *carpe diem*:

com la merda s'esmuny en estirar la cadena,
així són de fugissers els plaers
que la vida ens depara, els amors, tot això.

(how shit slips away when you pull the chain, / that's how fleeting pleasures are / that life has in store for us, loves, all that.)

In this case, in the last tristich he can introduce a more serious – and at the same time ironic –reflection on death:

ens van parir amb merda i altres amenitats semblants,
i el nostre darrer acte o darrera voluntat
serà també una cagada gratuïta, uns orins.

(we were born with shit and other similar amenities, / and our last act or last will / it will also be a free shit, some urine.)

What had begun – it seemed – with an eschatological tug culminates in a serious note about the humid and smelly circumstances of the act of giving birth and the total and uncontrollable physical release at the time of death. By an inversion of registers, the low one substituting for the high one, the excrements become unusual chronotopes through which the transformations of a human being throughout a day are expressed, in the first part of the poem, and throughout life, in the second part.

In another poem, Horaciana VII, Estellés relativizes the transcendence of death and the fear of death and reduces it to a few sensations: a wind blowing, reading, and the naked body of his wife, and he thinks again in terms of survival, of what will remain in this world after our passage:

pense, potser, en ella però sense dramatisme.
com qui sent l'oreig ens uns brins, com qui nota
que li porten els ulls mentre llegeix, un dia,
com qui un dia mira el nu de l'esposa, fatigat dels parts.
que restarà de nosaltres?

(I think, perhaps, of her but without drama. / as those who feel the wind in a few strands, as those who notice / that his eyes are lead while reading, one day, / like one who one day looks at his wife's nakedness, tired of giving birth. / what will be left of us?)

Without a metaphysical or dramatic position, Estellés proposes the same philosophical concepts, the same eternal questions about the meaning of life, the relationship with the afterlife, in seemingly discordant terms, but with great effectiveness, inspired by very basic constituents of what is glimpsed in everyday life. Death and life go hand in hand and enlighten each other.

Pleasures and Pain

As is well known and Jaume Medina has studied so well, in many books Estellés pretends to impersonate the voice of well-known Latin poets in a distinctive version of pastiche. According to David H. Rosenthal, "[t]he book's title, *Horatians*, is mostly ironic: an indirect reference to the phony classicism (which the poet Francesc Parcerisas has categorized as "realismo fascista" or "fascist realism") that the Spanish state was pushing after the civil war. The reference to Horace is nevertheless a genuine one. It evokes both the Latin poet's satires and his vivid descriptions of

Mediterranean rural life. Estellés's Mediterranean landscape is at once a real and a poetically created place, full of both brutal passions and literary fantasy" (89).[7] This device has at least two effects. The first we can consider as a manifestation of the *umheimlich*, the uncanny, in Freud's terminology. What is sinister according to Freud is familiarity, the fact that something belongs to our world, and therefore the impossibility of not seeing it. The sense of disturbing is activated when something seemingly unimportant awakens repressed content that comes from previous experiences related in particular to childhood or the discovery of sexual consciousness. Freud combined two concepts here: fear of the familiar and intellectual uncertainty. The German word *heimlich* includes the dialectic of privacy and intimacy that is inherent in bourgeois ideology. The sinister (*umheimlich*), understood as the strange, the unfamiliar, the unpleasant, the foreign, is superimposed on the second sense, less common of *umheimlich* as the revealed, that which ceases to be secret. That is, what should have been a secret is revealed by mistake. In Freudian terminology, *umheimlich* indicates the repressed return. In the case of Estellés, the connection between past and present, Latin and contemporary Valencian poetry, sets in motion this phenomenon of revelation of repressed or secret aspects: politics and sex.

A second, more direct effect is the fact that Estellés's impersonation of Latin poets is that it allows him to speak of nearby realities, or about the present, posing behind the voice of another, in a manoeuvre of confusion devised to fool censorship. In these cases, the approach to everyday life takes on a special level. It is a complex operation, mixing realities and verses that seem ancient but that refer to present time, when these poems were written, in the midst of a dictatorship.

In "Res no m'agrada tant …" (I don't like anything so much), that is *Horacianes*'s first poem, the poet praises the roasted pepper. The poem thus elevates to a symbolic category one of the simplest and tastiest dishes in popular Valencian cuisine. He associates it with carnal, sensual pleasures. The line "res no m'agrada tant" refers to food as one of life's most important pleasures. We are in the realm of everyday life: "m'agrada molt el pimentó torrat" ... / "l'enrame d'oli cru amb un pessic de sal i suque molt de pa, com fan els pobres." ("I really like the roasted paprika" … / "the mixture of raw oil with a pinch of salt and a lot of bread, like the poor do.") Through an operation of exaltation and elevation of the gestures of the moment of getting ready to eat a pepper, the author seems to want to communicate to us simplicity and humility in the face of life. As is usual in his poetic world, Estellés makes various associations between gastronomy on the one hand, and sexuality and eroticism on the other, which is one of the most repeated leitmotifs in his work: "sinó amb aquella carn mollar que té" ... / "l'expose dins el plat en tongades incitants" ... "de vegades arribe a l'èxtasi, a l'orgasme" (but with that soft meat it has / I expose it on the plate in tantalizing strokes ... sometimes I reach ecstasy, orgasm). He is tempted by the pleasure of eating in the same way he feels tempted by sexual pleasure. In the poem he also establishes an association between gastronomy and religion. In an almost irreverent movement he compares the moment of tasting the food with the gesture made by a Catholic priest in the Eucharist: "després en un pessic / del dit gros i el dit índex, amb un tros de pa, / agafe un tros de pimentó, l'enlaire àvidament, / eucarísticament" (then in a pinch / of the thumb and forefinger, with a piece of bread, / I take a piece of pepper, lift it eagerly, / eucharistically). In this way readers are deliberately confused by the mix-up of two ceremonies. To elevate the condition of the simple meal to a sacred condition, of communication between heaven and earth, he introduces something that belongs to the register of the magical or the sacred. In Estellés's work the confusion of tone is very characteristic. It is perceived in the use of peculiar vocabulary, mixing cultured words with other popular and colloquial, even crude, ones that lead the reader to premeditated confusion. Thus, in these poems the colloquial expression *me'l fot* introduces a discursive tone in which the intention of the Valencian poet regarding the spontaneous, colloquial, and popular externalization of words is clearly reflected. In the same way, we can see a very abundant use of adjectives, offering countless nuances in the way they describe everything around them: "oli cru / pimentó torrat / cante, llavors, distret / crosta socarrada / tongades incitants" (crude oil / roasted pepper / sing, seeds, distracted / flaky crust / tantalizing tones). The colloquial aspect, with an emphasis on everyday life, is detectable in the same metrical model chosen, free verse, without rhyme, with the use of lowercase letters as in all the poems of *Horacianes*. The apparent formal disorder only underscores the idea of simplicity, spontaneity, and breaking with the demanding, rigid, and complicated rules of conventional poetry, which seeks to make a poem easy, accessible, and comprehensible to all.

In Horaciana LVI Estellés raises a debate between mayonnaise and allioli that he resolves in insulting terms, emphasizing masculinity:

jo defensava l'allioli,
aquell sabor, la seua trèmula solidesa.
tu, al contrari, defensaves la maionesa
adduint testimonis cultíssims de *gourmets*.
t'he de dir, malgrat tot, que la maionesa
és sols un allioli que va eixir maricó.

(I defended the allioli, / that flavour, its trembling solidity. / you, on the contrary, defended mayonnaise / quoting highly educated testimonials from gourmets. / I have to tell you, despite everything, that mayonnaise / it's just an allioli that turned out to be a fag.)

The difference between both sauces serves to contrast an exquisite culture of refined tastes – "testimonis cultíssims de *gourmets*" (highly educated testimonials from gourmets) – with one of popular taste: "aquell sabor, la seua trèmula solidesa" (that flavour, its trembling solidity).

In yet another poem, Horaciana XV, "Si més permés ..." (If I am allowed to ...), Estellés repeats a reconstruction of childhood memories linked to a primitive world, made of small pleasures:

si m'és permés,
evocaré dies de la infantesa.
furtava els fruits dels arbres
me'ls menjava dins el dacsar,
fresc com un celler aleshores.
i sentia llunyana, pels carrers del meu poble,
la veu del meu pare que venia peix i cridava les veïnes.

(if I may, / I will evoke days of childhood. / I stole fruits from the trees / I ate them in the cornfield, / cool as a cellar then. / and I heard distant, through the streets of my town, / the voice of my father selling fish and calling the neighbours.)

These are images that Estellés repeats again and again: the theft of fruit and hearing the voice of his father far away. In this way he mixes two senses, taste and hearing, in a time that seems immemorial to him: stealing and selling, eating and feeling. The comparison "el dacsar, / fresc com un celler aleshores" (the cornfield, / cool as a cellar then) prepares the double sense of distance linked to the father's voice: "sentia llunyana" (I heard distant). Distance has two meanings: he does not see his father, and the poet evokes an already extinct time.

The celebration of a vanished world is noticeable in Horaciana XXXV. Living in a more primitive and elementary world, which is the mythical time of *Horacianes*, involves cultivating, acting as a farmer:

M'estime molt de bon matí, treballar al meu hort,
les bledes, les lletugues, els raves, les tomaques;
regue els breus solcs a poalades lentes,

arrenque les brosses nocives.
Avui deia el diari que ha arribat l'home a la lluna
m'he girat a mirar-la, vinclat sobre el solc;
no he vist res i he continuat.

(I love early in the morning, working in my garden, / Swiss chard, lettuce, radishes, tomatoes; / water the short furrows with slow buckets, / pull out the noxious weeds. // Today the newspaper said that man has arrived on the moon / I turned to look at her, bound on the furrow; / I saw nothing and continued.)

Here, unlike in other cases, the poem does not mix the times – classical antiquity and present in a contemporary world – but a rural, pre-industrial world, even mentioning the space race, the landing on the moon. He can also present an ideal of daily life that is now – at that time – already impossible and that corresponds to a lost world, that of his ancestors. It is the world of yesterday that has gone forever. However, with the arrival of human beings on the moon, he introduces a contemporary moment, distorted by the – supposedly – farmer's sly mistrust.

In other poems, such as Horaciana XLII, Estellés develops a song to life from a variant of the *aurea mediocritas*, the ability to settle for small things and avoid excesses:

m'he estimat molt la vida,
no com a plenitud, cosa total,
sinó, posem per cas, com m'agrada la taula,
ara un pessic d'aquesta salsa,
oh, i aquest ravanet, aquell all tendre,
què dieu d'aquest lluç,
és sorprenent el fet d'una cirera.
m'agrada així la vida,
aquest got d'aigua,
una jove que passa pel carrer
aquest verd
          aquest pètal
                    allò
una parella que s'agafa les mans i es mira als ulls,
i tot amb el seu nom petit sempre en minúscula,
com aquest passarell,
                              aquell melic,
  com la primera dent d'un infant.

(I loved life very much, / not as fullness, total thing, / otherwise, let's say how I like the table, / now a pinch of this sauce, / oh, and that radish, that tender garlic, / what do you say about this pike, / the fact of a cherry is surprising. / I like life like this / this glass of water / a young woman passing by on the street / this green / this petal / that / a couple holding hands and looking into each other's eyes, / and all with his little name always in lower case, / like this walkway, / that navel, / like a child's first tooth.)

Little pleasures of home cooking correspond to a love of life, hedonism under control. Pleasure is reduced to gastronomic elements encompassing sauce, garlic, hake, cherry, water, or the sensuality of bodies – a young woman, a couple. The accumulation culminates, as Francesc Parcerisas reminded us, with the vindication of smallness: "i tot amb el seu nom petit sempre en minúscula" (qtd. in Parcerisas 54; and everything with its small name always in lower case). This line has a synecdoche effect and confirms that all these elements of everyday life that he has been listing have this common denominator. Pleasures, however, present the catalogue of gestures, foods, of an endangered world. They show an interest in the infra-ordinary aspects, many of which correspond to a lost world.

Self-Reflective Writing

In the third section of another book, *Coral romput*, Estellés presents one of the keys to understanding his poetry and much of his literary project. He introduces crickets as an unpoetic symbol, which refer in a suggestive and intuitive way to the will to recover a lost paradise: "Hi ha en els versos que escric, entre tots els meus versos, / certs mots que encara tenen un no sé què de grills … Però jo sé que tinc el cor tot ple de grills, / i també les butxaques, i si escric és per ells,/ per aquesta nostàlgia que tinc d'un món verdíssim" (143–9). (There are in the verses that I write, among all my verses, / certain words that still feel like crickets … But I know that my heart is full of crickets, / and also my pockets, and if I write it is for them, / for this nostalgia I have for a very green world.) In these verses we are presented with the key to understanding the equidistance between a peasant world, which corresponds to the time of his childhood, and the urban world, which corresponds to the time of his adulthood. At the same time, his call to smallness makes us realize the meaning of his project:

Tinc ganes, unes ganes horribles, d'olorar
això: el fem dels estables amuntegat en un

camp d'aquells que recorde de sobte a Beniferri.
Una olor que m'indica aquells camins, finíssims,
que feien, en les caixes de sabates, els cucs
de seda per damunt de tomellos ben secs.
La caixa de sabates amb un forat damunt. (Estellés, *Coral romput* 120–6)

(I have, I have a horrible desire, to smell / this: the dung of the stables piled into one / field of those who suddenly remember Beniferri. / A smell that shows me those paths, very fine, / what the silk moth did in the shoe boxes / of silk on top of well-dried thyme. / The shoe box with a hole in it.)

As usual, Estellés shows us his ability to poetize tiny elements: worms and the shoe boxes where they live – objects of infra-ordinary life, marks of a childhood. The poet remembers how his father arrived home with a garbage bag full of what he had grabbed by the handfuls on the roadside to feed his rabbits and sometimes unknowingly also ended up carrying crickets inside. The crickets' cries break the silence of the night, "a plànyer-se'n, potser, a sentir-se petits, / molt més petits encara, i abandonats, i sols, / lluny dels camps, lluny del marges, com jo lluny del meu poble" (*Coral romput*, 132–4; to mourn, perhaps, to feel small, / much smaller still, and abandoned, and alone, / far from the fields, far from the banks, like me far from my town). His father had forced his family to respect the crickets, and now for the poet as an adult, crickets become words in a singular metaphorical process:

Els grills que no he matat, però que ja s'han mort,
potser ara se'm tornen paraules, de vegades,
igual que els cucs de seda, morint, s'esdevenien
papallones petites, amb un tacte domèstic,
vagament cereal, cosa de cada dia.
Hi ha en els versos que escric, entre tots els meus versos,
certs mots que encara tenen un no sé què de grills:
jo sé ben bé quins són, i estic content, i calle. (Estellés, *Coral romput* 138–45)

(The crickets that I have not killed, but have already died, / maybe now words come back to me sometimes / just as silkworms, dying, became / small butterflies, with a homely touch, / vaguely cereal, everyday thing. / There are in the verses that I write, among all my verses, / certain words that still sound like crickets: / I know very well what they are, and I'm happy, and shut up.)

The notion of crickets becomes the reference point for a lost world. They are a metaphor that includes nostalgia:

> No sé si tinc el cap tot ple de grills, com diuen.
> Però jo sé que tinc el cor tot ple de grills,
> i també les butxaques, i si escric és per ells,
> per aquesta nostàlgia que tinc d'un món verdíssim
> de xiquets agafant les móres d'albarser
> i de xiquets que seien al rastell per les nits
> d'estiu i li tiraven quatre pedres a un gos,
> de xiquets que furtaven melons, bresquilles, figues
> i després se n'anaven a menjar-se-les dins
> un dacsar, i menjaven, i dormien després,
> i després es tiraven a nedar a la sèquia
> i es secaven al sol i ballaven grotescs
> damunt l'herba del marge, i eren obscens, i ingenus.
>
> (Estellés, *Coral romput* 146–58)

> (I don't know if my head is full of crickets, as they say. / But I know that my heart is full of crickets, / and also the pockets, and if I write it is for them, / because of this nostalgia I have for a very green world / of children picking blackberries / and of children who sat on the rake at night / of summer and they threw four stones at a dog, / of children stealing melons, brussels sprouts, figs / and then they went to eat them inside / a cornfield, and they ate, and then slept, / and then they would go swimming in the ditch / and they dried in the sun and danced grotesquely / on the grass of the margin, and they were obscene, and naive.)

In this last stanza he clearly expresses the loss of a world and the propaedeutic function of poetry as a catalogue of gestures, smells, and activities that belong to a vanished world. This is not an isolated example; this theme can be recognized throughout the work of Estellés. The magmatic sense of poetry that I have commented on before, based on the opinion of Yves Bonnefoy, acquires its maximum manifestation here.

Francesc Parcerisas pointed out two important aspects of Estellés's poetic project: the need to record what is happening around him in an avalanche of writing, to give existence to things based on writing them; and the need to link this activity that we could describe as "scriptographic" with what, Parcerisas tells us, is the daily routine of work, the act of writing, which has meaning and justification in itself (Parcerisas 58). It should be added that Estellés is also interested in an awareness of the time during which he wrote and the conditions in which a situation of repression and censorship affects writing under a dictatorship. He writes in Horaciana LI:

aquest any miserable,
m.cm.lxiii. d. de c.,
serà molt recordat i molt amargament.
vicent ventura, desterrat a munic o parís;
joan fuster, a sueca;
– diuen pel veïnat que escriu de nit a màquina, i

circula un tenebrós prestigi –;
sanchis guarner recorre, perplex, la ciutat;
jo escric i espere a burjassot,
mentre pels carrers de valència
la gent, obscena, crida i crema un llibre.

(this miserable year / m.cm.lxiii. a.d., / it will be remembered very bitterly. / vicent ventura, exiled to munich or paris; / joan fuster, in sueca; / – they say in the neighbourhood that he types at night, and // a dark prestige circulates –; / sanchis guarner walks around the city, perplexed; / I write and wait in burjassot, / while on the streets of valencia / obscene people shout and burn a book.)

The four greatest representatives of the Valencian literary society in the 1960s, Vicent Ventura, Joan Fuster, Manuel Sanchis Guarner, and Estellés himself, the ones who articulated an idea of being Valencian, are presented as writing, or without being able to write, from different locations, living in external or internal exile, in the city or in the countryside. And the poem culminates in denouncing the fascist acts of book burning, particularly of one book, Joan Fuster's *Nosaltres el valencians* (1962). The poem can be read, as Ferran Carbó did, as an expression of exile, but it can also be seen in terms of the infra-ordinary, attentive to a deaf or silent music that is repressed, sung by the sound of typewriters that try to express the truth about a repressed country.

Literature and society, or literature with the value of civic responsibility, are constant in Estellés. In yet another poem, words become an essential working material for the writer. Words organized like a stone dry wall help to save a language and defend it from erosion and any attack:

molt més que un temple, bastiria
amb les meues paraules, aspres i
humils, una marjada com aquelles

que vaig veure un dia a mallorca.
les pedres, sàviament organitzades,
amb una organització ben sòlida,
contribueixen a salvar de l'erosió
la terra batuda pels vents marins.
m'agradaria, amb una semblant assemblea
de pedres, preservar amb els meus mots
un idioma, un país, una forma de vida,
i que ningú no sapigués mai quin és el meu nom,
com tampoc hom no sap el nom de l'autor d'una marjada.
(Horaciana LXX, 204)

(much more than a temple, I would build / with my words, rough and / humble, a dry wall like those / that I saw one day in mallorca. / the stones, wisely arranged, / with a very solid organization, / they help save from erosion / the land blown by sea winds. / I would like, with a similar assembly / of stones, preserve with my words / a language, a country, a way of life, / and that no one would ever know what my name is, / just as one does not know the name of the author of a dry wall.)

In this way he calls for an anonymous and collective conservation task. The profession of dry-wall builder is equivalent to that of a writer and by extension to that of any speaker of the language. This is made even clearer in the poem "Assumiràs la veu d'un poble" (You will assume the voice of a people), which belongs to the book *Llibre de meravelles* (2015; Book of marvels). Here the poet assumes and expresses his commitment to be the voice of the silenced people to which he belongs. He does so by mixing records from three different semantic fields. First, Joan Maragall's conception of poetry, the theory of the "paraula viva" (living word): "Tu seràs la paraula viva,/ la paraula viva i amarga" (Andrés Estellés, *Llibre de meravelles* 317; You will be the living word, / the living and bitter word). Second, a biblical discourse that equates the poet with the biblical prophets, responsible for communicating the message of Yahweh:

Assumiràs la veu d'un poble
i serà la veu del teu poble,
i seràs, per a sempre, poble,
i patiràs, i esperaràs,
i aniràs sempre entre la pols,/ et seguirà una polseguera.
....
I tindràs fam i tindràs set,
no podràs escriure els poemes

i callaràs tota la nit
mentre dormen les teues gents,
i tu sols estaràs despert,
i tu estaràs despert per tots. (Andrés Estellés, *Llibre de meravelles* 317)

(You will assume the voice of a people /and it will be the voice of your people, / and you will be, forever, a people, / and you will suffer, and you will wait, / and you will always go among the dust, / a dustbin will follow you ... // And you will suffer hunger and thirst, / you won't be able to write the poems / and you will be silent all night / while your people sleep, / and you alone will be awake, / and you will be awake for all.)

And finally, he becomes the poet, somebody who has a civic and political mission:

No tot serà, però, silenci.
Car diràs la paraula justa,
la diràs en el moment just.
No diràs la teua paraula
amb voluntat d'antologia,
car la diràs honestament,
iradament, sense pensar
en ninguna posterioritat,
com no siga la del teu poble. (*Llibre de meravelles* 318)

(It will not all be silence, however. / For you will speak the just word, / you will say it at the right time. / You will not say your word / with the will of it becoming an anthology, / because you will say it honestly, / angrily, without thinking / at no later date, / as it is not the one of your people.)

In this poem we recognize Estellés's way of being popular, but it is based on the double meaning: the "living" value of the word, and the condition as a guide that the poet Estellés acquires.

A Poet of Infra-realities

As Joan Fuster said, "ell no és el 'poeta realista' de l'esquema dogmàtic, ni de bon tros. Podem qualificar-lo de 'poeta de realitats,' i endavant. Per aquest cantó, facciosament narratiu, l'Estellés esdevenia 'col·loquial'" ("Nota" 33). (He is not the "realist poet" of the dogmatic scheme, not by a long shot. We can describe him as a "poet of realities," and so on.

From this point of view, factionally narrative, Estellés became "colloquial.") In fact, Estellés is a colloquial poet, meaning that he uses a language that is characteristic of family conversation, and not because he is opposed to literary or written language as classical rhetoric wanted, but because he inaugurates interest in the infra-ordinary that I mentioned at the beginning. Theorists of everyday life claim that this, as obvious as it is, is a clandestine notion. According to Lefebvre, it is the common denominator or the connective tissue of all possible acts and thoughts of human beings. It is through daily life that we enter into a relationship of transformative action with nature, we learn about friendship and love, we learn to communicate with others, we can formulate and be aware of the rules, and we feel desires, pains, and emotions. We are unaware of the moment that we are born, but we can foresee death. We know that sooner or later the unknown, our last sigh, will arrive.

Vicent Andrés Estellés through poetry drew a delicate self-portrait with collective implications and expressed a sense of place that included the inhabitants of a strip of land near the Mediterranean Sea who spoke a common language, with habits, sense of places, or a smallness that was the soundtrack of their lives, the eyes and ears of everyday life. In the same way that Antoni Gaudí, helped by his faithful Jujol, created an original *trencadís* by incorporating into public spaces fragments of ceramics that were witnesses of the private life, thus the poems of Estellés are made of fragments of things, of lives, of passions – of the infra-ordinary essence of everyday life.

5

Churches and Trams

Die Motore unterm Boden rattern,
Von den Leitungsdrähten knattern
Funken.
Scharf vorüber an Laternen, Frauenmoden,
Bild n Bild, Ladenschild, Pferderitt, Menschenschritt –
Schütternd walzt und wiegt der Wagenboden,
Meine Sinne walzen, wiegen mit!:
Voller Strom! Voller Strom!
Der ganze Wagen, mit den Menschen drinnen,
Saust und summt und singt mit meinen Sinnen.

Gerrit Engelke, "Auf der Straßenbahn" 8–9

(The motors rattle under the floor, / From the wires rattle / Sparks. / Sharp past lanterns, women's fashions, / Picture after picture, store sign, horse ride, human stride – / Shaking, the carriage floor rolls and weighs, / My senses roll, weigh with!: /Full current! Full of electricity! / The whole wagon, with the people inside, / Hums and sings with my senses.)

In this chapter and the following one I devote my attention to two instances of the everyday: the presence and the use of public transportation in the cities of modernity. I will deal with several examples in the city of Barcelona but I think they can be easily extrapolated to other cases through the industrialized world. We spend much of our lives going places: commuting, jogging, travelling for business or pleasure. The time of travelling gets somehow lost or is forgotten because our destination and the reasons for our movement are more important than the travel itself.

In a 1944 movie – *Double Indemnity* directed by Billy Wilder – there is a shrewd insurance investigator, played by Edward G. Robinson, who discusses a case: a pair of lovers have murdered the woman's husband. The investigator says to his associate (who happens to be the assassin): "They've committed a murder and it's not like taking a trolly ride together where they can get off at different stops. They're stuck with each other and they've got to ride all the way to the end of the line, and it's a one-way trip, and the last stop is the cemetery" (Wilder). In the next scene the two lovers meet secretly at a supermarket, where they hope nobody will notice them. They speak while walking through the aisles. As the man tries to get out of the deal, the woman, with her sunglasses still on, answers harshly: "Nobody is pulling out. We went into this together and we're coming out at the end together. It's straight down the line for both of us. Remember." Of course, in the next scene, the assassin, Robinson's associate, remembers his line that likens the situation of two in a murder to two in a trolley ride.

In the open scenes of another great movie, *Black Orpheus* (1959) directed by Marcel Camus, Orpheus and Eurydice meet in a tram that is crossing downtown Rio de Janeiro, which is sizzling with preparations for the carnival. Orpheus is the tram driver; Eurydice is a poor young peasant woman who has just arrived at the city and is lost and dizzy with so many new feelings and sensations. By the end of the movie, she will have been killed in the tram yard.

In these two examples I find two things quite conspicuous. First, that riding a tram could be used as a metaphor for a difficult human situation, a usage that speaks about the powerful impact of public transportation on the human imagination, once it had become a conspicuous element of urban landscape in modernity. Modern cities offer a whole array of situations and objects that can be used to express the shock of the new (trams) and its coexistence with the old (churches). On many occasions this imagery, which mixes the past and the future, tends to present conflicting assessments about the present. Second, that a romantic liaison could be started in a tram. Cities of modernity offer spaces where the mixing of social classes and opposite sexes is much easier than it was in previous times. It is also notable that a conversation about a murder can take place in a supermarket. It is quite eloquent of how spaces are used in a variety of ways in modernity.

Artists and writers have tried to express the experience of the modern city, its spaces, the clash of simultaneity, and the anonymity provided by public spaces. I discuss here in some detail the following issues: the use of trams as places and objects with a symbolic meaning, based on the juxtaposition of the old and the new (the classic mythological figures of Orpheus and Eurydice travelling on a tram); trams as vehicles for the metaphorical discussion of problems and situations that arise in modernity; the sensations and experiences provoked in the modern world, ranging from fear of dizziness, negative attitudes, visceral rejection, to the innocent and candid acceptance of the urban experience; and the tram as an element that synthesizes the contradiction between the random and the systematic that is characteristic of life in the city.

French scholar Pierre Sansot, in *Poétique de la ville*, paid attention to "[l]es transports de la ville" (199–206). According to him, the means of transport are almost characters. In public transportation we notice an emphasis on solitude, waiting periods, and anticipation of the city. The controller, as we will see in the case of Salvat-Papasseit, plays a mysterious role. Trams and buses are a structure within the city, but they have the particularity of being an isolated space. It is a moving interior, the floor of which is like a terrace or an observation point: mixed among the masses, we can observe people on foot or in other vehicles. It is also a volume that stands out in the urban landscape without reaching the height of houses and public buildings. The first trams were a dangerous bulwark. An article by Santiago Rusiñol reminds us of this fact. He wrote a sarcastic opinion on the changes that modernity was introducing to the Barcelona landscape, using the tram as a measure of those changes. In "El progrés i les criatures" (Progress and children) he evoked an unfortunate accident in which a tram killed a child. After seeing angry people burning the murderous object, he comments with an alternative pedagogical note: "Potser no és excés de motors i remolcs, el que hi ha, sinó excés de criatures. Potser en comptes de maleir els frens i les vies, el que hauríem de procurar és posar *freno* a l'espècie per *vies* malthusianes" (Rusiñol 217). (Perhaps it is not an excess of engines and trailers, what is there, but an excess of creatures. Perhaps instead of cursing the brakes and the tracks, what we should try is to stop the species by Malthusian methods.)[1] Trams, however, create a different unity of the city (that of the neighbourhoods and the settlements) by means of transportation maps, which are full of colours and circuits that have nothing to do with regular city maps. The tram is a sign of urban modernity, an urban replica of train, and involves an expansion of the city; it does not limit it but introduces new openings.

Trams remind us of the new forms of transportation that were introduced in the modern city and of the impact they had on the formation of a new model of society. Trams provided not only a new form of communication and transport but also a mobile space in which people shared time doing nothing, forced to be in contact with strangers. Trams were invented in the 1880s and were a very popular means of transportation in European and American cities until the 1960s. In Eastern Europe they have never disappeared. Currently, with the growing concern for the environment and the need for faster ways of mobility in congested areas of urban centres, a new interest in trams has emerged. In Barcelona they stopped circulating in 1973, and only the Tramvia blau (Blue tram) remains, for the amusement of children and tourists (Flórez-Bosque and Ibáñez Puente). A very contentious new line has been built, but it does not travel across the city centre due to the strong opposition of people living in well-to-do districts. Trams, however, also offer an unequivocal connection between the old and the new, as their early versions were a mixture of nature and mechanical engineering. Until the turn of the century, when they became electric, trams were carriages made of wood and metal that ran on tracks, pulled by horses or mules.

Trams tend to invade urban space and also establish a correlation between the centre and the periphery. In addition, the massive presence of means of transport of industrial traction introduces a temporary referent. Trams, with their heavy appearance and the electrical apparatus that surround them, tend to monopolize the streets through which they pass and are considered very dangerous. Getting on a tram is a special way to contemplate the city and certainly another way to look at shops, as the city itself becomes a spectacle or a "passage" filled with shops offering their merchandise. Passengers watch people and the movement of cars from a privileged grandstand. The moving city looks like a mobile shop window in front of the passenger. We can relate it to a variant of Baudelaire's flâneur, who – as noted by Walter Benjamin – sees the streets as a landscape or a room and finds refuge in the crowds of the big city (Benjamin, "Paris" 156–8).

Trams express the triumph of the machine and the arrival of new modes of transportation, which allowed the development of an industrial society. These modes of transport (the bus, the tram, and the underground) allowed the rise of situations that have been studied in detail by sociologists such as Georg Simmel and cultural historians such as Walter Benjamin. The impact of the masses on the individual, the fact of being an unknown among one's fellow citizens, is a kind of experience that developed in modernity. For those who had lived most of their lives in small towns, the decision (or being forced) to move to a big city was a life-changing experience, and it meant living under the pressure of constant psychological stimuli. In connection with new urban situations, a series of literary and artistic topoi arose: the solitude of the individual; the Baudelairean flâneur who evolved, in the Catalan context, into Josep Carner's *badoc* (beholder), as we will see in this chapter; encounters with unknown people (the gaze, the visual flirt); new spaces such as the railway, trams, and social venues (cafes, theatres); and the marginalization of artists and writers (Simmel; Benjamin, "Paris").

Churches and Trams in Barcelona: Ways to Modernity

When Antoni Gaudí was criticized for his awkward reform of the presbytery in Palma de Mallorca's cathedral, he answered, according to popular legend, in pure Gaudinian style: A tram is also a work of art (Carner, *Les bonhomies* 69). Gaudí is best known for the powerful Sagrada Família temple, still under construction, which can be read as a life-size illustration of some of the conflicts introduced by industrialization. Ironically, Gaudí was killed by a tram in 1926 while he was on his way to the Sagrada Família construction site. Churches and trams were ever-present items in modern cities throughout the industrialized world, but perhaps in Barcelona they epitomize the beauties and pitfalls of life in modernity. I would like to explore some of the conflicts expressed by these two symbols as they are used by several artists and writers.

Turn-of-the-century Barcelona was a city booming with industrial activity. Industrialization had introduced many changes in its daily life, bringing hordes of immigrants from nearby and remote mountain towns. The city would soon be known as one of the most conflict-beset in Europe, ruled by the clash between groups of anarchists and a very religious, conservative bourgeoisie. In 1850 the city walls had been torn down, opening up new space for expansion. Ildefons Cerdà's Eixample gave the city much-needed space for new dwellings. It was in this new part of the city that two different objects – churches and trams – became powerful symbols of the contradictions and necessities of the modern world.

Catholic churches are spaces dedicated to devotion, temples in which people have gathered since Roman times. In the case of Barcelona, the old city is dotted with churches, and all have powerful connections to the city's past: the cathedral, Santa Maria del Mar, Església del Pi, and Betlem, to name just a few. New temples spread dramatically in the new neighbourhoods created during the nineteenth century, mainly in the Eixample. One of them, the Sagrada Família, had a powerful meaning in the social fight between unionized workers and factory owners that characterized the industrial world.

Besides being a new means of transportation, trams helped shape a new society, providing not only a different way to communicate and go places but also a mobile space in which people could share time without doing anything, forced into contact with each other. Furthermore, trams, with their massive presence and electrical power, are quite dangerous, tend to monopolize the street, and, together with trains and automobiles, became symbols of modernity. They offered an unequivocal connection between the old and the new; in their earlier versions they were metallic horse-drawn carriages representing a mixture of nature and mechanical engineering. Until the turn of the century, when they became electric, trams were just a carriage put on a rail and pulled by horses. With their massive presence, trams invaded urban space and also established a correlation between the urban centre and the periphery (suburbs).[2]

In the imagination of inhabitants of turn-of-the-century Barcelona, churches and trams were powerful symbols connected to two different worlds, their juxtaposition a reminder of the clash between past and present, between forces resisting change to the status quo and those fighting for renewal and progress. That clash took place at the social, religious, and political levels, with serious repercussions in the arts and literature of the time.

Churches and trams can be related to the equation established by Jean Starobinski in an article in which, through a reading of Baudelaire's first poem in the "Tableaux parisiens" section of *Les fleurs du mal*, he defined a concept of modernity based on the coexistence of two worlds, represented by chimneys alongside architectural spires. He detected what is most characteristic of modernity, the coexistence of elements of two very different worlds and times in one single space. That coexistence takes place in the modern city, where people are constantly aware of the lack of nature (whence the longing for parks and gardens)[3] and the overwhelming presence of industry. Starobinski also pointed out the special position of the poet-observer, who sees things from far away and belongs neither to the universe of religion nor to that of labour: "la perte du sujet dans la foule – ou, a l'inverse, le pouvoir absolu revendique par la conscience individuelle" (26; the loss of the subject in the crowd – or, conversely, the absolute power claimed by the individual consciousness). In this sense the equation of churches and trams has a powerful new meaning. They relate to very different conceptions of the world, but they share an urban space, and the very contradiction of their coexistence makes that space unique. Literary and artistic reaction to this coexistence establishes a particular moment in cultural history.

Many of the best literary works and paintings about Barcelona in the early twentieth century and beyond reproduce with striking fidelity the many changes in the process of modernization. The sharp contrast between a passion for the church or the tram (or an assimilation of both) becomes a remarkable point of interest.[4] In Barcelona, anarchists were summarily executed for burning a church or throwing a bomb into a religious parade. The bourgeoisie paid for church renovations and inspired the building of one of Europe's last cathedrals, the Sagrada

Família, as a way to show their class cohesion against unruly enemies. Some would blame all social disgraces on trams (and the like), and others would use them as the epitome of modernity, thereby elevating them to an almost religious status.

Starting in 1860, the new Eixample neighbourhood was a perfect space in which to build churches, develop a network of trams, and experience new sensations. Ildelfons Cerdà designed the new urban space. He was a member of congress for the Progresista Party and was much attracted by the problems of the working classes, as demonstrated by his book *Teoría general de la urbanización* (López Guallar 90–124). Two areas were immediately fashioned in the new neighbourhood, left and right of the Eixample. On the right side were exclusive residential buildings. On the left were hospitals, markets, a prison, a fire station, and so on – that is, all the services for a growing metropolis.

The building of the Eixample was an extraordinary occasion, which required an exercise of naming. Barcelona, the former capital of an ancient independent region, did not enjoy any autonomy at the time, so naming became a device of self-recognition, which romantic writer Victor Balaguer used to draw a sort of historical map of Catalonia's past, as discussed in my introduction. The Eixample became an arena for architectural experimentation. Gaudí, together with other leading architects in turn-of-the-century Barcelona, such as Domènech i Montaner and Puig i Cadafalch, shaped what is now one of the most striking *modernista* sections of any city in Europe. Antoni Gaudí (1852–1926) was very much involved in the invention of the new city. The Eixample is the area in which he built most of his apartment buildings, as well as the Sagrada Família. Churches became special buildings at a time of social unrest, as a means of defending the higher classes' territory and standard of living. The Sagrada Família, a modern-age cathedral, was funded by a private religious organization, the Spiritual Association of Devotees of Saint Joseph, a saint promoted throughout the nineteenth century as a symbol for those defending "family values" such as the sacred family and manual labour. The church had been planned from its origins as a "cathedral of the poor," but later its name was changed to "New Cathedral" (Solà-Morales 27), and it is a by-product of the reaction against industrialization.

The Sagrada Família is the building that best epitomizes Gaudí's impact on the city and the city's obsessive juxtaposition of the old and the new. From 1883 Gaudí was in charge of the construction, replacing the first architect, and the project became a lifelong obsession for him. His contribution is an iconic program, explaining through visual symbols the mysteries of the faith. The cathedral was supposed to have three facades (the birth, death, and resurrection of Christ) and eighteen towers (twelve apostles, four evangelists, the Virgin Mary, and Christ). Lateral chapels would symbolize baptism and penitence, the theological virtues, and the sorrows and joys of Saint Joseph (Carandell; Lahuerta 324–35).

In 1906 Maragall visited the Sagrada Família and wrote a keen reading of the new temple under construction, which he viewed as a compromise between destruction (the challenge presented by social unrest) and construction (that the challenge offered by religious redemption):

> Y el templo se me apareció, como siempre, como a tantos, como una gran ruina; o como un gran palomar, que dijo una niña a su primera vista ... Pero a mí me penetra más la sensación de ruina; y me halaga, porque sabiendo que aquella ruina es un nacimiento, me redime de la tristeza de todas las ruinas; y ya desde que conozco esta construcción que parece una destrucción, todas las destrucciones pueden parecerme construcciones. (Maragall, *Obra catalana* 727)[5]

> (And the temple appeared to me, as always, as it did to so many, like a great ruin; or like a great dovecote, as a little girl said at first sight ... But the sensation of ruin penetrates me more; and it flatters me, because knowing that this ruin is a birth, it redeems me from the sadness of all ruins; and since I know this construction that looks like a destruction, all destructions can look like constructions to me.)

Maragall continues his visit and realizes that metaphorically there is more light inside than outside, as he goes through a process in which he imagines that the stone has turned into light. This attention to elements from nature when he describes the building is remarkable because it is essentially what he did in one of his most famous poems, "Oda Nova a Barcelona" (*Obra catalana* 175–7; New ode to Barcelona). The poem is divided into two parts. In the first, the poet engages in a dialogue with the city and with a previous poem, "Oda a Barcelona" (1883; Ode to Barcelona), by Jacint Verdaguer. In the second part, the revolutionary events of July 1909, the Tragic Week, interrupt the poem. What was a placid dialogue written in alexandrine quatrains becomes an admonition to the city of Barcelona, written in free verse, in which the poet tries to elucidate virtues and failings associated with the city, concluding:

> Tal com ets, tal te vull, ciutat mala:
> és com un mal donat, de tu s'exhala:
> que ets vana i coquina i traïdora i grollera,

que ens fa abaixa el rostre,
Barcelona! i amb tos pecats, nostra! nostra!
Barcelona nostra! la gran encisera! (Maragall, *Obra catalana*, 177)

(As you are, as I want you, bad city: /it is like a given evil, it is exhaled from you: / that you are vain and naughty and treacherous and rude, / that makes us look down, / Barcelona! and with your sins, ours! ours! / Our Barcelona! the great enchantress!)

Before that final stanza he had introduced an allusion to the Sagrada Família:

A la part de Llevant, místic exemple,
com una flor gegant floreix un temple
meravellat d'haver nascut aquí,
entremig d'una gent tan sorruda i dolenta,
que se'n riu i flastoma i es baralla i s'esventa
contra tot lo humà i lo diví.
Mes, enmig la misèria i la ràbia i fumera,
el temple (tant se val!) s'alça i prospera
esperant uns fidels que han de venir. (Maragall, *Obra catalana* 789)

(In the Eastern part, mystical example, / like a giant flower a temple blooms / amazed to have been born here, / in the midst of such a sultry and evil people, / that laughs and blows and fights and blows off / against everything human and divine. / But, in the midst of misery and rage and smoke, / the temple (for what it's worth!) rises and prospers / waiting for the faithful who must come.)

In the 1906 text, Maragall saw the temple as a dovecote, but now it becomes a mystical flower, symbol of the city's redemption, as he also stated in articles of the same period (see Maragall, *Obra castellana*; Bou, "'Amor redemptor'").

Churches were not only sacred spaces for the dominant religion and for public gatherings to celebrate Mass but also a symbol hated by the working class. At a time of acute social unrest, churches became targets for attacks by extremist groups. Joan Ullman has explained that a latent force in any Catholic society is the layperson's natural resentment of the clergy's privileged position. In Barcelona and in Spain at large there was much animosity against the clergy because of their dominant role in the education of the wealthy, their vast amount of property, and vague suspicions about their obscure system of financing (Ullman 27–47). According to Ullman, approximately eighty religious buildings (including churches, schools, residences, and convents) were burned down during the Tragic Week of July 1909 (326). Joan Maragall recalled a moving experience he had while attending Mass at a burned-out church. In this case, he establishes a parallel with the first Christians and uses the occasion to discuss his principle that hate should be fought with love (*Obra castellana* 777). Nature (a dovecote, a flower) and architecture (Sagrada Família), destruction and construction, sins and redemption – these are some of the terms Maragall uses to express his feelings about life in the new city. And in doing so, he invokes modernity's double face.

Trams were objects very much present in the urban landscape. The shock of the new, of social unrest, was resolved by Maragall through metaphors inspired by nature. Some writers, however, used the example of trams to express the uncertainty of modernity. In 1905, Maragall wrote an article entitled "L'últim xiscle" (The last whistle) in which he expressed in striking terms how modernization was affecting daily life. In this case the "last whistle" designates the one blown by the last steam-drawn train on the Sarrià line. The poet hears the whistle as a farewell to old ways of living, the ones associated with early industrialization. Maragall interprets the arrival of electric traction as a goodbye to a more humane society: "Era una joguina dels ciutadans de Barcelona que el veien passar amb una mitja rialla enternida, sabent que aquell carril no duia cap malícia" (*Obra catalana* 265; It was a toy for the citizens of Barcelona who with a hearty half-laughter saw the train pass, knowing that that train carried no malice). But trains, trams, and later the metro were not just a toy. As indicated by *costumista* writer Robert Robert in the mid-nineteenth century, the new means of transportation became a fixture in the urban landscape:

> L'animació del passeig de Gràcia, a l'estiu, comença amb el dia.
>
> Abans que els òmnibus vagin i vinguen, ja hi transita gran munió de jornalers, que amb pas lleuger, àgils de cames i sans de color, s'encaminen a Barcelona, amb el gec al coll (si en porten) i l'esmorzar embolicat en un mocador de quadros blaus.
>
> Al mateix temps baixa, amb ells, gent que vénen a vendre pollastres, forcs d'alls i cebes, pebrots i tomàquets, esbergínies i ous i fruites …
>
> Aquest moviment dura fins a la força del calor, en què baixa un poc, mes no cessa, puix són moltes les persones que, per motius que deuen ser molt poderosos, se'n van amb el pic del sol a dinar a algun siti a on, per arribar-hi, per força es té d'atravessar el passeig de Gràcia; de modo que tot se torna òmnibus, *centrals*, cotxes, crits de calessers, xurriacades, pols i gatzara dels joves ferms, que se'n pugen a dalt, sota la vela, a on se torren baix el pretext de què allí hi corre millor l'aire. (R. Robert 17–18)

(The animation of Paseo de Gràcia, in the summer, begins with the day.

Before the omnibuses come and go, there is already a large crowd of day labourers passing by, who with a light step, nimble legs, and healthy complexion are on their way to Barcelona, with a coat around their neck (if they have one) and a breakfast wrapped in a blue-checked handkerchief.

At the same time, people come down, with them, to sell chickens, forks of garlic and onions, peppers and tomatoes, eggplants and eggs, and fruit …

This movement lasts until the strength of the heat, in which it drops a little, but does not cease, because there are many people who, for reasons that must be very powerful, go with the peak of the sun to have lunch somewhere for which, to get there, you have to cross Passeig de Gràcia; so that everything becomes an omnibus, power stations, cars, shouts of coachmen, squeals, dust and noise of the steadfast young men, who go up there, under the sail, where they roost under the pretext that the air runs better there.)

And about the *badocs* (flâneurs) who watch the progress of the works on Passeig de Gràcia, Robert writes:

No n'hi ha cap que tingui casa, mes tots estan enterats de la calitat del morter i els jornalers que hi treballen: són els que fan córrer per Barcelona aquest eixam de notícies que, bones o dolentes, per tot circulen sobre els ventatges i desventatges de l'*ensanche* (hem de dir ensanche!). (R. Robert 20)

(None of them has a house, but they all know about the quality of the mortar and the day labourers who work there: they are the ones who make this swarm of news run through Barcelona that, good or bad, circulate everywhere about the advantages and disadvantages of *ensanche* – we should say *ensanche*!)

Another realist author, Joaquim Riera i Bertran, wrote in 1892 a story set in a tram, the chance encounter with his old landladies, which ends with the intervention of a municipal policeman (171–84).

Emilia Pardo Bazán's naturalist approach in the story "En tranvía" (1901; On the tram), splendid and truculent, is another excellent example in which the Galician writer presents a woman who explains the misfortune of her life, because she has been abandoned by her husband and left alone with a blind son:

– Tenga ánimo, mujer – le dije enérgicamente –. Si su marido es un mal hombre, usted por eso no se abata. Lleva usted un niño en brazos … para él debe usted trabajar y vivir. Por esa criaturita debe usted intentar lo que no intentaría por sí misma. Mañana el chico aprenderá un oficio y la servirá a usted de amparo. Las madres no tienen derecho a entregarse a la desesperación mientras sus hijos viven.

De esta vez la mujer salió de su estupor; volvióse y clavó en mí sus ojos irritados y secos, de horrible párpado ensagrentado y colgante. Su mirada fija removía el alma. El niño, entretanto, se había despertado y estirado los bracitos, bostezando perezosamente. Y la mujer, agarrando a la criatura, la levantó en vilo y me la presentó. La luz del sol alumbraba de lleno su cara y sus pupilas, abiertas de par en par. Abiertas, pero blancas, cuajadas, inmóviles. El hijo de la abandonada era ciego. (Pardo Bazán, "En tranvía" 204)

("Cheer up, woman," I told her forcefully. "If your husband is a bad man, don't be discouraged. You are carrying a child in your arms ... for him you must work and live. For that little creature you must try what you would not try for yourself. Tomorrow the child will learn a trade and will serve you as a shelter. Mothers have no right to give themselves up to despair while their children are alive."

This time the woman came out of her stupor; she turned and fixed her irritated and dry eyes on me, with their horrible bloodshot and hanging eyelids. Her fixed gaze stirred the soul. The child, in the meantime, had woken up and stretched out his little arms, yawning lazily. And the woman, grabbing the child, lifted it up and presented it to me. The sunlight shone brightly on his face and pupils, wide open. Open, but white, curdled, immobile. The child of the abandoned woman was blind.)

Chance and Trams: Symbolist Visions

According to Stephen Kern, trams played two important roles in the modern city: they helped to enlarge the city's size, as the suburbs and nearby towns were linked to the centre, and they contributed to the mixing of social classes (191–3). Two writers, Joan Salvat-Papasseit and Josep Carner, incorporated some of those themes into their literary work from very different aesthetic perspectives. They both dealt with the possibility of being close to an unknown woman for a significant period of time.

We can relate some poems to the poetry of experience (Langbaum). Poetry proposes to reproduce a lived or imagined experience, grasping its process to derive, as a synthesis, a judgment of moral implications. The poem, however, can be related to a very long tradition, that of falling in love suddenly (the coup de foudre or love at first sight), a tradition that has been studied in detail by Jean Rousset in *Leurs yeux se rencontrèrent*. Carner's poem seems to intertextually evoke this tradition in the rhymes of lines 14–16: *copsada* (grasped) and *llambregada* (glance).

As is well known, on 6 April 1327, Petrarca met Madonna Laura: "Era il giorno ch'al sol si scoloraro … Trovammi Amor del tutto disarmato, / ed aperta la via per gli occhi al core, / che di lagrime son fatti uscio e varco" (Petrarca; It was the day, that the sun extinguished … / Amor found me completely disarmed / And saw the way to my heart open through the eyes / which have become door and passage for tears). These lines resonate in poem LXVI by Ausiàs March:

Amor, Amor, lo jorn que l'Ignocent
per bé de tots fou posat en lo pal
vós me ferís, car jo em guardava mal,
pensant que el jorn me fóra defenent. (March, 325)

(Love, Love, the day that the Ignocent / for the good of all he was put on the stake / you would hurt me, because I did not protect myself, / thinking that the day was defending me.)

And they resonate in the Baudelaire of "À une passante" ("To a Woman Passing By"), which is possibly much closer to Carner's experience and anecdote:

La rue assourdissante autour de moi hurlait.
Longue, mince, en grand deuil, douleur majestueuse,
Une femme passa, d'une main fastueuse
Soulevant, balançant le feston et l'ourlet;

Agile et noble, avec sa jambe de statue.
Moi, je buvais, crispé comme un extravagant,
Dans son oeil, ciel livide où germe l'ouragan,
La doucer qui fascine et le plaisir qui tue.

Un éclair … puis la nuit! – Fugitive beauté
Dont le regard m'a fait soudainement renaître,
Ne te verrai-je plus que dans l'éternité?

Ailleurs, bien loin d'ici! Trop tard! Jamais peut-etrê!
Car j'ignore où tu fuis, tu ne sais où je vais,
O toi que j'eusse aimée, ô toi qui le savais! (Baudelaire, *Oeuvres complètes* 92–3)

(The deafening road around me roared. / Tall, slim, in deep mourning, making majestic grief, / A woman passed, lifting and swinging / With a pompous gesture the ornamental hem of her garment, // Swift and noble, with statuesque limb./ As for me, I drank, twitching like an old roué, / From her eye, livid sky where the hurricane is born, / The softness that fascinates and the pleasure that kills, // A gleam … then night! O fleeting beauty, / Your glance has given me sudden rebirth, / Shall I see you again only in eternity? // Somewhere else, very far from here! Too late! Perhaps never! / For I do not know where you flee, nor you where I am going, / O you whom I would have loved, O you who knew it!) (Wagner, 112)

A similar situation, yet with a very different outcome, is portrayed by Josep Carner in several of his poems, particularly in "La bella dama del tramvia."[6] Carner had a moral and political agenda and was carefully pointing out what needed to be changed in urban life. He traced a real map of urban fruition when he wrote about changes in the city in "L'anunci lluminós" (Electric advertisement) and how people spend summer nights, or when he rejoiced with Gaudí's legends.

In the early twentieth century Josep Carner combined two poetical tones: one amorous and more frivolous, such as the tone in the poems of *La paraula en el vent* (1914); and another one humorous, such as the tone in *Auques i ventalls* (1914). As Joan Ferraté rightly recalled, in the latter the strict theme is "the Catalan country"

presentat pel poeta com l'àmbit social que el fonamenta humanament i que ell accepta sense cap altra reserva que les que no pot deixar d'introduir-hi el seu esforç de recreació imaginativa … És, en tot cas, la cara de la seva experiència més objectivada en estils de vida que no li pertanyen com a bé personal exclusiu, però que no deixen de formar part del seu ésser efímer, allò que el poeta ha rescatat en aquestes dues seccions ["Lloc" i "Auques i ventalls"] per tal de donar-ho al lector com a possessió comuna, i potser com a testimoniatge de la solidaritat original entre els dos, que roman a la base de tota divergència ulterior en el procés de personalització que serà el curs vital de cadascun d'ells. (Ferraté 20)

(presented by the poet as the social sphere that grounds him as a human being and that he accepts without any reservations other than those that he cannot help introducing in his effort of imaginative recreation … It is, in any case, the face of his most objectified experience in lifestyles that do not belong to him as an exclusive personal good, but that do not cease to be part of his ephemeral being, what the poet has rescued in these two sections ["Lloc" and "Auques and fans"] in order to give it to the reader as a common possession, and perhaps as a testimony of the original solidarity between the two, which remains the basis of all further divergence in the personalization process that will be the life course of each of them.)

These two books introduce the reader to Carner's world, a world that can be shared by most readers of the original poems. As Manent pointed out, it is a world filled with humour and love for the city of Barcelona (165, 168). However, Ferraté introduces an amendment:

> I irònica i tendra és, al capdavall, tota la poesia de Carner. Això vol dir que no és el seu humorisme allò que caracteritza aquest llibre de Carner, sinó més aviat la gamma de pretextos que hi preval, que pertanyen tots a la rutina possible i a l'ordre de curiositats normals en un home de vida ciutadana ... no pas gens diferent del que devia ser el Carner que el va escriure en el temps que el va escriure. És la ciutat i els seus habitants i els seus apèndixs i els habitants dels seus apèndixs allò que, juntament amb el cicle de les estacions al qual obeeix l'ordenació dels seus poemes, determina i qualifica més que res l'humor propi d'*Auques i ventalls*, que en ell mateix no és gens diferent de l'humor característic de la poesia de Carner de cap a cap de la seva obra. (Ferraté 20–1)

> (And ironic and tender is, after all, all of Carner's poetry. This means that it is not his humour that characterizes this book by Carner, but rather the range of pretexts that prevails in it, all of which belong to the possible routine and to the order of normal curiosities in a man of city life ... not at all different from what the Carner who wrote it must have been at the time he wrote it. It is the city and its inhabitants and its appendages and the inhabitants of its appendages that, together with the cycle of the seasons to which the arrangement of his poems obeys, determines and qualifies *Auques i ventalls*'s own humour more than anything else, which in itself is not at all different from the characteristic humour of Carner's poetry throughout his work.)

This opinion – if I read it correctly – is closer to a succinct phrase by Jordi Llovet when he was referring to the "indefugible passió de Carner – clau de la seva poètica – pels elements més universalment discrets de la Catalunya antropològica" (5; Carner's inescapable passion – key to his poetics – for the most universally discreet elements of anthropological Catalonia).

Carner himself wrote in the introduction to *Auques i ventalls* some helpful information: "L'autor d'aquest llibre té una convicció, que no gosaria dir a segons qui, i és que el present recull no deixarà d'oferir un interès arqueològic a les vinents tongades de la humanitat. Es de creure que els venidors tindran la gentilesa de considerar-hi dues senyalades característiques del nostre temps, que és possible que el datin" ("Advertiments" 119). (The author of this book has a conviction, which he would not dare to say to anyone, and that is that the present collection will not fail to offer archaeological interest to the coming turns of humanity. It is to be believed that the sellers will have the kindness to consider two marked characteristics of our time, which it is possible to date.) The second of these characteristics was "un insistent civilisme, que no arriben a mascarar del tot les seves modalitats facecioses o els seus jocs efímers i canviants. Creu l'autor, que l'humorisme és cosa altament civil, però és que, de més a més, aquest llibre ha estat escrit indolentment al marge de una amable vida ciutadana, amb una especial cordialitat per ses metamorfosis i fins amb una convicció indisputable de sos bells esdevenidors" ("Advertiments" 120; an insistent civility, which does not manage to completely mask its comical ways or its ephemeral and changing games. The author believes that humour is a highly civil thing, but the fact is that, in addition, this book has been written indolently on the sidelines of a friendly citizen's life, with a special cordiality for its metamorphoses and even with an indisputable conviction of your beautiful futures). And he riveted it with a rhetorical question: "Serà ben escaiguda la visió de la ciutat en trasmudança?" ("Advertiments" 120; Will the vision of the city in transmutation be appropriate?).

In "La bella dama del tramvia" (The beautiful lady of the tram) Carner describes a mysterious young lady travelling in a tram. The poet sees her from a stop, surrounded by very different people, "sota un gran feix de plomes" (under a huge bunch of feathers). He poses himself questions about the identity of the mysterious woman, and in the final two stanzas he comes up with a moral conclusion. Following is the entire poem, the 1957 version in *Auques i ventalls*, although the original edition dates from 1914:

I Si ran de la parada veieu el *tram* passar
tot ple de *smarts* o gent de la pescateria,
sota un gran feix de plomes eternament hi ha
la bella dama del tramvia.
II La nua el seu ermini, gelós com un serpent;
sa gorja mal coberta la voluptat exhala;
deurà parlar, quan parli, melodiosament;
és de París o Guatemala.
III Tot d'una que l'heu vista, s'allunya a l'infinit
dins el brogit del tròlei i de la baluerna,
i es decandeix llavores la flama del sentit.
Ah, si hi pugéssim, ¿fóra eterna?
IV Oh, no! La bella dama, de plomes sota un feix,
val més que amb sa llegenda s'allunyi, gens copsada;
si gaire l'escatíem no fóra tanmateix
com la sobtà la llambregada.
V Car ella cal que baixi quan arribem – ço és,
que aquella maniobra subtil resulta vana –

o resta, i és de Gràcia, i de segur diu *pues*,
sollant la parla catalana.
VI I no hi ha més manera: la dama se'ns ne va
o bé un detall la minva i un mot la deshonora.
Aneu a peu, poetes, cercant de somiar
l'alta bellesa duradora.
VII Jovent, oh tu que cerques la joia o el renom!,
no cuitis a adorar-los, que el dol et colpiria.
Sovint les esperances que fan d'esquer són com
la bella dama del tramvia.

(Carner, *Poesia* 175–6)

I (If beside the stop you should see the tram pass by
full of "smarts" or people from the fish store,
under a huge bunch of feathers, there is eternally
the beautiful lady of the tram.
II The knot of her ermine fur, jealous as a snake;
her throat, badly covered, exhales voluptuousness;
she might speak, and whenever she should speak, melodiously:
she is from Paris or Guatemala.
III As soon as you have seen her, she flees into infinity,
into the car and the metallic mass,
and then the flame of meaning is extinguished.
Ah, if we were able to get closer, would she be eternal?
IV Oh no! The beautiful lady, of feathers beneath a bunch,
is worth more as she leaves, her aura intact, little seen;
if we should pursue her, she wouldn't be the same
person we saw at first.
V For she must get off as we get on – that is,
that either our subtle manoeuvre is in vain,
or she stays, and she will be from Gracia, and surely she says "pues,"
staining Catalan language.
VI And so, there is no other solution; the lady leaves us
or else a detail diminishes her and a word dishonours her.
Go on foot, poets, searching for a dream
the high, enduring beauty.
VII Youth, oh you who search for joy and renown!,
do not care to adore those things, for the lament would strike you.
Often hopes that serve as bait are like
the beautiful lady of the tram.)

The poem, at first glance, is a tour de force.[7] Written in seven stanza quartets consisting of three Alexandrian verses and one octosyllabic, with a chained rhyme, it helps to create a light rhythm. The vocabulary chosen by the poet, an extremely refined and selected lexicon, including forced neologisms and archaisms, is close to what Lausberg characterizes as *vetustas* (old fashioned). It places us, thus, in a time, a very specific linguistic atmosphere. This lexicon, in spite of the process of purification that it underwent in successive editions (1914, 1935, and 1957), is still very strong in the definitive version, of 1957. We can see it: line 1, *tram*; line 2, *smarts* (well dressed, an Anglicism); line 5, *nua*; line 10, *brogit;* line 11, *decandeix*; line 14, *copsada*; line 15, *l'escatíem*; line 16, *llambregada*; line 17, *beutat defall* was in the 1914 and 1935 versions; and line 20, *sollant*.

In the first stanza the lady is presented as inside the tram, surrounded by men of various backgrounds ("*smarts* o gent de la pescateria," line 2), as seen by an anonymous observer from the tram stop, the voice that says the poem. The second stanza introduces the voluptuous character of the lady, again through the synecdoche to which she adds a comparison ("La nua el seu ermini gelós com un serpent") which introduces a biblical allusion (Eve), with external and internal references concentrated on the lady's neck: adorned with an "ermine" or melodious speech. There is a double play: the lady has a mysterious beauty in the way she dresses and talks. He concludes the second stanza by introducing the topos of exoticism, as the anonymous observer presumes that the lady "is from Paris or Guatemala," thus exaggerating a process of idealization that has been introduced in imagining the speech of the lady with a verb in the future tense, *deurà parlar* (she should speak).

Stanza III presents two possibilities of solution to the situation. In the first lines the vision is a passing effect, and the lady disappears: "s'allunya a l'infinit / dins el brogit del tròlei i la baluerna" (she flees into infinity, / into the car and the metallic mass). An image in line 11, "la flama del sentit" (the flame of meaning), introduces the idea of falling in love at first sight. Line 12 raises the second possibility, of getting on the tram and approaching the lady, and this leads to a rhetorical question: "Ah, si hi pugéssim, ¿fóra eterna?" (Ah, if we were able to get closer, would she be eternal?). Stanza IV presents a first response to this denial. Line 13 retrieves the synecdoche of line 3 – "La bella dama, de plomes sota un feix" (The beautiful lady, of feathers beneath a bunch) – and warns of the danger of getting too close to beauty and of the possibility of it disappearing.

Carner uses here a literary cliché that romantic poet Francesc Bartrina had already put into play in poems such as "Davant de Portvendres," a poem in which, according to Joaquim Molas, "reprèn la idea de la il·lusió, de l'ideal, que hem de deixar lluny, perquè, si l'aproximem, se'ns quedarà a les mans" (Molas 198; takes up the idea of the illusion, of the ideal, which we must leave far away, because, if we approach it, it will remain in our hands). In that case the poet is on a boat, contemplating the landscape of Portvendres from a distance and considering it to be of great beauty. He considers that as one gets closer, one loses one's beauty, which is regained when one moves away from it:

Camina lo vapor. Una muntanya
veig allà lluny que el sol amorós banya …
Ja la veig a prop meu. No és tan hermosa
com creia ma il·lusió sempre ambiciosa …
………………………………………
Camina lo vapor. Sembla que aquella
al allunyar-se es va tornant més bella.
Que bella és! … Vull gosar de sa hermosura …,
i lo vapor camina i no es detura. (Molas 189–200)

(The steam ship moves. A mountain / I see far away that the loving sun is shining … / I can already see her near me. She's not that beautiful / as my ever-ambitious illusion believed … / The steam ship moves. / As it moves away it becomes more beautiful. / How beautiful she is! … I want to boast of her beauty …, / and the steam ship moves away and does not stop.)

Going back to Carner's poem "La bella dama del tramvia," stanza V introduces a double explanation of the negation we read in stanza IV through a disjunctive phrase: the decision to not approach beauty, while maintaining idealization, or to approach it and face the harsh reality: "o resta, i és de Gràcia i de segur diu *pues*, / sollant la parla catalana" (lines 15–16; or she stays, and she will be from Gracia, and/ surely she says "pues," / staining Catalan language). The first part of the following stanza reflects this double possibility of solution: "I no hi ha més manera: la dama se'ns ne va/ o bé un detall la minva i un mot la deshonora" (lines 21–2; And so, there is no other solution; the lady leaves us / or else a detail diminishes her and a word dishonours her). It is worth mentioning that the versions of 1914 and 1935 was much more straightforward in this denunciation: "la dama corre avall / o bé de dispesera tot d'una pren la fila" (lines 21–2; the lady runs away / or all of a sudden she looks like a landlady). But in the final version Carner has preferred to emphasize her speech as the element that uncovers the lady's social origin: speech dishonours her. Stanzas VI and VII are concluding and include some advice, ranging from the literal to the symbolic level. The last six lines of the poem introduce three levels of morality. Thus, the admonition "Aneu a peu, poetes, cercant de somiar / l'alta bellesa duradora" (23–4; Go on foot, poets, searching for a dream / the high, enduring beauty), a warning that makes the 1914 and 1935 versions look lighter – "Anem a peu, poetes, car la beutat defall / en el topant on hom s'enfila" (Let's walk, poets, because beauty disappears / at the moment where you climb). It could be read literally as "anar a peu" (to go on foot), but also in a figurative setting: not getting on the tram implies living in beauty, in illusion, in a world of idealization.

The final stanza, VII, contains a moral lesson, the broadening of the advice addressed only to the poets who announced the final two lines of the previous stanza. Now it is no longer addressed only to poets but is generalized to the vocative "Jovent" (Youth). Against a life lived in dream and idealization, the poetic voice advises one to live with feet on the ground. And the skilful modifications of the nominal group "la bella dama" (the title of the poem in the first edition, of 1914, which was extended to "La bella dama del tramvia" in the second edition, the one from 1935) confirm and condense this sense in the final comparison: "Totes les esperances de l'avenir són com / la bella dama del tramvia" (All hopes for the future are like / the beautiful lady of the tram). This conclusion goes beyond the anecdote of "the beautiful lady of the tram" and places us at the category level. The variations of the nominal group "beautiful lady" are a very productive isotopy: in line 4 it is "la bella dama en el tramvia" (the beautiful lady in the tram), which it is reduced to "la bella dama" (the beautiful lady) in line 13, and even more so in line 21, "la dama" (the lady). In the final line, 28, we read "la bella dama del tramvia" (the beautiful lady of the tram), which recovers the phrase of the poem's title. The change of preposition, *in* for *of*, synthesizes this process of symbolic identification between lady and tram and, in fact, of conversion into a symbol of illusion (joy, renown, hopes), riveted by the use of an adverb, *com* (like), in a rhyming position in line 27. Thus, Carner's skill allows us to read the poem in these various stages: the process of association between lady and tram, from a completely urban scene (the pretext), presents the fleeting beauty, the ideal, the illusion, the dream, or the lesson of greatness, relativity, and scepticism. There is a movement from the particular to the general: from *poets* to *youth*; from *lady in* to *lady of*. In the conclusion there is a piece of advice for poets and young people about the danger of appearances. In this case the vision of a beautiful lady riding a tram incites questions and raises many doubts. They are transmitted to the fellow traveller or reader, and in this way the encounter in a tram becomes a device for a meditation on the dangers of trusting appearances and beauty. What in the beginning was a distinctive urban experience becomes the excuse for a moral rumination.[8]

Carner's poem also refers to a personal mini-tradition. In *Les planetes del verdum* we read prose titled "La ciutat sense ara" (The city without now), in which trams represent the multiplicity of Barcelona's urban life. It is in the centre of the town that encounters of the subversive forces, those of rupture, the playful ones, take place. Josep Carner caught it sharply in this prose, in which he highlighted the character, bringing together the differences, of the centre of the city:

> A la Plaça de Catalunya van a raure tots els tramvies barcelonins: per allà passen les cubanes que van a Sant Josep de la Muntanya, els alemanys que van a Sarrià, les monges que van a les Corts, les gallinaires que van al Poble Sec, les dolces dames barcelonines que segueixen la via Gràcia-Rambles, les peripatètiques indígenes que van a la Ronda de Sant Antoni, les franceses que van al Lyon d'Or, la gent que ve i va del port i les estacions: gent amb raquetes, gent amb paquets, gent llegint diaris, gent que té tard, gent que té mandra, gent mudada per al teatre; criatures que ploren o s'enfilen, criades, militars, senyors d'anell i de cigar. Tota aquesta gent tomba per la Plaça de Catalunya, centre estèril de Barcelona. ... A la Plaça de Catalunya, la ciutat no hi té cap ara. (Carner, *Les bonhomies* 69–70)

> (All the Barcelona trams stop at Plaça de Catalunya: Cuban women going to Sant Josep de la Muntanya, Germans going to Sarrià, nuns going to Les Corts, chicken coops going to Poble Sec, pass by there; the sweet Barcelona ladies who follow the track Gràcia–Rambles, the peripatetic Indigenous who go to the Ronda de Sant Antoni, the French women who go to the Lyon d'Or, the people who come and go from the port and the train stations – people with tennis rackets, people with packages, people reading newspapers, people who are late, people who are lazy, people dressed for the theatre; crying or climbing creatures, maids, military, ring and cigar lords. All these people tumble through Plaça de Catalunya, the barren centre of Barcelona ... In Plaça de Catalunya, the city does not have one now.)

In a prose piece of the same book, "La dama folrada" (The stuffed lady), Carner describes a beautiful lady who passes by and causes the following effect: "El celibatari és encara en adoració, i el somni passa inassolible" (*Les bonhomies* 45; The bachelor is still in worship, and the dream is unattainable). In "Idil·li en tramvia" (Idyll on the tram), collected in *La creació d'Eva i altres contes*, a prose by Carner – of dubious taste we would say from a gynocritical reading perspective – he introduces an unknown lady on a tram, and after uttering a whole series of doubts about her nationality, beauty, et cetera of the lady, he realizes that "[e]ra coixeta" (*La creació d'Eva* 83; she was lame).

Eugeni d'Ors, in a 1909 *glosa*, alludes to a woman symbol, the one who travels in all the *ripperts* of the city, a symbol of a Barcelona or Catalonia that he perceives to be an enemy of her classicist thought: "a qualsevol temptativa d'ideal ens ha perseguit amb els mals mots de son argot, de *sss* xiulades, i arrossegants! *'Catalaniztas!' 'Mudarniztas'* … *'Zebas'*… – és ella la gran nosa, la gran resistència, la fossa comuna dels nostres benvolers" (Ors 1180). (Any attempt at an ideal has been haunted by the bad words of slang sleep, *sss* whistles, and creepy! *"Catalanizt!" "Mudarnizts"* … *"Zebas"* … – she is the great nut, the great resistance, the common grave of our good intentions.) In essence, both Carner and Ors only expand, in ideological terms, what realist writers had written half a century earlier.

Avant-Garde Experiences

Other writers and artists were much more forcefully enthusiastic about modernity and its new objects. Torres Garcia and Rafael Barradas, both natives of Uruguay, spent a few years in Barcelona in the early twentieth century and painted many urban landscapes filled with trams and other remarkable objects of the industrial city: electric billboards, cafes, seas of faces, the experience of simultaneity. This was their personal reinterpretation of cubism, which they called *vibracionismo*.[9]

In Salvat-Papasseit's poetry the city landscape is depicted by someone who is obviously in love with modernity. In a letter Salvat-Papasseit wrote that he felt "intoxicated by the city" (*Epistolari* 161–2); in another one, when he was living in a sanitarium outside of Madrid, he wrote, "I am missing a piece of Catalonia's sea, and our magnificent harbour, and even our old daily streets" (*Epistolari* 161–2).) In the end, besides being impressed by Italian futurism and its love of engines, he contemplated the landscape, and his is a landscape characteristic of the proletariat. That can be seen in his books *Poemes en ondes hertzianes* (1919; Poems in hertzian waves) and *L'irradiador del port i les gavines* (1921; The irradiator of the port and the seagulls).

In Salvat-Papasseit's poem "54045," the number of a *capicua* (palindrome) tram ticket, a number with superstitious undertones, the tram is linked to a phallic image: "La dinamo turgent mou els priaps de foc / en CIRCUMVAL·LACIO" (*Obra completa*, 60; The turgent dynamo moves the 'priaps' of fire / in CIRCUMVALATION). At the same time he reproduces perfectly the sensation of isolation inside the multitude:

Es que jo sóc igual per cadascú
en el passatge
Fa fàstic que tothom sap estranger
i es segur que aquest vell coneix el meu nom

(I am the same for everyone / in the tram / It's disgusting that everyone knows foreign languages/ and I'm sure this old man knows my name.)

And by the final line, the passenger fears for his own safety:

M'he palpat bàrbarament
si m'han pres la cartera
A fe que no en portava amic (Salvat-Papasseit, *Obra completa* 60)

(I felt myself barbarically / if they took my wallet / To be sure I didn't bring my friend.)

He also draws with words, in a sort of calligram, a well-known monument in one of Barcelona's central squares, the Arc de Triomf, a monument that was used as the main entrance to Barcelona's 1888 world exhibition. The first edition of *Poemes en ondes hertzianes* (1919) was illustrated by Joaquin Torres Garcia, with an abundance of trams and references to electricity. Needless to say, Salvat-Papasseit and Torres Garcia's position is very favourable to modernity and one of its most pervasive symbols, the tram. In other poems such as "Bitllet de quinze" (Fifteen ticket) and "Encara el tram" (Still the tramway) Salvat-Papasseit develops a literary motif, the encounter with a lady in the tram. What is remarkable about his case is that he pays a lot of attention to describing the action itself, the moment, without paying attention to the details of what is really going on, as is the case with Carner's poems. The poet wonders about the gaze of a young woman reading a book. After paying attention to several parts of her body, he decides to step down from the tram and carry with him the mystery of her eyes.

The city represented in some of J.V. Foix's poetical proses in *Gertrudis* (1927) and *KRTU* (1932) is little related to Salvat-Papasseit's machinist and futuristic model. Under the pressure of Dadaist-inspired oneirism the result is more violent and chaotic. In many cases it is concentrated in one neighbourhood, the Sarrià Vell (Old Sarrià), which is transformed into a dreamworld. In three cases the tramways are used to fix an original image because this element of the city is appropriate for the expression of the drop scenes, filled with quick and unexpected mutations, with grotesque figures, where we find objects such as shoes and umbrellas, which symbolize the world's uselessness and absurdity. In "Plaça Catalunya-Pedralbes" we read:

> Acabava de llençar el meu bitllet quan l'inspector, bufat, em refusà l'excusa: calia abonar de nou el trajecte. Contra el costum fou ell mateix qui em lliurà rebut: un manyoc de bitllets multicolors em floria de sobte entre mans mentre l'inspector em befava amb cadència perquè distingís el meu. El seu esguard voraç em xuclava les rels del cabell i em sentia per moments esdevenir calb. Hauria aixecat el braç amenaçador, si la fúnebre sensació de tenir-lo amputat sota l'aixella no m'hagués aturat la voluntat i enterbolit el seny el qual s'obstinava a engrandir una llàntia groga que l'inspector lluïa arran mateix d'un botó amb imatgeria d'ex-vot ...
>
> Allunyats de la parada, vaig mirar enrere i em vaig adonar que en aquell paratge no hi havia instal·lació tramviària. El tram, sense rodes, amb la carrosseria esbotzada i el tròlei malmès, tenia l'aspecte de fer anyades a desdir que es podria sobre l'areny a l'embat del temps. (Foix 32–4)
>
> (I had just thrown away my ticket when the inspector, full of self-importance, refused my excuse: I would have to pay for the journey again. Contrary to the usual practice, he himself gave me a receipt. A bunch of multicolored tickets suddenly bloomed in his hands as he demanded derisively that I pick out mine. His voracious stare sucked the roots from my scalp, and I soon felt I was growing bald. I would have raised my arm menacingly if the lugubrious feeling of getting it amputated at the armpit hadn't sapped my will and clouded my judgment. I persisted in exaggerating a yellow lamp that the inspector was shining right next to a button with ex-voto imagery ...
>
> As the stop receded, I looked behind and noticed that no tram cable was installed. The tram, minus wheels, its coachwork smashed and its poles broken, looked as if it had spent too many years rotting in sand, beaten by weather.) (Foix 33–5)

Menacing tram inspectors are likened to gigantic human figures, which appear in other texts. The disappearance of the rails stresses the nightmarish status of reality as the poet imaginatively experiences it.

Fear of the City

Many critics have pointed out that life in the big city is a hideous experience: "Fear, revulsion, and horror were the emotions which the big city crowd aroused in those who first observed it," writes Walter Benjamin. And he adds some important comments about movement in the big city: "Moving through this traffic involves the individual in a series of shocks and collisions. At dangerous intersections, nervous impulses flow through him in rapid succession, like the energy from a battery. Baudelaire speaks of a man who plunges into the crowd as into a reservoir of electric energy. Circumscribing the experience of the shock, he calls this man 'a kaleidoscope equipped with consciousness'" (Benjamin, "On Some Motifs" 174–5). In the 1950s this was still a forceful impression. Colometa, the main character in Mercè Rodoreda's *La Plaça del Diamant*, had literally this kind of feeling. In the novel, Gràcia's Carrer Gran is the street that separates the poor from the rich and also divides two periods in Colometa-Natalia's life. On several occasions Colometa has a life-threatening encounter with trams, and they all happen on the Carrer Gran. In the most desperate moment of the novel, when Colometa is about to kill her children and commit suicide, a tram almost kills her. She sees blue lights, a reference to war and to dislocation:

> Vaig respirar com si el món fos meu. I vaig anar-me'n. Havia de mirar de no caure, de no fer-me atropellar, d'anar amb compte amb els tramvies, sobretot amb els que baixaven, de conservar el cap damunt del coll i anar ben dret cap a casa: sense veure els llums blaus. Sobretot sense veure els llums blaus. (Rodoreda, *La Plaça* 192)
>
> (I breathed as if the world was now mine. And I left. I had to make sure I didn't stumble, didn't get knocked over, had to take care with the trams, particularly the ones coming downhill, not lose my nerve and go straight home and not see any blue lights.) (Rodoreda, *In Diamond Square* 199)

Her adverse reaction to the urban environment must intensify before it can dissipate. All signs of modern life scare her:

> Vivia tancada a casa. El carrer em feia por. Així que treia el nas a fora, m'esverava la gent, els automòbils, els autobusos, les motos … Tenia el cor petit. Nomes estava bé a casa. (Rodoreda, *La Plaça* 217)
>
> (I lived shut up at home. The street frightened me. As soon as I poked my nose outside, the people, cars, buses and motorbikes terrified me … I turned tail. I was only happy at home.) (Rodoreda, *In Diamond Square* 221)

In one of the most moving episodes of the novel, after her daughter's wedding, Colometa leaves her new house at dawn and walks through the neighbourhood where she had spent her youth, her early years of deep pain and fight for survival. Finally, she dares to go across the

Carrer Gran, a street that repeatedly had been too imposing for her. This time she masters the situation; she is finally in control of her life, and Rodoreda shows the character going across the street as if she were crossing a river:

> I quan vaig arribar al carrer Gran vaig caminar per l'acera de rajola a rajola, fins arribar a la pedra llarga del cantell i allí em vaig quedar com una fusta per fora, amb tota una puja de coses que del cor m'anaven al cap. (Rodoreda, *La Plaça* 248)
>
> (And when I was in the High Street I walked along the pavement, racing from one flagstone to the next, until I reached the long kerbstone where I stood as stiff as a board on the outside, but with a stack of things rushing from my heart to my head.) (Rodoreda, *In Diamond Square* 259)

The street crossing is presented in a way that reminds readers of Maragall's metaphors about the Sagrada Família, and it shows the strong intertwining taking place between nature and the city. Then a tram comes and helps her overcome her irrational fear of open spaces and, most important, of her past:

> Va passar un tramvia, devia ser el primer que havia sortit de les cotxeres, un tramvia, com sempre, com tots, descolorit i vell –i aquell tramvia, potser m'havia vist córrer amb en Quimet al darrera, quan vam sortir com rates boges venint de la placa del Diamant. I se'm va posar una nosa al coll, com un cigró clavat a la campaneta. Em va venir mareig i vaig tancar els ulls i el vent que va fer el tramvia em va ajudar a arrencar endavant com si m'hi anés la vida. I a la primera passa que vaig fer encara veia el tramvia deixat anar aixecant espurnes vermelles i blaves entre les rodes i els rails. Era com si anés damunt del buit, amb els ulls sense mirar, pensant a cada segon que m'enfonsaria, i vaig travessar agafant fort el ganivet i sense veure els llums blaus … I a l'altra banda em vaig girar i vaig mirar amb els ulls i amb l'anima i em semblava que no podia ser de cap de les maneres. Havia travessat. I em vaig posar a caminar per la meva vida vella fins que vaig arribar davant de la paret de casa, sota de la tribuna. (Rodoreda, *La Plaça* 248)
>
> (A tram clattered by, it must have been the first out of the garage, a run-of-the-mill tram, like them all, battered and old; perhaps that tram had watched me running with Joe in hot pursuit, when we scampered like mad mice from Diamond Square. And I felt something irritating my neck like a pea rattling in my eardrum. I felt queasy and closed my eyes and the

> draught from the tram helped move me on as if my life depended on it. And with my first step I could still see the tram which was leaving a trail of red and blue sparks between its wheels and the rails. It was as if I was blindly walking above the abyss, thinking every second that I was about to fall, and I crossed to the other side gripping the knife tight and not seeing any blue lights … And once I was over I turned round and looked with my eyes and all my heart and thought it couldn't possibly be true. I had made it to the other side. And I started walking through my old life until I was opposite our old house, under the bay window.) (Rodoreda, *In Diamond Square* 259–60)

The tram is not only seen as an object that has witnessed her past. At the same time, its fantastic appearance – "aixecant espurnes vermelles i blaves entre les rodes i els rails" (leaving a trail of red and blue sparks between its wheels and the rails) – allows Colometa to overcome her fear of the future, her morbid attraction to the past. That is, being able to go across the street without any fear means that she is in control of her own life since trams are no longer menacing objects.

The distinction between churches and trams makes us aware that they coexist in an industrialized metropolis and have very different meanings. As Marc Augé's distinction between places and non-places suggests, a certain place can be considered a space if it can be defined as relational, historical, and concerned with identity (Augé, *Non-places).* It does not take long to decide which of the two is a place – obviously, the church – and which one is a non-place, the tram. One is a powerful symbol that stresses the relationship to the past of a certain society, its millenary religious traditions; the other represents an open door to the future. One of the characteristics of the modern city is a different sense of spaces as an outcome of the combination of spaces with history and of spaces that are completely new. Slowly, trams, which used to be non-places, have become as relational, historical, and concerned with identity as any other space, thanks to the efforts of writers and painters. Churches and trams coexist in modernity, and they are excellent examples of links to the past and of open gates to the future. Many of these writers and painters, when in need of a characteristic trait in the urban landscape of Barcelona, always include a tram, which happens to run near a church. This coexistence becomes a sort of fixture of modernity.

Architecture and urban planning create new spaces. And art and literature, following the leadership of the city's inhabitants, illustrate a wide range of problems: coexistence of the past and the present, emergence of new characters and situations, strollers, flirting on trams, and fear of trams, which are turned into mythological, atavistic monsters.

The title of Salvat-Papasseit's poem "54045" expresses the importance of chance and fortune in the encounters on the tram that Carner elevated to a moral category. What is remarkable is the difference between Salvat-Papasseit and Carner. Salvat-Pappasseit devotes much attention to describing the action itself, the moment, without discussing in detail what it means, unlike what happens in Carner's poems. Salvat-Papasseit bestows less attention to the modernity of the moment but manages to elaborate a moral reflection on the situation.

Trams represent modernity. They are excellent examples of the relationship to the past and of the doors to the future. In fact, if we take up the quote from Billy Wilder's film *Double Indemnity*, we can rewrite it and affirm that the coexistence of this double meaning attributed to trams must be read, not as a journey without return but as a round trip. It is not a single-track route but a two-way route. Trams act as powerful symbols of the many unions with the past, and open the doors to a post-industrial future. This coexistence becomes, in the words of Jean Starobinski, a symbol of modernity, its successes and failures.

6

Thresholds in Barcelona's Metro

In June 2013, I visited – with my son – the exhibition celebrating the 150th anniversary of the Tren de Sarrià (Sarrià Train), formerly known as Els Ferrocarrils Catalans (Catalan Railways). The exhibit took place at the site of a former cinema called Avenida de la Luz (Avenue of Light). Since 1979 the railway has become a public-owned company, and it is now called, less compromisingly, FGC, Ferrocarrils de la Generalitat de Catalunya (Generalitat of Catalonia Railways) (Tren de Sarrià). I was unpleasantly surprised by the self-celebratory nature of the exhibition and how little attention was given to a critical reading of the past. Trying to explain the meaning of FGC to my son, I immediately recalled a variety of texts that provided a different version of Barcelona's metro. I also thought of all those hidden underground empty spaces, or those redesigned for a new use, that populate our cities. It was easy to make the connection because we were at the site of a former cinema and next door to the former and once flamboyant avenue bearing the same name that was inaugurated in 1940 and closed in disarray in 1990. It had been converted into a place for drug dealing and treacherous encounters and was now a dreary Sephora store.

My attention is devoted to three interrelated issues: the layout of Barcelona's network and its meanings; the disappearance of some metro stations and underground spaces such as connecting corridors; and Barcelona subway life as portrayed in literary texts. The texts under consideration have something in common: they depict metro riding as an experience analogous to exploring the inner self, exposing the many absurdities in life. In addition, they draw upon mythological references to imbue the metro experience with a more positive aura. The writers also pay attention to the lack of natural light in the underground and the confluence of people from many backgrounds and circumstances within a closed space, thus creating a sort of temporary melting pot that stresses divergence and conflict. They acknowledge the dialectical interrelations between the built environment and the urban consciousness, leaving room for oppositional forms of consciousness (Masterson-Algar, "The subte" 70). David Pike's threshold concept provides a helpful explanation for the topography of the "vertical city" because "it figures the ways in which the two spaces (aboveground and underground) overlap and the ways in which they remain fundamentally different" (*Metropolis* 64). The texts and spaces examined provide a threshold that "figures the moments that link aboveground and underground, where what is hidden emerges into visibility" (Pike, *Subterranean Cities* 16).

Notes on Barcelona's Metro System

The metro system of a city is a unique piece of its environment that links two aspects of urban space. As stated by Lewis Mumford, "the modern city plan involves a coordination of the super-surface city with the sub-surface city" (qtd. in Williams 52); there is a direct connection between our wide knowledge of the surface and very limited knowledge of the urban underworld. According to Ashford, "[t]he Underground is a transitional form, linking the alienated space of production created by the Industrial Revolution to the fully virtual spaces of late capitalism that emerged following the Cold War" (2). Development of Barcelona's underground transportation has been the result of disparate initiatives and bad planning, which shows through in its topsy-turvy layout and current condition.[1] Tracing the many changes that Barcelona's rail system has undergone reveals that even as the metro came to be a mirror of collective wishes and frustrations, it persistently lacked coherence.

The first application for the construction of a railway between Barcelona and the nearby town of Sarrià was filed in 1851, three years after the opening of the first railway line connecting Barcelona and Mataró. The Sarrià train began operating in 1863, the same year as the London Underground did. It was a short line, only 4,600 metres in length, starting in what is today known as the Plaça de Catalunya (Catalonia Square) and crossing Barcelona through the villages of Gràcia and Sant Gervasi to arrive in Sarrià, at the foot of the Collserola mountain. For many decades the trains were operated by steam locomotives, but in 1905, with the gradual development of the Eixample district, they were upgraded to electrical locomotives, as described by Joan Maragall. In his article "L'últim xiscle" (The last cry) Maragall stresses change and loss, and thus disappearance of a way of life:

> L'endemà – ja ho havia llegit en el diari – l'endemà començava la *tracció elèctrica*. Ja no'l sentiriem xiular mai més aquell tren de Sarrià: aquell xiscle era un adéu; el tren se'n anava no cap a Sarrià, sino cap ala eternitat: no'l tornariem a sentir mai més. (Maragall, *Escrits en prosa* 155)

> (The next day – I had already read about it in the newspaper – next day began electric traction. Since we would not listen ever again to the train of Sarrià whistle: that was a goodbye scream; it was not the train to Sarrià, but to eternity: we would not listen to it ever again.)

The Sarrià train became the first electric railway in Catalonia. The engineer Carles Emili Montañés convinced Frederick S. Pearson, an engineer from Lowell, Massachussetts, to purchase the Sarrià–Barcelona line and its extension towards Vallès. In 1912 it was incorporated as Ferrocarriles de Cataluña (Catalonia Railways). In 1917 the company opened the double track to Sant Cugat del Vallès. In 1919 the line reached Terrassa, and in 1922, Sabadell. The line ran on the surface until 1929 when the section Catalunya–Muntaner was buried. In 1953 a branch from Gràcia to Avinguda Tibidabo was inaugurated. The urban lines became L6 and L7 (Tren de Sarrià). When the line was buried, it caught the attention of a sharp-sighted journalist named Gaziel, who in a memorable article, "Pequeña elegía urbana" (Little urban elegy), evoked his personal relationship with the Sarrià train. In the article he recalls the forty years since he started using the line, the impact of industrialization on ways of life, and, ending with a characteristic Gaziel observation, longing or imagining (or assuming) what the future may bring:

> ¿Es un sueño? No; es algo parecido: cuarenta años de vida … Al constatar sus extraordinarias mudanzas es forzoso sentir que, en nuestra brevedad, todo lo que fuimos en el seno de esa vida municipal gigantesca, se borra paulatinamente, y nuestra propia vida se va convirtiendo poco a poco en estampas del tiempo pasado. (Gaziel, "Pequeña elegía urbana")

> (Is it a dream? No. It is something similar: forty years of life … When acknowledging its extraordinary changes you must feel that in our brevity, everything that we witnessed within that giant municipal life is gradually erased, and our life is gradually becoming prints from the past.)

Gaziel's elegy for a time past emphasizes the speed at which changes occur, resulting in a fragile awareness of transience: we are meant to be swallowed and disappear. He does not notice the fact that there is an important transformation taking place in city life: the underground swallows a former surface train. Demolition and erasure bring with them a sudden appreciation of what is no longer there, and this is a distinctive feature of our experience of the modern cityscape: "perpetual change erases memory" (Gilloch and Kilby 6). The endless quest for novelty merges into the flow of undifferentiated, empty time in which the past is consigned to oblivion by the present, and, perhaps most importantly, it may fleetingly reappear as a disturbance that gives a shock to today's passer-by (Gilloch 300). This peculiarity is particularly eloquent in the slow transformation of a city's underground life. Circulating underground, that line lost its character as an urban train and became a real metro.

Gran Metropolitano de Barcelona (Barcelona's Big Metro, known as Gran Metro) was created on 26 May 1921 to construct and operate a subway line, now called L3. On 30 December 1924 the section between Lesseps and Catalonia was inaugurated (Reyes). It had a length of 2,470 kilometres and four stations. Initially the project was to connect La Bonanova with Estació de França, but this never materialized. In 1926 a new branch was added. From Aragó station one branch would go to Liceu (it later became L3), and the other one to Correos (The Post). This second branch was converted in the 1980s into L4.

Metro Transversal began as an underground electric traction railway with the goal of establishing a transversal connection between the stations of the Barcelona–Tarragona and Barcelona–France railway lines (currently the underused Estació de França, France's Station) and the other train stations: Estació del Nord (North Station), Estació Magòria (Magòria Station, from which there is a narrow-gauge railway to Berga), and Estació P. Catalunya (used by Ferrocarrils Catalans, Catalan Railways). The first section was built to link the city centre with the Plaça d'Espanya (Spain's Square), the site of the 1929 world fair. The official opening of the first section (Bordeta–Catalonia) took place on 10 June 1926. It was named Metro Transversal to differentiate it from the Gran Metro and was 4,063 kilometres long and had nine stations. The station Espanya at that time had the world's largest station vault (27 metres). Because of its origins (connecting train stations), a particularity of this metro line is the use of the Iberian gauge of 1,672 millimetres, which makes it one of the widest in the world. Carriages from this line cannot circulate on other Barcelona lines. Between 1935 and 1950 there were no new stations built. In 1959 a new short line known as L5 was built, and in 1973 the L4 was added (Salmerón i Bosch; Schwandl; Guerola).

The return to democracy in 1977 made the public use of the Catalan language possible and enabled a call for self-government. Thus, it introduced significant changes in Barcelona's metro system. Local authorities had more direct control over planning decisions. During the 1980s there were substantial changes, in terms not of growth but in the identity of the system and the ability to do long-term planning. First, Lines III and IIIb (Pueblo Seco–Zona Universitaria) became the new L3. Roman numerals became Arabic numerals respecting the old numeration. Colour-coded lines were introduced, and finally several station names were either translated into Catalan or renamed. The rationalization of public transportation included the creation of the T10 card, which was accepted on all metro lines and buses. The following chart summarizes the most important name changes.

Line	Former name	New name
L1	Navas de Tolosa	Navas
	Triunfo Norte	Arc de Triomf
	Bordeta Cocheras	Santa Eulàlia
L3	Ciudad Universitaria	Zona Universitària
	Palacio	Palau Reial
	Roma Estación Renfe	Sants Estació
	Parlament	Poble Sec
	Pueblo Seco	Paral·lel
	Aragó	Passeig de Gràcia
	Diagonal–Paseo de Gracia	Diagonal
L4	General Mola	Verdaguer
	Ribera	Ciutadella
	Pedro IV	Bogatell
	Luchana	Llacuna
L5	Buxeras	Can Boixeres
	Maladeta	Can Vidalet
	San Ramón	Collblanc
	Dos de Mayo	Hospital de Sant Pau
	Viviendas del Congreso	Congrés

Overall, these changes reflect two trends: an attempt to correct a politically tainted heritage, and a push towards recuperation of symbols after a long fascist dictatorship that had pointedly erased any traces of Catalan language and culture wherever possible. Two examples are particularly significant in this respect. First, the name of General Mola, one of the generals who had rebelled against the republic, became that of Verdaguer, Catalonia's famous poet from the Renaixença (Renaissance); and second, the name of Dos de Mayo, a commemoration of the Madrid rebellion against Napoleon, of little importance in Barcelona, became that of Hospital de Sant Pau, a landmark of *modernista* (Art Nouveau) architecture.[2] In a comparison of the metro layout, extension of lines, and amount of stations of Barcelona with those of other cities of similar size, there are a number of stark differences ("List of Metro Systems").

The history of Barcelona's metro could be said to be a tale of wishes and frustrations. If one considers the gaps between the project's conceptions, the desires of the planners, and the results that were obtained, it is clear that something strange has happened; the old saying that "the Barcelona metro was developed by the enemy" is not so far from reality. A few examples should suffice to convey the magnitude of the disaster. There is no direct link between the city centre and Estació de França, which was for many years the main railway station in the city. Gran Metro was built with the idea of establishing that link, but this never happened, and travellers had to walk eight hundred metres to reach the station from the nearest metro stop. In figure 7 we read a remarkable example of wishful thinking: riders "only" need to take a four-minute walk to reach the Correos station from Estació de França. Connections between many stations seem to be the work of shrewd labyrinth designers. Most notably is the connection between L3 and L4 in Passeig de Gràcia (formerly Aragó), where subway users are supposed to walk underground for more than five hundred metres, or the connection between L7–L8 and L1 in Catalunya, where users have to walk for miles or navigate dangerously through incoming L3 trains and rushing passengers. This kind of basic metro map hides a more complex reality that the universal use of colour-coded lines and a rendition of paths in the city's real space tend to conceal.

Comparing these five maps (figures 7–11), one sees the changes successively introduced into the layout of the network. Lines avoid the old part of town (only two lines cross it), and there is no direct link across the northern part of the city, thus increasing the isolation between different lines. The adoption of international standards with Beck's model to represent a metro network hides this gloomy reality (Pike, *Subterranean Cities* 21–33).

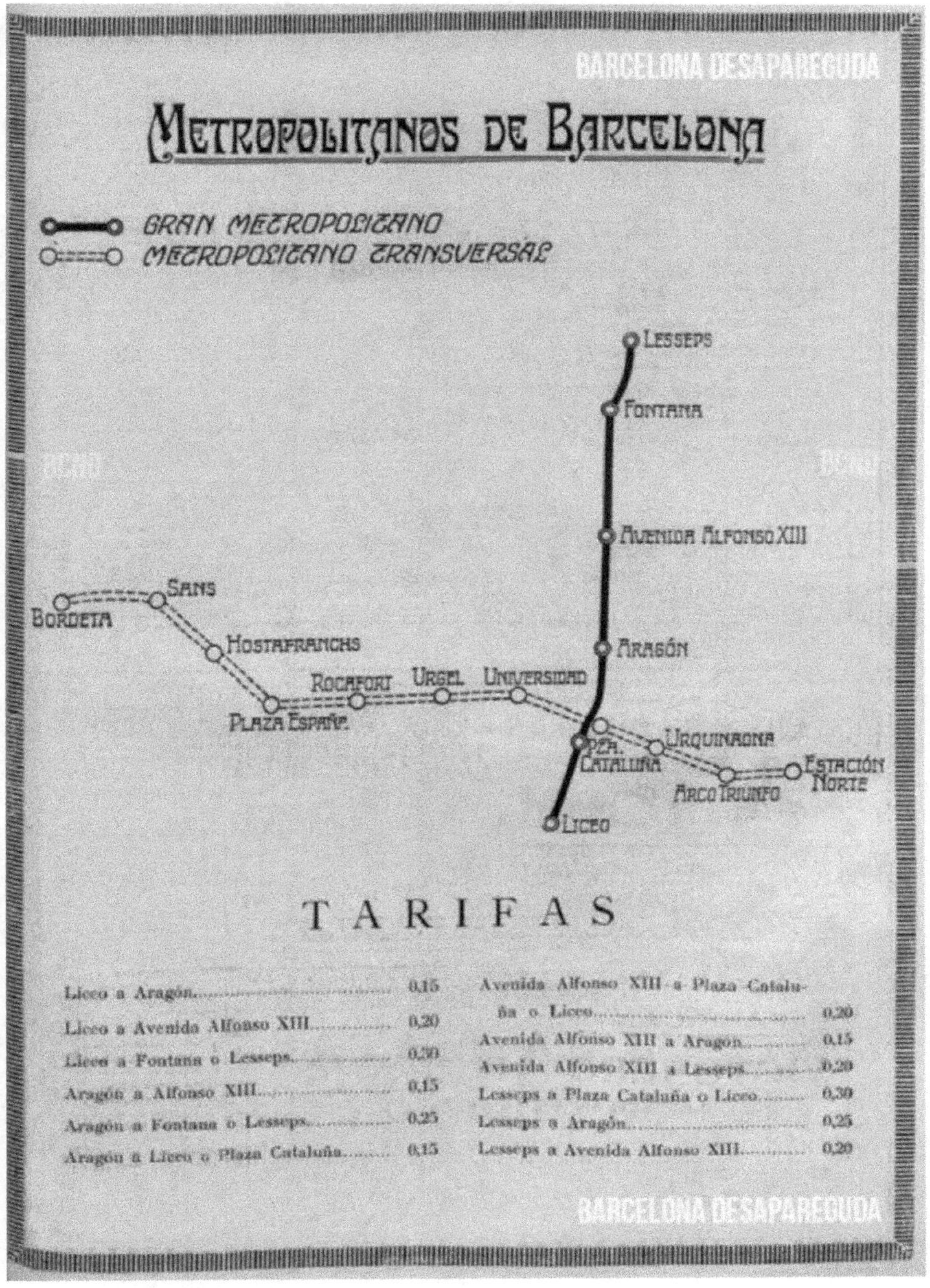

Figure 7. Barcelona Metro Map, 1925

Figure 8. Barcelona Metro Map, 1940

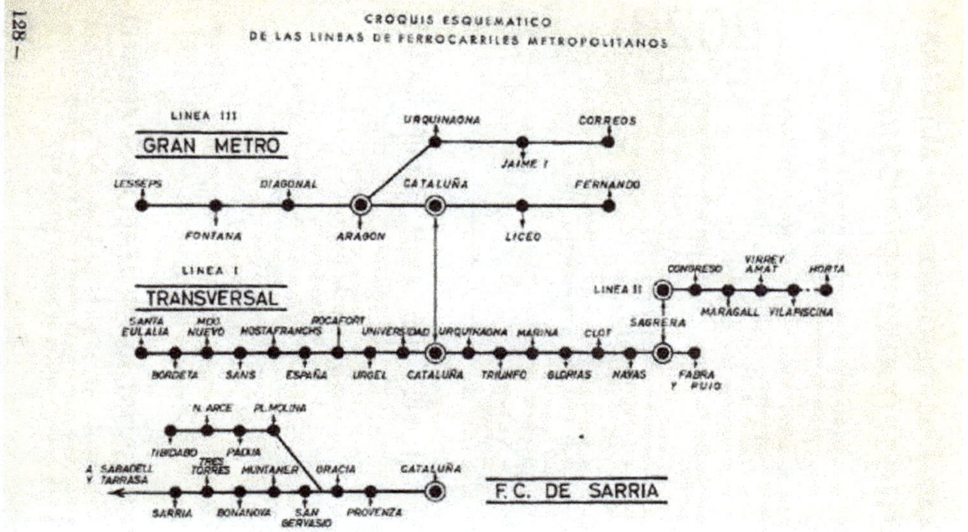

Figure 9. Barcelona Metro Map, 1966

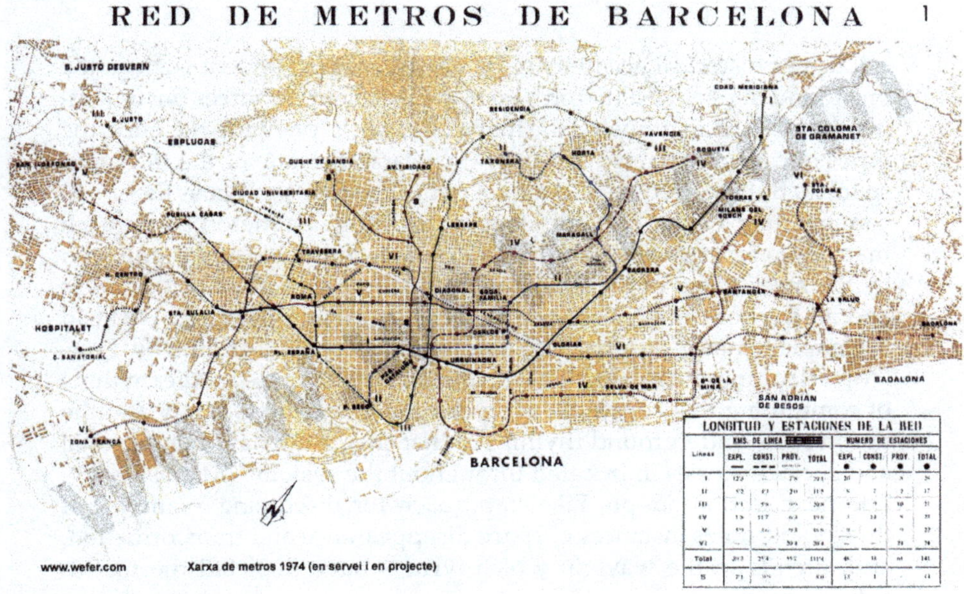

Figure 10. Barcelona Metro Map, 1974

Figure 11. Barcelona Metro Map, 2023

Current historical accounts of Barcelona's metro system such as the one found in Carles Salmerón's book are excellent resources documenting the birth of an industry, the many changes in planning the lines, the types of cars and trains used over the years, the state of the fleet, and so forth. But we need an alternative critical history to discuss the shortcomings and errors of traditional cartography. Salmerón's approach matches Lefebvre's notion of planned space, conceived and dominated by the mechanism of the state: the infrastructure of trains and tunnels and all the personnel necessary to keep the metro operating. We need a complementary approach to this planned space. As put by Pike, "[o]verlapping and interacting with this conceived space are the rhythms of commuting that constitute everyday life in the modern city and the unforeseen, underground rhythms of that city … overlapping personal and social histories imbricated throughout the system" (*Metropolis* 13). The next section adopts Pike's approach for discussing examples of thresholds, notes instances of space disappearance and transformation, and attends to the ways in which writers have depicted the metro-riding experience.

Reading Metro Maps

Current maps of Barcelona's metro hide the transformation of the network. They are meant to help current users navigate the system, without any mention of what is hiding underneath such as unused connecting corridors and closed stations. Many of these spaces still exist but they have been erased or transformed, and with them disappear memories and a way of living in the city. Current subway maps testify to a history of mismanagement and of missed opportunities, to a failure to create a city with a more coherent, useful, and practical transport system. They hide the intricacy and difficulties of building the system, completely erasing the past. Alternative mapping is required if these transformations are to become visible, if a history lesson is to be written into the city map. One example is what Víctor Balaguer did when he wrote *Las calles de Barcelona* (1865; The streets of Barcelona), his proposal to name the still-silent (unnamed streets) plan of Barcelona envisioned by Ildelfons Cerdà, thus naming the Eixample streets according to historical references as a way to revive a neglected Catalonian past (Quintana, "Didàctica"; Subirana).

Radical cartography or counter-mapping is an attempt to map against dominant power structures. It must provide products that satisfy the basic criteria of mapping: maps that are useful, usable, and persuasive. It has to introduce elements or approaches that are inaccessible, invisible, or perhaps even undesirable as seen through the lens of the existing schema (Denil). The separation between the city above ground and the city under ground is a "topographical mnemonic" based on the symbolic topography of a single social space (Pike, *Metropolis* 63). Likewise, a new approach to Barcelona's metro map would reveal trends of disappearance and establish a cartographic picture of the past.[3] Literature, however, provides us with tools to map the experience and recall it from a diachronic and critical perspective.

Urban metro systems are an integral part of the lives of commuters and as such are ambiguous spaces, both familiar and threatening, reliable and unpredictable, crowded yet isolating, decisively subterranean yet linked to the geography of the city that lies above. An important tool in metro riding is the map we use to navigate a system. Subway networks are a special case in point when one is discussing the everyday. Marc Augé stressed the fact that subways link both physical spaces and human beings with all their complexity: "Le métro relie des points algébriques, des lieux et des êtres" (*Le Métro* 15; The metro connects algebraic points, places, and things). The everyday is not a region, a town, or a show that can be represented: without objective status, it only exists through practices that, by revealing its existence, make it happen. According to Blanchot, indeterminacy is the everyday's defining characteristic. The everyday escapes – that is its definition; it is the hardest thing to uncover (Sheringham 16). Metro maps may present a different window into the everyday.

When looking at a metro map, we deal with two basic principles of typography: legibility and readability (Tracy 31). *Legibility* refers to perception, and *readability* to comprehension. On the one hand, legibility means, for example, that colour-coded lines are easily discernible between each other, and station names can be read without difficulty. On the other hand, readability implies communicating a meaning as directly as possible, for example getting from point A to point B, what Duke Ellington's song "Take the A Train" expresses so well. What I am pursuing here is another level of readability, one closer to Marc Augé's analysis. Augé points to daily rituals and other repetitive acts that metro users perform, thus explaining how the metro functions as a distinctive social space, with specific codes, rules, and habits. Getting to know a city by using the metro is a journey taken in accompanied solitude, a voyage through space and through a kind of geographically mapped collective unconscious. As Kafka wrote in his diary, the metro was a way to capture the essence of Paris (Nervi).

The metro network underpins the city, offering an experience of urban space that is very different from any other because it provides a restricted underground view that is contingent on the topographical reduction of the city to a web of lines and correspondences. Augé comments on the way in which metro riders organize their experiences in space and time: "Subway riders basically handle nothing more than time and space, and are skilled in using the one to measure the other" (*In the Metro* 15). This is what Cortázar shows in "El perseguidor" (The pursuer), where the main character reflects on the way in which the metro brings a temporal flexibility into being. Johnny remembers moments of his life – many moments in his timeline, which encompasses fifteen minutes – that are now compressed into just a minute and a half, the time between two stops. This ability to mix different temporalities suggests the subway as a small time machine; it stops, spreads, and takes us through a lonely temporal journey. For Cortázar, with the subway we immerse ourselves in a world created for observation and imagination. He looks at the metro as if it were a labyrinth under the earth, something that allows him to access another kind of time: "sólo en el *métro* me puedo dar cuenta porque viajar en el *métro* es como estar metido en un reloj. Las estaciones son los minutos" (*Cuentos Completos* 233). (Only in the *métro* I am aware because riding the *métro* is like finding oneself in another kind of time. Stations are minutes.)

Gilles Esposito, in a sort of Oulipian play with words, has created an anagrammatic version of Paris's metro, "Plan anagrammatique du metro de Paris / Prisa," turning each metro station into an anagram. Here are a few examples:

> Bibliothèque François Mitterrand = Fier, l'errant don Quichotte s'imbiba (Lit de brebis fort antimonarchique)
> Saint-Germain des Prés = Garnements à dissiper
> Saint-Michel = Il est machin
> Mairie des Lilas = Iris à médailles
> Porte des Lilas = Le spot sidéral
> Gare d'Austerlitz = Les gaz du traître
> Les Halles = Less a hell

An Oulipian author, Jacques Jouet, wrote a book entitled *Poèmes de métro*. He writes: "Un poème de métro est un poème composé dans le métro, pendant le temps d'un parcours. / Un poème de métro compte autant de vers que votre voyage compte de stations moins un." (A metro poem is a poem composed in the metro, during the time of a journey. / A metro poem has as many verses as your journey has stations minus one.) It is similar to "Subterrània" (Eutròfics), a song made with a list of all Barcelona metro stations organized according to rhythm and phonetics.

The play with rhythm and phonetics is also very characteristic in the second kind of text about metro riding. A poem by Jacques Prévert, "Le contrôleur," in *Paroles* (Words) stresses some features in the condition of metro riding and identifies the intense anonymity of this experience. The poem reminds us of a few characteristics of travel by subway: short journeys in the company of people one does not know, thus emphasizing anonymity; a combination of bright lights in stations and the darkness of tunnels; the monotony of the journey; the scrutiny of fellow travellers; reading; sleeping; and daydreaming. Another example in point is Serge Gainsbourg's "Le poinçonneur des Lilas," a song that stresses the difficulty of working underground, without any sunlight and doing a monotonous activity. Gainsbourg describes a profession that is no longer in existence, adding a sort of historical perspective to metro riding. The song is immersed in late-1950s French culture with all the emphasis on the attraction of North American culture and ways of life. He mentions the American dream as opposed to the tedious situation, and he even refers to a metro combination that is not possible to make any more because of the new layout of Line 3 in the Paris metro:

J'suis l'poinçonneur des Lilas
Arts-et-Métiers direct par Levallois
J'en ai marre j'en ai ma claque
De ce cloaque. (Gainsbourg)

(I am the puncher at Lilas station / Reach directly Arts-et-Métiers by Levallois / I'm sick I'm sick / Of this cesspool.)

Gainsbourg points to his condition of extreme boredom with the rhyme *claque/cloaque*, underlining the fact that the metro runs parallel to the sewer system.

While Prévert and Gainsbourg point out an everyday long gone and forgotten, acting as notaries of disappearance, other texts incorporate, with a lucid accuracy, instances of the everyday such as the contemplation of the crowd or one's anonymity in it. Ezra Pound's poem "In a Station of the Metro" (1913) is a brilliant example of brevity and intensity:

The apparition of these faces in a crowd;
Petals on a wet, black bough.

Pound describes watching faces in a metro station in Paris. The image denotes a dark subway platform, filled with the people who look like flower petals on a flower branch. It is an example of the imagist style, using only a few descriptive words without any verbs. One cannot but think of Kurt Tucholsky's 1930 poem "Augen in der Großstadt," which evokes a chance encounter occurring in the U-Bahn and S-Bahn trains:

Wenn du zur Arbeit gehst
am frühen Morgen,
wenn du am Bahnhof stehst
mit deinen Sorgen:
dann zeigt die Stadt
dir asphaltglatt
im Menschentrichter
Millionen Gesichter:
Zwei fremde Augen, ein kurzer Blick,
die Braue, Pupillen, die Lider – (Tucholsky 379)

(When you go to work / in the early morning / when you stand at the station / with your worries: / there the city reveals to you / asphalt clear / in a human crater / millions of faces: / two unknown eyes, a quick glance, / the brows, pupils, eyelids –)

Tucholsky highlights the brief eye contact: two eyes meet briefly, affinity is noticeable, but only for a very brief moment, exactly as long as the eye contact holds:[4]

> Ein Auge winkt,
> die Seele klingt;
> du hast gefunden,
> nur für Sekunden.
>
> (An eye winks, / the soul rings; / you have found, / only for seconds,)

The conclusion of the poem indicates the speed and the disappearance of the other:

> Was war das?
> Von der großen Menschheit ein Stück!
> Vorbei, verweht, nie wieder. (Tucholsky 379–80)
>
> (What was that? / Of the great humanity a piece! / Over, dead end, never again.)

Ramon Solsona's novel *Línia Blava* (2004) seems to develop Marc Augé's view that on the metro "we constantly brush up against the history of others … without ever meeting it" (Augé, *In the Metro* 10). The narrator describes a metro ride along the entire Line 5 in Barcelona, emphasizing the subway as a place where there is an inability to establish communication with others due to a self-imposed set of rules derived from the subway's system of connections and coincidences. The novel is organized by chapters whose titles chart the names of metro stations along Barcelona's blue line. The plot consists of parallel biographies, each one hiding its own little drama, using flashback, suspense, and an omniscient narrator who imagines the future of every single character he observes. Some lives end up intersecting, without any consequence. The novel recreates a form of mental activity or philosophical speculation in which many of us engage when facing unknown people: we may guess who they are, what their troubles are, what their futures may be, or even when they might die. Solsona's narrator builds a sort of kaleidoscope and focuses on a few characters that he observes; he deduces trends and imagines a past, inner feelings, and coincidences among them. A man and a woman – one a prostitute, the other an adopted immigrant from Central Africa – are interacting via a love cyberchat. The beginning and the end of the novel are organized around a threshold, stressing life outside the underground by paying attention to the free flight of birds, and thus denouncing the concealment and lack of fresh air below ground. There is also a self-reflective moment at the end of the novel when the narrator turns the tables around and offers to exchange views: "Potser ella també ha fet volar la imaginació i, mentre tu li atribuïes una història, ella te n'atribuïa una altra" (300; Maybe she also has played with her imagination, and while you made up her story, she made up another one for you). In this way, the observer becomes the observed character. In the novel there is also a play with the metro map. A very well-known underground route is linked to imagined private lives, and in the process human experience intersects with urban underground geography. With painstaking detail he narrates how to use the metro card and also the similarities between the Sagrera and Horta stations that may lead to confusion: "el viatger es desconcerta, té la sensació de retrobar-se a l'estació de partida" (71; the rider feels puzzled and may think that he is back at the station of departure).

As depicted in Solsona's novel, metro riding is a major example of the monotony present in everyday life. There is a certain degree of consistency as "[m]ost of the singular itineraries in the subway are daily and obligatory" (Augé, *In the Metro* 8). Time and space constraints are crucial in defining the essential structures of subway riding, but there are also "daily and obligatory" burdens that have a value at the individual level and are also experienced by the other riders. Augé focuses on socially significant uses of time and space offered by metro riding, as well as the way in which these uses accommodate themselves to the specific symbolic matrices that are more noteworthy along particular lines, or as regards particular stations. For instance, he examines the naming of metro stations after military victories (Austerlitz and Solférino in Paris; Waterloo in London) and wonders whether this attests to the co-presence of history in our everyday lives or the unreality of history (*In the Metro* 16). Just as the monuments and squares of the city surface cease to have a meaning for those who pass through them every day, the historical connotations of familiar metro station names tend to disappear with time. In fact, they create new associations, series of names that sound almost as full sentences or paradigms, united according to their musicality or by just chance.

A recent song by a Catalan rock band, Nens Eutròfics, explores this possibility: "Subterrània" is a long list of all Barcelona metro stations organized according to rhythm and phonetics: "Fondo, Fabra i Puig, Pàdua, Sant Martí / Selva de Mar, Horta, Gornal, Joanic" (Eutròfics).[5]

This list, bordering Leo Spitzer's chaotic enumeration, provides a phonetic and puzzling version of Barcelona's metro map that can be read as a provocation, a sort of wake-up call to reread in a different way a map encapsulating the space of everyday monotony. Moreover, the chaotic list of metro stations reminds us of the distinction between the world as seen from above ("hierachized and conceptualized") and the world as seen from below, one that "revels in the sensation of its proximity to chaos" (Pike, *Subterranean Cities* 11). The subway map can be used in other innovative ways, such as a trigger for memories, a sort of pocket mirror in which will be reflected instantly birds from the past: "Sometimes the chance happening of an itinerary (of a name, of a sensation) is enough for distracted travelers suddenly to discover that their inner geology and subterranean geography of the capital city meet at certain points, where dazzling discoveries of coincidences promote recall of tiny and intimate tremors in the sedimentary layers of their memory" (Augé, *In the Metro* 4). As Augé puts it, riding the metro creates new itineraries, therefore new topographies, mixing the past and the present, "a slice of life of which the subway map, in the schedule we carry inside ourselves, reveals only a piece, the aspect simultaneously the most spatial and the most regular, but about which we know well that everything was or seemed to be in order" (9). The metro map indicates a blending of individual lives with those of others, private and public life, personal and collective stories. Another singer, Miquel Pujadó, has written a song titled "Pels intestins de la ciutat" (Through the city's intestines) in which he lists names of stations and makes them rhyme with actions and objects related to the metro riders he observes. Pujadó begins his song by stressing the monotony of metro riding, the weariness of the riders, a situation that allows extreme mingling of people from very different social origins and backgrounds. He stresses the mixing of worlds and of humanity that takes place underground. Pujadó's text adds a notion of the everyday. After a crucial metaphor ("city's intestines") he reveals the blending that takes place: mixed, crossing, weariness, intersections, tangent, secant, colliding, hence stressing the lack of cooperation between human beings. Hostility and indifference characterize human attitudes underground. He also builds riddles and plays on words based on the musical combination of metro station names, alternating lines of two or three station names with lines of interrupted reflection on metro riding:

Arc de Triomf, Fondo, Espanya
Hi ha gent vulgar, gent estranya.
Poble Sec, Sant Roc, Entença

L'un parla sol, l'altre pensa.
Can Serra, Glòries, Vallcarca
Hi ha qui va llegint el *Marca*. (Pujadó)

(Arch of Triumph, Fondo, Spain / Some people are vulgar, some are strange. / Poble Sec, Sant Roc, Entença / One speaks alone, the other thinks. / Can Serra, Glòries, Vallcarca / Some read *Marca*.)

Of special note is the reference to what riders read: sports newspapers or highbrow authors such as Joyce or Rodoreda. Later in the song Pujadó focuses on the metro as a cage, the encounter with different people, one rider speaking to himself or herself, others thinking, reading, exhausted or dreamy workers, the smell of sweat, being stepped on, pickpocketing, suicides, the pressure of bodies, distrust of immigrants, metro musicians, lack of blue sky, dreams, routine, views of a passing beautiful young woman, indifference. He ends with another metaphor: the metro map (the riddle of metro station names) as an unfathomable grid, a giant word puzzle:

Via Júlia, Cornellà
Resignem-nos a deixar
Besòs Mar, Trinitat Vella
no resolta la graella
Sagrada Família, Encants
d'aquests encreuats gegants. (Pujadó)

(Via Júlia, Cornellà / Let's resign ourselves to leave / Besòs Mar, Trinitat Vella / the grid unresolved / Sagrada Família, Encants / of this giant crossword.)

Pujadó's text introduces the underground as an unsolved problem, a hieroglyphic or labyrinth that one needs to solve. In both examples of poetry (Nens Eutròpics and Pujadó), chaotic enumeration emphasizes the puzzling effect of the city on the surface. Their reorganization of station names opens a threshold that further amplifies this confusing meaning, calling attention to personal and social histories of riders and how they read the network.

It is useful to recall Pike's analysis of the underground and the labyrinth: "The underworld follows neither the standard rules of time – for it endures eternally and mingles every epoch in its depths – nor those of space – for it is dark, supernatural, and labyrinthine in its construction" (*Subterranean Cities* 191–2). This personalized version of the underground city map relates to personal and general history and, in the words of Michel de Certeau, makes us the sole exegetist of a certain legacy: "Places are fragmentary and inward-turning histories, pasts that others are not allowed to read, accumulated times that can be unfolded but like stories held in reserve, remaining in an enigmatic state, symbolizations encysted in the pain or pleasure of the body" (Certeau 108). We might relate this last consideration to what Certeau pointed out about city walking, which applies to metro riding and metro plan reading: with the use of synecdoche and asyndeton "[i]t practices the ellipsis of conjunctive loci" (101). Riding and reading become part of an intertwined activity characterized by its disjoint unity. The metro map becomes a sort of metro book. Moreover, it can be related to Rosalind Williams's observation that "the subterranean environment is a technological one – but it is also a mental landscape, a social terrain, and an ideological map" (21).

Julio Cortázar reflects on metro rides and plays with the different meanings of the words used to indicate an exchange station, *changes/correspondances/combinaciones*: "En Inglaterra y Estados Unidos, las correspondencias se llaman *cambios*, y en mi país *combinaciones*. Cualquiera de las tres palabras contiene cargas análogas, insinúan mutación, transformación, metamorfosis" ("Bajo nivel"; In England and the United States, correspondences are called *changes*, and in my country, *combinations*. Any of the three words contains analogous charges, insinuating mutation, transformation, metamorphosis). For him, riding a subway is a life-changing experience that only a happy few can detect. He refers to how to travel under the city changes the rider's perception. In yet another excerpt he points to the different experience of freedom that one human being can perceive with the underground experience:

> Pasajeros y trenes se mueven dentro de la misma relojería predeterminada, y es entonces cuando las potencias de la superficie se adormecen y puede suceder que accedamos a otros niveles; al liberarnos de la libertad, el metro nos vuelve por un momento disponibles, porosos, recipientes de todo lo que la libertad de la superficie nos priva, puesto que ser libres allá arriba significa peligro, opción necesaria, luz roja, cruzar en las esquinas mirando del buen lado. (Cortázar, "Bajo nivel")
>
> (Passengers and trains move within the same predetermined clockwork, and it is then that the powers of the surface become numb and it may happen that we access other levels; by freeing ourselves from freedom, the subway makes us available for a moment, porous, recipients of everything that the freedom of the surface deprives us of, because being free up there means danger, necessary choice, red light, crossing at the corners, looking on the right side.)

With the paradox *liberarnos de la libertad* (free ourselves from freedom) he makes us aware that only the metro ride can bestow an experience of this kind.

What we have seen in the first section reflects the real underground city, one constructed with uncertainties and errors. We also detect instances of disappearance that portray a hidden map under the visible city. All this leads me to three conclusions. First, the metro map indicates a different portrait of the city because physical geography is reduced to a list of names and their connecting, coloured lines. We may travel through a metro line for years without knowing exactly what is on top of a specific station above us. Second, metro maps/rides create a different sense of time and a different way of reading. Third, it is a special setting for everyday life where communications, interaction, acquire a different status. The legibility of the metro plan hides a problematic way of reading, one that only by looking at its hidden meanings can we fully understand those plans.

Disappeared Spaces: Vanishing Metro Stations

Michel de Certeau stated that proper names in the city link acts and footsteps, opening meanings and directions. They are symbolic devices that organize "the topoi of a discourse on/of the city (legend, memory, and dream) in a way that also eludes urbanistic systematicity" (105). As we have seen before with the changes in station names, proper names associated with space (toponyms, metro stations) make habitable or credible a place that is beautified with a word. They recall or conjure the ghosts (dead or allegedly missing) that are still moving, crouching on the actions and bodies in motion, imposing an injunction arising from the other (a history), and altering the functionalist identity, creates on the spot of this erosion a non-place that undermines the law of the other.

In the case of metro networks there is a special condition of ghost stations, or Geisterbahnhöfe, a term used to describe the stations on Berlin's U-Bahn and S-Bahn metro networks that remained closed during Berlin's division, from 1953 to 1989. It was an extreme situation in which passengers travelled through ghost stations, crossing the wall and encountering an underground world with a blurred temporality and geography (Links). Similarly in Paris, during the Second World War the French government closed all but eighty-five stations of the city's network. The majority of stations were reopened after the war, although some less profitable stations remained closed. Some of these closed stations have been used as sets for films (J. Robert; Symbioz). Similar examples can be found in other cities: City Hall station in the New York subway, decorated by Guastavino (Brennan); and the Chamberí station in Madrid, which in 2008 was restored and became a Metro Museum (Masterson-Algar, "Digging Madrid").

An analogous situation has taken place in Barcelona. Some metro stations and even an underground shopping mall have disappeared. The stations include Bordeta, Correos, and Fernando. Bordeta was closed as it was deemed unnecessary, being too close to Santa Eulàlia. Correos was part of the former L4 section at the end of Pau Claris; it was inaugurated in 1934 as a temporary station until metro network was extended to Estació de França, and in 1972 it was closed because of its proximity to the Barceloneta station. The old stairs to the station can be seen in front of the main facade of the post office building. Fernando station is located between Liceu and Drassanes stations; it opened in 1946 and closed in 1968 for being very near the Liceu station and to enable extension of Drassanes station. Other stations never opened: Banco, Gaudí, and Travessera. Banco, built in Plaça Antonio Maura, was never opened to public use. According to popular belief it was made for the money train, which ran only at night, carrying shipments of the money raised in all metro stations to the former Banco de España Barcelona's headquarters (now Caixa Catalunya). The station had a direct access to the vault of the bank ("Estacions fantasmes"). This station was built fifteen years before the advent of the metro in Barcelona. It was envisioned as part of the Reforma works of 1908 to open a fast way – Via Laietana (see figure 12) – of communication between the Eixample and the port of Barcelona. The demolition was supposed to open an avenue 80 metres wide and 900 metres long. Planners built two tunnels under the new avenue, hoping that they could be of use in a future underground metro system in the city. Over a decade later, and with the first metro line already operational, construction work began on a station that became known as Banco. However, the work was never finished. The engineers of the time made some serious miscalculations. According to Álex Reyes, they built the platforms at the same level as the track, because they thought the metro would be like an underground tram. They neglected to take into account the machinery underneath, which meant they were later forced to lower the level of the track so that trains would be able to move along them.

Gaudí station can be seen on L5 between Sagrada Família and Hospital de Sant Pau stations. The station was completely built in 1968, with platforms, walkways, and escalators, but it was never opened. Located near the Sagrada Família, it was supposed to be a link with the old Line 2 and provide easy access for tourists, but when the Sagrada Familia–Horta section of L5 was built, it no longer made sense to open Gaudí. At the top level of the station are the headquarters of the associations

Figure 12. Opening of Via Laietana

of retired workers from Transports Metropolitans de Barcelona ("Estacions fantasmes"). It is remarkable that three of those stations (Correos, Gaudí, and Banco) correspond to important landmarks in Barcelona. Gaudí was the leading architect of the *modernista* movement, and it is ironic that not a single metro station commemorates him. The other stations are linked to facilities – banking and the postal service – stressing yet again the odd way in which Barcelona's metro system has been developed either without a plan or as an idiosyncratic solution to political needs. Line 9, the latest addition to Barcelona's metro network, has been born with a ghost station (Solé). Interestingly, in his novel Solsona denounces an uncompleted ghost station. At the time, the station would have been named Cardenal Reig, which prompted his comment that "s'afegirà a la tradició clerical d'un nomenclàtor ple de sants, de cardenals i bisbes" (218; it will be added to the tradition of clerical names of streets full of saints, bishops, and cardinals).

Another remarkable case of disappearance is that of a connecting corridor built under Pelai Street. Jaume Sabater envisioned Avenida de la Luz (Avenue of Light; see figure 13) as an underground street, taking advantage of a disused tunnel excavated during the Universal Exhibition of 1929. It became the first underground shopping mall in Europe, which initially was to be extended to Urquinaona Square (Xalabarder). There was a public toilet that became a site for gay sexual encounters; a manufacturer of wafer biscuits with an aroma that filled all the mall; a Pedro Montroy Masana wine shop, with a large mannequin dressed as an Aragonese pouring wine into a boot; a *futbolín* (foosball); and a cinema that for many years showed double features and later became an X-rated theatre. After being closed for many years, most of the mall is presently a dull Sephora store (figure 14) and serves as a showcase of the city's transformation and its fading personality at the hands of globalization. The theatre space is used occasionally as an exhibition area by FGC. Singer Loquillo, in his record "¿Dónde estabas tú en el 77?" (1984; Where were you in 1977?), included a song evoking the decadence of Avenida de la Luz in 1984 before it was closed.

> Avenida de la Luz
> Es un buen lugar para acabar borracheras.
> El *Heartbreak hotel* de mi ciudad.
> El mito de ciudad sumergida,
> a estas horas se vuelve real.
> Estás solo, date cuenta, estás solo.
> Avenida de la luz, no me mires con piedad.
> Voy cegado por la luz de mi libre soledad.

....
Avenida de la luz, el desierto empieza aquí. (Trogloditas)

(Avenue of Light / / It is a good place to stop drinking. / The heartbreak hotel in my city. / The myth of a submerged city, / at this time it becomes real. / You are alone, you must realize, you're alone. / Avenue of Light, do not look at me with pity. / I'm blinded by the light of my free loneliness. / … / Avenue of Light, the desert begins here.)

Echoing the emphasis on solitude and the end of love in Elvis Presley's song "Heartbreak Hotel," Loquillo stresses a blinding solitude at night and the fact that it encapsulates a submerged city, two of the main oxymoronic elements in the disappeared space: an avenue of light underneath the city, darkness under earth.[6]

The first paragraph of a short prose piece by Pere Gimferrer evokes fluorescent light as a mark of difference between two metro systems. Comparing FGC and the metro, he evokes the subway experience as a moment of serenity in a hurried city life, focusing particularly on noise and the sense of imprisonment associated with travelling under the earth. The disparity in terms of lighting seems to refer to the connecting corridor between FGC and Gran Metro where Avenida de la Luz was once located:

Tot, al contrari, és, per definició, fosquedat i vida lucífuga, i claror neutra de clínica amb llums de neó si deixem l'àmbit del tren de Sarrià i ens endinsem a l'immens coval del Metro. És ací, verament, la caverna orba i remota, el ventrell fosc de la ciutat, els pulmons que esbufeguen en la negror soterrada. Lloc de passadissos immensos, on la gernació, espessa, flueix en silenci, sense cridòria, a un ritme igual, només amb una fressa constant de passos que bressen l'oïda. (Gimferrer 329)

(Everything, however, is by definition life by light and darkness, light and neutral neon clinical atmosphere when we leave the Sarrià railway area and enter the immense Metro cave. It is here, indeed, the blind and remote stomach of the dark city, lungs that puff in underground darkness. A place with immense corridors, where a thick crowd flows quietly, without shouting, at a steady pace, with a constant noise of steps that sings to the ear.)

The emphasis here is on illumination. The underground city is perceived as the bowels of a body, with the masses moving mechanically in silence, echoing images from Fritz Lang's *Metropolis*.

Figure 13. Avenida de la Luz (Avenue of Light), 1940

Figure 14. Sephora Store, 2013 @Enric Bou 2013

Gabriel Ferrater's poem "Amistat del braç" (Arm's friendship) evokes the unexpected promiscuity created during a subway ride. Of some attention is his metric choice (ten-syllable lines), which creates a sturdy rhythm, and how he expresses the heinous nature of inexperience and poor sensitivity by a young man, the voice in the poem. The allusion to the noise he hears when the carriage stops, breaking the sleepiness of the absent-minded protagonist:

El metro anava ple. Jo m'agafava
al barrot niquelat vora la porta.
Tenia el braç tibat, i tolerava
aquell pes tebi, persistent, a l'avantbraç.
Quedàvem poca gent quan vaig girar-me.
Era molt jove. Lletja i pobra, descarnada,
com una prima cabra mogrebina
que premia amb el front, tancant els ulls,
abalançada per tota carència,
un braç encara de ningú, lliure i promiscu,
i no veia que ja algú es reprenia
i s'isolava al seu davant. Jo, massa jove
també, no havia après a reconèixer-me
en l'acceptació més que en la tria.
Vaig abandonar el braç, que no fos meu,
i no els vaig mirar més, anguniat
fins a l'estació, i el súbit trenc
d'una corda del cello, la més baixa. (*Les dones* 46)

(The subway was packed. I was grabbing / the handrail by the door. / I had my arm tightened, and I endured / that warm, persistent weight on my forearm. / There were few people left when I turned around. / She was very young. Ugly and poor, emaciated, / like a thin Maghreb goat / pressing with her front, her eyes closed, / leaning without energy, / one arm still free and promiscuous / and she did not realize that someone was already standing up / and he was isolating himself in front of her. I was too young / and I had not learned to recognize myself / in the acceptance rather than choice. / I left that arm, which was not mine, / and I did not look at them any more, distressed / until we reached the station, and the sudden noise / of a cello string, the lowest one.)

In the poem one can detect an echo of Baudelaire's "À une passante" (To a passerby), but more precisely of Jaime Gil de Biedma's poem "Amistad a lo largo" (Lasting friendship). The cello sound indicates the train's sudden stop, but also it may indicate a significant break experienced by the protagonist when the described situation occurs, because it interrupts the natural flow in the relationship of the protagonist with others and in particular with young women, breaking away from innocence. Through the final metaphor, "the poem becomes the formulation of an emblematic youth experience" (Cornudella 43) and also of a moment of uncertainty and separation. The metro passenger car is used as an unexpected setting for proximity and intimacy combined with distance and unfamiliarity. It is a very familiar situation: a young man travelling in a packed metro car realizes that somebody is leaning against his arm. When the train reaches the final stop, the young man realizes that it is a young woman, "ugly and poor, emaciated," who with her eyes closed (half asleep?) in front of him creates this unforeseen intimate contact. Because of the young woman's nature ("like a thin Maghreb goat"), we may infer that the poet evokes an encounter with a prostitute in a vanished metro stop, Fernando, at the heart of Barcelona's infamous red-light district, Barrio Chino. Ferrater's poem transforms the everyday, focusing on an event that could not have occurred in the streets above ground and that relates to the idea of the underground as "the physical and conceptual trash heap of the modern world above" (Pike, *Subterranean Cities* 5).

Vanished metro stations are related to readability and maps. They belong to a different category of city design, a conceptualization of the city that creates new senses and realities. Moreover, vanished metro stations belong to the reign of ruins, and they should be related to a sort of recuperation of the Renaissance's attraction for ruins. Brian Dillon has examined the twentieth-century ruin as the preserve of countless urban explorers and enthusiasts of decaying concrete who show their obsession in countless websites devoted to haunted asylums, silent foundries, vacant bunkers, and amputated subway stations. He explains that "[t]he ruin … seems almost a means of mourning the loss of the aesthetic itself" (6). Abandoned metro stations are ruins of an industrial past, a result of extremely expensive decisions in city planning that came to sticky ends, and ghosts of forgotten spaces below earth that politicians and city-branding experts alike love to forget. They are witnesses to a way of life that has already disappeared, traces of former everyday activities. Maybe it is literature (and cinema) that remains one of the ways of preserving a forgotten past and consequently giving an account of disappearance and creating a catalogue of everyday life activities and locations. They are thresholds that help explain the transformation of underground urban space.

Mythological Views of Metro Riding

The sheer amount of literature, film, and popular music devoted to depicting the metro-riding experience is truly impressive (Pike, *Subterranean Cities*; Ashford). I am especially interested in one manner of depiction that opens a threshold of a different nature: evocations of the subjective experience that takes place during a metro ride, in particular the comparisons with mythological situations in an obvious effort to uplift the banality of the situation.[7] The use of classical mythology to elevate such an everyday activity is noteworthy. It could be linked to the way in which early railways cloaked their novelty in classical garb (Pike, *Subterranean Cities* 36), and it is a reminder of the vertical structure of modern technology and ancient mythology (Williams 67). Many texts about travelling by public transportation focus on the fact that they are short journeys in the company of strangers, thus emphasizing anonymity, the combination of bright lights in stations with the darkness of tunnels, the monotony of the journey, and the scrutiny of fellow travellers, as well as reading, sleeping, and daydreaming. David Welsh indicated two main themes of such travel: "the *infernal,* in which the subterranean railway was perceived as a form of hell, abyss or underworld; and secondly, the utopian, in which the underground helps to integrate the modern metropolis by offering new freedoms" (qtd. in Ashford 2).

Catalan avant-garde author Joan Salvat-Papasseit devoted several poems to the experience of tram and metro riding from a futurist perspective (Gavagnin 207). His emphasis is on limited space and time, that of the short travel, chance encounters, and observation of female fellow passengers. Salvat is fascinated by the mixing of futurist industrial objects and the everyday, which provides a unique perspective to observe and suffer modernity. Eroticism always plays a role in Salvat's poetry. A poem such as "Bitllet de quinze" (Fifteen ticket) finishes with a surprise: a breastfeeding woman squirts a passenger with milk. The observation from an almost voyeuristic perspective dominates the suspicions generated by the observation of the "girl of the tram":

Que les cames se't veuen
i la mitja és ben fina;
i tot el tram ets tu.
Però els ulls no se't veuen. (*Obra completa* 147)

(I see the legs / and the pantyhose is very thin; / and you become the entire tram / But one cannot see your eyes.)

The title of the poem "54045" refers to the palindromic ticket number, a sign of good luck. He combines a double cubist perspective – exterior and interior – evoking the experience of travelling by tram with attention to the details of the route (Arc de Triomf) and the presence of figures of control (inspector and ticket collector). These figures provoke anxiety and discomfort, dispelling his condition of anonymity in the crowd.

This kind of approach to the experience of public transportation becomes the centre of two similar poems written in Paris, linked to the metro there. The fact that Barcelona did not have a metro until 1924 explains why, when Salvat visited Paris in 1921, he reacted with such eagerness, writing these two poems.[8] Interestingly, he rides the Nord–Sud, which was central to the avant-garde activities linking Montmartre and Montparnasse. The line's name was borrowed by Reverdy for an avant-garde review (Pike, *Subterranean Cities* 64). The poems by Salvat are "Passional al metro reflex n.° 1" (Pasional on the subway reflection no. 1) and "La femme aux oranges reflex n.° 2" (Woman with oranges reflection no. 2), included in *L'irradiador del port i les gavines* (1921; The port radiator and the seagulls). In the first one he uses exactly the same terms as in "54045" to describe the passenger car as a mythological monster with a powerful sexuality, personified by Priapus, the god of fertility. "La dinamo turgent mou els príaps de foc" (*Obra completa* 60; The roaring engine moves the fiery Priapus) in "54045" becomes "Antinous donzell príap perdut" (72; Antinous a young lost Priapus). By metonymy and apposition he names a young lover in the metro, alluding to priapism and sexual arousal provoked by a female rider, Penelope. In the poem he describes a seduction between Antinous and Penelope that culminates when Penelope does not pay attention to her clothing and Antinous eats a rose right at the moment that the metro is under the Seine river: "justament en passant sota la serp del Sena direcció Saint-Lazare" (72; right under the Seine's snake in the direction of Saint Lazare). Completing the sexual connotations of the character's name (from the *Odyssey*) and priapism, the river is perceived as a snake. In the second poem the poet's lover rides the metro, sings what the poet calls the "metro song," and performs a striptease under the earth according to different metro stations, thus indicating a movement or a ride in the line Nord–Sud:

I així la meva amada
ve assetjada a desdir:
Per això és que baixa a Rennes
es deixa la cotilla a Saint Michel,
i s'ajeu al meu bany de purpurina.
Banyera del NORD-SUD! (Salvat-Papasseit, *Obra completa* 73)

(And thus my lover / is harassed: / That's why she steps out at Rennes / leaves her corset at Saint Michel / and lies down in my glittery bathroom. / Bathtub of the NORD–SUD!)

When the song ends, she shows her breasts to the other passengers. It is remarkable that Salvat includes, in the middle of the sentence, the name of a metro station, Château d'Eau, which is part of the Nord–Sud line, and at the same time introduces the idea of squirting:

Finava la cançó quan la *femme aux oranges*, direcció
Château d'Eau, s'ha descobert la brusa i ha ensenyat els
mugrons
que eren com una llàntia de cremell. (*Obra completa* 73)

(When the song was ending, the *femme aux Oranges*, direction / Château d'Eau, has unbuttoned her blouse and shown her / nipples / they were like a wax candle.)

In both poems an intimate scene between the lovers is depicted in a very public space. They are inscribed in a series, and they suggest another situation of the everyday that is noticeable in metro riding: the stark contrast between private and public, eye seduction, the creation of traces of our movements under earth that are not recognizable from the exterior. The movement of the metro, associated with the snake river, has strong sexual connotations.

Julio Cortázar's short story "Manuscrito hallado en un bolsillo" (Manuscript found in a pocket) focuses on the possibility of a communication being established after a slight touch between two passengers. His story seems to develop Marc Augé's sentence according to which on the metro "we constantly brush up against the history of others … without ever meeting it" (*In the Metro* 10), developing a story based on the inability to establish communication with other fellow passengers due to a self-imposed set of rules linked to the subway's system of connections and coincidences.

Finally I will briefly discuss a few examples of texts that use the metro-riding situation as a metaphorical evocation of the harshness in life. T.S. Eliot's poem "East Coker," section 2 in *Four Quartets*, contains a reference to subway riding as a descent into the underworld (Ashford): "Or as, when an underground train, in the tube, stops too long between stations / And the conversation rises and slowly fades into silence / And you see behind every face the mental emptiness deepen / Leaving only the growing terror of nothing to think about" (Eliot).

Written during the Second World War, the poem discusses stopped time in an unknown place, in complete darkness. The presence of silence, the stress on emptiness, with a moment of terror, is remarkable: "nothing to think about." As stated by Atkins, the speaker of "East Coker" is "in darkness, lacking a firm 'foothold,' approaching an abyss, and all the while menaced by enchantments and alluring lights" (34).[9] Eliot inspired Spanish poet Carlos Barral when he wrote his poem *Metropolitano*. According to a critic he wrote it "como poema unitario cuyos temas están ordenados según un sistema de acumulación, de recurrencia de ciertas sensaciones de la experiencia urbana" (Barral 33; as a single poem whose topics are organized according to an accumulation system, a recurrence of the urban experience sensations). Poems such as "Portillo automático" (Automatic gate) show from different angles the gap between vital rhythm and chronological time, the mutual incomprehension of the sexes, inequality, and partition caused by existence and the awareness of disaster (Barral 33). In the poem Barral depicts metaphorically the Paris metro's *portillon*:

Y luego que el portillo se ha cerrado,
Después de sumergidos,
Cuando pasan las alas y nos rozan
Que reconozco su metal tan cerca,
Entonces, cuando,
        ahora, casi
en este momento, se producen
los primeros peldaños, la avenida
que lleva de uno a otro bajo el mundo. (Barral 92)

(And when the gate is closed, / After immersed, / When the wings pass and rub us / I recognize their metal so close, / So when, / Now, almost / at this time, materialize / the first steps, the avenue / taking from one to another under the world.)

Similarly, Narcís Comadira in *Un passeig pels bulevards ardents* (1973; A walk by the burning boulevards) uses two versions of the metropolis (London) that are told in a sequence of narrative and textual displacements, in a texture that tends towards collage. He describes with detail the closing of the doors and peeping at your neighbour's newspaper at the time of the 1973 oil crisis:

Van tancar-se amb neguit les portes corredores,
darrere les muralles protegíem

somnis encara dolços de llençols,
olor de matinada, de taronja,
esma i instint i basarda de llum.

El dolar s'ensorrava entre tipografies.
Cada pausa era un surt a la memòria,
cada rostre un parany, cada ull, estrany,
esfumats pensaments i pells boiroses,
només mitges paraules. Tanca't, tanca't
al món com una porta corredora. (Comadira 18)

(The sliding doors drew shut uneasily, / Behind the walls we clung to / Dreams still soft from sheets, / A morning smell, the scent of oranges, / Instinct, sixth sense, the fear of light. / The dollar collapsed among the small print. / Each pause was a jolt to memory, / Each face a snare, each eye a stranger, / Blurred thoughts and foggy skins, / Only half-words. Shut out, shut out / The world as with a sliding door.)[10]

Comadira evokes the moment in early morning, feeling loneliness in the crowd, and establishes a neat correspondence between the sliding doors (metro and world) as a metaphor of oppression. In the final lines of the first section he escapes through the escalator, reaching for light, abandoning a place where human beings are only shadows.

In the novel *Los mares del sur* (1979; The southern seas) Manuel Vázquez Montalbán introduces an elaborate description of fellow passengers on a metro line that reaches the outskirts of the city. With painstaking precision he describes the lower classes packed in a metro carriage: "El metro, cualquier metro, es una animal resignado a su esclavitud de subsuelo. Parte de esa resignación impregna los rostros aplazados de los viajeros, teñidos por una luz utilitaria, removidos levemente por el vaivén circular de la máquina aburrida" (110; The subway, any subway, is an animal resigned to its underground slavery. Part of that resignation permeates the deferred faces of the travellers, tinged by a utilitarian light, slightly stirred by the circular swaying of the dull machine). For the main character in the novel, riding the underground again implies a travel in time, going back in time, and visiting his humble origins:

Recuperar el metro fue recuperar la sensación de joven fugitivo que contempla con menosprecio la ganadería vencida, mientras él utiliza el metro como un instrumento para llegar al esplendor en la hierba y la promoción. Recordaba su cotidiana sorpresa joven ante tanta derrota recién amanecida. Recordaba la conciencia de su propia singularidad y excelencia rechazando la náusea que parecía envolver la mediocre vida de los viajeros. Los veía como molestos compañeros de un viaje que para él era la ida y para ellos de vuelta. Veinte o veinticinco años después sólo era capaz de sentir solidaridad y miedo. Solidaridad con el viejo barbado de tres días y vestido con traje bicolor, con una mano enganchada al skay pringoso de un portafolios lleno de letras protestadas. Solidaridad con las cúbicas mujeres samoyedas que amurcianaban una incoherente conversación sobre el cumpleaños de tía Encarnación. Solidaridad con tanto niño pobre y pulcro llegado tarde al obsoleto tren emancipador de la cultura. Ejercicios del lenguaje. Diccionario Anaya. Muchachas disfrazadas de Olivia Newton-John, en el supuesto caso de que Olivia se vistiera aprovechando las liquidaciones fin de temporada de grandes almacenes de extrarradio. Muchachos con máscara de chulos de discoteca y músculos de condenados al paro. Y a veces la reconfortante osamenta de un subejecutivo de inmobiliaria con el coche averiado y el propósito de utilizar transportes públicos para adelgazar y ahorrar para medios whiskies de mediana calidad, servidos por un insuficiente camarero con caspa y uñas negras sin otro encanto que saber llamarle a tiempo don Roberto o señor Ventura. El miedo a ser todos víctimas de un mediocre y fatal de la pobreza a la nada. (Vázquez Montalbán, *Los mares* 109–10)

(To go back to the subway was to recover the feeling of a young fugitive who looks down on the defeated livestock, while he uses the subway as an instrument to reach the splendour in the grass and promotion. He remembered his daily youthful surprise at so much freshly dawned defeat. He remembered the awareness of his own uniqueness and excellence rejecting the nausea that seemed to envelop the mediocre life of the commuters. He saw them as annoying companions on a journey that for him was the outward journey and for them the return. Twenty or twenty-five years later he was only able to feel solidarity and fear. Solidarity with the three-day-old-bearded old man in a two-tone suit, one hand hooked on the smeary imitation leather of a briefcase full of protested bills. Solidarity with the cubic Samoyed women who amurciated an incoherent conversation about Aunt Encarnación's birthday. Solidarity with so many poor and neat children who arrived late to the obsolete emancipating train of culture. Language exercises. Anaya dictionary. Girls disguised as Olivia Newton-John, in the event that Olivia dressed up by taking advantage of the end-of-season sales at department stores in the suburbs. Guys with masks of disco pimps and muscles of the doomed unemployed. And sometimes the comforting bones of a real estate sub-executive with a broken-down car and the intention of using public transport to lose weight and save for medium-quality whiskies, served by an insufficient waiter with dandruff and black nails with no other charm than knowing how to call him Don Roberto or Mr Ventura in time. The fear of being all victims of a mediocre and fatal trip from poverty to nothingness.)

It is a sub-world, dirty, that reminds of public restrooms, where the masses of riders move like a machine, according to one written scenario:

> El mundo era un paisaje de estaciones semejantes a retretes sucios recubiertos por azulejos tiznados por la invisible suciedad de la electricidad subterránea y de los alientos agrios de las masas. La gente que subía y bajaba parecía cumplir el ritual de un relevo previamente acordado para justificar el rutinario ajetreo de la máquina. (Vázquez Montalbán, *Los mares* 110)
>
> (The world was a landscape of stations resembling dirty toilets covered with tiles stained by the invisible filth of subway electricity and the sour breaths of the masses. The people getting on and off seemed to fulfil the ritual of a prearranged relay to justify the routine hustle and bustle of the machine.)

The monotony and vulgarity of the space can be redeemed in other cases. Gimferrer also uses classic mythology in converting the metro-riding experience into a metaphorical evocation of the harshness in life. In "La vida subterrània" (Life underground), included in his *Dietari complet*, he points to the mechanical aspects of metro carriages surrounding the rider in a terrible noise that creates numbness. He also draws a fundamental distinction between the underworld and the surface: the prevalence of darkness and the shocking encounter with light when one reaches the street. It is a way of portraying one significant aspect in the view from below (Pike, *Subterranean Cities* 11):

> Però ja som en un vagó i hi ha un brunziment rítmic de pistons i carrils, èmbols i rodes; el metall, fent espurnes, colpeja, ràpid, el metall, i ens atueix els sentits aquest ressò fondíssim. Perdem, talment en un avió, la mesura del temps i de l'espai; cada cop ens serà, després, una sorpresa la claror sobtada del carrer. (Gimferrer 329)
>
> (But we're in a car and there is a rhythmic sound of pistons and rails, valves and wheels; metal, producing sparks, hits, fast, metal, and this way the deep sound sleeps us. We lose, as in a plane, the sense of time and space, and every time the sudden light of the street surprises us.)

The vertical aspect of metro riding is suggested through the association with flying in an airplane and losing sense of time and space. Gimferrer also points to the mythological characterization of the underworld by making associations with Roman mythology and Greek philosophy with references to Proserpina and Plato:

> El viatge – com si haguéssim davallat al dominis de Proserpina, o tal vegada a la caverna de Plató – hauria hagut de purificar-nos. En el silenci individual – silenci de la vida personal de cadascú, suspensió momentània, en un parèntesi – aquests minuts, amb la vastedat del brogit de les locomotores subterrànies colpint, velocíssimes, la foscor del túnel, ens donen el que la vida diària ens estalvia sovint: un lleure per meditar sobre el lloc de l'home en el cicle còsmic, que alhora l'enclou, l'envolta i li és extern. (Gimferrer 329)
>
> (The trip – as we had fallen in the domains of Proserpina, or perhaps Plato's cave – should have purified us. In individual silence – silence in the personal life of each one of us, in a momentarily suspended parenthesis – these minutes, with the vast roar of the engines hitting at great speed the underground tunnel's darkness, give us what daily life often spares us from: a leisure to meditate on man's place in the cosmic cycle, that at the same time encompasses, surrounds and is external to him.)

Thanks to the references to Proserpina's underworld and Plato's cave, the subway-riding experience is elevated to a more sophisticated level, and we can understand why the metro can be an unlikely refuge for a philosophical meditation about the place of human beings in the universe. Proserpina introduces the association with the underworld realm. With her mother, Ceres, along with the springtime growth of crops and the cycle of life, she refers to death and rebirth, or renewal. There is also a contradiction between public and private space, the world over and under the city. Gimferrer's metro ride adapts a heroic allure, achieving a rare success: finding a very public and noisy place in which there is room for metaphysical meditation. As stated by Williams, "the subterranean environment is a technological one – but it is also a mental landscape, a social terrain, and an ideological map" (21). Gimferrer's prose acknowledges and combines all three environments. Both authors provide a glimpse into instances of disappearance (privacy, quietness) through the mixing of private and public spaces, or linking aspects of the vertical city.

Conclusion

Imagery of the underground is grouped into two distinct yet complementary categories: "a discourse of segregation and elimination, and a discourse of incorporation and recycling" (Pike, *Metropolis* 6). Although

Pike applies this categorization to nineteenth-century London and Paris, it still bears some truth in the case of Barcelona, with its backwardness and late arrival to modernity, and the authors discussed here exemplify both trends. Paying attention to the metro-riding experience leads one to reflect upon the disappearance of buried and forgotten urban spaces. In fact, one must reflect on the rapidity with which urban space evolves in contemporary cities, which only adds to the unravelling of memories that the city space evokes and the ways in which it affects everyday life, changing imperceptibly how we are in the world and how we relate to our environment. Zoë Thompson has stated that "the aesthetics of disappearance is intrinsically linked to the aesthetics of change as urban spaces evolve" (162). Unravelling hidden spaces, and their presence in a physical and emotional network, helps to create a map of the city and of its inhabitants' past, exploring space and becoming witness of the changes in everyday life. The awareness of the metro maps introduced by the songs examined, the attention to hidden and disappeared underground spaces in other texts, and the drive to connect the metro experience with mythological references all are crucial components in the cartography of disappearance.

The topics discussed here are fragmentary thresholds that reflect the real underground city, one constructed with uncertainties and errors. We have observed instances of misreading, disappearance, and transformation through mythological references that portray a hidden map under the visible city. As cartography is more than a selected list of names and their connecting coloured lines, Barcelona's metro map can be read in different ways, thus providing a different portrait of the city. Metro maps and rides create an unusual sense of time and an unusual way of reading the underground and its relationship with the surface. The underground is a special setting for everyday life in which communications and human interaction acquire a different status. The legibility of the metro map belies a problematic way of reading. It is only in attending to the metro's hidden meanings that we may fully understand the map, thus catching a glimpse of our past and present everyday.

7

Forms of Thanatourism: José Pla and Josep M. Espinàs

Tenho visto alguma coisa do mundo, e apontando alguma coisa do que vi. De todas quantas viagens porém fiz, as que mais me interessaram sempre foram as viagens na minha terra.

(I've seen something of the world, and I'm writing down some of what I've seen. Of all the journeys I've made, the ones that have always interested me the most have always been the journeys in my homeland.)

Almeida Garrett, *Viagens na minha terra*

Viele werke der Alten sind Fragmenten geworden. Viele werke der Neuern sind es gleich bei der Entstehung.

(Many works of the ancients have become fragments. Many of the works of the newcomers are like this when they are created.)

Friedrich Schlegel, *Charakteristiken und Kritiken*

Space Mapping

Human beings relate to the space that surrounds them, projecting in their mind an intellectualization of what they see, what they experience. The physical reality, the dimensions sent by the senses (primarily sight), become a mental projection. When it comes to dealing with space, humans do so from two complementary perspectives: one narrative, the other schematic. When we have to explain to someone how to get from one point to another, we do it with a list of instructions (go right, turn left, etc.) or with a sketch of the movements to follow on a map. They are but metaphors that help us read the world. A technical word like *odology*, derived from *hodos*, a Greek word meaning "road, path, journey," is very useful in referring to our relationship with the physical environment. The word comes from an experimental psychologist, Kurt Lewin, who used it to characterize the "lived space," that is, the space in which an individual lives or the space as it is perceived by the user. This space is opposed to the geometric space of maps and plans, to the rational and homogeneous, measurable Euclidean space. Odology prefers walking more than the path walked, the sense of geography more than metric calculation. Human beings struggle between two desires: to settle or belong somewhere and to find a new field of action elsewhere (Careri). This opposition of spaces expresses the debate between permanence and mobility, between living in one's own country and living in exile.

These two attitudes can be compared to the two different approaches to visiting a city that Miguel Tamen proposed in "A Walk about Lisbon." One possibility, "feeling the atmosphere," involves just walking and looking. The other is the aesthetic obligation of the tourist who walks around with a list of things to visit and that serves as a measure of the success of the trip. The ineffable and infallible *Michelin Guide* proposes a star system, which has become a lodestar for tourists, with a description of the obligations of what to do in each place they visit (Tamen 35). In many writers' work we recognize an internal struggle between aimless walking and stability. Writers such as Ramón Gómez de la Serna and Joan Maragall were aware of their vital space throughout their lives – rooted in one place, in Madrid, Buenos Aires, or Barcelona, but always looking for new horizons. At the rhythm of personal passions and political crises, they adapted to their environment and gradually modified the way in which they experienced space and manifested it in their literary works.

Francesco Careri's book provides some of the coordinates for a cartography of urban space from the perspective of the walker. In *Walkspaces: El andar como práctica estética* (2002; Walkspaces: Walking as an aesthetic practice), Careri affirms that it is in the twentieth century that walking has acquired the status of a pure aesthetic act. His thesis is that a history of walking can be constructed as a form of urban intervention, which contains the symbolic meanings of the primary creative act: "roaming as architecture of the landscape, where the term *landscape* indicates the action of symbolic as well as physical transformation of anthropic space" (20).

We can distinguish three significant moments, perfectly homologated, of transformation in the history of art whose turning point has been an experience related to walking. Careri indicates the transition from Dadaism to surrealism (1921–4), the transition from the Letterist International to the Situationist International (1956–7), and the transition of minimalism to land art (1966–7). Following this chronological precision, it is possible to distinguish ways of travelling through urban space that in turn generate a conception of it: the banal city of Dada and the unconscious and dreamlike city of the surrealists; the playful and nomadic city of the Situationists; and Robert Smithson's Entropic City. If the entropologist is the dissolution scientist, his work must confront that of the encyclopedist. While one builds structures and systems, the other maps the process and studies the signs of its disintegration.

Lévi-Strauss drew up the basic rules of discipline. The more complex the cultural organization of a society, the more entropy it produces. The more developed the structure, the greater its disintegration. Thus, while "primitive" or "cold" societies (whose mechanism Lévi-Strauss compared to that of a clock) produced little or no entropy, "hot" societies (assimilated to combustion engines) produced enormous quantities (Charbonnier).

Thus, the modes of appropriation of urban space would include Anti-Walk, associated with Dada activities, which in 1921 organized a series of "visit-excursions" in Paris to the most banal places in the city. In 1924 the Parisian Dadaists also organized a wandering in the open country. Then they discovered a dreamlike and surreal component in their walk and defined this experience as a "wandering," a kind of automatic writing in real space capable of revealing the unconscious areas of space and the dark parts of the city.[1] In the 1950s Letterist International developed the "Theory of the Dérive" (drift). The Land Walk began in 1966, when *Artforum Magazine* published the story of Tony Smith's journey on a highway under construction. Land art is a reworking through the journey of the archaic origins of landscaping. In 1967 Robert Smithson finished *A Tour of the Monuments of Passaic*.

These new ways of dealing with space can be summarized as "transurbancia" (transurbance). The reading of the current city from the point of view of wandering is based on the "transurbances" carried out by Stalker in some European cities from 1995. Between the folds of the city, spaces of transit have grown; they are territories in constant transformation over time. In these territories it is possible to overcome the millenary separation between nomadic spaces and sedentary spaces. Careri states: "Actually, nomadism has always existed in osmosis with settlement, and today's city contains nomadic spaces (voids) and sedentary spaces (solids) that exist side by side in a delicate balance of reciprocal exchange. Today the nomadic city lives inside the stationary city, feeding on its scraps and offering, in exchange, its own presence as a new nature that can be crossed only by inhabiting it" (24). This allows us to adopt a flexible and open attitude towards the limited conception of urban space, admitting the complexity of the concurrent nomadic and sedentary nature.

Portuguese author Cardoso Pires walks the city of Lisbon and writes a book echoing the narrative entitled *Der Spaziergang* (1919; *The Walk*), by Robert Walser. As he walks, Walser alternates reflections and considerations about himself, the environment around him, literature, and the people he knows with dialogues with other characters. Walser considered himself to be a professional walker: "In short: thinking, scrutinizing, digging, mistreating, reflecting, writing, researching, researching, and walking, I earn my daily bread as hard as anyone" (69) Amato stated: "Walking establishes intimate contact with place. It attaches us to a landscape – its trees, rocks, hills, and riverbanks. It makes us in good measure the streets and paths we walk. It puts us in contact with local communities. Walking coagulates time, expands distance, and makes places dense and prickly with details and complexities. It expands and defends localities against the reductionism and systematization of roads, commerce, government, and mass culture. It makes the case for individual localities in an era of rampant globalism" (*On Foot* 276).

Cardoso Pires evokes the district of Chiado, which represents the environment to which the author belongs. His personal involvement in the comment on the fire that ravaged this neighbourhood in 1988 is evident:

> Hoje, quando atravesso esse rosto corrompido de Lisboa vejo-o como uma ferida aberta na nossa memória coletiva. Mais ainda: é um pouco da memória de mim mesmo que ficou destroçada porque também eu subi o Chiado em diferentes idades dos meus livros e com amigos de diferentes gerações. Assim, por mais rápida que seja a cicatrização destas paredes fantasmas, sei que ficará para sempre um fumo, uma sombra dolorosa a Largo do Carmo enquanto cenário da revolução, coração de uma Lisboa que finalmente tinha caído nas mãos do povo, que se tinha apropriado das ruas para fazer delas «o palco da hora que libertou um país». (Cardoso Pires 71)

> (Today, when I cross that corrupted face of Lisbon I see it as an open wound in our collective memory. Even more: it is a bit of the memory of myself that has been shattered because I too have walked up Chiado at different ages in my books and with friends of different generations. So, no matter how quickly these ghost walls heal, I know that there will forever remain a smoke, a painful shadow of Largo do Carmo as the scene of the revolution, the heart of a Lisbon that had finally fallen into the hands of the people, who had appropriated the streets to make them "the stage of the hour that freed a country.")

In 2000 Rebecca Solnit published *Wanderlust: A History of Walking*, an incomplete account of the topic she was trying to cover but nevertheless an insightful reflection on contemporary walking, particularly in the United States, where suburban culture has substituted walking for the home treadmill. Her account is also incomplete because she does not pay any attention to the strong tradition, that of German walkers and naturalists who account for a substantial amount of walking and travel literature. Thus, she does not include the German term *Fernweh*, which can be translated as "nostalgia for distance," a common expression in German that describes the human desire to leave the known circumstances (of everyday life) and open up to the vast outside world. The word *Fernweh* literally stands for the opposite of *Heimweh* (nostalgia), the desire for the homeland or home.

In this chapter I cover a special version of *Fernweh*, the one that brings you to nearby realities, which are observed as if they were distant ones. We could consider a famous book by Almeida Garrett, *Viagens na minha terra* (1846), as one of the first expeditions to explore the nearest reality in Iberian literature. This is a mixed work, fundamental to building a Portuguese national identity, because it tells of the author's journey to the Portugal of his time. It is an internalized landscape from which arise many historical or fantastic episodes related to themes that the author expresses: the violence of the war, the hoax of the gothic novel, and the anti-religious criticism about the parasitism of the friars. It is no coincidence that Garrett's book opens with a significant epigraph, a quotation from Xavier de Maistre's book *Voyage autour de ma chambre* (1794): "Qu'il est glorieux d'ouvrir une nouvelle carrière, et de paraitre tout-à-coup dans le monde savant un livre de découvertes à la main, comme une comète inattendue étincelle dans espace!" (6; How glorious it is to open a new career, and to appear suddenly in the scholarly world with a book of discoveries in hand, like an unexpected comet sparkling in space!). On the one hand, the *Voyage autour de ma chambre* clearly parodies the published accounts of great travellers of the eighteenth century in its proposal to describe a journey of discovery through the apparently non-exceptional and banal reality of the everyday; and on the other hand, it is similarly connected to the well-developed genre of the imaginary journey that tended to present wonderful, often allegorical and dreamlike places and inhabitants, whose exoticism is in stark contrast to the setting of the book by De Maistre. Lawrence Sterne had previously used the example of *Don Quijote* to warn about the stupidity of travelling to unknown places: "I am of opinion, That a man would act as wisely, if he could prevail upon himself, to live contented without foreign knowledge or foreign improvements, especially if he lives in a country that has no absolute want of either – and indeed, much grief of heart has it oft and many a time cost me, when I have observed how many a foul step the inquisitive Traveller has measured to see sights and look into discoveries; all which, as Sancho Panza said to Don Quixote, they might have seen dry-shod at home" (244).

Most of Chinese travel literature was written to commemorate pleasure outings. An important variety refers to trips that are not physical but imaginary and made without reaching a real destination. The most important examples are *muyou* (eye travel), *shenyou* (spiritual travel), *xinling Zhi you* (mental travel), *woyou* (stretched travel, i.e., "travel from an armchair"), and *mengyou* (dream travel). These terms refer to a kind of imaginary roaming that takes place in a person's mind. There is a rich tradition of these works in China. The term *woyou* was coined by a famous painter, Zong Bing (375–443):

> He [Zong Bing] loved mountains and waterways, and delighted in excursions to faraway places. In the west he made his halting place Mount Lu in Jingzhou and on the south he climbed up Mount Heng. There he made himself a hut in the hope of following the example of the hermit [Shang] Ziping but instead fell ill and had to return to Jiangling. He said with a sigh: "I am old and ailing: I fear that I can no longer wander among famous mountains. Now I can purify my heart by contemplating the Dao, and do my roaming from my bed." All that he had visited he depicted in his chamber. (Wang 3)

A journey to proximity is comparable to the journey in an armchair. Bernd Stiegler has studied this type of travel, which may seem like an oxymoron because travelling requires us to leave home. Yet anyone who has been lost for hours in the descriptive pages of a novel or in the compelling images of a film knows the true feeling of having explored and experienced a different place or time without ever leaving home. Without the need to have a passport, to change currency, or to pass a security check, the luxury of travelling in an armchair is accessible to all of us. The type of trip that interests me is the one that is done in a dimension that resembles De Maistre's trip: the trip to one's own country. In room travel, as in the journey to proximity, there is a relationship with the concept formulated by Viktor Shklovsky on the theory of artistic estrangement, that is, the artist's vision of a common object from an unusual perspective. This is exactly what happens: we move away from apparently familiar spaces to observe them closely with the applied eye of an ethnologist, to explore them as if we were seeing them for the first time or to see them in a new light.[2] This kind of conceptualization was disseminated by Jean-Didier Urbain in books such as *Ethnologue mais pas trop*, where we read that the function of an ethnologist of proximity is to "éxotiser l'endotique": "la sémiologie sociale et culturelle de proximité serait ... ce voyage dans le présent permettant de débarquer sur un immense continent perdu attendant ses explorateurs, un monde invisible aux yeux de ses habitants, libre et inconnu par vacance de vigilance, d'intérêt ou de conscience de soi" (169–70; the social and cultural semiology of proximity would be ... this voyage in the present allowing one to disembark on an immense lost continent waiting for its explorers, a world invisible to the eyes of its inhabitants, free and unknown by vacancy of vigilance, of interest or of conscience of oneself). Using the opposition between endotic and exotic established by Georges Perec, we can recognize the strangeness in what we already know. Urbain's idea of "discovering" seeks what is obvious, adopting an explorer's attitude in our best-known environment. It is about relating nearby worlds:

> [L]e voyageur de l'immédiat est un entremetteur: un rencontreur des mondes. Ils les fait se rejoindre, se parler les uns les autres, voyant, par analogies, mises en abyme et autres correspondances, l'immense dans l'intime, l'immémorial dans l'éphémère, le lointain dans le proche, l'exotique dans le banal et du panorama dans le microscopique, à l'instar de Francis Ponge, qui voit un firmament dans un coquille d'huître. (Urbain 175)

> ([T]he traveller of the immediate is a matchmaker: a meeting of worlds. He makes them meet, talk to each other, seeing, by analogies, *mise en abyme* and other correspondences, the immense in the intimate, the immemorial in the ephemeral, the distant in the near, the exotic in the banal, and the panoramic in the microscopic, like Francis Ponge, who sees a firmament in an oyster shell.)

As we know, travelling has had educational value since ancient times. Between 1660 and 1840, the Grand Tour facilitated the knowledge of the classical and Renaissance world by the wealthy classes of northern Europe during a trip to Italy. The vast majority of travellers have been considered for their social origin, although they do not always know where they are and, when they come into contact with people and cultures other than their own, they never fully know the place they visit and always need the help of a guide. In a characteristic manoeuvre, being away from home accelerates the interaction with the other, the observation of lands, habits, exotic languages, allowing the traveller to know himself better, without knowing at all, or only superficially, the place visited (Fussell; Leed; Pratt; Liebersohn). Things change radically when one is exploring neighbouring territories that are already known (Brenner; Buzard). Some of the romantic travellers such as Wordsworth in *Guide to the Lakes* (1810) and Pedro Antonio de Alarcón in *La Alpujarra: Sesenta leguas a caballo precedidas de seis en diligencia* (1874), instead of going in search of new discoveries or feeling attracted to afar destinations, often oriental, decided to do the opposite: discover the exotic in nearby places and recover medieval ruins. Seeking to preserve a national heritage, Baron Taylor wrote twenty-one volumes of *Voyages pittoresques et romantiques de l'ancenne France* (1821–78). Romanticism confirmed an interest in the medieval as a way of opposing the massive growth of cities and the birth of industrialism, and it claimed the exotic, the unknown, and the distant as the most authentic way of exploiting the power of the mind to imagine and escape from reality (C. Thompson). The romantic writers of the nineteenth century and Iberian writers of the 1960s fall into the two categories established by Kowalewski: "the authors may be celebrating the local and unfamiliar or – in a long tradition of social exploration – exposing and investigating conditions at home that most would prefer to ignore" (13). In these books the two categories detected by Kowalewski are highlighted: celebration and denunciation.

A travelogue is a literary form that does not easily accept classification, as it occurs at the crossroads of several genres. J. Chupeau stated: "La double nature – narrative et descriptive – du récit de voyage … révèle surtout l'ambiguïté d'un genre partagé entre les exigences souvent contradictoires de la documentation et du récit" (qtd. in Monga 50; the double nature – narrative and descriptive – of a travelogue … reveals the ambiguity of a literary genre divided between the contradictory needs of documentation and narration). In this kind of travelogue there is a need to incorporate graphic documents to illustrate the "foreignness" of everyday life. There is a certain juxtaposition of elements, as these experiences are very close to what James Clifford calls "the surrealist moment in ethnography," the moment in which it is possible to make comparisons in an "unmediated tension with sheer incongruity" (146).

I will analyse the case of two authors who explore nearby territories, areas of proximity – that is, their own country. They are Josep Pla and his *Viaje en autobús* and Josep M. Espinàs with his many examples of "viatge a peu" (journey on foot). Both authors agree on a rejection of faster and more modern forms of trasnport and provide manifestos in favour of slowness. To travel into one's own country was not invented by Josep Pla, who after the civil war and in the midst of the Second World War did not have many places left to visit. Before him, particularly during Romanticism, many writers had done this. What is remarkable in the case of Pla is that in his first postwar trip he used an established narrative form to explore with closed eyes, to see what he wanted to see, and to eliminate what was objectionable. His attempt is related to explorations of the country made by romantic writers, who are looking for ruins, as evoked by Novalis in a famous poem, "Ans Kloster in Ruinen": "Da liegst gefallen bist du nun, / Zerstöret mächtigern von der Zeit" (Novalis 469; There you lie now fallen / destroyed by the power of time).

Viaje en autobús is a key book in Pla's body of work because it was the first of his books to be published after the collapse following the civil war, and it implies the replacement of attention to cosmopolitanism by a peasant's world view. A beret replaces the elegant hat and thus becomes an effective synecdoche of blunt ideological transformation. Two of the most popular books published in the forties, *Viaje en autobús* (1942; Travel by bus) and *Viaje a pie* (1949; Travel on foot), correspond to Josep Pla's postwar autarkic attitude: travelling by bus or on foot implies a sort of critical return to the world of the traveller's origins.

Many travellers take an elegiac attitude. Susan Sontag observed that "[o]ne of the recurrent themes of modern travel narratives is the depredations of the modern, the loss of the past: the report on a society's decline" ("Model Destinations" 699). As noted by Paul Fussell, the traveller is between two extremes: the explorer seeking the unknown and the tourist seeking what has been packaged and wrapped for them with effective advertising. The true traveller is located between those extremes: "It is between these two poles that the traveller mediates, retaining all he can of the excitement of the unpredictable attaching to exploration, and fusing that with the pleasure of 'knowing where one is' belonging to tourism" (Fussell 39). Josep Pla did not discover anything new, but he confirmed what he already knew. His journey deals with celebration and atonement, observing disappeared forms of life, a world that no longer exists, but that after the war's upheaval seems to have re-emerged. It is a kind of journey into the past. And not only that. *Viaje en autobús* is a journey that is not a journey. It can be read as fragments of a visit to the ruins of the past, realizing Schlegel's assertion: "Many works of the ancients have become fragments. Many of the works of the newcomers are like this when they are created" (Schlegel 169). Some chapters were published in *La Publicitat* or *Destino* and reorganized later so that they made sense between the covers of a book. As always happens in the work of Pla, the book is a bric-a-brac with materials from different sources (Bonada 195; X. Pla "Introducción").

Readings of a Book

Several scholars have taken an interest in studying Josep Pla's book *Viaje en autobús*. Among them it is worth noting Santos Sanz Villanueva and his prologue to the 2003 Spanish edition, and an extensive, well-informed, and revealing article by Lluís Quintana (2007), which serves to highlight the evils of canon construction. He is interested in two aspects:

> Por un lado, la discusión acerca del lugar que ocupan, en la "cultura española" ... aquellos escritores que no escriben en castellano ... Por otro lado, la discusión acerca del lugar que ocupan, en el ámbito de las distintas literaturas, aquellos escritores que escriben en más de una lengua. Así, el desconcierto que produce presentar a Pla como escritor en castellano se debe, por una parte, a una consideración parcial y sesgada de lo que sea el hispanismo; y por la otra, al criterio restrictivo que tiene cada una de las literaturas, para las cuales un autor sólo puede pertenecer a una literatura. Pla no puede ser escritor en castellano porque la literatura en castellano (comúnmente denominada española) lo ha olvidado y porque la literatura en catalán (o catalana) lo ha retenido. (Quintana, "El *Viaje*" 122)

> (On the one hand, the discussion about the place is occupied, in "Spanish culture," ... by those writers who do not write in Spanish ... On the other hand, the discussion about the place is occupied, in the sphere of different literatures, by those writers who write in more than one language. Thus, the bewilderment produced by presenting Pla as a writer in Spanish is due, on the one hand, to a partial and biased consideration of what Hispanism is; and on the other hand, to the restrictive criteria of each of the literatures, of which an author can only belong to one. Pla cannot be a writer in Spanish because literature in Castilian (commonly called Spanish) has forgotten him and because literature in Catalan (or Catalan) has retained him.)

This paradox has an easy solution if one uses a polysystemic approach. But that is not what interests me here. *Viaje en autobús* was a real bestseller. According to Quintana (and partly Sanz Villanueva), the explanation for the book's success must be linked to Pla's political and social attitude adopted at that time. Quintana states that "es un libro sólida y fundamentalmente reaccionario. No fascista, pero reaccionario, quizá algo más radical que el 'profundo conservadurismo' que le encuentra Sanz Villanueva" ("El *Viaje*" 125; is a solidly and fundamentally reactionary book. Not fascist, but reactionary, perhaps somewhat more radical than the "deep conservatism" that Sanz Villanueva finds in it). Indeed, the book rebels beyond nostalgia and against progress, changes, and transformations, the desire of human beings to grow. Pla writes apropos of the republic and war without mentioning them: "Las Revoluciones ajan las cosas. En España, hoy, hasta los árboles parecen sobados y manoseados" (J. Pla, *Viaje en autobús* 12; Revolutions make things look worse. In Spain, today, even the trees look worn and manhandled). He compares the peasant's life, "frugal, virtuosa, sencilla" (163; frugal, virtuous, simple), with life in the big city in the chapter "La Maresma, suburbio" (La Maresma, suburb). A chapter that contradicts his own biography is impressive and amazing, "Las falsas ilusiones" (False illusions), in which he refers to a young peasant who studied in Barcelona. Gallofré said that another reason for the book's success is that under the most varied episodes there is always a constant, relentless complaint against the misery of the time: shortages, rationing, poor-quality products. Pla need not hide convictions. According to Sanz Villanueva, Pla's discourse has some key ideas that he keeps repeating: "la vida es un proceso difícilmente comprensible ...; la naturaleza es una fuerza amoral y ciega; la existencia está dominada por la circularidad del tiempo ...; la desigualdad es consustancial a la especie humana" (29; life is a process that is difficult to understand ...; nature is an amoral and blind force; existence is dominated by the circularity of time ...; inequality is consubstantial to the human species). Lluís Quintana pointed out yet a third factor that justifies the success of *Viaje en autobús*. In 1942 Catalonia was trying to recover, like the rest of Spain, from the disaster of the civil war, but it also had an identity problem. Catalans in exile, both abroad and within the region, knew well the identity they wanted: the one that had been taken from them and that they both continued to call "Catalanism." For Franco's Catalans, the problem was a bit more complicated: it was about building a new Catalonia, within the new Spain, and its intellectuals were trying difficult combinations that, in the long run, would prove useless. For Catalans who had supported Franco and also found his complicity with the Axis powers irresponsible and his furious anti-Catalanism unnecessary, that is, for people like the Destino group and its readers, the problem was even more difficult: "La solución más inmediata fue un difuso barcelonismo, sucedáneo muy rebajado del catalanismo, que tenía su correspondiente desarrollo en otros ámbitos del territorio, como son el Ampurdán y el Maresme en este libro" (Quintana, "El *Viaje*" 125; The most immediate solution was a diffuse Barcelonism, a very lowly substitute for Catalanism, which had its corresponding development in other areas of the territory, such as Empordà and Maresme in this book). In the words of Maria Josepa Gallofré, "barcelonisme" became a sign of identity, part of a manoeuvre of "reconstruction" (78). The opinions of the illustrious critics who have been interested in the book are partly right. But there is one aspect that I am interested in highlighting: reading it as a travel book and elucidating its main characteristics.

Invitation to a Trip

Viaje en autobús is deliberately timeless. The "cuatro palabras" that Pla set as prologue indicate the coordinates of space and the tastes of the trip proposed to the reader. The prologue works as some kind of author-reader agreement:

> Hasta ahora, he tenido la desgracia de no poder presentar a mis lectores un libro sobre algún país remoto, exótico y extraordinario. En mis libros, no hay mosquitos, ni leones, ni chacales, ni objeto alguno sorprendente o raro. Confieso sentir, por otra parte, poca afición por el exotismo. Mi heroísmo y bravura son escasos. Me gustan los países civilizados. Desde el punto de vista de la sensibilidad me daría por satisfecho plenamente si pudiera llegar a ser un hombre europeo. He sido siempre aficionado a la "mateotte" de anguilas, a la becada en canapé y a la perdiz mediterránea. (J. Pla, *Viaje en autobús* 9)
>
> (Until now, I have had the misfortune of not being able to present my readers with a book about some remote, exotic, and extraordinary country. In my books, there are no mosquitoes, no lions, no jackals, no surprising or rare objects. I confess, on the other hand, that I have little fondness for exoticism. My heroism and bravery are scarce. I like civilized countries. From the point of view of sensibility I would be fully satisfied if I could become a European man. I have always been fond of the "matteotte," woodcock in canapé and Mediterranean partridge.)

But in this book – although he does not say so – Pla disclaims Europe and is only interested in his version of the *plat pays*. He is well aware of the changes that have taken place in the world. With characteristic malevolent irony he states: "En nuestro país había tres pretextos esenciales para pasar la frontera: la peregrinación a Lourdes, la luna de miel y los negocios" (J. Pla, *Viaje en autobús* 9; In our country there were three essential pretexts for crossing the border: the pilgrimage to Lourdes, the honeymoon, and business). He blames those who travel during their honeymoon or who try to see the world during a business trip. With Europe in war and Spain in ruins he offers an innovative solution:

> Lo esencial, para aprovechar un viaje es tomarlo como finalidad misma. Andar por el mundo un poco al azar es muy agradable. Viajar sin tener un objeto concreto, es una auténtica maravilla. Yo siento que podría curarme de todos mis vicios y de todas mis virtudes, caso de que tenga alguna; lo que no podré dejar jamás es mi recalcitrante vagabundaje. Hay que viajar

para descubrir, con los propios ojos que el mundo es muy pequeño, y por tanto que es absolutamente necesario hacer un esfuerzo para dignificar la visión hasta llegar a ver las cosas en grande. (J. Pla, *Viaje en autobús* 10)

(The essential thing to take advantage of a trip is to take it as a purpose. To wander around the world a little bit at random is very pleasant. To travel without having a concrete object is a real marvel. I feel that I could cure myself of all my vices and all my virtues, if I have any; what I will never be able to give up is my recalcitrant wandering. You have to travel to discover, with your own eyes, that the world is very small, and therefore it is absolutely necessary to make an effort to dignify your vision until you can see things in a big way.)

He contradicts himself, however, in explaining the many virtues of travelling:

Hay que viajar para darse cuenta de que una pasión una idea, un hombre, sólo son importantes si resisten una proyección a través del tiempo y del espacio. No hay nada como alejarse un poco para curarse de la psicosis de la proximidad, de la deformación de la proximidad, de la que todos estamos atacados. Hay que viajar para aprender – a pesar de todo – a conservar, a perfeccionar, a tolerar. (J. Pla, *Viaje en autobús* 10)

(You have to travel to realize that a passion, an idea, a man, are only important if they resist a projection through time and space. There is nothing like moving away a little to be cured of the psychosis of proximity, of the deformation of proximity, of which we are all afflicted. It is necessary to travel in order to learn – in spite of everything – to preserve, to perfect, to tolerate.)

In these paragraphs he hides the paradox and contradiction of his approach because he does not stray far from an intimate reality and his journey's goal is to discover a near world. He also recognizes that this decision has been unwanted, imposed by abnormal circumstances: "En fin, ya que no se puede viajar como antes, hay que viajar de todos modos. Aquí está el fruto de mis recientes, insignificantes vagabundajes. Viajando en autobús, el vuelo es gallináceo" (J. Pla, *Viaje en autobús* 11). (Anyway, since you can't travel like you used to, you have to travel anyway. Here is the fruit of my recent, insignificant wanderings. Travelling by bus, the flight is gallinaceous.) He ends the introduction with a blunt confession about the true purpose of his writing: "Finalmente espero – y esto es cosa mía – que este libro será leído dentro de cien años cuando algún curioso – y espero, gustoso – erudito trate de resucitar la vida que estamos arrastrando – el temporal que estamos capeando" (11; Finally I hope – and this is my own doing – that this book will be read a hundred years from now when some curious – and, I hope, tasteful – scholar tries to resurrect the life we are dragging along – the storm we are weathering). He expects the book to be a document of a sinister period.

Against Hurry and Progress

In the first chapters, or in the last chapters, Pla makes the reader believe that he is making a "trip," with various references to the means of transport and stray references to his route. In a more systematic way he describes the people he finds on the bus or in the towns he visits. The starting point is a chapter timely titled "Emprendemos la marcha" (We are on the move), in which he is very attentive to means of transport: old buses and trains. He writes with little hope or enthusiasm about a world of hungry people. Travelling by bus allows Pla to contemplate the world from a nearby point of view. It allows him to brag about the lack of rush. He is an idle flâneur in search of surprises, who can make the trip at his own pace. In addition, at various times he exhibits time control, refusing to fall for rush imperatives, something that in his mind belongs to an already disappeared world: "La urgencia, como la prisa, como la premura, son cosas absolutamente desprovistas de sentido. En lo único que hay una prisa notoria es en aumentar los precios" (*Viaje en autobús* 22; Urgency, like haste, like pressure, is absolutely meaningless. The only thing in which there is a notorious haste is in increasing prices). After the civil war, rush has disappeared; the driver is worried because he has been waiting for more than ten minutes to pick up a jug of milk at a crossroads. The bus driver asks Pla if he is in a hurry. "A mí, realmente, me es igual – le digo –. Yo comprendo que usted se preocupe del horario. Pero los demás, apañados estaríamos si nos inquietáramos, en esta época, por estas nimiedades! Desgraciado, amigo, el que en estos tiempos que vivimos tenga prisa" (28). ("I don't really care," I say. "I understand that you are concerned about the timetable. But the rest of us would be in trouble if we were to worry, in this day and age, about such trifles! Woe betides anyone who is in a hurry in these times we live in.") In the same chapter he makes a stern defence of slowness and a denunciation of people from a bygone era who exhibit haste and bad manners associated with rush. Denying some constraints from a previous time allows Pla to justify a renunciation of being always in a hurry, which he considers a terrible imposition of the age in which he lives (30). The conclusion is in favour of a life governed by the slow pace of seasons, and a return to atavism. As we can see, the emphasis is on this time, in the present. Hurry and speed are anachronisms. Needless to say, we can detect an echo of Ordine's and Esquirol's proposals that I have discussed at length in chapter 4.

Related to haste, Pla, still thinking about the distinction between a world of the past and one of the present, expresses in the first text, "Emprendemos la marcha" (We are on the move), a warning about happiness and, in the manner of Seneca, a warning against excess (*Viaje en autobús* 17). In the conclusion of the book we read another admonition, in the chapter titled "Epílogo, perplejidad" (Epilogue, bewilderment): "Hasta ahora nos habíamos figurado, tanto nos lo habían dicho, que la felicidad de los pueblos y de los hombres radicaba en el progreso indefinido. Ahora nos dicen lo contrario: que la felicidad está en el regreso, en volver atrás" (185). (Until now we had imagined, we had been told so many times, that the happiness of peoples and men lay in indefinite progress. Now we are told the opposite: that happiness lies in going back, in going backwards.) Josep Pla, who was a true conservative, introduces the idea of catastrophe as the result of the civil war and the previous era of debauchery:

> Muchas personas han creído, en efecto, que estábamos pasando la época más brillante de la historia, el momento en que el género humano en tanto que impulso progresivo ha llegado al cénit. Sin embargo … ha venido la catástrofe. Catástrofe que ha sido más trágica que todas las anteriores porque el progreso material ha podido aumentar su nocividad hasta el infinito. Nuestra época contará con las catástrofes más grandes, más dolorosas, más aparatosas del paso del linaje humano sobre la tierra. (J. Pla, *Viaje en autobús* 187–8)
>
> (Many people have believed, in fact, that we were passing through the most brilliant epoch in history, the moment when the human race as a progressive impulse has reached its zenith. However … the catastrophe has come. A catastrophe that has been more tragic than all the previous ones because material progress has been able to increase its harmfulness to infinity. Our epoch will have the greatest, most painful, most spectacular catastrophes in the history of the human race on Earth.)

The use of a euphemism such as *catastrophe* serves to mention the Second Spanish Republic, the civil war, and the revolution, thus avoiding compromising words that attract the attention of censorship.

This first book published after the war also has an approximately subversive rhetorical element, rejecting the verbal pomp of the new regime.

Jordi Gracia indicated that Pla's approach to writing, similar to the first Camilo José Cela's approach, rejected the rhetoric and grandiloquence of Francoism's language in the early postwar period, sick of perpetual inflation. Gracia adds: "construeixen una retòrica de la banalitat, una cerimònia del despullament" (49; they construct a rhetoric of banality, a ceremony of undressing). It is from this perspective that one assessment of *Viaje en autobús*, by Dionisio Ridruejo, can be understood as one of the most effective books of incantation or demystification of the rhetorical environment of the postwar period (50).

Nature and Gastronomy

Another important characteristic of Josep Pla's writing is his attention to aspects of eating and food. Josep Pla's Epicurean attitude lead him to contemplate nature, a refuge, and, in relation to it, to defend aspects of gastronomy. Nature provides the rigidity of the cycles of the year, the link with an immovable tradition. In the chapter "Tardes de viaje" (Afternoons of travel) he talks to a young lady. He asks her which she prefers: letters, science, or a steak with potatoes. The girl does not hesitate and chooses the third option. We are in the years of hunger and rationing to which he continually refers. Pla feels overwhelmed by the girl's impressive sincerity and takes refuge in contemplating the landscape (*Viaje en autobús* 33–4). Pla tends to digress. In the chapter "Los mercados, hoy" he talks again about hunger and the recent transformations of the world. The evocation of gastronomy makes him notice the changes, and he sings the elegy of an already-gone, better past. Carnival arrives, and he remembers the good food of yesteryear. Speaking of mushrooms, he laments the opulent pre-war custom of eating dishes that are out of season. The colour of the mushrooms makes him dream of still lifes that are impossible to attain. And the colour serves him in making a meta-literary proposal about what and how to write (185).

His proposal comprises a variety of outbursts against the illusion of progress. In the chapter "Abundancia de fotografías" (Abundance of photographs) he feels it is regrettable that in his time a passport photograph is needed to make any bureaucratic operation. He deplores the inflation of graphic documents about people. Anticipating the approaches of Roland Barthes and Susan Sontag, he complains about the impossibility of a person resembling himself: "Si hay dos cosas distintas son dos fotografías de un mismo ser humano realizadas en minutos de diferencia" (*Viaje en autobús* 123; If there are two different things, they are two photographs of the same human being taken minutes apart). Thus he identifies *studium* – "le goût pour quelqu'un ou quelque chose" (Barthes, *La chambre claire* 48; the taste for someone or something) – and *el punctum* – "la piqûre, un détail poignant" (*La chambre claire* 49; the sting, a poignant detail). Sontag says that the individual who seeks to register cannot intervene, and that the person who intervenes cannot then faithfully register, because the two objectives contradict each other: "To photograph is to appropriate the thing photographed" (Sontag, *On Photography* 4). The sly comment (that in the future photographs of illustrious peoples will be confused with those of their relatives) allows Pla to conclude: "Y la confusión que de nosotros mismos sentimos, ¿no aumentará ante la cantidad exorbitante de fotografías que de nuestra persona van apareciendo?" (*Viaje en autobús* 123; And won't the confusion we feel about ourselves increase with the exorbitant number of photographs that appear of us?). It is another way of claiming the uses of the past, the anonymity of public figures.

Another notable aspect in this rejection of the present is the manoeuvre to present himself as an old-young man or as an old grumpy man. The paradox is that Pla is only forty-five years old. We can confirm this, for example, in the chapter "Los caprichos" (The caprices). At an inn, after an argument with the maid, he manages to have the sheets changed that seemed dirty to him. He comments: "Esas son escenas de la vida vulgar, es decir, de la vida básica. Lo que en ellas sucede afecta a todo lo demás, aun a lo más elevado" (*Viaje en autobús* 125; These are scenes of ordinary life, that is, of basic life. What happens in them affects everything else, even the most elevated). Then an acquaintance makes him taste a wine that turns out to be sour. And he complains about it with a harsh reaction:

> – Es usted un cascarrabias, un caprichoso, un pesado … Me entretengo en esas aparentes insignificancias porque una de las raíces de nuestra manera de ser está afectada por esas reacciones y coloreada por esas frases. A mí me gusta coincidir con todo el mundo siempre que la coincidencia pueda producirse sobre calidades probadas y ciertas. (J. Pla, *Viaje en autobús* 127)
>
> ("You are a curmudgeon, a capricious one, a bore" … I dwell on these apparent insignificances because one of the roots of our way of being is affected by these reactions and coloured by these phrases. I like to agree with everyone as long as the agreement can be on tried and true qualities.)

Travelling by bus, Pla stops at discreet, good-quality inns. A reflection on the cold allows him to introduce comments on the general unpredictability of the country (*Viaje en autobús* 49). These are the lessons of a peasant addressed to the urbanite: you lack fireplaces. His perspective as a peasant facilitates his rejection of the city and cosmopolitanism (90). The comparison between the city lights and the glow of the fireplace serves as a metaphor and gives rise to a very careful description that concludes once again with the vindication of the past, the evocative capacity of the wood fire. Pla's thesis is that living as a farmer allows us to be closer to civilization or, rather, to the idea of civilization that he is defending in this book:

> – Ni amigo, señora, ni enemigo. Estamos ante una realidad: de las grandes ciudades han desaparecido, en los días que vivimos, todas las ventajas que la civilización había concentrado en ellas. Y esto es cierto no sólo en nuestro país, sino en todo el Continente. En cambio, cuando entro en una casa de campo me parece pisar un terreno mucho más firme, penetrar en un refugio en el que se conservan todavía algunos residuos de civilización. En el campo puede uno satisfacer aún aquel mínimo de necesidades cuya carencia coloca al hombre frente a la Naturaleza en una posición irrisoria y ridícula. En las ciudades, en las grandes ciudades, esto es ya imposible. Le hablo en nombre de la modestia, de las personas modestas como yo, es decir, de la inmensa mayoría. (J. Pla, *Viaje en autobús* 91)

> ("Neither friend, madam, nor enemy. We are facing a reality: from the big cities have disappeared, in the days we live in, all the advantages that civilization had concentrated in them. And this is true not only in our country, but in the whole continent. On the other hand, when I enter a country house, it seems to me that I am stepping on much firmer ground, entering a refuge in which some residues of civilization are still preserved. In the country one can still satisfy that minimum of needs, the lack of which places man in a derisory and ridiculous position vis-à-vis Nature. In the cities, in the big cities, this is no longer possible. I speak to you in the name of modesty, of modest people like me, that is to say, of the immense majority.")

Trip to the Past

In *Viaje en autobús*, a "dissonant heritage" appears, that is, the "hurtful" heritage. We recognize this in the memory of past events, which is not easy to reconcile with the values of the present and its translation into an everyday experience. It is very evident that, when he visits various villages, Pla evokes some famous people who had lived there. They are all dead and represent little heroes of a disappeared Catalonia. Lluís Quintana, quoting Castellet, recalls that when one visits the heroes of the past, "the tone is Proustian" ("El *Viaje*" 131). That appreciation, inspired by Castellet, of a "Proustian" Josep Pla does both Pla and Proust a disservice because the comparison is a little more complex. A remark by Sanz Villanueva shows us what is missing in Pla's book: there are no material traces of the war that at the time could hardly go unnoticed even to a superficial and absent-minded observer (39). The attention that Pla devotes to these *homenots* (overmen) is not accidental. They represent a pantheon of illustrious second-division characters, perhaps the only ones he dares to evoke without arousing the attention (read the wrath) of the occupiers and censors.

Let us review the authors and try to understand why Pla is paying attention to them. Juli Garreta, who died in 1925, is presented as a watchmaker and sardana composer: "Garreta – como nadie – nos ha hecho comprender estas cosas tan íntimamente ligadas a nuestra sensibilidad. Con su música ha contribuido a que nos diéramos cuenta de cómo estamos hechos por dentro" (J. Pla, *Viaje en autobús* 27). (Garreta – like no one else – has made us understand these things that are so intimately linked to our sensibility. With his music he has contributed to make us realize how we are made inside.) Amadeu Vives, a zarzuela composer who died in 1932, stands out for his Catholicism. He interrogates the woman in charge of his archive to explain his conservative religious position (*Viaje en autobús* 58). In conclusion he makes her speak in words that are closer to Pla's: "Mi sensibilidad llega escasamente a figurarse el cielo como una tierra sin escorias, sin peso, alta y etérea. Pero mi punto de referencia constante es la tierra. La vida puede ser noble y agradable, no lo cree usted? Es un valle de lágrimas, que tiene sus inconvenientes y sus encantillos" (61). (My sensibility barely manages to imagine the sky as an earth without dross, weightless, high and ethereal. But my constant point of reference is the earth. Life can be noble and pleasant, don't you think? It is a vale of tears, which has its drawbacks and its charms.) Pla also stops at the house of the philosopher Ramon Turró, who died in 1926. There he visits the library and sees a portrait of Mariano Cubí. This reminds him of a book from 1851 that he has been seeking for a long time, *Al pueblo español, sobre las causas que hacen el comunismo imposible y el progreso inevitable* (To the Spanish people, on the causes that make communism impossible and progress inevitable). The next day he talks to a woman who had known Turró (and who is calm because he confessed before he died). He asks if there are any manuscripts, correspondence, and his query provokes a forceful response. During the war, communists ransacked the house and killed a nephew of Dr. Turró, who was also a priest and with whom she lived. She said, "The papers disappeared" (108–9). Then Pla tries to read a half-erased headstone. He concludes:

> La memoria del doctor Turró se irá perdiendo. En su pueblo natal ya no queda apenas rastro de su paso por la tierra. Sin embargo, yo creo que la memoria del doctor Turró es digna de ser conservada por algunas razones. En el doctor Turró se concentra el más grande esfuerzo personal que se ha hecho en este país contra el kantismo. Los resultados de este esfuerzo me importan menos que la posición misma. Si no queremos naufragar en el caos intelectual y sentimental hemos de aprovechar las experiencias de todos los que sintieron este mismo peligro. (J. Pla, *Viaje en autobús* 109)
>
> (Dr. Turró's memory will fade away. In his hometown there is hardly any trace left of his time on earth. However, I believe that the memory of Dr. Turró is worthy of being preserved for some reasons. In Dr. Turró is concentrated the greatest personal effort that has been made in this country againstKantianism. The results of this effort matter less to me than the position itself. If we do not want to be shipwrecked in intellectual and sentimental chaos, we must take advantage of the experiences of all those who felt this same danger.)

Afterwards Pla visits Blanes. There he asks about Joaquim Ruyra, who died on 15 May 1939. The conversations he begins suggest, at the end of the chapter, an admiration for the writer. The conversations highlight the routine and the double version of reality, the distance between the sexes. He exemplifies this with an episode in which he was taken in a horse-drawn carriage from the station to the village (*Viaje en autobús* 132). And he regrets once again the lack of passion for preserving the past that he detects in the country:

> ¡Que lástima que la gente recuerde tan poco las cosas! Uno va detrás de las sombras de los hombres que uno ha querido y admirado y generalmente no se encuentra nada. Uno busca sobre todo los reflejos de los momentos dramáticos de la vida de estos hombres y cuando se tiene la ilusión de que el reflejo está cerca, uno lo ve disolverse en el vacío incierto del pasado … No se conservan en este país, ni las viejas correspondencias amorosas. Nadie gusta de cultivar su memoria. Tabla rasa. Empezar de nuevo cada día. Todo es nada. Sin duda por esto queda a menudo este país como estúpidamente aniñado. (J. Pla, *Viaje en autobús* 134)
>
> (What a pity that people remember things so little! One goes after the shadows of the men one has loved and admired and one usually finds nothing. One seeks above all the reflections of the dramatic moments of the lives of these men, and when one has the illusion that the reflection is

near, one sees it dissolve in the uncertain emptiness of the past ... In this country, not even the old love correspondences are preserved. Nobody likes to cultivate their memory. Clean slate. Starting over every day. Everything is nothing. Undoubtedly for this reason this country often remains stupidly childish.)

Pla also remembers Pep Ventura, a native of Figueres who died in 1875. And he does an excursus on the sardana: "Para comprender las sardanas, el atolondramiento y la inconsciencia de la juventud son inservibles. Se requiere estar casado y a ser posible padre de familia" (*Viaje en autobús* 173; To understand the sardanas, the daze and unconsciousness of youth are useless. It is necessary to be married and if possible a father of a family).

These five characters do not represent a model for the future. They are minor figures, except for Ruyra, in a cultural imaginary or in a recovery project for Catalan culture after the war. But they are visited as if they were in a cemetery, and Pla writes the text of their tombstones, the tombs of a bygone era, the remains of a shipwreck of colossal dimensions.

Josep M. Espinàs's Exploration of the Nearby

Josep M. Espinàs is the author of twenty-one travel books that consistently express a postmodern attitude of retrieving the past, observing non-central places, and rejecting the rush. He has travelled on a VéloSoleX (a French invention of the postwar period, a bicycle with a small engine, a precedent to today's electric bicycle) and has made most of his journeys on foot. His two most extreme journeys are documented in *Seguint tot l'Ebre amb un primitiu Velosolex* (1961, but published only in 2003; Following the entire Ebro with a primitive VéloSoleX) and *Viatge pels grans magatzems* (1993; A trip to the department store). In the introduction to *A peu per Andalusia: Sierra Mágina; La frontera cristiano-musulmana* (2003; On foot through Andalusia: Sierra Mágina; The Christian-Muslim border) he declared his criteria for choosing the areas to travel on footand to write his books. They must be non-tourist areas, away from the big itineraries, with a certain regional identity and where some features characteristic of Andalusian life would not have been lost. He travels, like Josep Pla, but for different reasons, to a cemetery. In the 1990s Espinàs distinguished himself as a traveller by writing about a series of treks to remote regions in Catalonia and Spain. His visit to the department store completes, with irony, his series of visits to forgotten places. Espinàs's case is quite remarkable because he has done these kinds of travels and written about them at two separate times, in the 1950s and, much later, after 1990.[3]

Espinàs was a journalist of immense popularity in his native Catalonia, and in recent years he has walked through desolate regions in western Catalonia and remote Spanish provinces. In 1990, for example, he published *A peu per la Llitera: Viatge a la frontera de la llengua* (On foot through the Llitera: Journey to the border of language) and, more recently, *A peu per Castella: Terres de Sòria* (1999; On foot through Castile: Lands of Soria), *A peu per Aragó: El Somontano* (2006; On foot through Aragon: The Somontano), *A peu per l'Alt Camp* (2007; On foot through the Alt Camp), and *A peu per Múrcia* (2009; On foot through Murcia). In 1991 he defined his literary activity as travelogue writer in the following terms:

> I la sensació que tinc és que aquests llibres de viatges són la integració dels dos altres aspectes del meu ofici. Finalment puc ser narratiu – dibuixar personatges i paisatges, explicar sensacions, crear climes, treballar un ritme, aprofitant una realitat viscuda. Ni ficció pura ni periodisme estricte d'observació i reflexió. (Espinàs, "Pròleg" 11)

> (And the feeling I have is that these travel books are the integration of the other two aspects of my craft. Finally, I can be narrative – draw characters and landscapes, explain sensations, create climates, work on a rhythm, taking advantage of a lived reality. Neither pure fiction nor strict journalism of observation and reflection.)

It is both a special version of journalism (not only observation and reflection) and pure fiction. Espinàs travelled on foot through Catalonia and Spain for more than thirty years.[4] What difference is there between time and the reasons for *Viatge al Pirineu de Lleida* (1957; Trip to the Pyrenees of Lleida) and his latest, *A peu per Múrcia* (2009; On foot through Murcia)? What was once pure social interest is now closer to ecology. After a long break he started walking again in 1989. Let us glimpse fragments of his logbook. He does not travel on foot with a keen eye for landscaping. He says it very clearly: "hi vinc a ser emotivament forçat per la vida que flueix espontàniament al meu voltant. No fabrico el que vull que passi en aquests llibres, només narro el que passa pel camí de les hores viscudes" (*A peu per la Terra Alta* 66). (I come here to be emotionally forced by the life that flows spontaneously around me. I don't fabricate what I want to happen in these books; I just narrate what happens along the way of the hours lived.) Looking at the human data, he observes not details of the walks but human impressions – light sociology. It is fieldwork at its best, noted by a good-natured *badoc*, attentive to change and the enormous dangers of extinction from which the country suffers. He is more interested in stopping to make a vermouth and start the conversation: this is how the magical sounds of the Catalan language between Catalonia and Aragón (La Franja) and the worries of the people of the countryside are evoked in front of us. The travel book is a genre with followers among local readers. Espinàs has a restricted code and he applies it with enough wisdom: a mixture of objective observations and personal data, sentimental escapades. They are not great literary pieces, but they attract us for the testimonial value they offer, about the situation of a place located in a *finisterre*, linguistic and social. At a time when newspapers and social gatherings were so full of disastrous premonitions about the future of the Catalan language, his travels provide an intimate report of how it has been preserved in an area without a state or the Generalitat.

It is no less surprising how summer walks, which Espinàs has turned into a personal subgenre of travel literature, can change so dramatically as the expedition's location changes. Espinàs ingeniously remade the romantic arrangement of the essences of his own land and the popular spirit, replacing them with visits to places far from the centres of tourist attraction, places that did not exist for the centres of political decision making. Thus, he has visited the frontier of the language, areas outside the circuits of invention of tradition, or just burned by one of the usual summer disasters. In the book *A peu per Castella*, Espinàs continues to travel on foot, but in doing so through Castile, a section of Soria, in search of a different landscape, the dry land of the great mosaic of wheat, he allows the reader to discover significant differences with his own reality. If his previous books were built from the dialogue with the people he met along the way, in this case the few people there are, who are not very communicative, considerably condition the result. The Castilian wasteland, due to its pure human geography or its collective deduction, makes the encounters extremely difficult, and the result is a more descriptive text, of an economy of means that brings it closer to the desert that he visits. The other significant change, perhaps related, is introspection. The narration of the journey is counterpointed by frequent reflections on the reasons for walking and writing: "aquest és l'ofici que més m'agrada: anar a peu per tenir temps de trobar allò que no es busca" (*A peu per Castella* 103; this is the job I like best: walking to have time to find what is not sought). He also evokes the memory of his first trip with Camilo José Cela to the Lleida Pyrenees. He mentions that he had already taken the reader to Castile in his – for many – best novel, *Combat de nit*. If before he was riding a truck, now the slowness of walking, the wisdom of the years, makes it easier to observe lonely places, and he can better capture and share with the reader how he discovers the secret of the colours and smells of a different land.

Any serious reader of all of his travelogue series *A peu per …* knows that Josep M. Espinàs has an effective criterion for choosing the places he visits: remote areas of the world, far from the hustle and bustle of tourism. What began as a small adventure, in parallel with Camilo J. Cela, has become a whole program of conservation and a testament to the history of everyday life. Cents (of *pesetas*) are now in euros. People do not emigrate to Barcelona but return to the villages. In the book *A peu per Andalusia* the chosen villages are from the Mágina mountain range, in the province of Jaén, which has inspired the mythical place in the novels of Antonio Muñoz Molina. The traveller confesses to us that he has gone to Andalusia to listen. He is surprised by the natural grace of speakers, given the variety of Spanish that he reproduces with a made-up version of a phonetic transcription. The journey on foot returns us to the essences. Espinàs is amazed at how easily one can live with just a few things. He examines specific experiences that mechanical means of transportation do not let us enjoy: every trip has a smell that accompanies the traveller. That is why he enjoys the little paradise of peace on the road. He is aware that he is walking along the border between Moors and Christians, which he still observes in their many castles. From village to village Espinàs goes along paths and incorporates brief notes on the orography, the state of nature that he finds along the way. But he specializes in the humblest branch of human geography: "Els pobles són les meves fites, els meus objectius. Els paisatges són escenaris de pas" (*A peu per Andalusia* 24; Towns are my goal, my objectives. Landscapes are passing scenarios). The encounter with people, the conversations that the author knows how to provoke, are always the juiciest part of these trips. Episodes like those of the faces of Bélmez, or the one of the *maquis* of Torres (the native town of Judge Garzón), are most remarkable. But there is also a note of nostalgia, a journey into the "journey on foot." Numerous self-referential notes prove it. One critic detects:

> El passeig adopta el ritme del pensament i després de la prosa. Amb el temps, els natius s'han anat sorprenent que algú viatgi a peu. Lentitud, curiositat, paciència i sobrietat són factors claus per donar veu a un lloc, una gent, un tros de vida. El camí és una acció higiènica per desprotagonitzar-se. Ens porta a la diversitat humana. Cal copsar-la amb paraules precises. (Guixà)

> ([Espinà's] walks adapt to the rhythm of thought and then to his prose. Over time, the natives have been surprised that someone travels on foot. Slowness, curiosity, patience, and sobriety are key factors in giving voice to a place, a people, a piece of life. The path is a hygienic action to efface oneself. It brings us to human diversity. You need to grasp it with precise words.)

This remark is similar to what Jean-Jacques Rousseau wrote in his *Confessions*, "I can only meditate when I am walking. When I stop, I cease to think; my mind only works with my legs" (ix). Perhaps a distant model for Espinàs was Robert Walser's *Der Spaziergang* (1917; *The Walk*). This is a text that covers the time frame of a day, centred on a walk that a stroller takes from morning to sunset in a town in German Switzerland. *Der Spaziergang* is a sequence of sketches (or short dialogues) and natural scenarios that the walker encounters; people, things, nature, are offered to him, suggesting several reflections – on nature, existence, architecture, literature, art in general, writing, the role and ethics of the writer, children and their future as adults, the new that advances, and social inequalities. Once out of the house, he is taken by "a joyful wait for everything that could have come to meet me or present myself" (12). He greets a well-known professor; discusses with a bookseller and asks him to show him the most read, most admired, best-selling, and most valid book of the moment; has a long talk with a tax officer; and engages in a fierce dialectical duel with his tailor.

A Trip with a VéloSoleX

As mentioned before, in 1957 Espinàs went to the Pyrenees with C.J. Cela and published his own account of their trip, parallel to Cela's version.[5] In 1960 he published his memories of a trip through the Pyrenees from coast to coast.[6] The following year he followed the Ebro River using a second-hand VéloSoleX. In the year 1961 the impact of tourism and mild industrialization began to be noticeable in Spain, but not in the Ebro River area. That is why following the river from its origins in Santander to the Mediterranean echoes a geographical description he learned in his school days: "El Ebro nace en Fontibre, cerca de Reinosa, provincial de Santander" (*Seguint tot l'Ebre* 8; The Ebro rises in Fontibre, near Reinosa, in the province of Santander). He is astonished when reading an inscription on stone with some words by right-wing philologist Marcelino Menéndez y Pelayo:

> La áspera sierra que guarda en sus humildes peñascales la cuna del histórico río que a toda la península da nombre y que después de saludar los férreos lindes de la Vasconia y besar el muro triunfal y sagrado de Zaragoza viene a rendir tributo a vuestro mar en la ribera tortosina simbolizando en su majestuoso curso la unidad suprema y la diversidad fecunda de la historia patria. (Espinàs, *Seguint tot l'Ebre* 11)
>
> (The rough mountain range that keeps in its humble crags the cradle of the historical river that gives its name to the whole peninsula and that after

> greeting the iron boundaries of the Vasconia and kissing the triumphal and sacred wall of Zaragoza comes to pay tribute to your sea in the Tortosa shore, symbolizing in its majestic course the supreme unity and the fertile diversity of the patriotic history.)

During his trip Espinàs pays attention to signs of a world that is fast disappearing: worn-out road signs that lead to nowhere, and all the rural activities occurring without any signs of industrialization. It is a world about to disappear, still without tourism. A man makes *albarcas*, shoes made out of a tree log. Espinàs is witness to the end of a world, when he reflects on the town of Miranda de Ebro, where the river has been replaced by rivers of another nature, roads and railways: "Miranda és la clau de la total decadència de l'Ebre com a via de comunicació I de transport. Els immòbils rius d'asfalt I de rails ferroviaris que aquí s'han construït han triomfat totalment. Hi navega el turisme I el comerç" (*Seguint tot l'Ebre* 57). (Miranda is the key to the total decline of the Ebro as a means of communication and transport. The immobile rivers of asphalt and railway tracks that have been built here have completely succeeded. Tourism and trade sail there.) Near Mequinensa he contemplates the works for a huge dam to produce electrical energy and that will swallow an entire energetic town (113) One could say that Espinàs is foreseeing what Jesús Moncada, a native of Mequinensa, wrote in his literary works of the 1990s, particularly in *Camí de sirga* (1995). Moncada's novel narrates the loss and destruction of a space that was, at once, private (personal) and collective. In the complex process of recovery he manipulates time, devising a new way of including it in the narrative. Thus, the memories of some characters seep into those of others, reflecting the weight of collective memory. Indeed, the novel is permeated by a sense of destruction, which can be found on nearly every page. It is particularly palpable, for instance, in the novel's first and final pages. While it is Moncada's personal use of time that makes his story credible, this credibility is also heightened by the story's unity in time. Moncada recreates a sort of mythical time, which was cut short in 1971 by the disappearance of the original Mequinensa. In so doing, he both reconstructs the collective memory and manages to create a different sense of time in which the past and present are interwoven.

In the final pages of *Camí de sirga*, Moncada tells of the disappearance of Mequinensa, threatened by the waters of the Ebro River. He does so by reproducing the funeral procession for Carlota de Torres, which he links to the demolished buildings and shuttered bars. The town's imminent total destruction is suggested by the replacement of human life with encroaching nature. What Moncada does in this novel is akin to what Marianne Hirsch has called "postmemory." According to Hirsch, "postmemory is distinguished from memory by generational distance and from history by deep personal connection. Postmemory is a powerful and very particular form of memory precisely because its connection to its object or source is mediated not through recollection but through an imaginative investment and creation … Postmemory characterizes the experience of those who grow up dominated by … stories of the previous generation shaped by traumatic events" (22). Moncada uses postmemory in two ways: as the narrator and by imposing it on his characters (Bou, "Time and memory").

When Espinàs arrives at Tortosa, he is puzzled at seeing an old man dressed in traditional attire.

> [H]e vist en un carrer absolutament posat al dia, un vellet tortosí que passejava vestit a la manera tradicional. Els pantalons, la faixa, la camisa, no eren el vestuari d'una agrupació folklòrica. He hagut d'arribar al final del meu viatge, i en una Ciutat i no en una aldea, per veure el primer home, en tot l'Ebre, fidel a la indumentària dels seus avantpassats. (Espinàs, *Seguint tot l'Ebre* 130)
>
> (I saw in an absolutely up-to-date street an old Tortosa man walking around dressed in the traditional way. The trousers, the belt, the shirt, were not the costumes of a folkloric group. I had to reach the end of my journey, and in a city and not a village, to see the first man, in all of the Ebro, faithful to the clothing of his ancestors.)

The final words in the book evoke a sense of nature and solitude:

> Altra vegada en marxa, cap a llevant. La soledat és absoluta entre la terra plana i el cel llis. És un país de joncs, d'alguns matolls pobres, batuts pels vents. I dels ànecs sedentaris i les aus migratòries. El temps sembla aturat. Només un ritme, el de les veus de les granotes … Ara, una gran massa d'aigua sota un cel immens. No es mou res, no sento cap soroll. Les onades del mar trenquen contra el riu que baixa, feixuc i poderós. La mirada em queda fixada en la línia d'escuma que es dibuixa i s'esborra, una vegada i una altra. (Espinàs, *Seguint tot l'Ebre* 138–9)
>
> (On the move again, heading east. The loneliness is absolute between the flat earth and the smooth sky. It is a country of reeds, of some poor scrub, beaten by the winds. And sedentary ducks and migratory birds. Time seems to stand still. Only a rhythm, that of the voices of the frogs … Now, a great body of water under an immense sky. Nothing moves, I don't hear

> any noise. The waves of the sea break against the flowing river, cumbersome and powerful. My gaze remains fixed on the foam line that is drawn and erased, again and again.)

This is the ending of one of his lesser-known expeditions, but one that defines the way Espinàs looks at disappearance.

Thanatourism

In recent years, the exploration of nearby places has become quite a popular type of travel, in which the traveller explores a well-known reality with the perspective and techniques of travel to exotic places, resulting in a thorough exploration of everyday life. Josep Pla's *Viaje en autobús*, as we have seen, is a contradictory book. It is a book that expresses a rejection of postwar situations and manifests itself in a blurred and indirect way against autarky; at the same time, it denies progress and speaks out against the dangers of modernity. Acting as if he were a farmer, disguised with a beret, and travelling by bus, this forty-three-year-old Pla, a fairly young writer, explores the country with an eye on the past, going deeper and deeper into it. Pla's journey technique is to move around, making turns, without a fixed goal; as Guy Débord theorized about psychogeography, he practises *la dérive* (drifting), a way of wandering around a place with an attitude of discovery, connecting a network of experiences and encounters. He travels with little attention to the route and with much more attention to the effects of the disaster (civil war), trying to recover some essences that he seems to recognize in an idealized life as a farmer. It is an approach in which one must move through the different moods of a space (a city, neighbourhood) and be guided by impressions, by the subjective effects of these places. Drifting also involves a contradiction, a letting go, and a knowledge and calculation of possibilities.[7] This is one of the techniques of Pla's journey, moving around in circles, letting himself be carried away by psychogeography. According to Guy Débord, "[l]a psychogéographie se proposerait l'étude des lois exactes, et des effets précis du milieu géographique, consciemment aménagé ou non, agissant directement sur le comportement affectif des individus" (11; psychogeography would propose the study of the exact laws, and the precise effects of the geographical environment, consciously arranged or not, acting directly on the emotional behaviour of the individuals). Lluís Quintana indicated:

> La acción transcurre en una época imprecisa: no se especifica el día, ni el mes ni el año, pero a través de informaciones esporádicas podemos ver que

el libro empieza en invierno (por ejemplo "Tardes de viaje") y siguen luego las otras estaciones: primavera ("La primavera"), verano ("Los mercados, hoy") y otoño ("Otoño"); como en las viejas alegorías, la tierra aparece muerta, renace, florece y se hace fecunda, y se prepara otra vez para la muerte. Los primeros capítulos transcurren en las tierras más ásperas del Ampurdán y los últimos en las más amables del Maresme. ("El *Viaje*" 38)

(The action takes place in an imprecise period: the day, month, and year are not specified, but through sporadic information we can see that the book begins in winter (for example "Travelling afternoons") and then follows the other seasons: spring ("Spring"), summer ("The markets, today"), and autumn ("Autumn"); as in the old allegories, the earth appears dead, is reborn, blooms and becomes fertile, and prepares again for death. The first chapters take place in the roughest lands of the Empordà and the last ones in the gentler lands of the Maresme.)

Secondly, both journeys narrated by Josep Pla and Josep M. Espinàs have a funereal character. They are dedicated to recovering characters, experiences, and values from the past. Unknowingly, they are in the orbit of what has been known since 1996 as dark tourism or thanatourism, the study of tourism in places of death. Foley and Lennon (1996) used the term *dark tourism*, and AV. Seaton (1996) *thanatourism*. Then came other terms: *Black Spot tourism* (Rojek), *morbid tourism* (Blom), *grief tourism*,[8] or, in Dann's version, *milking the macabre* (61). A more recent definition states that *dark tourism* is "the act of travel to sites associated with death, suffering and the seemingly macabre" (Stone 146). There is generally unanimity in saying that visits to places of death are made not only for a morbid attraction but also because there is a deep bond with the visitor. As Tarlow says, *dark tourism* means "visits to places where tragedies or historically noteworthy death has occurred and that continue to impact our lives" (48). Josep Pla does this type of travel in two ways: he is attentive to lost forms of life, which he evokes and reconstructs for the reader; and he evokes minor figures from the prewar Catalan cultural world, figures he finds in a cemetery that is the whole country, and he complains about the lack of attention to memory, to the memory of the dead. Espinàs pays attention to a society that is fast changing and is replacing old ways of life.

I mentioned earlier that the construction of the book by Pla – and the one by Espinàs – fits Friedrich Schlegel's concept of the fragment. The book is fragmentary with respect to the original texts and is an extract of fragments of a present and disappeared reality. It can be related also to the idea of ruin. Pla visits both ruins of a past and funerary monuments. Ruins are highly evocative forms of the fragment, and they operate according to their logic: they suggest something absent and in fact occupy an ambivalent space between the total past and the partial past, the presence of which they affirm and deny. Ruins mean loss and absence, which are, however, a visible evocation of the invisible, the appearance of disappearance. And yet, in so far as the ruins are preserved, they suggest perseverance: the possibility, at least, of resistance to the evils of time and history. The notions of hope, commemoration, and restoration are inherent in ruin (Thomas 42). Pla's and Espinàs's pilgrimages through areas and experiences of disappearance are characteristic of an atavistic gaze, one interested in the fragment, the ruin, the funerary monuments of a vanished past. In the case of Pla, his journey has an undeniable political value and mourning and is an original practice of thanatourism. Espinà's travelogues excel in visiting hidden areas of Catalonia and Spain, in witnessing a world that is fast disappearing. His text becomes an epitaph, the inscription on a tomb. In the case of Pla, it has an undeniably political mourning value. In the case of Espinàs, it is a light elegy, closer to ecology.

8

Beggars Can't Be Choosers: From Autarky to Globalized Gastronomy in Spain

In this chapter I address five different ways in which food speaks to us: Emilia Pardo Bazán's uses of food as an expression of a post-colonial dire situation; a surrealist approach in Buñuel's cinema; table manners as discussed by Larra; the shortage of food and hunger that was an obsessive and persistent reality during the Spanish Civil War and post-war period of the twentieth century; and the recent sophistication and cosmopolitanism of Spanish cuisine due to the transformation of the country by the presence of immigrants. I am interested in highlighting the passage from a culture of survival during the civil war and the Franco regime to one of greater abundance and sophistication with the arrival of democracy. The current recognition of Spain as one of the gastronomic destinations in the world modifies part of a historical and cultural past, which includes the ethnic transformation experienced by Spanish society. From the perspective of food studies, one can examine the relationships of the individual with food and analyse how this association produces a large amount of information about a society.

The well-known Spanish saying *A buen hambre no hay pan duro* (Beggars can't be choosers) is useful to introduce a reading of the diverse strategies around food from a Hispanic perspective, taking into account the challenging peripheralization of Iberian Hispanic studies, valuing the peripheral thing as a geographical, cultural, and ideological positioning. As the English say, "beggars can't be choosers." In the realm of everyday life, food is a key aspect. Food can be read as synecdoche in action, a part of human experience that can metaphorically replace the whole of social life. Its very definition helps to establish customs, traditions, and identities that soon acquire a central character and that can no longer be absent when it comes to imagining a place, a people, or a culture.

The concept of *foodscape* refers to a metaphorical landscape of foods and their production methods and cultural associations, as well as to the physical settings, dining etiquettes, human interactions, and atmospheres, all of which express different familiar and novel situations. The notion of foodscape has attracted wide academic attention in both social and natural sciences, including nutrition, health, urban geography, public policy, consumer studies, and food sciences. It is an aggregative concept interconnecting the place, identity, culture, foodstuff, service, and humans. Scholars are thus provided with relational thinking about these actors. In cultural studies, foodscape helps us understand how people consume and experience food in interaction with environments and social-cultural contexts (Zhu et al. 2022).

Food has played a key role in some of the great classics in Spanish and Catalan literature, such as the *Book of Sent Soví* (1324), *Tirant lo Blanc* (1490), *Don Quixote* (1504), and *Lazarillo* (1554). The contemporary recognition of Spain as one of the gastronomic destinations in the world erases this historical and cultural past. This identification also forgets the very ethnic transformation that Spanish society has undergone. Alfredo Martínez Expósito in *Cuestión de imagen: Cine y Marca España* has analysed recent films in which he verifies the presence of "discursos y valores promovidos por la Marca España" (speeches and values promoted by the Spain Brand) that materialize in the "renovación del país, la recuperación vanguardista de tradiciones locales, una ética del pluralismo y la diversidad, o la vindicación de sexualidades no normativas" (204; renewal of the country, the avant-garde recovery of local traditions, an ethic of pluralism and diversity, or the vindication of non-normative sexualities). To those one could add the gastronomic imagination and the many uses it has had in recent years.

From the perspective of food studies, one can examine the individual's relationships with food and analyse how this association produces a wealth of information about entire individuals and societies. The food choices available to people, either as individuals or as a group, can reveal views, passions, prior knowledge, budgets, and idiosyncrasies. Food choice tells the stories of families, migrations, assimilation, resistance, and change, as well as group or personal identity. Food studies encourages us to delve deeper into the everyday life related to food and forces us to find a deeper meaning in this everyday practice. By examining the what, where, how, and why of our food choices and eating habits, we develop a better understanding of ourselves and others.

Complementing the foodscape concept, other very useful critical concepts have been developed in recent years with which to discuss food as it relates to the everyday. It was Hauck-Lawson (1998) who introduced the concept of *food voice* and suggested that what one eats or decides not to eat communicates aspects of a person's identity or sensitivity in a way that words alone cannot. We owe to Kittler, Sucher, and Nelms (2012) the term of *food habits* (also known as *food culture* and *modes of eating*) to describe holistically how humans use food – from the way in which it is chosen, how it is bought and distributed, to how it is prepared, served, and eaten. These authors studied the importance of the eating-habits process, something that is unique to human beings. They wondered why people spend so much time and invest so much energy, money, and creativity in food.

The English saying "You are what you eat," a variation on Brillat-Savarin's "Dis-moi ce que tu manges je te dirai ce que tu es" (19; Tell me what you eat and I'll tell you what you are), exemplifies the idea of food linked to identity and also concentrates two of the key questions in any investigation of this kind: "What is the meaning of the food I have on my plate?" and "How do you define who I am?" In cultural terms, what one eats defines what one is and is not. Food choices from different cultural groups are often connected to ethnic behaviours and religious beliefs: vegan, carnivore, halal, or kosher. Kittler, Sucher, and Nelms refer to the influence of eating habits on an individual's personal identity, stating that "eating is a daily reaffirmation of cultural identity" (4). Many people relate foods of their culture or childhood, with very good and positive feelings and memories. Food is part of who we are and what we do. It is related to our families and has a special meaning for each person. Food from our culture, from our family, often becomes the food of refuge that we seek as adults in times of frustration and stress.

Chocolate and Recipes in Pardo Bazán

In recent years, attention to food has become an extraordinary field of study. So-called food studies raise a number of crucial questions: What impact does food have on the environment? What are the ethics of eating and food? How does food contribute to systems of oppression? How are foods symbolic markers of identity? At the same time, researchers ask questions that are fundamental to human existence: Who chooses what we eat and why? How is food traditionally prepared and where is the boundary between authentic culinary heritage and invented traditions? There are also questions about the spatialization of foodways and the relationship to place. This led to the development of the foodscape concept, introduced in the early 1990s, and the related practice of foodscape mapping. Pardo Bazán offers some great examples of food concerns. Her cookbooks were analysed by María Paz Moreno ("*La cocina española*"; "Beyond the Recipes"), and Gareth Wood has analysed her situation in the "Biblioteca de la Mujer" (Women's library. In the articles she published at the turn of the century in *La Ilustración Artística* (besides being very opinionated about the Spanish-American war), she paid attention, among other things, to chocolate and Lenten fasting.

Chocolate, including the difficulties in obtaining it, how it is eaten, and where, is an expression of the symbiosis between metropolis and colonies, but at the same time it is a synecdoche of what has been lost. In the article "Artículo … Ex colonial" (January 1899), written after the 1898 Spanish-American war, Pardo Bazán uses a product such as chocolate, present on every table in Spain, as a symbol of what the country has lost:

> Es natural que os hable de cosas de poca monta, pero no quisiera que dijeseis que también de poca substancia: y el chocolate es de las más substanciosas que se me ocurren. Además, el chocolate, en las actuales circunstancias, no carece de simbolismo. En él están cifradas nuestras glorias y nuestras desventuras. Cuando ganamos á América, revelamos al mundo el chocolate; cuando la perdimos definitivamente, lo primero que notamos en la esfera de la economía doméstica, es que el cacao se ha puesto por las nubes … El chocolate fue nuestro vellocino de oro. Al invadirnos el te (el té, sajón más que chino), podemos dar por consumada nuestra anulación ante la historia futura. (Pardo Bazán, *De siglo a siglo* 150)

> (It is natural for me to talk to you about small things, but I would not want you to say that they are also of little substance: and chocolate is one of the most substantial things I can think of. Besides, chocolate, in the present circumstances, is not without symbolism. Our glories and our misfortunes are encoded in it. When we discovered America, we revealed chocolate to the world; when we lost it definitively, the first thing we noticed in the sphere of domestic economy was that cocoa had gone through the roof … Chocolate was our golden fleece. When tea (tea, Saxon rather than Chinese) invaded us, we should consider that our disappearance in future history has already happened.)

Pardo Bazán takes the opportunity to confront chocolate with tea, as epitomes of the *castizo* (American) and the Anglo-Saxon, also establishing a parallelism between the loss of the centrality of chocolate and the fortunes of Spain as a country and its position in the world:

> Cuando se ufanaban con el chocolate nuestras mesas, nuestra bandera flotaba al aire tan orgullosa, tan respetada, tan gaya de color. – Eran los tiempos del jubón, del coleto, de la valona, de las espadas de taza, de los chambergos con cintillo de pedrería; eran después los del tontillo, de la casaca, del espadín de acero, del calzón corto, de la media de seda que

dibuja la pierna torneada y nerviosa … – Eran los tiempos en que el grave jerónimo, el docto benedictino, el capuchino de luenga barba, concurrían á la merienda ó refacción familiar de las casas ilustres, y los criados, á las cinco en punto, entraban las salvillas, las bandejas, las mancerinas cargadas de bizcochos, de tortas, de polvorones, de tazones chinescos ó jícaras de plata rebosando hirviente soconusco, cuyo aroma serla capaz de resucitar á un muerto – á un muerto español, naturalmente. – La deliciosa bebida era el tema de aquellas colaciones clásicas, pero tema tan enriquecido con variaciones golosas y aun artísticas, que él sólo formaba un aspecto peculiar, acaso el más sibarítico de nuestro vivir. (Pardo Bazán, *De siglo a siglo* 150)

(When our tables were boasting with chocolate, our flag floated in the air so proud, so respected, so colourful, and so gaudy: those were the times of the doublet, the coif, the *valona*, the rapiers, the chamberlain with a rhinestone headband; then there were the times of the *tontillo*, the *casaca*, the steel rapier, the short breeches, the silk stocking that outlines the turned and nervous leg …. – Those were the times when the grave Hieronymus, the learned Benedictine, the Capuchin with the long beard, attended the afternoon tea or family meal in the illustrious houses, and the servants, at five o'clock sharp, brought in the *salvillas*, the trays, the *mancerinas* loaded with cakes, of *polvorones*, of Chinese bowls or silver cups overflowing with boiling *soconusco*, whose aroma would be capable of resurrecting a dead person – a Spanish dead person, naturally. – The delicious beverage was the theme of those classic meals, but a theme so enriched with gourmand and even artistic variations that it formed only a peculiar aspect, perhaps the most sybaritic of our life.)

The parallelistic construction allows her to associate the triumphal moment of chocolate with military attire and also with moments and modes of chocolate tasting. Chocolate was the centre of an industry and craftsmanship to facilitate its consumption:

Para el chocolate trabajaban los alfares de Talavera y Alcora, modelando y pintando esas mancerinas de graciosa forma salpicadas de menudas florecillas, que hoy buscan los coleccionistas con interés. Para el chocolate se labraba la plata de Méjico, relevando en ella rosas de resalte y festones y astrágalos que contorneaban la maciza salvilla trípode. Para el chocolate se grababan en la Granja los cristales transparentes como el mismo aire. Colmados de la rica agua de fuente, se disolvía en ellos el perfumado azucarillo, cuyos remansos de espuma apartaba la cucharilla desdeñosa antes de que la bebida llegase á los labios … Desde que ha venido el té a encalabrinarnos los nervios, acabáronse los Churrucas y no queda un Álvarez de Castro ni para señal. (Pardo Bazán, *De siglo a siglo* 150–1)

(For chocolate, the potters of Talavera and Alcora worked, modelling and painting those gracefully shaped cups sprinkled with small flowers, which today collectors seek with interest. For the chocolate, the silver of Mexico was carved, with roses, scallops, and astragalus that outlined the solid tripod silverware. For the chocolate, the crystals, transparent as the air itself, were engraved in the Granja. Filled with rich spring water, the perfumed sugar cubes were dissolved in them, whose foamy rivulets were pushed away by the disdainful spoon before the drink reached the lips … Since tea has come to get on our nerves, the Churrucas have gone and there is not even an Álvarez de Castro left for a token.)

The two final metonymies allow her to emphasize, on the one hand, the contrast between the bravura of yesterday and the cowardice of the present. On the other hand, chocolate seemed ideal if accompanied by home-made products, rather than by industrial products that we can assume are of foreign origin:

Al chocolate, en vez de indigestas pastas é insípidas galleticas, le acompañaban conservas en caja, de esas que todavía se elaboran en los conventos, y dulces de almíbar, caseros y de un sabor inolvidable. La brillante pasta de membrillo, la compleja tropezada, la perada, el limoncillo amargo, la melosa guinda, el translúcido espejuelo, el rubio cabello de ángel, el melocotón dorado, se lucían en tacitas de cristal con asa ó en platillos de loza, al presente guardados en las vitrinas. Había quien, menos espiritual, reforzaba el chocolate con magras de jamón granadino, ó lo glosaba con un par de huevos estrellados. (Pardo Bazán, *De siglo a siglo* 151)

(Chocolate, instead of indigestible pastries and tasteless cookies, was accompanied by preserves in boxes, the kind that are still made in convents, and home-made syrup sweets with an unforgettable flavour. The bright quince paste, the complex *tropezada*, the perry, the bitter lemon grass, the syrupy cherry, the translucent *espejuelo*, the blond angel hair, the golden peach, were displayed in glass cups with handle or in earthenware saucers, now kept in the showcases. There were those who, less spiritual, reinforced the chocolate with a few slices of Granadian ham, or garnished it with a couple of fried eggs.)

And as for the moment of tasting, we see that it requires a parsimonious gesture, a calmness, which is not granted to tea:

> Lo indudable es que el chocolate nunca se tomó desparramándose la gente jícara en mano, ni al vuelo, de pie y como en viaje, al modo que se toma el té; el chocolate siempre se gozó á pulso, con solemne mesura; el chocolate exige sentarse, y mejor si es un eran sillón de los llamados fraileros, con su cordobán, sus clavos de asterisco, sus brazos anchos y su asiento profundo. (Pardo Bazán, *De siglo a siglo* 151)
>
> (Undoubtedly, chocolate was never drunk by people walking around with a jug in hand, nor on the fly, standing up and as if on a trip, the way tea is drunk; chocolate was always enjoyed with a pulse, with solemn moderation; chocolate requires a seat, and better still if it is an armchair of the so-called *fraileros*, with its *cordobán*, its asterisk nails, its wide arms, and its deep seat.)

An additional problem is that of counterfeiting, when cocoa is replaced by starch:

> He aquí por qué no se ha podido restaurar el chocolate. Se aspira á ello; se intenta, en la buena sociedad, sustituir el té, tan cursi, tan burgués, tan resobado, con el chocolate, mucho más noble; pero se tropieza siempre con el inconveniente de que se paga chocolate y se compra fécula. Detrás del té y del chocolate hay un problema histórico; no se restaura una bebida sin restaurar un mundo, sin restaurar una época, sin restaurar una nación. Nuestro menguado sino nos condena á té y pastas ... porque nos conduce á imitar, á perder lo que fue bueno de nuestro pasado, sin encontrar ni instituir lo que es óptimo en el presente de otros pueblos. (Pardo Bazán, *De siglo a siglo* 154)
>
> (This is why it has not been possible to restore chocolate. One aspires to it; one tries, in the good society, to replace tea, so corny, so bourgeois, so poor, with chocolate, much nobler; but one always runs up against the inconvenience that one pays for chocolate and buys starch. Behind tea and chocolate there is a historical problem; one cannot restore a beverage without restoring a world, without restoring an epoch, without restoring a nation. Our diminished destiny condemns us to tea and pastries ... because it leads us to imitate, to lose what was good in our past, without finding or instituting what is optimal in the present of other peoples.)

She concludes sententiously with an extreme defence of the ancien régime, kings and nobles, as the best tasters of the colonial drink:

> No, el chocolate no se prestará nunca á los *buffets* de las actuales reuniones, donde los hombres se agolpan quitando el sitio á las damas, y donde se

> pide en voz alta lo que se desea, ni más ní menos que en un bar ó en un baile público. El chocolate nació para ser ofrecido con reverencia A la señora por el caballero de empolvada peluca. No consiente el chocolate prisas, ni descomedimientos, ni empujones, ni excesiva libertad de maneras. Es un cortesano, es un señor el chocolate. Bebida de emperadores, de prelados, de pontífices, de reyes, de bellezas calzadas de blanco, con tacón alto y girándulas de diamantes, exige para enfriar aire de abanico de marfil con pinturas Watteau, para limpiarse servilleta blanquísima, para entremés pulidos versos moratinianos …
>
> Es una elegancia más que desaparece, un artículo más del que se ha apoderado la industria, poniéndolo en manos de todos, pero en tal estado que no lo conocerá la madre que lo parió, justificando la donosa y colérica exclamación del huésped barato, que al remojar un mendrugo en polvo de teja disuelto con agua, gruñe: "A cualquier cosa llaman chocolate las patronas ..." (Pardo Bazán, *De siglo a siglo* 155)
>
> (No, chocolate will never lend itself to the buffets of today's meetings, where men crowd around, taking the place of the ladies, and where they ask aloud for what they want, no more or less than in a bar or at a public dance. Chocolate was born to be offered with reverence to the lady by the gentleman with the powdered wig. Chocolate does not allow rushes, nor discomforts, nor pushes, nor excessive freedom of manners. It is a noble, chocolate is a gentleman. Drink of emperors, of prelates, of pontiffs, of kings, of beauties dressed in white, with high heels and diamond *girandoles*, it requires, for cooling air, an ivory fan with Watteau paintings; for cleaning, a white napkin; for hors d'oeuvres, polished Moratinian verses …
>
> It is one more elegance that disappears, one more article of which the industry has taken possession, putting it in the hands of all, but in such a state that the mother who gave birth to it will not know it, justifying the witty and choleric exclamation of the cheap guest, who when soaking a crust in tile powder dissolved with water, grunts: "To anything the ladies of the house call chocolate …")

As recognized by Joyce Tolliver, "in this way, Pardo Bazán shows us that it is precisely through the domestic – or more exactly, through a feminine-code 'thick description' of everyday practices – that her readers can begin to fully understand the economic significance and the deeper cultural meaning of the War of 1898" (229).

In March 1896 Pardo Bazán complained about the disappearance of Lent – "¿Existe la Cuaresma?" (Does Lent exist?) – and took the opportunity to denounce the falsehood of those who pretended to practise fasting during Lent, as one of the most neglected precepts, together with the vigil with abstinence. She laments that the menus of the inns and eating houses present oysters linked with partridges, and lobsters together with capons. Even in the houses on Fridays, chops and the stew persevere: "apenas si los días más señalados de la Semana Santa se come de vigilia" (*De siglo a siglo* 19; hardly in the most important days of the Holy Week do people fast). All the Spaniards have a pretext not to fast. The great cooks add meat substance and beef marrow to the fasting soups, deceiving the diners who come out, blessing them, and repeating with the most delicious candour: "'¿Ha visto usted qué comida de pescado? Mantiene lo mismo que una de carne. ¡Lo que pueden la habilidad y la ciencia do un buen cordón bleu!'" (19; Have you seen such a fish meal? What skill and science can do with a good cordon bleu!). Pardo Bazán is hopelessly Catholic and conservative. She associates the lack of respect for the precept of fasting with profanity and blasphemous expressions (18–19).

Pardo Bazán completes the article by comparing the richness of the Lenten menu in Galicia and the mediocrity of the one in Madrid. She defends the freshness and variety in her homeland as opposed to Madrid's.

> La lista de una comida de vigilia no sólo es fácil, sino golosa, en tierras del Noroeste, donde el mar cría y sazona tan delicados manjares. En el país gallego el marisco ofrece variedad increíble, y son tan numerosos los géneros de pescado blanco y azul, que se considera habilidad el conocerlos por sus nombres y saber cogerlos y diferenciarlos. (Pardo Bazán, *De siglo a siglo* 21)
>
> (The list of a vigil meal is not only easy, but gourmand, in lands of the Northwest, where the sea breeds and seasons such delicate delicacies. In the Galician country, seafood offers an incredible variety, and there are so many types of white and blue fish that it is considered a skill to know them by name and to know how to catch and differentiate them.)

She makes a defence of the blue fish that is very much to the taste of today's dieticians:

> Aunque sólo existiese la sardina, con el gusto que tiene al salir de las olas, sería llevadera la Cuaresma. La sardina no es viajera: quiere, según el dicho popular, que se oiga desde el puerto donde la redaron el chirrido de la sartén en que la fríen; á la corte llega la sardina denegrida, acardenalada, sin la gentil curvatura que guarda su plateado cuerpo mientras está la carne fresca y sólida; los madrileños ignorarán siempre lo que es una sardina si no van á probarla á orillas del Cantábrico. (Pardo Bazán, *De siglo a siglo* 21–2)

> (Even if only the sardine existed, with the taste it has when it comes out of the waves, Lent would be bearable. The sardine is not a traveller: it wants, according to the popular saying, to be heard from the port where it was caught, the creaking of the frying pan in which it is fried; the sardine arrives at the court denigrated, *acardenalada*, without the gentle curvature that keeps its silvery body while the meat is fresh and solid; the people of Madrid will always ignore what a sardine is if they do not go to taste it on the shores of the Bay of Biscay.)

According to Pardo Bazán, in a city such as Madrid, far from the ocean, the gastronomic offer is much more limited:

> En Madrid, el seco bacalao, las ascéticas lentejas y el garbanzo disfrazado con verde capuchón de acederas en potaje, son el recurso de los que aún acatan el precepto. Las colaciones constituyen un problema de economía doméstica. Patatas, alcachofas, berenjenas, judías, se empeñan en remedar á otros manjares más nutritivos, y se rebozan y se rellenan de pan para fingir que no son verduras, algo semejante á lo que manducaban los primitivos anacoretas, á quienes debemos recordar para no sentir tanto las leves mortificaciones del estómago. (Pardo Bazán, *De siglo a siglo* 22)

> (In Madrid, dry cod, ascetic lentils and chickpeas disguised with a green cap of sorrel in stew, are the resource of those who still abide by the precept. The snacks constitute a problem of domestic economy. Potatoes, artichokes, eggplants, beans, are determined to imitate other more nutritious delicacies, and they are battered and stuffed with bread to pretend that they are not vegetables, something similar to what the primitive anchorites used to eat, whom we should remember so as not to feel so much the slight mortifications of the stomach.)

Her interest in food is not surprising. Years later Pardo Bazán was to be the author of two notable cookbooks: *La cocina española antigua* (1913) and *La cocina española moderna* (1917). In the prologue of the first of these volumes she apologized for the little time she had been able to devote to household activities: "si no he trabajado más en este interesante ramo, la culpa ha de achacarse á que nunca me sobra un minuto para hacer cosas sencillas y gratas, – un pastel de ostras, por ejemplo" (*Cocina española* 14; if I have not worked more in this interesting field, it is because I never have a minute to spare to do simple and pleasant things – an oyster pie, for example). She then confirms the symbolic value (Fischler) that the importance of food has in the knowledge of a country:[1]

> La cocina, además, es, en mi entender, uno de los documentos etnográficos importantes ... La alimentación revela lo que acaso no descubren otras indagaciones de carácter oficialmente científico ... Cada época de la Historia modifica el fogón y cada pueblo come según su alma, antes tal vez que según su estómago. Hay platos de nuestra cocina nacional que no son menos curiosos ni menos históricos que una medalla, un arma o un sepulcro. (Pardo Bazán, *Cocina española* 14)
>
> (The kitchen, moreover, is, in my opinion, one of the most important ethnographic documents ... Food reveals what perhaps other officially scientific inquiries do not discover ... Each epoch of history modifies the stove and each nation eats according to its soul, perhaps more than according to its stomach. There are dishes of our national cuisine that are no less curious or less historical than a medal, a weapon, or a tomb.)

She concludes:

> Que la cocina española propiamente dicha tiene su sello, lo demuestra, entre otras cosas, su extensión y evolución en América. En Cuba, en Méjico y en Chile abundan los platos hoy nacionales, que revelan á las claras lo hispánico de su origen y la aplicación de los elementos ibéricos al nuevo ambiente. Algunos he incluido en este tomo. (Pardo Bazán, *Cocina española* 15–16)
>
> (That Spanish cuisine itself has its own stamp is demonstrated, among other things, by its extension and evolution in America. In Cuba, Mexico, and Chile there is an abundance of national dishes that clearly reveal the Hispanic origin and the application of Iberian elements to the new environment. I have included some of them in this volume.)

She also surprises the reader with a statement of her proto-feminism, which is overturned by her sense of class:

> Lo más femenino de este libro es la recomendación con que voy á terminar el prólogo. En las recetas que siguen encontrarán las señoras muchas donde entran la cebolla y el ajo. Si quieren trabajar con sus propias delicadas manos en hacer un guiso, procuren que la cebolla y el ajo los manipule la cocinera. Es su oficio, y nada tiene de deshonroso el manejar esos bulbos de penetrante aroma; pero sería muy cruel que las señoras conservasen, entre una sortija de rubíes y la manga calada de una blusa, un traidor y avillanado rasero cebollero. (Pardo Bazán, *Cocina española* 17)
>
> (The most feminine aspect of this book is the recommendation with which I will end the prologue. In the recipes that follow, the ladies will find many

where the onion and garlic come in. If you want to work with your own delicate hands in making a stew, try to have the onion and garlic handled by the cook. It is her job, and there is nothing dishonourable about handling those bulbs of penetrating aroma; but it would be very cruel for ladies to keep, between a ring of rubies and the openwork sleeve of a blouse, a treacherous and villainous onion aroma.)

These examples of the incorporation of aspects of food in Pardo Bazán's journalistic work confirm not only the descriptive or decorative use of food but also the deep meaning she attributes to it from a post-colonial perspective, even to highlight the differences between centre and periphery or to help define a concept of femininity.

Bell-Ringers and Bread Crumbs in Buñuel's Films

Luis Buñuel's cinema is built around an exploration of the subconscious, which goes hand in hand with psychoanalysis within the surrealist movement. In some of his great films food occupies an essential place. Buñuel (influenced by Dalí) included many scenes with food throughout his career as a film-maker. Sea urchins played an important role at the beginning as a substitute for female sexuality. "Poema de las cositas" (in the version he copied in a letter to García Lorca) established the association between the crustacean and female sexuality: "Los dos pechos de mi amiga: el uno es un movidísimo avispero / y el otro una calma garota / Los pequeños erizos, los pequeños erizos, los pequeños erizos, los pequeños erizos, / los pequeños erizos, los pequeños erizos: pinchan" (Dalí 68–9; The two breasts of my friend: the one is a very busy hornet's nest / and the other a calm sea urchin / The little sea urchins, the little sea urchins, the little sea urchins, the little sea urchins, the little sea urchins, the little sea urchins: they sting). One of the sequences of *Un chien andalou* confirms this association. In a series of fades that correspond to the filmic version of the multiple images, we see how the hand with ants melts into the armpit hair of a young woman lying in the sun on a beach; the armpit becomes a sea urchin whose tips oscillate slightly; and it becomes again a woman's armpit (shots 56 to 60). Dalí used them also as an allusion to William Tell (the apple being replaced by a sea urchin on his head), when Buñuel was expelled from his family in 1929, after getting together with Gala (Bou, *Daliccionario*). Sea urchins were the favourite food of Dalí's father and of the artist himself. When Dalí and Buñuel were scouting for locations for *L'age d'or* in Cadaqués, Buñuel shot a four-minutes film entitled *Menjant Garotes*. Salvador Dalí's father appeared in the film, eating sea urchins in a very ritualistic fashion. The short film highlighted the centrality of eating, from the first stages of Buñuel's filmography, and the implications of it.

On many other films Buñuel incorporated food not just as a mimetic device but with surrealistic implications. In *Viridiana* (1961), in which appear some of Buñuel's great themes, such as the contrast between God (man, spirit) and the world of the flesh, the centrality of food is exemplified through a particularly significant sequence: a sacrilegious and irreverent dinner. The beggars occupy the house where Viridiana and her cousin live (after the death of their uncle and father), and the beggars prepare a dinner that becomes a parody of Leonardo da Vinci's *Last Supper* thanks to a photographic group portrait. In fact, it is a false portrait because it is done – as the children did – with an eschatological gesture: one of the women in the group lifts her skirt and shows her panties to the group. This is how Buñuel inverts evangelical iconography. It is a way of mercilessly portraying the vices of bad religiosity, of the hysteria of false asceticism, which denies corporeality, instincts, and the animality of the human being. This and other scenes are excellent illustrations of a statement by Buñuel:

> El misterio, elemento esencial en toda obra de arte, falta, por lo general en las películas. Ya tienen buen cuidado autores, directores y productores de no turbar nuestra tranquilidad abriendo la ventana maravillosa de la pantalla al mundo libertador de la poesía … El cine es un arma maravillosa y peligrosa si la maneja un espíritu libre. Es el mejor instrumento para expresar el mundo de los sueños, de las emociones, del instinto … El cine parece haberse inventado para expresar la vida subconsciente. (Buñuel 66)
>
> (Mystery, an essential element in any work of art, is missing, usually in movies. Authors, directors, and producers are already careful not to disturb our tranquility by opening the wonderful window of the screen to the liberating world of poetry … Cinema is a wonderful and dangerous weapon if it is operated by a free spirit. It is the best instrument to express the world of dreams, emotions, instinct … Cinema seems to have been invented to express subconscious life.)

Buñuel expresses many instances of subconscious life in all his films. In *Tristana* (1970), filmed in the city of Toledo (a vague reference to the "Orden de Toledo" from his time at the Residencia de Estudiantes), Buñuel is particularly concerned about the importance of gastronomy. The critics of *Cahiers du Cinéma* pointed out sixteen occasions where food is present in the movie. Luis Buñuel contradicted that number in an interview (Pérez Turrent and de la Colina 158), saying that he only found three scenes with food in them. The scene of the encounter between the bell-ringer and Tristana stands out: at one point, a close-up shows crumbs in a pan and a slotted spoon with which they are being served. Then the off-field voice of the ringer is heard, explaining to Tristana, "These crumbs are from the ringer, miss," to which she adds, "But that skimmer?" "Also," answers the ringer. This particular exchange of words does not appear in the script. In this absurd and disconcerting dialogue the irony is detected with the manipulation of language that the surrealists so liked (Poyato Sánchez 745). It is a kind of significant delusion in which things are said without saying them. Here the reference to food concentrates attention. As Antonio Monegal explained, when Buñuel introduces elements that, as in *Tristana*'s dialogue, do not contribute anything to the economy of narration but, on the contrary, distort it, he is carrying out an exercise of catachresis that leads to the reading of those elements from strictly poetic criteria (Monegal-Brancos 154). The sequence of the bell tower and the crumbs has a corollary in Tristana's later dream in which it produces another brilliant association: the bell clapper, with clear phallic connotations, has become Don Lope's severed head, in a sublimation of the castration that announces the liberation of the young woman.

A third example is provided by *Le fantôme de la liberté* (1974). Buñuel repeated many times that he had made the film in collaboration with Karl Marx (the title refers to the first line of *The Communist Manifesto*), but the title is also a personal nod to a phrase in *La Voie lactée* (1969): "Free will is only a whim! In any circumstance, I feel that my thinking and my will are not in my power! And my freedom is only a ghost!" In the film there are many situations that are characteristic of Buñuel, such as eroticism seen as perversion, necrophilia, eating while in the bathroom, pedophilia, incest, sadomasochistic flogging, foot fetishism, voyeur priests, and many other varieties of the taboo. One of the most surprising sequences is the inversion between the dining room and the toilet. Guests at a dinner are sitting around the table over toilet bowls, in which they are defecating. They ask permission to get up and go individually to a small private room where they eat disorderly. Buñuel thus highlights and denounces the construction of the sense of what is natural and what is a cultural convention.

We see then that in Luis Buñuel the crumb of allusions to food reaches poetic and symbolic meanings or is an instrument for his denunciation of the contradictions of bourgeois morality. The crumbs of the ringer are used as a provocative comment on repressed sexuality and unsatisfied desires.

Customs and Manners at the Table

There is a gray area in which articles on customs (*costumbrismo*) and purely gastronomic writings coexist. Articles that pursue social change coexist with culinary writings by authors such as Dr Thebussem and with other works such as recipe books and manuals. At first, gastronomic writings of the nineteenth century aimed to illustrate or advise on matters of food, cooking, and protocol; years later, Thebussem's gastronomic chronicle and criticism became associated with leisure and consumption rather than with questions of society. Food, customs, festivities, restaurants, and dishes are integrated into Thebussem's articles as part of the life experience of the characters, which contributes to re-treating the intimate and social environment of the time. The express mention of cuisine, dishes, recipes, and food contributed to a broadening of the gastronomic cartography of the nineteenth-century foodscape, with mostly sociocultural comments and criticism, and evidenced a subject whose evolution led to a journalistic specialization of its own (Blanco Hernández). Sánchez-Llama has pointed to the role (even if unsuccessful) of Larra's articles in shaping a modern bourgeoisie in Spain: "The good taste of the emergent bourgeoisie – a social class identified in the Spain of 1830 with liberalism – is important in order to articulate a reformist project of cosmopolitan inspiration. Codes of etiquette or culinary habits, consequently, are relevant both for asserting the bourgeois distinction and for accentuating the parodic traits of its traditionalist detractors" (Sánchez-Llama 208).

In one of the best-known articles by Mariano José de Larra, "El castellano viejo," the author insists on another aspect of food and the everyday: a country without education shows its rudeness at the table. It "presents a detailed X-ray of the cultural habits of an openly nationalist middle class resistant to the introduction of any foreignizing novelty (Sánchez-Llama 209). As shown by James Mandrell, this *costumbrista* article has a clear textual dependence "point by point" on "Observaciones sobre la cortesanía" (1820; Observations on courtesy) by José de Urcullu (Mandrell 79).

In "El castellano viejo," Fígaro (one of Larra's pseudonyms) receives an invitation to lunch at the house of his friend Braulio, and he describes the lunch in such a way that it becomes one of the most hilarious pieces of Larra's entire body of work, focusing on the manners of the people sitting at the table. He looks at meal times by giving a hyperbolic version of Spanish customs. It is already four in the afternoon and they have not started. Braulio's wife makes some excuses: "con tanta visita yo he faltado algunos momentos de allá dentro y …" (Larra 89; with so many visitors I have missed a few moments from there and …). They end up eating at five. Right away Fígaro describes the ritual of eating at Braulio's house, the little formality he wants to give to the event: "– Sin etiqueta, señores – exclamó Braulio, y se echó el primero con su propia cuchara" (89; "Without compliments, gentlemen," Braulio exclaimed, and he served himself first with his own spoon). After the soup comes the cooked assortment "de todas las sabrosas impertinencias de este engorrosísimo, aunque buen plato; cruza por aquí la carne; por allá la verdura; acá los garbanzos; allá el jamón; la gallina por derecha; por medio el tocino; por izquierda los embuchados de Extremadura" (91; of all the tasty impertinences of this most cumbersome, albeit good dish; some meat here; over there the vegetables; here the chickpeas; there the ham; the hen on the right; in the middle the bacon; on the left the sausages of Extremadura). The narrator comments:

> ¿Hay nada más ridículo que estas gentes que quieren pasar por finas en medio de la más crasa ignorancia de los usos sociales; que para obsequiarle le obligan a usted a comer y beber por fuerza, y no le dejan medio de hacer su gusto? ¿Por qué habrá gentes que sólo quieren comer con alguna más limpieza los días de días? (Larra 91)
>
> (Is there anything more ridiculous than these people who want to seem to be extremely well educated in the midst of the most crass ignorance of social customs; that to give you gifts they force you to eat and drink, and they don't leave you the means to do what you like? Why will there be people who only want to eat with some more cleanliness on special days?)

Fígaro realizes that his *Lebensraum* has been occupied at the table as his neighbours gradually invade it with spoils and other remains that they leave on the tablecloth. A boy to his left "hacía saltar las aceitunas a un plato de magras con tomate, y una vino a parar a uno de mis ojos que no volvió a ver claro en todo el día" (Larra 91; made the olives jump onto a plate of lean meats with tomato, and one fell into one of my eyes, that I did not see clearly again for the whole day); a fat man on his right side "había tenido la precaución de ir dejando en el mantel, al lado de mi pan, los huesos de las suyas, y los de las aves que había roído" (91; had taken the precaution of leaving on the tablecloth, next to my bread, the bones of his own, and those of the birds that he had gnawed on); the opposite guest "se había encargado de hacer la autopsia de un capón, o sea gallo" (91; had carried out an autopsy on a capon, or maybe of a rooster) and also dropped some leftovers: "en una de las embestidas resbaló el tenedor sobre el animal como si tuviera escama, y el capón, violentamente despedido, pareció querer tomar su vuelo como en sus tiempos más felices, y se posó en el mantel tranquilamente como pudiera en un palo de un gallinero" (91; in one of the attacks the fork slipped on the animal as if it had scales, and the capon, violently thrown off, seemed to want to take flight as in its happiest times, and perched on the tablecloth calmly as it could on a stick from a chicken coop). The narrator reflects in dismay on the neighbours who offer him food to eat with their own hands or a drink from their glasses: "el niño se divierte en despedir a los ojos de los concurrentes los huesos disparados de las cerezas" (93; the boy amuses himself by firing cherry pits into the eyes of those present). Another guest makes him taste the exquisite manzanilla (dry sherry), which he had refused, in his own glass, which retains the indelible signs of his greasy lips; towards the end of the meal, his neighbour smokes a cigar like a chimney: "mi gordo fuma ya sin cesar y me hace cañón de su chimenea; por fin, ¡oh última de las desgracias!, crece el alboroto y la conversación; roncas ya las voces, piden versos y décimas y no hay más poeta que Fígaro" (93). (My fat man smokes incessantly and makes me a cannon from his chimney; finally, oh last of the misfortunes!, the uproar and the conversation grows; the voices are already hoarse, they ask for verses and ten-line stanzas and there is no other poet than Fígaro.) It is no wonder that when he finishes eating, he runs away, scared:

> –¡Santo Dios, yo te doy gracias, exclamo respirando, como el ciervo que acaba de escaparse de una docena de perros y que oye ya apenas sus ladridos; para de aquí en adelante no te pido riquezas, no te pido empleos, no honores; líbrame de los convites caseros y de días de días; líbrame de estas casas en que es un convite un acontecimiento, en que sólo se pone la mesa decente para los convidados, en que creen hacer obsequios cuando dan mortificaciones, en que se hacen finezas, en que se dicen versos, en que hay niños, en que hay gordos, en que reina, en fin, la brutal franqueza de los castellanos viejos! (Larra 93)
>
> ("Holy God, I thank you," I exclaim, breathing like the deer that has just escaped from a dozen dogs and can hardly hear their barking any more; from now on I do not ask you for riches, I do not ask you for jobs, or honours; protect me from home-made treats and from birthdays celebrations; protect me from these houses where a treat is an event, where only a decent table is set for the guests, where they think they are giving gifts when they give mortifications, where courtesies are made, where verses are said, where there are children, in which there are fat people, in which reigns, in short, the brutal frankness of the old Castilians!)

Larra, nevertheless, ridicules the culinary habits of social groups that propose an anachronistic anchor for Spain in the remote past. As stated by Sánchez-Llama, "[t]he author's satire signals the imperative necessity of introducing cosmopolitan gastronomic tendencies" (208). The obvious vulgarity of this Spanish middle class becomes *grosera* (rude). It is important to note that "the absence of urbanity during the banquet organized by Braulio and the rustic presentation of the food offered in the meal reveal a mental predisposition that associates alleged Spanish purity with the manifestation of primitive instincts uncontaminated by any kind of artifice" (Sánchez-Llama 210). Larra also affirms the lack of vital authenticity noticeable in social groups that are hostile to any transformation of good culinary taste. Cosmopolitan reform and genuine vitality define a perspective whose textual development associates liberalism with the practice of gastronomic habits that were in keeping with the exigencies of modern consciousness in the nineteenth century (Sánchez-Llama 208).

In another article by Larra, "La fonda nueva," he develops a similar strategy, showing the lack of care for the food's presentation in the inn, the mediocre condition of what is offered to the public, and the non-existent urbanity of the waiters (Sánchez-Llama 216). The lack of vitality and the non-existent authenticity of such businesses show the urgent cosmopolitan reformation that the author considers unavoidable in Spanish society.

It is not very difficult to relate Larra's approach to so many other reflections on the unseemly and rude behaviour of his compatriots, as if it were a preview of Jaime Gil de Biedma's famous verses when he referred to his countrymen as "intratable pueblo de cabreros" (intractable goatherd people). In this case, we do not recognize a food voice but a strong apprehension towards certain types of behaviour through the denunciation of Hispanic manners, in accordance with a strong critical tradition that Juan Goytisolo enumerated in *Reivindicación del Conde Don Julián*. In this following fragment a certain Lord Carpeto appears, as the symbolic representative of Castile Spain. His name is derived from the adjective *carpetano*, which means "of the Kingdom of Toledo." Lord Carpeto is starving because, in his quest to ensure the purity of the Spanish language, he cannot eat any of the dishes whose name has an Arab origin:

> [Y]o, señor, soy gramático, y miro por la pureza del idioma mucho más que por mi vida, estudiando de noche y de día y tanteando la complexión del carpeto para acertar a curarle cuando cayere enfermo: y lo principal que hago es asistir a sus comidas y cenas, y dejarle comer de lo que me parece castizo y quitarle cuanto etimológicamente es extraño … vea el señor gramático de cuantos manjares hay en esta mesa cuál me hará más provecho y cuál menos daño y déjeme comer dél sin que me le apalee, porque por mi vida de carpeto, y así Dios me le deje gozar, que me muero de hambre, y el negarme la comida, aunque le pese al señor gramático y el más me diga, antes será quitarme la vida que aumentármela vuesa merced tiene razón, señor carpeto. (Goytisolo 363–6)
>
> (I, sir, am a grammarian, and I look after the purity of the language much more than my own life, studying by night and by day and testing the

complexion of the *carpeto* to be able to cure him when he falls ill: and the main thing I do is to attend his lunches and dinners, and let him eat what seems to me to be traditional and take away what is etymologically strange … let the grammarian see which of the many delicacies on this table will do me the most good and which will do me the least harm, and let me eat them without him beating me, because for the sake of my life as a *carpeto*, and so God grant me to enjoy it, I am dying of hunger, and to deny me food, even if it is hard for the grammarian and he tells me the most, it would be better to take my life than to increase it, you are right, Mr Carpeto.)

The presence of Arab language is evident in Spanish language. This is an example of the hybrid character of Spanish itself. The scene was analysed by Linda Gould Levine in her book *Juan Goytisolo: La destrucción creadora*. In the novel, Goytisolo uses the dialogue between Sancho and the doctor in *Don Quixote* and parodies it (Gould Levine 137). He creates a scene in which he replaces the doctor with the grammarian and in which the forbidden foods are no longer those that are harmful to the stomach, as in *Don Quixote*, but those that are etymologically foreign:

[N]o hay cosa peor en el mundo que una olla podrida con albóndigas y unas gotas de aceite: y respecto a los postres de vuesa merced ni uno siquiera le puedo autorizar: el flan, a causa del caramelo: el helado, por contener azúcar: la macedonia, por el jarabe: en cuanto al exquisito sorbete que acaban de servir a vuesa merced, la duda ofende: es etimológicamente foráneo y, abandonando al carpeto en la plena y solemne posesión de su hambre, galoparás de nuevo por el próspero y floreciente reino de la Paz, el Desarrollo y el Orden y provocarás catástrofes financieras y desastres bursátiles mediante la brusca supresión de aranceles y tarifas, la abrogación inesperada y radical de todas las barreras de aduana a los comerciantes que miden y pesan los dejarás sin fanegas, quintales, arrobas, azumbres, quilates privarás de álgebra a las escuelas y a las contabilidades de cifras y galoparás y galoparás e incorporarás a tus huestes alguaciles y alféreces, almirantes y alcaldes requisarás las bebidas alcohólicas despoblarás las construcciones de albañiles derribarás tabiques, secarás acequias, motivarás infecciones y epidemias al desbaratar el arduo, laborioso sistema de alcantarillas y galoparás y galoparás sin tregua por el vasto y asolado país, y cuando la ruina sea completa y la bancarrota absoluta, te pararás frente al mapa de la Península y apuntarás aún con tu varilla de ballena ah, se me pasaba : y quítenme de ahí ese Guad-el-Kebir! (Goytisolo 198–9)

(There is nothing worse in the world than a rotten pot with meatballs and a few drops of oil. And as for your worship's desserts, I cannot even authorize one: the flan, because of the caramel; the ice cream, because it

> contains sugar; the fruit salad, because of the syrup; as for the exquisite sorbet that has just been served to your worship, the doubt offends; it is etymologically foreign, and, abandoning the carpet in the full and solemn possession of its hunger, you will gallop again through the prosperous and flourishing kingdom of Peace, Development, and Order and you will provoke financial catastrophes and stock market disasters by the abrupt suppression of duties and tariffs, the unexpected and radical abrogation of all customs barriers to traders who measure and weigh; you will leave them without bushels, quintals, arrobas, azumbres, you will deprive the schools of algebra and the accounting of figures and you will gallop and gallop and you will incorporate as your hosts marshals and ensigns, admirals and mayors, you will requisition alcoholic beverages, you will depopulate the buildings of masons, you will demolish partitions, you will dry up irrigation ditches, you will cause infections and epidemics by disrupting the arduous, laborious system of sewers, and you will gallop and gallop relentlessly through the vast and ravaged country, and when the ruin is complete and the bankruptcy absolute, you will stand in front of the map of the Peninsula and point even with your whale rod – ah, I missed it: and take that Guad-el-Kebir away from me!)

It prohibits then the marinade, saffron, eggplants, carrots, spinach, meatballs, and artichokes, which accompany (contaminate) the rice, olives, partridges, and rabbits of the Spanish table. By removing all words of Arabic derivation from the Spanish language, Goytisolo shows ironically the importance and abundance of Arabic terminology in Spanish and the "impurity" not only of the Spanish language but also of the food. In Larra and Goytisolo, food habits acquire definitely a symbolic status. Food culture and modes of eating describe the way humans use food, how it is served and eaten, and its profound signification.

Civil War and Autarky: Vindication of the Essential Kitchen

Joan de Déu Domènech published in 2012 a distinctive book, *La batalla de l'ou: De quan passàvem gana (1936–1939)* (The egg battle: When we were hungry), which deals with hunger in Catalonia during the civil war. In the book he discusses the egg battle, but he also includes aspects of the famine endured during the war, that sparked the conception of alternative recipes: bread with oil, *almortas* (grass peas), carob beans, rabbit herbs, and other subsistence foods. One of the chapters is dedicated specifically to the egg battle, an initiative in January 1937 by the Generalitat's Department of Agriculture to compensate for the lack of eggs. With the idea of promoting the production of poultry and thus increasing the production of eggs, the "Egg Office" was created, one of whose slogans summarized the main objective: "in 1937, 100 chickens to each farmhouse and 6 chickens to every working woman" (Domènech 13). As Domènech explains, it was intended that, in addition to having chickens on farms, there should be chickens in cities, on every patio, balcony, terrace, or outing – a precedent for current urban gardens, in this case urban chicken coops. To achieve this, with food rationing one could choose between one egg a week for each person or feedstuff for the chickens. This "battle," like so many others of those difficult times, was lost.

One of the peculiar solutions to the shortage of food was the renewal of the home cookbook. A gastronomist invented a recipe for making a potato omelette without eggs or potatoes. At the end of 1938, Ignasi Domènech i Puigcercós, gastronomist and Catalan publisher, issued *Cocina de recursos*. It is a classic of subsistence cooking that shows that, in the absence of resources, imagination and ingenuity are capable of working miracles, as is the case with this potato omelette. In the absence of eggs, Domènech came up with the idea of replacing the egg with a paste of flour, bicarbonate, and water, while the potatoes were replaced by their skins or the white part of the rind of an orange. This ingenuity responded to an intimate desire:

> Como sentía hambre, mi primera ilusión era el poder recordar el delicado perfume de las tortillitas de patatas, con dos huevos, recién hechitas, y el cordero o pollos recién asados, los trozos de jamón, la ternera a la parrilla, y así mil manjares que en gran abundancia habían pasado por mis manos. ¡Contrastes de la vida, en que hasta los cocineros pueden morirse de hambre!" (I. Domènech, qtd. in Sella Montserrat 10)

> (As I was feeling hungry, my first illusion was to be able to remember the delicate perfume of potato tortillas, with two eggs, freshly made, and the lamb or freshly roasted chickens, the pieces of ham, the grilled beef, and thus a thousand delicacies that in great abundance had passed through my hands. Disparities of life, in which even cooks can starve!)

It is not surprising that Manuel Vázquez Montalbán described Ignasi Domènech as "the Menéndez Pelayo of Spanish culinary literature" (Vázquez Montalbán, qtd. in Serrallonga et al. 112). These cases represent the creation of a culinary dialect similar but different from the known dishes, as an imposition of the voice when facing a desolate present.

The difficulties and rationing during the civil war continued in the postwar period, and the deprivation did not end until the late 1950s.

Scarcity and hunger became normal. This was evidenced by Carpanta, a popular comic character created by Escobar, who was always starving and whose name according to the *Diccionario de la lengua española* means "Hambre violenta" (Guiral; violent hunger). During the years of autarky, ration cards abounded, symbols of hardship and dearth. The government controlled the distribution of merchandise, assigning each person a certain quantity of basic products, such as sugar, rice, oil, bread, and beans, which had to be collected with ration cards. These were established on 14 May 1939 and used until 1952. Those years have remained etched in Spanish collective memory as the "Years of Hunger." It was a long postwar period, marked by economic hardship, brutal repression, the close relationship with the Axis powers during the Second World War, and international isolation after 1945 (Arco Blanco 4).

The Spanish famine was furthered by a reduction in harvested areas and yields and a general decline in production. The imposition of poor wages and the rigid control of the workforce lowered costs but took away incentives to raise productivity (Arco Blanco 9). The scarcity was also linked to the black-market phenomenon, which was a reaction to the tight (and enduring) regime control over a variety of foodstuffs:

> The regime fixed the price of the majority of basic commodities, forcing their sale at an official price throughout the country. Scarcity, supply control and poor prices paved the way for the rise of a black market across the country for nearly all products subject to official control. In reality, the scarcity was somewhat fictitious: any item could be found in the black market if one had enough money to pay for it. Further, those with access to any state-controlled product could hide it from the authorities and sell it as *estraperlo* (illegally) in the black market. This was the case of many farm workers, who formed a key social pillar of support for the dictatorship and were able to control supply and [to] even profit from trading on the black market. (Arco Blanco 9)

Even though the lower classes were on the brink of starvation, struggling against the high cost of living and the spread of diseases, the middle classes were protected from such hardships. They were impoverished, but their lives were not at risk. According to Arco Blanco, hunger and famine are critical to explain the dynamics of political opposition to Francoism during the period. Resistance practices like *estraperlo* and the black market should be understood as a real fight for survival in the context of a famine triggered by the dictatorship's policies (Arco Blanco 26).

Distribution functioned with the assignment of a personal ration card, which, through coupons, set for each citizen the stipulated amount of basic food. The supply was provided by the Comisaría General de Abastos (General Commissariat of Supplies), which publicly announced each week the percentage, quantity, and price of the food awarded. Each person was assigned a vendor or grocery store. It was impossible to legally acquire any food that was not controlled by *racionamiento* (rationing); the black market, also known as *estraperlo* (a word composed of the last names of two individuals, Strauss and Perlaux, experts in forging casino roulettes in Spain in the 1920s), operated at prices well above what was established by the corresponding police station (Terán Reyes).

Néstor Luján wrote a remarkable article concerning *estraperlo*, entitled "Si no existiera el estraperlo" (If the *estraperlo* did not exist):

> En estas dos últimas semanas la Comisaría de Abastecimientos ha repartido lo siguiente: en la semana penúltima repartió un racionamiento compuesto de aceite refinado de ignoramos qué producto y desde entonces nuestra imaginación está intentando representarse cómo puede ser el aceite en bruto, a razón de un octavo de litro por persona, café a razón de cincuenta gramos y alubias, éstas de excelente calidad a razón de doscientos gramos. La última semana nos vimos favorecidos por azúcar blanco, bacalao, pasta para sopa y manteca vegetal. Ahora bien, considerando los precios de la carne, de los huevos, de la leche y demás comestibles inasequibles a la mayoría de los bolsillos modestos, desearíamos que estos racionamientos fueran acompañados de un folletito explicativo de qué platos pueden cocinarse con bacalao, pasta de sopa y azúcar blanco que es lo que pueden comprar las clases humildes o bien qué menús pueden construirse en una larga semana con aceite, café y alubias. (Luján, *La Barcelona* 35)
>
> (In these last two weeks the Commissariat of Supplies has distributed the following: in the week before last it distributed a rationing composed of refined oil, we do not know from what product, and since then our imagination is trying to imagine what the oil could be like, at the rate of one eighth of a litre per person, coffee at the rate of fifty grams, and beans, these of excellent quality at the rate of two hundred grams. Last week we were favoured with white sugar, codfish, soup paste, and vegetable shortening. Now, considering the prices of meat, eggs, milk, and other foodstuffs unaffordable to most modest pockets, we would like these rationings to be accompanied by a little booklet explaining what dishes can be cooked with codfish, soup paste, and white sugar, which is what the humble classes can buy, or what menus can be built in a long week with oil, coffee, and beans.)

Luján's originality is visible in his ironic claim of a cookbook specially written for this incongruous series of foods. He ended the article by praising *estraperlo* despite the official ban, because it allowed for other food combinations. The excerpt includes a list that must be read as a coded plea for missing meals in order to develop a full life in those difficult years.

An excellent chronicler of these times of hardship was Josep Pla. His epicurean attitude, which was limited by the historical moment, led him to contemplate nature, which is a refuge, and, in relation to it, to defend aspects of gastronomy. As we have seen in chapter 7, his *Viaje en autobús* chronicles the situation of hunger in postwar Spain. Josep Pla tells us of a world of hunger, with few hopes and even less illusions. Travelling by bus is for him an exercise in contemplation of the world by getting close to it. And such a trip allows one to brag about one's lack of haste. He is an idle flâneur looking for surprises. And he can make his journey at a personal pace. In addition, at various times he exhibits control of his time, renouncing falling under the dictatorship of hurry that seems to him to belong to a world and a moment that has long disappeared: "La urgencia, como la prisa, como la premura, son cosas absolutamente desprovistas de sentido. En lo único que hay una prisa notoria es en aumentar los precios" (J. Pla, *Viaje en autobús* 22). (Urgency, like haste, like rush, are absolutely meaningless things. The only notorious urgency is to raise prices.)

The postwar period involved the cultivation of a basic, elemental cuisine with few ambitions. The case of Josep Pla allows us to delve into the geographical aspect, so decisive in the European culinary field, where, every twenty kilometres, sauces or sweets change. Álvaro Cunqueiro was an extraordinary connoisseur of Galician culture. In books and thousands of articles he achieved a sublime union between gastronomy, scholarship, and rhetoric. If Pla bears witness to times of rationing, Cunqueiro announces the leap towards sophistication, which writers such as Néstor Luján in *Las recetas de Pickwick* (Pickwick's Recipes) and Manuel Vázquez Montalbán in multiple books and articles would develop to unsuspected extremes. A digression of Cunqueiro over cod allows him to synthetically establish the best recipes, as well as to establish a fundamental geographical distinction between north and south:

> El bacalao tiene un sabor característico y profundo, que se dilata en las amables compañías que se le conceden en la cocina, e impregna, suave y terco, el conjunto. Tolera el picante sin perder nada de su gracia, e incluso el tomate, ese enmascarador coquinario, más todavía que el perejil, que en la décima de Mauricio Bacarisse, disfraza las salsas "con fraudes a la mayéutica" … Alrededor del bacalao ha cuajado un espléndido y católico recetario, del que los pueblos hiperbóreos, noruegos o escoceses, no tienen

> ni idea. Lusitanos, españoles, franceses, somos los que sabemos comer bacalao, y nuestras recetas ilustran los grandes compendios de la cocina occidental. (Cunqueiro, *La cocina cristiana* 190)
>
> (Cod has a characteristic and deep flavour, which expands in the kindly company it is given in the kitchen, and permeates, soft and stubborn, the whole. It tolerates the spicy without losing any of its grace, and even the tomato, that kitchen masquerader, even more than parsley, which in the tenth of Mauricio Bacarisse, disguises the sauces "with frauds to the maieutics" ... A splendid and Catholic recipe book has developed around cod, of which the Hyperborean, Norwegian, or Scottish peoples have no idea. Lusitanians, Spaniards, French, we are the ones who know how to eat codfish, and our recipes illustrate the great compendiums of Western cuisine.)

In another article he examined the taste of well-cooked peppers:

> As cousas son coma son, e ás veces, as máis pequenas grandes misterios. Estas merendando unha pimentada, e no aceite de fritir os pimentos, que xa dixen que se lles bota sal da gorda, rebañas cun anaco de pataca, e co prebe apégaselle a ésta unha area de sal, que ven á boca, e o todo aumenta de sabor, ven ao paladar algo de fondo, i esquisito, que non ousas borralo cun grolo de viño. Son ises intres "chüen" dos "gourmets" da vella China, que Ezra Pound ademira coma algo de indudabre poética calidade e camiño do éstasis. (Cunqueiro, *A cociña galega* 34).
>
> (Things are as they are, and sometimes, the smallest are great mysteries. You are snacking on a pepperoni, and in the oil for frying the peppers, which I have already said is sprinkled with salt, you slice them with a piece of potato, and with the pepper a grain of salt is attached to it, which comes to the mouth, and the whole thing increases its taste, comes to the palate as something deep, and exquisite, that you don't dare erase it with a sip of wine. They are those "chüen" moments of the "gourmets" of old China, which Ezra Pound admires as something of undoubted poetic quality and path to stasis.)

Gourmet writers were interested in a history of food and culinary uses. Pla, Luján, Cunqueiro and Vázquez Montalbán are milestones of a tradition, of an almost professional activity to unveil the ancestral mysteries of the cuisine of a country.

A Sophisticated and Multicultural Spain

There is almost no space left in this brief gastronomic journey through the ages of Hispanicity for the strictness of contemporary times. It is worth indicating only a couple of phenomena, which have to do with the culinary coming of age. This has been exemplified, first, by the proliferation of award-winning restaurants, the sophistication of cookbooks, and the rise of star chefs (similar to archistars) such as Ferran Adrià, who became one of the special guests of *Documenta 2007*. The kitchen is ubiquitous in television shows and literature. A particular case is that of Manuel Vázquez Montalbán, a novelist, and cooking scholar in his own right, who in the Detective Carvalho series manages to shift part of the reader's interest from the mystery he has to solve to recipes. In one of his last texts from the year 2000, this fiction writer and culinary expert published a series of articles in *El País* under the title "De Portbou a Hendaya: La vuelta a la cazuela de España" (From Portbou to Hendaye: The return to the casserole of Spain), in which he discussed the culinary traditions of Spain at the end of the twentieth century. The curious thing about that series is that by focusing on traditions, he did not mention the new Spain that was changing under his eyes through the presence of massive immigration. As a result of the migratory phenomenon, a society that has been transformed by different tastes is emerging and experimenting with foreign culinary traditions that Vázquez Montalbán barely glimpsed.[2] This is even more remarkable in the case of an author who was always very attentive to the analysis of the social aspects of reality and was the author of a book such as *La cocina del mestizaje* (2002; The cuisine of miscegenation).

It is obvious that migrant cuisine has not yet had a direct influence on Spanish recipes, but it has had an influence on what restaurants have to offer. Perhaps it is too early to detect the paradox that Ray addressed in *The Ethnic Restaurateur*. Although those who are foreign born have numerically dominated restaurant jobs in cities in the developed world, their presence in the culinary field and their own perspective on taste modification are still absent in texts dealing with cuisine and culture. Since the 1990s, African and Latin American immigration to Spain has dramatically changed a society that was once homogeneous. The impact of this migration has created new spaces for communication and coexistence where food plays an important role, is a main actor, and has forced an important social transformation. In contrast to the indifference, misunderstanding, or rejection of the gastronomy of the immigrant seen in Iciar Bollaín's film *Flores de otro mundo* (Flowers from another world), some books and films reflect the attempts at gastronomic miscegenation. A valid example could be Fernando Colomo's film *El próximo Oriente* (2006), as I will discuss in chapter 9.

Another good example is the graphic novel *Gazpacho agridulce: Una autobiografía chino-andaluza* (2015) written by Quan Zhou Wu, a Chinese woman who was born in Andalusia and has become a designer and illustrator. She presents a comic reflection about the clash of the Chinese and Andalusian cultures. The title reveals the difficult combination of two gastronomical symbols of both cultures. The novel reviews many of the stereotypes and also the conflicts experienced by educated Chinese in Andalusia, who are wanting to maintain their own traditions: Chinese bazaars and restaurants, savings, a taste for brands, the idea of love. All these stereotypes are reviewed from a humorous perspective. Divided as if it were a Chinese restaurant menu, the book consists of four parts: *entrants* (starters), "Mini Zhous al estilo andaluz" (Mini Zhous Andalusian style); *primer plato* (first course), "Familia feliz agripicante" (Happy family spicy and sour); *segundo plato* (second course), "Hormigas bajan del árbol" (Ants come down from the tree); and *postre* (dessert), "Macedonia china" (Chinese Macedonia).

The work addresses different themes, several of which stand out, including the stereotypes about the Chinese community, interracial and intercultural relations, the construction and crisis of identity, and the dispute between integration into Spanish culture and conservation of Chinese culture. Quan Zhou Wu ironizes on various urban myths about the Chinese community, such as the use of dog meat in the food of Chinese restaurants (Zhou Wu 43). However, the book also unreservedly confirms other beliefs, such as that a high percentage of Asians – mainly Chinese, Japanese, and Koreans – do not tolerate alcohol well due to the lack of an enzyme that synthesizes it in the blood (Zhou Wu 112). Much of the humour in the novel comes from the hyperbolic and stereotypical representation of the Chinese mother, who appears as an authoritarian, demanding, thrifty, unaffectionate woman, obsessed with work, honour, and family. The vignettes show how the clash of food cultures is central to the process of adaptation by younger generations. Figure 15 shows the three sisters' preference for Spanish paella. Figure 16 addresses the mother's desperation when she realizes that her daughters do not comply with Chinese cultural rules.

Food plays an important role in interrogating specific forms of identity in modern literature. It can be linked to violence and aggression, death and dissolution, and it is also integral to positive literary representations of food gatherings. Food meetings provoke a sense of belonging and shared humanity that is achieved through acts of consumption and tends to always be precarious and provisional; grounded in shifting subjectivities and imaginary identifications, culinary community is at best a transient and ephemeral phenomenon in twentieth- and twenty-first-century fiction.

Food can be analysed in light of concepts that provide a discursive and intellectual framework such as hybridization, unhomeliness,

Figure 15. Historias del restaurante chino. https://gazpachoagridulce.tumblr.com/tagged/restaurantechino

displacement (liminality or standing between spaces), syncretism, xenophobia, and friction and/or conflicts between different generations of immigrants (Bhabha). Hybridism applied to the everyday, to the most basic of the everyday, which is food, implies talking about displacement. What sense does it make in gastronomic terms? In food one cannot set aside an ingredient, but must substitute it. In a similar way new cultures are formed. Among the many products that crossed the Atlantic and arrived on Spanish turf are tomatoes, vanilla, chocolate, various beans, and potatoes. They helped change food culture in the 1500s. Similarly, current migration movements have changed what people eat and how they interact with food culture. Immigrants' culinary practices and food habits travel with them. The sheer presence of women in second-generation migrations changes the type and quality of food in the homes they move into, and even more so with the arrival of the children. Migration has an impact on markets and on the display of local products that define a certain territory. Growing demand for exotic products leads to them becoming fully assimilated. It also changes the way produce is distributed. Small supermarkets, generally

Figure 16. Gazpacho agridulce

run by immigrants, supply the public with products from their countries of origin. Finally, restaurant menus offer crucial information about what is changing in a society as expressed by food. In Spain, couscous, a staple that disappeared in the 1500s, has been recently rediscovered. From diet shops it moved to Arab outlets that supplied immigrants, and today it is easily found in any big supermarket. It has also appeared on the menus of non-ethnic restaurants and as an optional accompaniment instead of rice, potatoes, or pasta in popular restaurants. On this issue, it may be helpful to recall what Terry Eagleton wrote in "Edible Ecriture": "food is endlessly interpretable, as gift, threat, poison, reward, barter, seduction, solidarity, suffocation" (Eagleton). Or we can add what Roland Barthes wrote: "What is food? It is not just a collection of products, litigable for statistical or dietary studies. It is also and at the same time a system of communication, a body of images, a protocol of uses, situations and conducts" ("Pour une psycho-sociologie" 979).

Eagleton and Barthes do not think in terms of hybridization, unhomeliness, or displacement, but they keenly remind us about the many meanings of food. The tomato imported from the Americas is an example of the decisive impact that a single ingredient has had on European cuisine. We should recognize coexistence strategies (as opposed to living permanently displaced). Today, thanks to how we travel, we work in contact with different worlds; all kinds of ingredients or instruments are exported and imported to reproduce the gestures of everyday life in a new place. This reality is evident, especially in the most essential things such as food, in the ingredients that everyone needs to prepare their food. There are some spaces that we can consider culinary satellites, such as mixed supermarkets in which we find all kinds of foreign foods, which are marginalized in separate areas of supermarkets, but at the same time they are engines of change in the host society.

Conclusion

So far we have detected five different tongues with which food speaks to us: Pardo Bazán's reflection on post-colonial issues by comparing chocolate and tea; the poetic use in a surreal way of the *migas de campanero* (ringer crumbs) in Buñuel; table manners; food shortages and hunger that were an obsessive constant for the authors of the picaresque or during the war and postwar period of the twentieth century; and the recent sophistication and immediate cosmopolitanism of Spanish cuisine. Mass immigration since the 1990s has meant the need to create new spaces for communication and coexistence. A moment of great transformation is occurring through the impact of this migratory phenomenon.

If the scarcity of the war years and the dictatorship produced speeches about the need for sacrifice and the duty of the citizen that affected both the public and the private sphere, recent immigration points to food and what it represents as an engine of social change. Gastronomic practices, traditional foods, ingredients, and new products are beginning to form part of a new horizon of daily expectations. The new space of colonial contact, this time in the metropolis, re-emerges and is formed through the daily gastronomic experience. In this encounter – or misunderstanding, shock, or rejection – the colonial experience finds a new field of cultural and literary analysis that helps us understand better the transformation of Spanish society in the twentieth and twenty-first centuries.

My brief evaluation shows that there was a long predominance of hunger and stale bread in Hispanic history and that the literary and film culture was in charge of accurately representing the predominance. In more recent times, as Vázquez Montalbán's books show us, there has been a double movement of sophistication (or European levelling) and miscegenation (or multiculturalism). The arrival of immigrants is changing the panorama of the gastronomic offers in Spain, and it is foreseeable that it will soon affect the culinary customs and uses of Spanish cuisine. To the saying quoted at the beginning, a reflection of times of crisis and autarky, one could oppose a phrase that my grandfather, a converted vegetarian, used to say, but giving it a slight twist that helps us understand the current situation and new consumption habits: "No como para vivir, sino que vivo para comer" (I do not eat to live. On the contrary, I live to eat).

9

Food and the Everyday in Spain: Immigration and Culinary Renovation

In the year 2000, fiction writer and culinary expert Manuel Vázquez Montalbán published a series of articles under the title "De Portbou a Hendaya: La vuelta a la cazuela de España," in which he discussed Spain's culinary traditions at the turn of the century without ever mentioning the new Spain that was changing under his eyes, through the presence of massive immigration. As a result, there is a transformed society with different tastes, one experimenting with foreign cooking traditions, that Vázquez Montalbán failed to picture. This is even more remarkable in the case of an author who always was very attentive to analysing social aspects of reality.[1] French novelist Jean-Claude Izzo has purposely incorporated in his novels this reality in the city of Marseille. Since the 1990s, African and Latin American immigration to Spain has dramatically changed a once homogenous society. The impact of this migration has created new spaces of communication and coexistence in which food plays an important role, is a major actor, and has forced a significant social transformation.[2]

Food played a significant part in Spain's history during the scarcity of the years of war and dictatorship. This produced discourses about the need for the sacrifice and duty of the citizen that affected both the public and the private sphere. The situation changed radically in the 1960s, the *desarrollo* years, and even more with the successful application for membership in the European Union. Successful Spanish cooks and flashy restaurants have been a part of the so-called revival of the Marca España, and they have swamped the land with television shows, culinary books, special sections in newspapers, blogs, and so forth and have made Spanish cuisine the subject of international attention.[3] Ferran Adrià's participation in *Documenta 12* in the year 2007 was a remarkable feat. Consequently, recent immigration waves have created a focus on food and what it represents as an engine of social change. Dining practices, traditional foods, ingredients, and new products begin to form part of a new horizon of everyday expectations.

I will present a reflection on two interrelated topics: the modification of eating habits in Spain, a key aspect of everyday life, through the presence of an enormous migration movement that started in the 1990s; and the intervention of migrant workers in the food chain, particularly in rural areas with heavy agriculture development such as Lleida and its surrounding towns. I will provide a reading of two recent texts, a film and a book, that deal with immigration and food issues. Both *El próximo Oriente* (2006; The Near East) by Fernando Colomo, and *La pell de la frontera* (2012; The border's skin) by Francesc Serés, offer significant evidence of the transformation through food of contemporary Spain. In these texts, food is a powerful weapon of social and physical control and encapsulates some of the many adjustments that have occurred in Spanish society. The kitchen, at home or at the restaurant, as a private or public space, becomes a setting to display the fine line between the familiar and the uncanny, between a domestic (thus safe) and a hostile environment. Louise Edwards has explained how in the context of immigration and changing food ways, new foodstuffs or food culture can be both exciting and threatening (Edwards et al. 297–308). It could be read as a variant to the omnivore's paradox: the ability of human beings to adapt, mixed with danger and curiosity. Immigrant's food allows travelling without using passports, a safe detour from daily routines without the dangers of Montezuma's revenge. Some unnoticed aspects of the food industry are denounced in Serés's book, which contains innovative portrayals of immigration and of the transformation of the country as a whole, always seen from a very intimate perspective.

Assimilation through Love and Food

Narratives and films on immigration to Spain have focused mostly on the transition from the home country to the destination, what according to Linhard we could call the shipwreck, that in many ways unleashes post-colonial spectres (Linhard 404), Here I focus on one example that pays attention to the aftermath of this transition, in particular the clash between food cultures once the arrival of immigrants has been somehow assimilated.[4]

The opening credits of Fernando Colomo's film *El próximo Oriente* conclude with a close-up on two elements that are essential to the development of the plot and its main threads. A young man (shortly afterwards, we will find out that he is Caín, one of the main characters) is cutting pieces of meat in the shop where he works, and a protest sign written in many languages is shown hanging from a balcony. It reads: "Papeles para todos." Before this we have seen glimpses of many multi-ethnic stores and situations that point to the changing nature of a society, most remarkably foreign food and publicity for cheap telephone calls to foreign countries. We see very few Spaniards because we are in the Lavapiés neighbourhood of Madrid, the heartland of a new society, and it shows. According to Michael Ugarte, "Lavapiés provides a perfect space for ethical reflection in the wake of the real and symbolic crossing" (181). In just two minutes, as indicated by Deveny, "Colomo packs in sixty shots of immigrants from all over the world in the streets of this neighbourhood as well as of storefronts that manifest this new world of immigrant Madrid: Cleopatra, India Style; Bisutería with half the sign in Chinese; Alimentación Bangla Town; Kurdistan Döner Kepab; Tangier Islamic Butchery (also in Arabic); and Bazra Import Export" (122–5). Perceptions of immigration have changed dramatically in the last few years. Not too long ago, Muñoz Molina presented a very negative vision of Madrid's Puerta del Sol in his novel *Los misterios de Madrid* (28).[5] This is not what happens in the case of Colomo's film, in which new Spaniards are presented as part of the regular urban landscape.

El próximo Oriente is set as a comedy, and thus the main characters are introduced in a comical way. The two brothers' names are Caín and Abel. In the opening scene Caín wears a T-shirt with an unusual writing: "Demasiado sexo nubla la vista" (Too much sex clouds the vision). He is waiting for his online date at a Bangladeshi restaurant. While Caín is waiting, Aisha, daughter of the owners, arrives. She has already assimilated into Spanish culture and mores and has an argument with her father, which shows her perfect command of Spanish and her integration into society. In half-broken Spanish her father reacts to her being out late at night: "Antes tu pedir permiso mi. Ser padre" (Before you ask my permission. I am the father). To which she reacts: "Soy mayor, soy independiente y tengo mi trabajo" (I am older, I am independent, and I have my job). From there everything goes wrong. The restaurant is run by a Bangladeshi family and they only serve ethnic food and, of course, not beer. Caín declares to his date that he wants to have children; it turns out that she already has a six-year-old. The woman leaves in a hurry, shocked by the conversation and what she is offered to eat.

In the next scenes we enter the core of the film: Aisha is pregnant by Abel, who in the meantime has moved with his wife and two children to Las Palmas in the Canary Islands. Through a slapstick situation, Aisha enters Caín's apartment looking for Abel, and she throws herself off the balcony into the street. Miraculously a container breaks her fall, saving herher. Aisha's family assumes that Caín is responsible for getting her pregnant. Caín accepts the responsibility and he receives a crash course on Islam from Aisha's father. After a few unconventional episodes he marries Aisha. During the wedding Shakir, Aisha's father, overhears a conversation between the two brothers about the cover-up and suffers an emotional shock.

Ana Corbalán's reading of the film suggests that it poses an inclusive dialogue between different cultures and that by representing the marginal world of Islam in Spain, the film establishes a contact point between two social groups that have been traditionally considered incompatible, and enables the construction of plural identities in a not mutually exclusive way (105–15). This is in line with most readings of the film,[6] but there is one aspect that has been overlooked: the role played by food and food-related attitudes and what they mean in an increasingly multicultural society.

Food-eating habits are at the centre of the film. In one instance, there is a conversation at the butcher's shop between Milagros, the owner, and Caín about the changing habits of their customers and how it is having an impact on their business. The conversation pictures the positive and negative aspects of Islam according to food:

> CAIN: … porque es que ya confundo a los indios de Bangladesh con los de Senegal, bueno es que ya los confundo hasta con los chinos …
>
> MILAGROS: Mira ahí te doy la razón, si es que parece que los extranjeros somos nosotros. Si fuera por ellos además no vendería nada, ni una escoba, con eso de que no comen carne de cerdo. […]
>
> MILAGROS: ¡Pero qué dices¡ ¡Si el islamismo no te deja comer cerdo! ¡Con lo rico que está el jamón! ¡Si reduce el colesterol!
>
> (CAIN: … because I already confuse the Indians from Bangladesh with those from Senegal, well, I even confuse them with the Chinese …
>
> MILAGROS: Look, I agree with you there, it seems that we are the foreigners. If it were up to them I wouldn't sell anything, not even a broom, since they don't eat pork. […]
>
> MILAGROS: What are you talking about! Islam doesn't allow you to eat pork! Ham is so good! It lowers cholesterol!)

This is a very good example of how the food choices of different cultural groups are often connected to ethnic behaviours and religious beliefs. It confirms what Kittler, Sucher, and Nelms have pointed out about the influence of food habits on an individual's self-identity as a crucial device: 'Eating is a daily reaffirmation of [one's] cultural identity' (Kittler et al. 4).

While Aisha's father is recovering at the hospital from the emotional shock he had at the wedding, municipal police close down the restaurant for breaking city health regulations. It is a *cese cautelar* (temporary closure). During the father's recovery, Caín convinces his other in-laws (only the women: the mother and three daughters) to become empowered (write, learn music, sing) and also to reopen the restaurant with a few changes: allowing alcohol consumption, female waitresses, and live music. They even breach a fundamental rule of Islam in borrowing money. A friend from the savings bank where Abel works comes to their subsequent financial rescue.

The transformation of their lives and their integration into Spanish culture is perceived in the changing names of the restaurant. Significantly the restaurant is renamed three times – Bangladesh becomes Taj Masala and finally Music Bar – coinciding with the evolution of the Muslim family. The last change reflects also the integration into a globalized, larger Anglo-Saxon world. In the process, Caín, besides becoming a husband, which was his dream at the beginning of the movie, acquires several skills, among them the ability to multitask as a father, contractor, and businessman. Seeing his new Muslim family threatened with embargo because of the city's fine and the weakness of the immigrant group provoked by the admittance of Aisha's father (the patriarchal authority) to a hospital, Caín takes command of the situation and saves his new family by asking for a bank loan to finance reforms at the restaurant. As the man in charge of the family, he convenes a meeting to establish the goals of each individual and provide the funds for them to be carried out. He encourages Aisha, her mother, and sisters Fátima and Reemah to engage in activities that contribute to the development of the family business, based on the exploitation of exoticism and their attachment to the land of origin, but also finding new motivations in life. For instance, the mother has always wanted to write. She engages in a creative writing course that allows a cameo appearance by renowned Valencian writer Juan José Millás. This teacher stresses that it is important not to mix life and fiction. One of the sisters learns to sing. Caín is empowered by assuming a patriarchal attitude that is a construct of stereotypical male roles both in Spain and in Muslim societies. He decides what the women will do and learn. He imposes on the Islamic women Spanish mores related to food, consumption of alcohol, and borrowing money. Meals and musical traditions rank high. The subtitle of the film gives us an interesting clue: *Una historia de amor al curry* (A curry love story). To solve the economic (and health) problems, the Bangladeshis, with the help of Caín, attempt to reform their ethnic restaurant. They fail in the effort, and it ends up being a very successful musical bar, to the shame of Aisha's Muslim father. The customs of the country of destination – Spain – are prominent and are at the root of many clashes.

As expected, the second generation has adapted to the language and customs of the host country, it has become their new habitus, and this causes a slight subversion of Shakir's patriarchal authority. He knows nothing of what happened during his long stay in the hospital, including the transformation of the small restaurant into a musical bar where his daughters perform.

A moment of crisis arises when Caín confesses to Milagros, the owner of the butcher's shop, that things are not going well at the restaurant and that they may have to close. Milagros is facing a similar tough decision: clientele is scarce because nobody wants to buy pork products. Cristobal-Abdul shows up and advises her to start selling some halal meat. Incidentally, Deveny considers him a "bridge character" to reduce the amount of "Otherness" in Muslims (123). This is a possible approach to relate to Colomo's adopted position: he is offering always through the movie a position of mixing cultures without conflict as a way of adapting to new realities.

The Peruvian band that is living in Caín's apartment is one of the weakest plot elements, but nevertheless it is useful to illustrate the clashing food cultures at play. When the musicians return to Caín's apartment, he makes his brother, Abel, fix them dinner. It is an excellent segment to illustrate the clash between food cultures. Abel has separated from his wife in Las Palmas, has gone back to Madrid, and tries to settle in his old apartment. He complains because he cannot find any pork produce in the fridge: "¿No hay jamón?" (No ham?) Thus he cannot cook the traditional Spanish dishes he wants to, and complains because in the fridge "no hay jamón, chorizo, cerveza" (no ham, chorizo, beer). In the end, Jorgito, the leader of the Peruvian music band, when leaving the apartment, says, "El huésped a los tres días apesta" (The guest after three days stinks), which reminds us of some popular sayings: "El huésped y el pez, a los tres días hiede" (The guest and the fish, three days later it stinks) or "Hostes i peix menut, al cap de tres dies put" (Guests and small fish, after three days, stink).

Caín fears that his brother will steal Aisha away from him, now that Caín and Aisha are starting to have a good – almost romantic – relationship. When he suspects that his brother is making advances towards Aisha and that she is not rejecting him, Caín flees the apartment and goes on a solitary walk around the city. Previously he has explained to Aisha that he once wanted to commit suicide (the image of the Viaducto de Segovia, a bridge used by suicidal people in Madrid, is in point), but he was unable to do it; instead, he should have killed his brother. At first, when he flees the apartment, Aisha thinks about him committing suicide; then she remembers that sentence and goes back to the apartment with her sisters and mother. In the meantime, Caín has returned to the apartment, having found a ham bone on the street, and is going up the stairs with the intention of killing his brother. The situation reminds the spectator of the biblical scene in which, according to popular belief, Caín killed Abel with the jawbone of an ass. It also reminds the spectator of a famous painting by Francisco de Goya, *Duelo a garrotazos* (Fight with cudgels), one of the series of Black Paintings now in the Museo del Prado, in which we see two men in the mud trying to kill each other. Or a more recent recreation of that scene in Bigas Luna's film, *Jamón, jamón*, the film that made Javier Bardem and Penélope Cruz famous. When Caín enters the apartment, he hears the baby crying and he drops his weapon to help the child, thereby strengthening his identification with his new situation as a father and husband.

Independence and emancipation through decisions are important because Caín has a subdued relationship with Abel. The latter is the dominant, while the former (who is older) plays along. Through the evolution of the plot Caín liberates himself of Abel's dominance. It is Caín's decision, to make things even more comical, that the name of Aisha's baby will be Adán. In a very simplistic way, but with an obvious didactic purpose, the characters of the two brothers take advantage of the inversion of Cain and Abel's archetypical behaviour to present opposing ideologies on immigration. Caín ends up accepting new people in the neighbourhood, and Abel represents the conservative, racist stance, which sees only immigrants as cheap labour willing to be exploited by a few euros. The film is sometimes overly optimistic. In the weeding scene between Caín and Aisha, intercultural dialogue becomes symbolic: it is an Islamic wedding in a Spanish courtyard, with Indian costumes, and with Peruvian musicians, Muslims, and Christians living together in perfect harmony.

The happy ending includes the victory of love, the solution of the quarrel between the two brothers, and a very kitsch final scene. The embrace between Cain and Aisha expresses very topically the family togetherness that is caused by a child born to an immigrant mother and a native father. This image can be read as a statement of solidarity, a call for the transformation of the Spanish mentality to be more open and to accept intermarriage, the reality of a multicultural society with food traditions and limitations such as new regulations for food consumption. To this we should add another ending. Milagros, the owner of a butcher shop that markets meat exclusively to Spanish taste, overcomes her apprehensions about the immigrants that seem to be occupying the neighbourhood. With the help of her new partner, Cristobal-Abdul, a Spanish convert to Islam, she tailors the butcher shop to the needs of the

Muslim community and caters to their demands by placing a sign on the door announcing the availability of "halal" meat prepared according to the Muslim rite. The positive result is that her business grows, and she accepts foreigners in the neighbourhood. The conversion of a very traditional and unattractive Bangladeshi restaurant into a modern music bar, and of a traditional Spanish butcher shop into a Muslim one, shows the weight of globalization and the role that women can take in this turn. The film plays with misunderstandings generated by contacts between very different cultures. Food, religion, and sex are central to the plot. Islam is the religion that is adopted by most of the Spanish characters. The final images in the movie play with this conversion, presenting Cristobal-Abdul with Aisha's father and Caín on a pilgrimage to Mecca.

Deveny points to the common narrative device of the lie becoming the truth, as Aisha realizes how good a person Caín truly is, and falls in love with him (125). In a similar way, there is a Spaniard becoming a Muslim, and Bangladeshi family that is forced to accept some food rules while living in Spain. Albeit there is a simplistic *buenista* (do-gooder) neocolonialist approach in this film, it provides food for thought: a denunciation of transformations in Spain and their difficulties. It is very different from other more recent approaches. A food show in Catalan on TV3, *Karakia* (2014),[7] emphasizes ethnic cuisine at the same time that it promotes cultural diversity in Catalonia. In this case, immigrants have the opportunity to show how they cook, thus teaching the audience about new cuisines and encouraging intercultural relations. The difference in approach may also show how attitudes in the country are changing.

Food and Immigration

Francesc Serés writes in his latest book, *La pell de la frontera* (The border's skin), about immigration in a very personal way. It comprises fourteen scenarios situated in the area where the author lived until he was eighteen years old. In the village of Saidí and surrounding areas – the Monegres, Fraga, Alcarràs, Soses, Mequinensa –the writer interviews some of its new inhabitants, paying special attention to immigrants who come from Mali, Senegal, Cameroon, Algeria, Morocco, Ukraine, Romania, and Bulgaria. Most of them work for local farmers and live in very precarious conditions: hazardous barns and warehouses that at any time could collapse and bury them among the ruins. The author approaches the working crews with a notebook and a camera. The book includes a selection of images shot by him under the unpretentious title "Petit manual d'interiorisme i d'arquitectura efímera" (Serés, *La pell* 141–56;

Small manual of interior design and ephemeral architecture). He is interested in their lives, health, livelihoods, and the journey they have taken to be here from so far away. Other approaches include a dialogue with a farmer who years ago hosted an emigrant family; memories from the time that the author was teaching immigrant children in Olot; a conversation with the employee of an agricultural multinational; and explanations about the book that the author makes in a writers' residence in upstate New York. Food is presented here in a desperate way and with a paradox. Immigrants do not have enough to eat, but they are a pivotal element that sustains the food industry in its early stages.

Serés started to write *La pell de la frontera* back in 2002. He incorporated autofiction, reportage, and autobiography. Serés is appalled by the change he is witnessing, a destruction that borders filthy ruins. His estimation of the situation is often so precise that it borders on cruelty. At some point he remembers seeing tractors and trucks filled with oranges, and vans filled with young immigrant men, in València. He calls it the Mediterranean fireworks: cranes moving around and up and down, and much building, "la pols sortia de les estructures de ciment i tot plegat semblava un castell de focs artificials" (Serés, *La pell* 166). But all of a sudden he changes his mind: "De lluny, emperò, semblava un cementiri, les làpides dels edificis a mig fer i tot de grues a sobre com si fossin les creus" (166; From a distance, however, it looked like a cemetery, the tombstones of the half-built buildings and all the cranes above them as if they were crosses). This is an original way of presenting a construction bubble in the making that provokes destruction, appearance and disappearance, the mourning of a lost world from the concussion of a new economy. Change creates new realities: "L'única certesa és el canvi, que aquí esdevé desgast" (159; The only certainty is change, which here becomes wear and tear).

Serés deals with the unseen effects of immigration. Having migrated himself from the rural areas, being a newcomer in big or small cities, he can easily perceive the changes in rural life, not from a strictly elegiac perspective but from a much more sophisticated one. He is particularly attentive to the transformation of agriculture. All those immigrants with or without jobs have remained hidden in the Lleida area, where their help is needed to harvest but also to do most of the work on the farms. In the title of the opening piece, "Història de les històries sense història" (History of stories without history), he points to the anonymity of the immigrant experience, to the impossibility of picturing the whole drama because they are illegal immigrants who may flee at any moment. He tells the story of Hakeem, a Moroccan teenager, and his family through the voice of an old man, Juli. He is appalled on the day that Hakeem first sets foot on the farm, and at one point, when Juli is not paying attention, Hakeem starts grabbing flour and the cows' fodder. Juli realizes that he is so hungry that he will eat anything. He then takes this sixteen-year-old under his wing, who works for him, and little by little Hakeem's family joins the teenager and helps Juli with the care of his bedridden mother. Suddenly one day three sub-Saharan young men come to ask for some food. Hakeem yells at them, unleashes the dogs, and throws stones at the three men until they run away. Juli sees everything but keeps quiet. A few days later Hakeem and all of his family disappear. Juli comments: "Volien feina, això sí, com tots els que desfilen per camins i magatzems, fileres d'homes suats i bruts que quan ja no hi ha res més demanen treballar quasi només a canvi de menjar" (Serés, *La pell* 29). (They wanted work, of course, like all those who parade along the roads and warehouses, rows of sweaty and dirty men who, when there is nothing else, ask to work almost exclusively in exchange for food.) Food is presented as a bargaining chip or as a commodity for the survival of a human being. The impossibility of communicating because of fear and cultural differences does not help to solve the problem.

One of the highlights of the volume is the scenario "Homes entre línies" (Men between the lines). Serés reminds us of the conversation he had with his friend Jordi, a food engineer, somebody who with his wide-ranging knowledge of new breeds can easily mock the so-called biological agriculture. Jordi compares his situation (working in Barcelona but with bosses in London) with what happens to peach trees: "els plantem aquí, però tota la genètica la fan els americans" (Serés, *La pell* 22; we plant them here, but all the genetics are done by the Americans). Through the conversation with this well-informed professional, Serés describes the effects that food innovation has on farming land. The workmanship of this activity is performed by the contingents of Africans, who, if they are lucky, work as day labourers in the fruit fields and live in dilapidated barns next to the fields. The transformations and changes in the physical environment determine human work: the traditional lifestyles of these regions, which were those that the author had known, disintegrate at the same rate that agriculture becomes "technified," industrial areas (without any industries) keep growing without any company in sight, and people keep arriving without finding the job they dreamed of. There is a colonization of sorts through the import of foreign crops. Peaches are genetically modified in California (like clothing and television series):

> Hi ha una nova koiné dels gustos i dels sabors, una fruita més dolça i rodona, una fruita que anivella els consumidors que pensen que si tothom

> té la mateixa poma, ningú no en tindrà cap millor que la seva. El nou comunisme: si les pomes són idèntiques, el consumidor no tindrà dubtes. I, això encara és més important, si els consumidors acaben sent idèntics, les pomes no tindran dubtes a l'hora d'escollir-los a ells, com passa amb els models de cotxe, les sèries de televisió o amb la roba. És molt difícil comprar tant sense vendre's una mica cada vegada. (Serés, *La pell* 222–3)
>
> (There is a new koine of tastes and flavours, a sweeter, rounder fruit, a fruit that levels consumers who think that if everyone has the same apple, no one will have a better one than theirs. The new communism: if the apples are identical, the consumer will have no doubts. And, this is even more important, if the consumers end up being identical, the apples will have no doubts when it comes to choosing them, as it happens with car models, television series, or clothes. It is very difficult to buy so much without selling oneself a little each time.)

Jordi warns the narrator that all fruit grown in Lleida – the major agricultural producing area in Catalonia – are foreign types that have replaced autochthonous ones. The scenario is ripe for the growth of slow food and a movement claiming the return of local kinds of fruit. Jordi is very attentive to the imposition of an industrialized agricultural system in recent years. He asserts that everything that does not have a regular and reliable consolidated production system will disappear. The clue is storage and conservation. In the past, agriculture was based on the family system; now it is an industry – "la cadena de muntatge" (Serés, *La pell* 232; the assembly line). Jordi presents the laws of the land in a new kind of agriculture setting: industry and anonymity against family traditions.

Jordi also talks about the first domestic animal, the goat, an animal that offers many advantages; it is a migrant animal, easily transferable, that could be used in many ways – protein factory, meat and milk, and finally it becomes a coat (Serés, *La pell* 233). He denounces how agriculture has become an international business ruled by US industries with transgenic solutions:

> ¿Saps la de varietats que s'han extingit per culpa de les millores genètiques? En gairebé totes les cadenes de distribució demanen les mateixes pomes. Estàndards, és clar. Granny Smith perquè té la pell diferent, Royal Gala, Fuji, Golden i una altra de vermella, la Top Red i l'Early Red One. (Serés, *La pell* 241)
>
> (Do you know about varieties that have become extinct because of genetic improvements? In almost all the distribution chains they ask for the same

apples. Standards, of course. Granny Smith because it has a different skin, Royal Gala, Fuji, Golden and another red one, the Top Red and the Early Red One.)

The last two scenarios in the book, "Els àngels que riuen" (Laughing angels) and "La fi del món tal com l'havíem conegut" (The end of the world as we knew it), have a characteristic Serés texture: he relates major social upheavals, dramatic changes to little events, changes in nature, mechanization of agriculture, in a metaphorical way. In "Els àngels que riuen" he refers, as he does throughout the book, to the changed nature of the landscape around his hometown: "Hi ha un paisatge de frontera que va des de la carretera de Tamarit fins al costat de l'A2 entre Lleida i fins que s'arriba als Monegres, zones àrides i plantacions que s'acaben o comencen en benzineres, polígons industrials més o menys actius, serres àrides, erms" (Serés, *La pell* 283). (There is a border landscape that goes from the Tamarit road to the side of the A2 between Lleida and until you reach the Monegres, arid areas and plantations that end or start at gas stations, industrial estates or less active, barren ranges, wastelands.) He introduces a landscape after a battle, abandoned by its owners, now that the economic crisis is at its height. He runs into a couple of immigrants, one of whom is going through an acute allergic reaction after eating a can of sardines. This allows the author to muse about his own miseries with food allergies, since before being born. He helps the two immigrants. He arrives at secured fields, lines of peach trees protected from birds and hail by nets (292). The fear of hail is compared to social and economic upheaval: "Parlo d'ara i d'aquí, de Saidí a Alcarràs, però també d'un present ubic i contemporani durant el qual hem mirat de teixir mil xarxes de seguretat per tal de conjurar el futur, en una mena de cel social, però la veritat és que els déus són grecs i no hi ha res previst" (293). (I'm talking about now and here, from Saidí to Alcarràs, but also about a ubiquitous and contemporary present during which we tried to weave a thousand safety nets in order to conjure up the future, in a kind of social heaven, but the truth is that the gods are Greek and nothing is planned.) Serés discusses the disappearance of what many in Spain perceived as the guaranteed social pillars of education, health, and safety. The crisis – a metaphorical hail – has gotten rid of everything, and there is no safety net available. Serés's critique underscores the impact of anonymous immigrants on food production and the colonization of local crops, thus showing the dark side of multiculturalism and globalization.

Throughout the book the author is genuinely concerned about the nature and the sense of what he is writing. He declares towards the end that trying to write about immigration is "intentar descriure un núvol" (Serés, *La pell* 304; to try to describe a cloud). Or that he is mesmerized by the little importance that the subject has, similar to constructing just a list: "No em queda res més per dir, d'aquí, mentre vaig escrivint m'adono que relato un inventari, res" (305; I have nothing more to say, from here, as I write I realize that I am recounting an inventory, nothing). The narrator repeats again and again this idea of little importance, of smallness (108). Serés has seen this landscape being transformed without almost perceiving it. While attending a writer's colony in upstate New York, he presents the idea of his book to a few fellow writers and a publisher in a very candid way: "Escric una mena d'història local, no sé ben bé com definir el llibre que escric" (54; I write a kind of local history, I don't quite know how to define the book I'm writing). A publisher in the group suggests that he should try to write a love story and include love letters. Serés is reluctant to write a love novel, or a book about the Holocaust, or even a historical novel. He keeps being mesmerized by the stories he is hearing that are always the same (54). He also uses military terms: the place where imigrants live is like a *trinxera*, a trench in the middle of the war line. In fact, Serés is unaware of the insurmountable task he has started, the difficulty of writing a book and finding the common traits among all these little life plots that he encounters and keeps writing about:

> Vida quotidiana i repetida al pati de baix; de tan petita, quasi invisibles, passes per davant i tot es torna borrós de tan clar com sembla. ¿Com es narra això? Els bolígrafs es gasten, les llibretes arriben a la darrera pàgina i la vida continua. (Serés, *La pell* 257)
>
> (Daily and repeated life in the courtyard below; so small, almost invisible, you walk past and everything becomes a blur from as clear as it seems. How is this narrated? The pens wear out, the notebooks reach the last page, and life goes on.)

The narrator acknowledges that he is dealing with the unseen, something that is not perceived, with a variable of what Georges Perec called the *infraordinaire* as opposed to the *extraordinaire*. Here we are also dealing with an unconscious refusal to see. One of the limitations when exploring the everyday is the difficulty of seeing what is so obvious. In this case, most observers refuse to see through racial and social stereotypes: "Sóc un estrany, de vegades només cal desplaçar-se uns mi·límetres del centre per caure als antípodes" (Serés, *La pell* 57; I'm a stranger; sometimes you only need to move a few millimetres from the centre to fall into the antipodes). Serés is in a place with no dignity, no glamour, in a desert land between Aragón and Catalonia, near the Monegres area. He tries to discover his own place and the place of immigrants in this desert.

As indicated, Serés is plagued with many doubts about the sense of his book that he shares with the reader. In the final two pages he links these narratives to some of his previous writing:

> [E]ls pitjors pronòstics que es llegeixen entre les línies de *La força de la gravetat* i de *La matèria primera* s'han complert. No és que s'hagin convertit en realitat, ja hi eren mentre als mitjans es descrivia una aparença de prosperitat, hi havia un tel tan fi com opac que pocs s'atrevien a esquinçar. Tot era de paper, només calia bufar una mica perquè comencés la pitjor crisi econòmica que es recorda i que ens marcarà a tots per molts anys. (Serés, *La pell* 307)

> (The worst prognoses that can be read between the lines of *La força de la gravetat* and of *La matèria primera* have been fulfilled. It is not that they have become a reality; they were already there while an appearance of prosperity was described in the media; there was a web so thin and opaque that few dared to tear it. Everything was on paper; you only needed to blow a little for the worst economic crisis in memory to begin and that will mark us all for many years.)

These are striking words that tackle the heart of the immigration problem in Spain's recent history. The transformation of the country through contrasting cultures, cheap labour that jumped into the construction bubble, the illusion of prosperity created by politicians and bankers alike, and a sinister coalition that has devastated Spain. Serés is keen in using subtle metaphors to refer to the everyday – "un tel tan fi com opac que pocs s'atrevien a esquinçar" (*La pell* 307; a fabric so fine and opaque that few dared to tear it), meaning by this the collective refusal to see what was happening before their eyes. In *La pell de la frontera* he focuses on immigrants, in a journalistic way, interviewing literally hundreds of them, getting to know their intimate journeys through anonymous stories. He even – as on many occasions in his narrative – refers in a self-referential way to what he is writing:

> El temps s'ha accelerat: la crisi ha estat fulgurant, la immigració ha modificat el mapa del país i la situació política ho canvia tot. Fins i tot als llocs que ofereixen més resistència: la plaça José Antonio es diu Joaquim Ibarz i el bar que hi havia està tancat. (Serés, *La pell* 307)

> (Time has sped up: the crisis has been blazing, immigration has changed the country's map and the political situation changes everything. Even

in the places that offer the most resistance: José Antonio Square is called Joaquim Ibarz and the bar that was there has closed.)

He sees some signs of hope through the timid renovation of historical memory, dedicating a square in Saidí to a journalist born there (Serés's hometown), a correspondent in Latin America for *La Vanguardia*, erasing the name and memory of the infamous founder of Falange, Spain's most prominent fascist party.

Serés links the immigrants' situation and experiences with "la independència, el tema dels temes" (*La pell* 307; independence, the subject of subjects). It is 11 September, Catalonia's national day, and Serés is trying to explain Catalonia's claim for independence to a group of immigrants in Lleida, who have seen many flags and cannot make sense of it. One of the immigrants has the right questions: "When will this happen? Isn't it too dangerous?" Serés is surprised because the kind of dangers that those immigrants have faced just to get to Spain are tremendous:

> ¿Crisi? ¿Risc? No sé com respondre a algú que s'ha jugat la pell com ho ha fet ell, algú que després de travessar cinc països ha saltat a l'Atlàntic en una barca per arribar a les Canàries i que ha anat de ciutat en ciutat fins a arribar a Lleida per acabar dormint al ras i treballar a la fruita. Tot plegat sense garanties, sense salvavides. (Serés, *La pell* 308)
>
> (Crisis? Risk? I don't know how to respond to someone who has risked his skin as he has, someone who, after crossing five countries, has jumped into the Atlantic in a boat to reach the Canaries and who has gone from city to city until he arrived in Lleida and ended up sleeping on the ground and working on the fruit. All without guarantees, without life preservers.)

These anonymous workers have been the pillar of the renovation in agricultural activities in Catalonia and Spain. By relating these pressing issues – the crisis, immigration, and Catalonia's claim for independence – Serés is linking three of the most urgent problems Spain is facing as a collective quagmire. Similarly to what happened in 1898, when Spain lost its last colonies, no one in the country seems willing to acknowledge the gravity of the situation.

La pell de la frontera shows the struggle for survival of people who have come from afar to do the jobs that unemployed natives do not want to do any more, and suggests the permeability of the border that separates us from the other. Armed with his pen and block, the author walks through inhospitable areas, and immigrants believe he is a policeman. Serés's book presents the toughest aspect of immigration: the fruit pickers and men working in the poultry and pig farms of Segrià. At the end of the book Serés discusses how immigrants have settled down with a minimum of adaptation to the environment. With acute sensitivity he has revealed the melting pot of the meeting point for immigration and the country's population, revealing that the border is no longer in the Strait of Gibraltar or the island of Lampedusa (Italy) or of Lesbos (Greece), but in our streets and fields, in the villages and cities within us, in an invisible symbiosis.

Francesc Serés's Lost World

Francesc Serés is a relatively young writer with a unique career in the Catalan literary field. With his trilogy *De fems i de marbres* (Of dung and marbles), he became the youngest author ever to receive the National Prize for Literature, in 2007. After this trilogy of novels he published two sets of short texts that continued to explore the territory and the world of work, halfway between literature and ethnography: *La força de la gravetat* (The force of gravity) and *La matèria primera* (The raw material). In his next three books he performed a twist: *Caure amunt* (Falling up) is a theatrical recreation of the life of three medieval Catalan authors; *Contes rusos* (Russian tales) is a metafictional tour de force; and the short stories in *Mossegar la poma* (Bite the apple) focus on married life.

As indicated by Jordi Marrugat, Serés followed the examples of Jesús Moncada and Maria Barbal, writing a critical representation of a rural world in a very original way (Marrugat 171–4). Serés, who was born in the Franja de Ponent, became an innovative narrator, similar to Moncada. His trilogy was based on an observation of changes in lifestyles and habits that had occurred so rapidly in modernity and postmodernity. In fact, in a text written in tribute to Moncada, Serés stressed that Moncada's great feat was to allow, thanks to literature, the survival of Mequinensa, a town that was to have been buried under water due to the Francoist policy of building dams. Speaking of Moncada, Serés highlighted that in his books one can perceive "l'imaginari col·lectiu" of the old town, and he added: "Una de les tasques de l'escriptor és mostrar el que els altres saben mirar però no saben veure ni llegir. Moncada situa al plànol tot allò que ja no és, el riu, els masos i, encara més, el poble, la descripció de les vides de veïns, avantpassats, enemics i familiars diversos (Serés, "Pilans" 2). (One of the writer's tasks is to show what others know how to look at but cannot see or read. Moncada places on the map everything that is no longer there, the river, the farms, and even more, the village, the description of the lives of neighbours, ancestors, enemies, and various relatives.)

Serés's trilogy is constructed as a narrative based on small episodes, stories seemingly unconnected to each other, the protagonist of which is "ningú, el viure dels qui som ningú" (Serés, *De fems* 50; nobody, the living of those who are nobody). They are the anonymous lives of those who are forgotten by history's main narrative, but who form the basis of it and suffer the ups and downs of history. This anonymous, collective biography covers crucial times in a region west of Lleida, including issues such as depopulation of the countryside and the misery of city life for those who have just arrived from small towns, and references to the Spanish migration to Barcelona to the sixties.[8] These caused an epochal transformation of a particular landscape that Hobsbawm has described with acute precision.

In his trilogy, because of his attention to the hidden everyday, "el que passa és que res no passa" (*De fems* 49; what happens is that nothing happens), Serés included remarkable comments on food and related topics:

> L'hora de dinar es coneixia aviat, les flaires dels sofregits o del brou de gallina pujaven puntualment pel buit de les escales, també la dels esquitxos de l'oli i la carn de corder ... ara als menjadors separats de les cuines no s'olora res, no arriba més que el sòlid o el líquid del menjar, les cases ja no fan olor de cuina. (Serés, *De fems* 80)
>
> (Lunch time was easy to detect, the scents of stir-fry or chicken broth came up punctually through the void of the stairs, also those of splashes of oil and lamb meat ... now in the separate dining rooms from the kitchens nothing is smelled, only the solid or liquid of the food arrives, the houses no longer smell of cooking.)

Here he depicts the separation of two crucial spaces that in the past in rural living were lived as one: kitchen and dining room. Elsewhere he shows the significance of the weekly town markets that he considers to be the centre of the world: "No hi ha cap altre lloc al món com el mercat, no n'hi ha cap altre perquè el món només té un centre, i el centre és un mercat curull de gent que es mou i es crida (Serés, *De fems* 171). (There is no other place in the world like the market, there is no other because the world has only one centre, and the centre is a crowded market of people moving and shouting.) Or in this excerpt: "escoltar els crits del xai que mataven en una parada a la vista de tothom i que en un tres i no res veies en forma de costelles tallades, de cuixa feta a talls, i el cap espellotat, preparat per anar al forn; dinar de diumenge, un cap per cap, festa. Festa de xai, de conills, de porcs. El mercat sempre ha estat el lloc de la festa i del sacrifici (173–4). (To hear the screams of the lamb that was slaughtered in a stall in full view of everyone and that in no time you saw it in the form of cut ribs, a thigh cut into pieces, and a mirrored head, ready to go to the oven; Sunday lunch, one for each, party. Feast of lamb, rabbits, pigs. The market has always been the place of celebration and sacrifice.)[9] These last two quotes reveal an elegiac view of eating habits and the food production chain in an industrial or pre-industrial mono-ethnic world. All this has disappeared, and the crisis was the perfect storm that made it happen.

In the short stories of *La força de la gravetat* (2006), Serés also shows meticulous attention to tiny aspects of everyday life: offices and factories; the presence of evil and sinister coincidences; and lives in the margins of a post-industrial society, such as those of a seller of perfumes, guards in a container storage area, and workers in foundries and an industrial bakery. There are references to food and the impact on the life and imagination of the people: "El preu" focuses on the importance of hunting and fishing. The narrator's grandfather cannot enter a restaurant because he is not properly dressed. He goes to buy a formal suit and then returns to the restaurant; once seated at the table and having ordered, he throws the table to the ground and leaves the restaurant without uttering a word. The book comprises seventeen stories with extremely minimalist plots carved with precise words, sharp and with obvious referents, in rural or urban suburbs, that picture "la perifèria moral de les vides subalternes" (Ollé, 13; the moral periphery of subaltern lives). Serés describes the microclimates of Catalonia in recent decades, with its rituals, rules, and shapes.

Food, Migrations: A Multicultural Spain?

As I have shown here, food and immigration are a important aspects of cultural studies. The new space of colonial contact, this time in the metropolis, somehow resurfaces (and is developed) through daily eating habits and experiences, with an impact on dialogue: agreement or disagreement, shock or rejection, a clash of cultures that provokes new unexpected situations. Paying attention to this aspect of the colonial experience, we can understand better the transformation of Spanish society of the twentieth and twenty-first century. Henri Lefebvre wrote that everyday life, in a sense residual, is defined by "what is left over" (*Critique* 97). Lefebvre viewed the everyday as the total of all lived experience of the ordinary, the recurrent: daily routes, tasks, work, and commuting to the workplace as well as vacation, funerals, the weekly visit to the cinema or dance hall, hobbies, family visits, and so on. That which he names as "what is left over" does not constitute a definition; first and foremost, it instead negatively describes everything that does not count in life as special or unique. It is an everyday marked by hybridity. According to Cornejo-Parriego, hybridity "constituye un fenómeno infinitamente diferido no sólo por ser un proceso abierto y progresivo, sino también por la mezcla que se produce con y entre colectivos en si mismos mestizos que impiden llegar a una noción estable y pura de cualquier denominación racial" (526; constitutes an infinitely differing phenomenon not only because it is an open and progressive process, but also because of the mixture that occurs with and among groups that are themselves mestizos, which makes it impossible to arrive at a stable and pure notion of any racial denomination). Immigration is provoking many changes in Spanish society as a whole. It is also testing the limits of accepting multicultural situations. The farther we are from the big city, the easiest it is to get lost and disappear and to accept the cruelty of a situation that affects the very core of the food industry: production and consumption. Serés amply exemplifies this issue, which could be linked to one aspect not developed here, what Krishnendu Ray calls the uneven relationship between "subordinate ethnic other and the self," that focuses on consumers and their desires. Ray calls attention to the paradox that a central discussion in food studies should be around the stories and subjectivity of the "ethnic food provider" (1). In developed countries, "although the foreign-born have numerically dominated the feeding occupations … we know relatively little about how the transaction in taste appears from their point of view" (15). Ray stresses the need to incorporate "immigrant bodies and conceptions into … discussions of taste" because it is the only way to understand that migrants have the resources "to turn the table on the dominant culture of taste" (194).

In cultural terms, in essence, what one eats defines what one is and is not. An important element in this type of research is the way in which food and eating habits contribute to the development and transmission of culture. Culture is defined as beliefs, values, attitudes, and practices that are accepted by members of a group or community. Culture is not inherited; it is learned. The food options from different cultural groups are often connected to ethnic behaviour and religious beliefs. I have detected two problems: the cultural shock caused by differences in eating habits for cultural and religious reasons; and the involvement of immigrants in the transformation of the agricultural production process and what people eat. Mass immigration since the 1990s has meant the need to create new opportunities for communication and coexistence. A moment of great transformation occurs because of this migration's impact.

If the scarcity of the years of war and dictatorship produced discourses about the need for sacrifice and duty of the citizen, affecting both the public and the private sphere, recent immigration points to food and what it represents as an engine of social change. Eating practices, traditional foods, ingredients, and new products begin to form part of a new horizon of everyday expectations. The new space of colonial contact, this time in the metropolis, re-emerges (and gets new forms) through daily eating experiences. At this point of encounter and misunderstanding, shock or rejection, the colonial experience is a new field of cultural and literary analysis that helps us understand better the transformation of Spanish society of the twentieth and twenty-first century.

Notes

Preface

1 My translation. Unless otherwise stated, all translations are mine.

Introduction

1 From a fictional perspective it is worth mentioning Albert Forns book *Abans de les cinc som a casa*.
2 https://cordis.europa.eu/project/id/295562.
3 Other examples would include Henry Petroski's, *The Evolution of Useful Things* (1992) and *The Pencil: A History of Design and Circumstance* (1989), or even Ben Highmore's latest book, *The Great Indoors: At Home in the Modern British House* (2014).
4 More on this in chapter 3.
5 https://www.weltderddr.de.
6 I also wondered why it is that in Spain nobody has dared to organize a similar exhibition on everyday life under the Franco regime. Forgetfulness? Amnesia? So many things still survive (like the smell of Zotal in the Renfe stations). The easiest answer is that Francoism is still very much present (just watch a RTVE newscast), but it must be a bit more complicated. Maybe the closest thing would be the RTVE very popular series *Cuéntame …* (Tell me …).

1 Defying or Defining the Everyday: Poetics of Everyday Life

1 https://elpais.com/politica/2019/07/27/actualidad/1564236891693662.html.
2 https://www.theschooloflife.com/shop/eu/tsol-press-small-pleasures-book/.20.

3 Joe Moran is also the author of two other books: *On Roads: A Hidden History* (2009), in which he explores the historical development and cultural resonances of Britain's road system; and *Armchair Nation: An Intimate History of Britain in Front of the Television* (2013), a social and cultural history of television viewing which explores how that act has changed the United Kingdom.
4 For a thorough discussion of this map see Bruno, chapter 7.
5 A similar concurrent project was developed by Ralph Rumney in Venice, "The Leaning Tower of Venice" (1959–1960). http://www.museodelcamminare.org/progetti/re_iter/rumney/rumney_en.html#intro2. As explained: "The Museo del Camminare (Museum of Walking), Venice, is located in the streets (calli) and squares (campi) of Venice, the largest and oldest pedestrian city in the world. It is from this outstanding open-air workshop that the museum aims to understand the 'art of Walking' (H.D. Thoreau), by enhancing and protecting its cultural meanings and asserting its fundamental human value at national and international level. The Museo del Camminare is non-commercial and aims to investigate and promote walking as a cultural, aesthetic, poetic, and political practice" (http://www.museodelcamminare.org/index_en.html).

2 Singing the Everyday, Signing or Signalling the World: On Catalogic Poems

1 https://condenaststore.com/featured/a-panel-called-creation-the-true-story-which-roz-chast.html.
2 This limited selection of poems deals with events in everyday life, parties, dinners, which are presented as moments of confusion, always introduced from the perspective of chaotic enumeration. Nevertheless, it is surprising that three poems in three languages and from rather different historical moments have much in common. One cannot help but think about so many other examples: Apollinaire's "Zone," Joan Salvat-Papasseit's "Tot l'enyor de demà," Rafael Alberti's *Roma peligro para caminantes* ("Si proibisce di buttare inmondezze," "Cuando Roma es cloaca"), and Gonzalo Rojas's "Materia de testamento." In *Orientalism* Edward Said discusses the nature of scholarship as an instrument of domination. To do so, he excoriates scholars of the Middle East for dividing into categories, classifying, indexing, and documenting "everything in sight (and out of sight)" (Said, 86). The kind of classification I am discussing here proposes a reverse organization of the world, one critical and anti-system, against the grain. Foucault rightfully stated that "no power can be exercised without the extraction, appropriation, distribution or retention of

knowledge. On this level, there is not knowledge on one side and society on the other, or science and the state, but only the fundamental forms of knowledge/power" (Foucault, qtd. in Sheringham 283).

3 For a discussion of the list as a paradigmatic form of non-narrative inscription see Young.

4 Something catalogic is a list or record of items systematically arranged and often including descriptive material. According to the Treccani dictionary, "Forma della poesia epica greca che ha per oggetto l'elencazione di persone o cose pertinenti ai fatti del ciclo epico: il Catalogo delle navi, nel secondo libro dell'Iliade; il Catalogo delle donne nel libro 11 dell'Odissea; il Catalogo delle donne attribuito a Esiodo, in 5 libri, con cui si identificavano le Eee o Eoie, elenco di miti riferiti al nome delle eroine uniti fra di loro con la formula di transizione ο η «o quale»." (Form of Greek epic poetry concerned with listing persons or things pertinent to the events of the epic cycle: the Catalogue of Ships, in the second book of the Iliad; the Catalogue of Women in book 11 of the Odyssey; the Catalogue of Women attributed to Hesiod, in 5 books, with which the Eee or Eoie were identified, a list of myths referring to the heroines' names joined together with the transitional formula ο η "or which.")

5 "Il y a dans toute énumération deux tentations contradictoires; la première est de TOUT recenser, la seconde d'oublier tout de même quelque chose; la première voudrait clôturer définitivement la question, la seconde la laisser ouverte; entre l'exhaustif et l'inachevé, l'énumération me semble ainsi être, avant toute pensée (et avant tout classement), la marque même de ce besoin de nommer et de réunir sans lequel le monde ('la vie') resterait pour nous sans repères: il y a des choses différentes qui sont pourtant un peu pareilles; on peut les assembler dans des séries à l'intérieur desquelles il sera possible de les distinguer" (Perec, *Penser/Classer* 167). (There are two contradictory temptations in any enumeration: the first is to list EVERYTHING, the second to forget something; the first would like to close the question definitively, the second to leave it open; between exhaustiveness and incompleteness, enumeration thus seems to me to be, before any thought (and before any classification), the very mark of this need to name and reunite, without which the world ("life") would remain for us without reference points: there are different things that are nonetheless somewhat the same; we can assemble them into series within which it will be possible to distinguish between them.)

6 It is also worth mentioning Borges's description of the universe in *El Aleph*: "Arribo, ahora, al inefable centro de mi relato, empieza aquí, mi desesperación de escritor. Todo lenguaje es un alfabeto de símbolos

cuyo ejercicio presupone un pasado que los interlocutores comparten; ¿cómo transmitir a los otros el infinito Aleph, que mi temerosa memoria apenas abarca? ... Por lo demás, el problema central es irresoluble: La enumeración, si quiera parcial, de un conjunto infinito. En ese instante gigantesco, he visto millones de actos deleitables o atroces; ninguno me asombró como el hecho de que todos ocuparan el mismo punto, sin superposición y sin transparencia. Lo que vieron mis ojos fue simultáneo: lo que transcribiré sucesivo, porque el lenguaje lo es. Algo, sin embargo, recogeré" (*Narraciones* 42). (I arrive, now, at the ineffable centre of my story, my writer's despair begins here. All language is an alphabet of symbols whose exercise presupposes a past that the interlocutors share; how to transmit to others the infinite Aleph, which my fearful memory barely embraces ... In any case, the central problem is unsolvable: the enumeration, even partial, of an infinite set. In that gigantic instant, I have seen millions of delightful or atrocious acts; none astonished me as the fact that they all occupied the same spot, without overlapping and without transparency. What my eyes saw was simultaneous: what I will transcribe successive, because language is. Something, however, I will gather.)

7 I am quoting "Tentative de description d'un dîner de têtes à Paris-France" according to the Pléiade edition (*Œuvres complètes* 3–12). The poem was published for the first time in 1931 in the journal *Commerce*, edited by Léon-Paul Fargue, Paul Valéry, and Valery Larbaud. Subsequent editions saw the light in 1935, 1946, and 1947. It was Saint-John Perse who pushed for the publication of a polemical poem; he had to do some arm-twisting, as he explained in a 1949 letter: "un signe de présence de Prévert me ferait vraiment grand plaisir. J'ai aimé ses *Paroles* et je souris encore au souvenir du petit coup d'État qu'il m'avait fallu effectuer à *Commerce*, en 1931, pour imposer son 'Dîner de têtes' contre l'avis de mes trois Aînés, les Conseillers en titre. (Là encore, j'imagine, nos pensées secrètement devaient se rejoindre.)" (*Œuvres* 1010). (A sign of Prévert's presence would give me great pleasure. I loved his *Paroles* and I still smile at the memory of the little coup d'état I had to carry out in *Commerce*, in 1931, to impose his "Dîner de têtes" against the advice of my three Elders, the senior Councillors. (Here again, I imagine, our thoughts must secretly have coincided.)

8 Unfortunately she misses the point because the song was written before the dictator's death.

9 Lists of characters are not alien to pop songs. In a Vinicius de Moraes tune, "Samba da Bênção" (Blessing samba), the poet manages to introduce a long list of samba musicians who preceded him and blesses them using a quasi-religious line: "A bênção, Pixinguinha / Tu que

choraste na flauta / Todas as minhas mágoas de amor / A bênção, Sinhô, a benção, Cartola" (The blessing, Pixinguinha / You who cried on the flute / All my love sorrows / The blessing, Sinhô, the blessing, Cartola).

10 Ovid's *Metamorphoses* is very different from Homer's *Odyssey* or *Iliad*. In Ovid's epic, which lacks both linear narrative and protagonist, inspiration comes from patterns that are much more fundamental to the human condition than narrative archetypes are.

3 Autopsies of Everyday Life

1 See, for example, a selection edited by Muñiz (2014). It is worth mentioning that there is still a large number of texts of exceptional quality that have never been published in book form.

2 See also Uzcanga.

3 See Navas; Quintana i Trias ("Joan Maragall"); and Cócola Grant.

4 See Cavallin: "En troisième lieu, les strophes du Cygne comme le premier chant des Métamorphoses s'écrivent sur un motif de construction. Tandis que le démiurge ovidien construit le cosmos à partir du vieux chaos de la matière, Napoléon III tire une ville impériale du chaos du vieux Paris. Dans le Cygne, l'apparition de l'Andromaque de Virgile s'inscrit dans cette réflexion sur la construction ou l'architecture. Si Baudelaire pense brusquement à elle alors qu'il traverse 'le nouveau Carrousel,' c'est que les chantiers du nouveau Paris lui rappellent le chantier de la ville qu'Hélénus, mari de la princesse troyenne, est en train de construire quand Enée la rencontre sur un rivage désert de l'actuelle Albanie. L'allusion au 'Simoïs menteur' illustre la méthode d'Hélénus. L'ancien esclave de Pyrrhus crée la ville de Buthrote à l'image de Troie détruite. Il construit 'une petite Troie, une copie faite sur le modèle de la grande Pergame,' 'simulataque magnis / Pergama.' Il appelle respectivement les deux fleuves qui longent la ville le Xanthe et le Simoïs, en souvenir des fleuves de la cité phrygienne. Sa translation onomastique imprime sur le support neutre de ce rivage inconnu une ville archétypique. Sous le roitelet bâtisseur, à la fois cadet d'Hector et sa copie en miniature, se profile la silhouette de 'Napoléon le petit,' singe et médiocre neveu de Napoléon 1er, transformant le vieux Paris en une ville impériale, conçue comme la figure du rétablissement de l'Empire. À l'exemple d'Hélénus produisant ex nihilo un simulacre de Troie, Napoléon III efface le 'bric-à-brac' du 'vieux Paris' et y substitue une idée de ville. Le démiurge des Métamorphoses, l'Hélénus de l'Enéide et l'empereur urbaniste, tous trois architectes et bâtisseurs, forment une séquence analogique qui invite à lire le poème comme une méditation sur l'acte créateur et donc sur la poïèsis" (342–3). (Thirdly, the stanzas of "The Swan" as the first song of the Metamorphoses are written on a construction

motif. While the Ovidian demiurge builds the cosmos out of the old chaos of matter, Napoleon III draws an imperial city out of the chaos of old Paris. In "The Swan," the appearance of Virgile's Andromache is part of this reflection on construction or architecture. If Baudelaire suddenly thinks of her as he crosses "le nouveau Carrousel," it is because the building sites of the new Paris remind him of the city that Helenus, husband of the Trojan princess, is building when Aeneas meets him on a desert shore of present-day Albania. The reference to the "liar Simoy" illustrates Helenus's method. The former slave of Pyrrhus creates the city of Buthrote in the image of destroyed Troy. He builds "a little Troy, a copy made on the model of the great Pergamos," "simulataque magnis / Pergama." He calls respectively the two rivers that border the city Xanthe and Simois, in memory of the rivers of the Phrygian city. Its onomastic translation stamps on the neutral support of this unknown shore an archetypal city. Under the little king, both Hector's younger brother and his miniature copy, stands the figure of "Napoleon the Little One," monkey [*singe* in the French original] and mediocre nephew of Napoleon I, transforming old Paris into an imperial city, conceived as a symbol for the restoration of Empire. Following the example of Helenus producing ex nihilo a simulacrum of Troy, Napoleon III erases the "bric-a-brac" of "old Paris" and substitutes it for an idea of a city. The demiurge of the Metamorphoses, Helenus of the Aeneid and the urbanist emperor, all three architects and builders, form an analogical sequence that invites us to read the poem as a meditation on the creative act and therefore on poiesis.)

5 As Benjamin said, "[t]he important thing for the remembering author is not what he experienced, but the weaving of his memory, the Penelope work of recollection. Or should one call it, rather, a Penelope work of forgetting? Is not the involuntary recollection, Proust's *mémoire involontaire*, much closer to forgetting than what is usually called memory? And is not this work of spontaneous recollection, in which remembrance is the woof and forgetting is the warf, a counterpart to Penelope's work rather than its likeness? For here the day unravels what the night has woven" ("The Image of Proust" 204).

6 One of the most striking literary cases is Petros Markaris's mystery novels and its main character, detective Costas Haritos. Through them Markaris depicts the social and economic transformation of Greece after the 2008 recession.

4 Vicent Andrés Estellés's *Trencadís*, or Attention to the Infra-ordinary

1 Cortázar also mentions Lezama Lima and draws a parallel between Lezama Lima's mode of expression and his own understanding of art: "Lo que entre ustedes ha hecho un Lezama Lima, es decir, asimilar y

cubanizar por vía exclusivamente libresca y de síntesis mágico-poética los elementos más heterogéneos de una cultura que abarca desde Parménides hasta Serge Diaghilev, me ocurre a mí hacerlo a través de experiencias tangibles" ("Acerca" 276; What Lezama Lima has done among you, that is to say, assimilate and Cubanize through exclusively bookish and magical-poetic synthesis the most heterogeneous elements of a culture that ranges from Parmenides to Serge Diaghilev, I can do through tangible experiences).

2 Cortázar was inspired by Poe's theory of short narrative (Mora 1987).

3 Perec also adds: "Il arrive pourtant qu'elles reviennent, quelques années plus tard, intactes et minuscules, par hasard ou parce qu'on les a cherchées, un soir, entre amis; c'était une chose qu'on avait apprise à l'école, un champion, un chanteur ou une starlette qui perçait, un air qui était sur toutes les lèvres, un hold-up ou une catastrophe qui faisait la une des quotidiens, un best-seller, un scandale, un slogan, une habitude, une expression, un vêtement ou une manière de la porter, un geste, ou quelque chose d'encore plus mince, d'inessentiel, de tout à fait banal, miraculeusement arraché à son insignifiance, retrouvé pour un instant, suscitant pendant quelques secondes une impalpable petite nostalgie" (*Je me souviens* 4). (It happens, however, that they come back, a few years later, intact and tiny, by chance or because we looked for them, one evening, among friends; it was something we had learned at school, a champion, a singer or a starlet who broke through, a tune that was on everyone's lips, a hold-up or a disaster that made the front page of the newspapers, a bestseller, a scandal, a slogan, a habit, an expression, a piece of clothing or a way of wearing it, a gesture, or something even smaller, inessential, completely banal, miraculously snatched from its insignificance, found again for a moment, arousing for a few seconds an impalpable little nostalgia.)

4 See also by Highmore *Everyday Life and Cultural Theory* and *Ordinary Lives: Studies in the Everyday*.

5 Inspired by Pablo Neruda's *Canto general*, to whom is dedicated the first of three volumes, *Mural del País Valencià* is also inspired by Neruda himself, Charles Baudelaire, Pablo Picasso's *Guernica*, Joan Miró's poster for the Congrés de Cultura Catalana (1975–7), and mural paintings by David Alfaro Siqueiros and Diego Rivera.

6 I quote the poems by giving the number of the Horaciana in Andrés Estellés, *Horacianes*.

7 Estellés's style could also be linked to an interest in Latin classics that is noticeable in twentieth-century Spanish literature. See Villena; Pérez García. A remarkable example in Italian poetry is Eugenio Montale, who operates with a special kind of intertextuality: "Figlio di un tempo

che ha ucciso anche i sogni o li ha trasformati in incubi, Montale è 'anticlassico' in un senso diverso da quello che la critica gli attribuisce generalmente: il suo amaro disincanto utilizza gli autori antichi come specchi irrimediabilmente incrinati dal trascorrere inesorabile del tempo, specchi che riflettono i lineamenti deformati di ciò che eravamo e che non riusciamo più a essere" (Nuzzo 177). (A child of a time that has killed even dreams or turned them into nightmares, Montale is "anti-classical" in a different sense from the one critics generally attribute to him: his bitter disenchantment uses ancient authors as mirrors irreparably cracked by the inexorable passage of time, mirrors that reflect the deformed features of what we were and can no longer be.)

5 Churches and Trams

1 See also Santiago Rusiñol's article "Apedrean un tranvía por haber atropellado a un niño" (A streetcar is stoned for running over a child), *La Vanguardia*, 4 September 1901.

2 As in most big cities throughout the industrialized world, trams had been a part of Barcelona's landscape since the early 1880s. At first they were called La Catalana or also Ripperts (or *tramvies lliures*) because they did not circulate on rails but were pulled by horses. They were used until the 1920s when they were bought by the company Los Tranvías de Barcelona SA. See Sempronio, 21–7. From 1899 onward there were trams with electrical engines. Les Tramways de Barcelone was a society, founded in 1905, that was directed by Mariano de Foronda y Gonzalez Bravo, Marques de Foronda, who later became director of the 1929 Barcelona World Fair.

3 Joan Puig i Ferreter wrote moving passages about his remembrance of nature and his hometown. While living in Barcelona, he would go to Ciutadella Park and enjoy nature there. "Dubto que ningú hagi estimat el nostre vell Parc com jo l'estimava aleshores. Després he sentit dir i he llegit que és lleig, ridícul, provincià. Jo no ho sabia llavors, i encara no ho sé ara. Quina sort que tenen aquells qui es poden mirar les coses amb ulls amorosos i no pas amb ulls estètics!" (151). (I doubt that anyone loved our old Park as I loved it then. Later I heard and read that it is ugly, ridiculous, provincial. I didn't know it then, and I still don't know it now. How lucky are those who can look at things with loving eyes and not with aesthetic eyes!)

4 Several drawings and paintings by Ramon Casas and Santiago Rusiñol focus on these events.

5 Also available in English translation. See Joan Maragall, *Homage to Barcelona: The City and Its Art, 1888–1936* (London: British Council, 1985). 265–7. I am most indebted to Lluis Quintana's vast knowledge of Maragall for his comments on this section.

6 Most poems in Carner's *Auques i ventalls* (1914) and many of his articles in *Les planetes del verdum* (1918) and *Les bonhomies* (1925) are comments on urban life experiences.
7 See an alternative reading that pays attention to formal and philological aspects of this poem (Ortín, "Sovint").
8 For an excellent review of the streetcar presence in Brazilian literature see Tosta.
9 See *Torres Garcia* and *Barradas*.

6 Thresholds in Barcelona's Metro

1 The opening of the southern segment in Line 9 is the last episode in a disgraceful history (Latorre; Deiros Quintanilla).
2 A comparison of name changes juxtaposing the city underground and the city on the surface would be useful. For name changes see Fabre and Huertas.
3 There have been initiatives to map Barcelona's underground from different perspectives than those of traditional maps (Valls).
4 For a comprehensive discussion of this situation in literature see Rousset.
5 The song can be related to poems based on a toponym list, such as Miguel de Unamuno's "Toponimia hispánica," Blas de Otero's "Espejo de España," Joan Brossa's *Poemes civils*, or Vicent Andrés Estellés's "Cos mortal" in *Llibre de meravelles*.
6 Following the example of London and Paris, the underground is used as the cinematic setting for thrillers such as Francisco Pérez-Dolz's *A tiro limpio* (1963). In two films – one by Bigas Luna, *Bilbao* (1978), and another by Francesc Betriu, *Sinatra* (1988) – Avenida de la Luz is used to emphasize separation and marginality of the film's characters. In all three cases, several scenes' images operate as witness of disappearance.
7 For an extensive list of stories on the metro in English, see "Tubes, Subways, and Cars" in Bleiler. Brooks provides a comprehensive approach to literature and art on New York City's subway.
8 Salvat-Papasseit died in 1924 and did not see underground transportation in his own city. In 1921, during his brief stay in Paris he wrote in a letter to a friend: "But the Metro is better. You see. Paris has become more than ever *avantgardiste*" (*Obra completa* 492).
9 Paul Theroux's "Subway Odyssey," a sort of travelogue on New York City's subway system, could be considered an extension of this way of looking at the metro.
10 Translation by Arthur Terry, https://www.anglo-catalan.org/downloads/joan-gili-memorial-lectures/lecture02.pdf.

7 Forms of Thanatourism: José Pla and Josep M. Espinàs

1 Louis Aragon in *Le paysan de Paris* presents the city as described from the point of view of a peasant who visits a big city (Simmel's proposal) and is a victim of the vertiginous nature of the modern. According to Careri, "the book is a sort of guide to the quotidian marvels concealed inside the modern city: It is the description of those unknown places and fragments of life that unfold far from tourist itineraries, in a sort of submerged, undecipherable universe (84).

2 According to Shklovsky, "[t]he purpose of art is to impart the sensation of things as they are perceived and not as they are known. The technique of art is to make objects 'unfamiliar,' to make forms difficult to increase the difficulty and length of perception because the process of perception is an aesthetic end in itself and must be prolonged" (16).

3 Espinàs's early travelogues have been linked to the example of Camilo José Cela and to social realism of the 1960s. See Gregori.

4 During his long literary career Espinàs published twenty-one travelogues: *Viatge al Pirineu de Lleida* (Barcelona: Selecta, 1957); *Seguint tot l'Ebre amb un primitiu Velosolex* (1961, published as a book in 2003); *Viatge al Priorat* (Barcelona: Selecta, 1962); *Viatge a la Segarra* (Barcelona: Dopesa, 1972); *A peu per la Terra Alta* (Barcelona: La Campana, 1989); *A peu per la Llitera: Viatge a frontera de la llengua* (Barcelona: La Campana, 1990); *A peu per l'Alt Maestrat* (Barcelona: La Campana, 1991); *A peu pels camins de cendra* (Barcelona: La Campana, 1994); *A peu per l'Alcalatén* (Barcelona: La Campana, 1996); *A peu pel Matarranya* (Barcelona: La Campana, 1996); *A peu pel Comtat i la Marina* (Barcelona: La Campana, 1998); *A peu per Castella* (Barcelona: La Campana, 1999); *A peu pel País Basc* (Barcelona: La Campana, 2000); *A peu per Extremadura* (Barcelona: La Campana, 2001); *A peu per Galícia* (Barcelona: La Campana, 2002); *A peu per Andalusia* (Barcelona: La Campana, 2003); *A peu per la Costa do Morte* (Barcelona: La Campana, 2004); *A peu per Mallorca sense veure el mar* (Barcelona: La Campana, 2005); *A peu per Aragó: El Somontano* (Barcelona: La Campana, 2006); *A peu per l'Alt Camp* (Barcelona: La Campana, 2007); and *A peu per Múrcia* (Barcelona: La Campana, 2009). For a more in-depth discussion see Armengol Gimeno.

5 Cela's version was published only in 1965.

6 "Los Pirineos de mar a mar, I: De Cadaqués a Ripoll," *Destino*, vol. 1, no. 200, 6 August; "Los Pirineos de mar a mar, II: De Ripoll a la Pobla de Segur," *Destino*, vol. 1, no. 201, 13 August; "Los Pirineos de mar a mar, III: El alto Pirineo de Lérida," *Destino*, vol. 1, no. 202, 20 August; "Los Pirineos de mar a mar, IV: Hacia Panticosa," *Destino*, vol. 1, no. 203, 6 August; "Los Pirineos de mar a mar, V: De Panticosa al valle de Ansó,"

Destino, vol. 1, no. 204, 3 September; "Los Pirineos de mar a mar, VI: El Pirineo vasco-navarro," *Destino*, vol. 1, no. 205, 10 September.

7 Two recent books have similar goals: to "travel" on foot through the anonymous outskirts of two major cities, Milan and London, in order to present an unexpected view of the big city. In *Tangenziali: Due viandanti ai Bordi della città* (2010) Biondillo and Monina observe the city from its extreme limits, clearly showing the many modifications introduced in the last Berlusconian decades. Iain Sinclair wrote in *London Orbital* (2002) about a real journey of brilliant discoveries in the limits of the most "fancy" London. He recounts his walk along the M25 as a kind of journey into the heart of darkness, an area full of golf courses, shopping parks, and industrial estates, which corresponds to Tony Blair's Britain. The tyres have buried the image of an idyllic England full of green parks and old women on bicycles. These two books are just the tip of the iceberg of broader dedication.

8 See www.grief-tourism.com.

8 Beggars Can't Be Choosers: From Autarky to Globalized Gastronomy in Spain

1 It is not far from the well-known definition by Brillat-Savarin: "La gastronomie est la connaissance raisonnée de tout ce qui a rapport à l'homme, en tant qu'il se nourrit. Son but est de veiller à la conservation des hommes, au moyen de la meilleure nourriture possible. Elle y parvient en dirigeant, par des principes certains, tous ceux qui recherchent, fournissent ou préparent les choses qui peuvent se convertir en aliments" (17). (Gastronomy is the reasoned knowledge of everything that has to do with man, in so far as he feeds himself. Its aim is to ensure the preservation of mankind, by means of the best possible food. It achieves this by directing, by certain principles, all those who seek, provide, or prepare things that can be converted into food.)

2 For a broader discussion of this issue, see chapter 9.

9 Food and the Everyday in Spain: Immigration and Culinary Renovation

1 Manuel Vázquez Montalbán published "De Portbou a Hendaya: La vuelta a la cazuela de España" as a series of articles in *El País* in August 2000. It would unfair to say that, being the son of immigrants, he did not pay attention to the transformation of Spain in many of his articles or novels, but maybe because it was too early and the effects were not yet visible in restaurants, he did not ruminate on the food effects of such

a social makeover. This is confirmed in personal communications from two Vázquez Montalbán experts (to whom I am most thankful), José F. Colmeiro and José Saval. Masterson-Algar's offers an up-to-date review of Spain's transformation (*Ecuadorians* 3–5).

2 There is very little research on this aspect. There are some sociological studies on the case of Latin American immigrants to Spain. See Romo and Gil.

3 At the time of the 1992 Olympics many magazines devoted special issues to Spanish food, thus starting a fad for *tapas* restaurants.

4 As shown by Masterson-Algar, Equatorian immigrants have been "expelled" from central areas of Madrid, thus enabling a sanitized and uniform vision of the capital city (*Equatorians* 88–122).

5 "[E]staba en el centro de Madrid, en el kilómetro cero, en el corazón mismo de España, y solo veía a su alrededor mendigos, tullidos, negros, marroquíes, indios de América del Sur que tocaban bombos y flautas, gente patibularia que trapicheaba en las esquinas, asesinos y salteadores en potencia" (28; He was in the centre of Madrid, at kilometre zero, in the very heart of Spain, and all he saw around him were beggars, cripples, blacks, Moroccans, Indians from South America playing drums and flutes, people who were hustling on street corners, murderers and potential robbers). See also Peñalta Catalán.

6 See also Deveny; Martín; or the opinion of Ricardo Arana Mariscal: "defiende … olvidar la postura 'nosotros-ellos' y reemplazarla por un enriquecedor 'todos'" (40; the film advocates … forgetting the "us-them" stance and replacing it with an enriching "all of us").

7 See *Karakia*, http://www.ccma.cat/tv3/karakia/.

8 According to Marrugat, the formula of this narrative trilogy – a recovery of a disappeared world from the consciousness of the individual, and the collective changes that have taken place – is similar to that of Spanish writer Julio Llamazares. In his second novel, *La lluvia amarilla* (1988), Llamazares tells of the depopulation of a village in the Aragonese Pyrenees, and in *Escenas de cine mudo* (1994) he shares with *De fems i de marbre* the use of photographs as activators of past memories.

9 See also "l'abandó progressiu de les terres" (Serés, *De fems* 244; the progressive abandonment of the lands); a Sunday's big meal with an open table "com si fos un llibre amb un faristol a sota" (253; like a book with a lectern underneath).

References

Abella, Rafael. *La vida cotidiana en España bajo el régimen de Franco*. Argos Vergara, 1985.

Agís Villaverde, Marcelino. "Hermenéutica de la vida cotidiana." *Pensar la vida cotidiana: Actas III; Encuentros Internacionales de Filosofía en el Camino de Santiago = Encontros Internacionais de Filosofía no Camiño de Santiago*, edited by Marcelino Agís Villaverde and Carlos Baliñas Fernández, Universidade de Santiago de Compostela, Servizo de Publicacións e Intercambio Científico, 2001, pp. 11–24.

Ahern, Stephen, editor. *Affect Theory and Literary Critical Practice: A Feel for the Text*. Palgrave Macmillan, 2019.

Alazraki, Jaime. "Enumeration as Evocation: On the Use of a Device in Borges' Latest Poetry." *Borges, the Poet*, edited by Carlos Cortínez, U of Arkansas P, 1986, pp. 149–57.

Amato, Joseph A. *Everyday Life: How the Ordinary Became Extraordinary*. Reaktion Books, 2016.

Amato, Joseph A. *On Foot: A History of Walking*. New York UP, 2004.

Andrés Estellés, Vicent. *Coral romput. Obra completa*, vol. 1, 3i4, 2014, pp. 383–426.

Andrés Estellés, Vicent. *Horacianes. Obra completa*, vol. 4, 3i4, 2017, pp. 123–215.

Andrés Estellés, Vicent. *Llibre de meravelles. Obra completa*, vol. 2, 3i4, 2015, pp. 221–322.

Andrés Estellés, Vicent. *Mural del País Valencià*. 3i4, 1996.

Arana Mariscal, Ricardo. *La inmigración en clave de comedia*. Bakeaz, 2007.

Arco Blanco, Miguel Ángel del. "Famine in Spain during Franco's Dictatorship, 1939–52." *Journal of Contemporary History*, vol. 56, no. 1, 2021, pp. 3–27.

Armengol Gimeno, Elisabet. *Els viatges a peu de Josep M. Espinàs*. PAMSA, 2015.

Asendorf, Christoph. *Batteries of Life: On the History of Things and Their Perception in Modernity*. U of California P, 1993.

Ashford, David. *London Underground: A Cultural Geography*. Liverpool UP, 2013.

Assmann, Jan. *Cultural Memory and Early Civilization: Writing, Remembrance, and Political Imagination*. Cambridge UP, 2011.

Atkins, G. Douglas. *Reading T.S. Eliot: Four Quartets and the Journey toward Understanding: Four Quartets and the Journey towards Understanding*. Palgrave Macmillan, 2012.

Audet, René. "Fuir le récit pour raconter le quotidien: Modulations narratives en prose contemporaine." *Temps Zéro*, no. 1, 2007, http://tempszero.contemporain.info/document84.

Augé, Marc. *In the Metro*. University of Minnesota Press, 2002.

Augé, Marc. *Bonheurs du jour: Anthropologie de l'instant*. Albin Michel, 2018.

Augé, Marc. *Le Métro revisité*. Seuil, 2008.

Augé, Marc. *Non-places: Introduction to an Anthropology of Supermodernity*. Verso, 1995.

Badiou, Alain. *Métaphysique du bonheur reel*. PUF, 2015.

Baecque, Antoine de. *La France gastronome: Comment le restaurant est entré dans notre histoire*. Payot, 2019.

Ballester Roca, Josep. "Dos elements poètics fonamentals en l'obra de V. Andrés Estellés." *L'aiguadolç*, no. 28–29, 2003, pp. 59–66.

Baquero Goyanes, Mariano. *Perspectivismo y contraste*. Gredos, 1963.

Bargh, J.A. "The Automaticity of Everyday Life." *The Automaticity of Everyday Life: Advances in Social Cognition*, edited by J.R.S. Wyer, Lawrence Erlbaum Associates, 1997, pp. 1–61.

Barradas: Exposició Antològica, 1890–1929. Generalitat de Catalunya – Gobierno de Aragón – Comunidad de Madrid, 1992.

Barral, Carlos. *Poesía*. Edited by Carmen Riera, Cátedra, 1991.

Barthes, Roland. *La chambre claire: Note sur la photographie*. Cahiers du Cinema-Gallimard-Le Seuil, 1980.

Barthes, Roland. *Mythologies*. Éditions du Seuil, 1957.

Barthes, Roland. *Oeuvres completes*, vol. 1. Seuil, 1993.

Barthes, Roland. "Pour une psycho-sociologie de l'alimentation contemporaine." *Annales. Economies, sociétés, civilisations*, vol. 16, no. 5, 1961, pp. 977–86.

Barthes, Roland. "Le troisième sens: Notes de recherche sur quelques photogrammes de S.M. Eisenstein." *L'Obvie et l'obtus: Essais critiques*, vol. 3, Éditions du Seuil, 1982, pp. 43–61.

Baudelaire, Charles. *Oeuvres complètes*, vol. 1. Gallimard, 1975.

Benjamin, Walter. *The Arcades Project*. Belknap P of Harvard UP, 1999.

Benjamin, Walter. "The Image of Proust." *Illuminations: Essays and Reflections*, Schocken Books, 1969, pp. 201–15.

Benjamin, Walter. "On Some Motifs in Baudelaire." In *Illuminations: Essays and Reflections*, Shocken Books, 1969, pp. 155–200.

Benjamin, Walter. "Paris, Capital of the Nineteenth Century." *Reflections, Essays, Aphorisms, Autobiographical Writings*, edited and with an introduction by Peter Demetz, Schocken Books, 1986, pp. 146–62.

Benjamin, Walter. *Selected Writings, Volume 2, 1931–1934*. Edited by Marcus Bullock and Michael W. Jennings, Harvard UP, 1999.

Benjamin, Walter. *Selected Writings, Volume 4, 1938–1940*. Harvard UP, 2003.

Benjamin, Walter. "Surrealism: The Last Snapshot of the European Intelligentsia." *Selected Writings, Volume 2, 1931–1934*, edited by Marcus Bullock and Michael W. Jennings, Harvard UP, 1999, pp. 207–22.

Benvenuto, Beppe. *Elzeviro*. Selerio editore, 2002.

Berger, Peter L., and Thomas Luckmann. *The Social Construction of Reality: A Treatise in the Sociology of Knowledge*. 1966. Penguin Books, 1971.

Bhabha, Homi. "The World and the Home." *Social Text*, no. 31/32, 1992, pp. 141–53.

Biondillo, Gianni, and Michele Monina. *Tangenziali: Due viandanti ai bordi della città*. Guanda, 2010.

Bishop, Michael. *Jacques Prévert: From Film and Theater to Poetry, Art and Song*. Rodopi, 2002.

Blanchot, Maurice. "Everyday Speech." *Yale French Studies*, vol. 73, 1987, pp. 12–20.

Blanco Hernández, Nuria. "La nota gastronómica y el artículo de costumbres." *Estudios sobre el Mensaje Periodístico.*, vol. 21, no. 2, July–December 2015, pp. 953–67.

Bleiler, Everett. *The Guide to Supernatural Fiction*. Kent State UP, 1983.

Blom, Thomas. "Morbid Tourism: A Postmodern Market Niche with an Example from Althorp." *Norsk Geografisk Tidsskrift / Norwegian Journal of Geography*, vol. 54, no. 1, 2000, pp. 29–36.

Bonada, Lluís. *L'obra de Josep Pla*. Barcelona: Ed. Teide, 1991,

Bonnefoy, Yves. *La longue chaîne de l'ancre*. Mercure de France, 2008.

Borges, Jorge Luis. *Narraciones*. Cátedra, 1998.

Borges, Jorge Luis. *Obra poética*. Sudamericana, 2011.

Borges, Jorge Luis. *Prosa completa*, vol. 2. Bruguera, 1980.

Bou, Enric. "'Amor redemptor'? Visions urbanes de Joan Maragall." *Joan Maragall, paraula i pensament*, edited by Josep-Maria Terricabras, Documenta Universitaria, 2011, pp. 237–57. Publicacions de la Càtedra Ferrater Mora, Noms de la filosofía catalana, 7.

Bou, Enric. *Daliccionario: Objetos, mitos y símbolos de Salvador Dalí*. Tusquets, 2004.

Bou, Enric. "Noucentisme 2.0: 'Palpitacions del temps'; De Guerau de Liost a Toldrà." *El Noucentime un nou discurs per al segle XXI: Actes del I Simposi Internacional sobre el Noucentisme 2014, Sitges 29 November, 2014*, edited by Vinyet Panyella, Consorci de Patrimoni de Sitges, 2018, pp. 259–82.

Bou, Enric. "On Rivers and Maps: Iberian Approaches to Comparatism." *New Spain, New Literatures*, edited by Luis Martín-Estudillo and Nicholas Spadaccini, Vanderbilt UP, 2010 pp. 3–26.

Bou, Enric. "Time and Memory: *Camí de sirga* and *Les veus del Pamano*." *Digithum*, vol. 15, 2013, pp. 73–9. http://digithum.uoc.edu/ojs/index.php/digithum/article/view/n15-bou/n15-bou-en.

Bou, Enric."Vicent Andrés Estellés, una inconformitat." *Serra d'Or*, vol. 20, no. 226–7, July–August 1978, pp. 57–60.

Bourdieu, Pierre. *Outline of a Theory of Practice*. Translated by Richard Nice, Cambridge UP, 1977.

Boym, Svetlana. *Common Places: Mythologies of Everyday Life in Russia*. Harvard UP, 1995.

Boym, Svetlana. *The Future of Nostalgia*. Basic Books, 2002.

Braga Marquilhas, Maria Rita. "Post Scriptum: A Digital Archive of Ordinary Writings (Early Modern Portugal and Spain)." https://cordis.europa.eu/project/id/295562.

Brennan, Joseph. "City Hall (IRT)." https://www.columbia.edu/~brennan/abandoned/cityirt.html.

Brenner, P.J., editor. *Der Reisebericht: Die Entwicklung Einer Gattung in Der Deutschen Literatur*. Suhrkamp Verlag, 1989.

Brillat-Savarin, Jean Anthelme. *Physiologie du gout*. Gallimard, 2017.

Brochu, André. *Roman et énumeration: De Flaubert á Perec*. Presses universitaires de l'Université de Montréal, 1996.

Brooks, Michael. *Subway City: Riding the Trains, Reading New York*. Rutgers UP, 1997.

Bruno, Giuliana. *Atlas of Emotion: Journeys in Art, Architecture and Film*. Verso, 2002.

Buñuel, Luis. "El cine instrumento de poesía." *Escritos de Luis Buñuel*. Editorial Páginas de Espuma, 2000, p. 66.

Buzard, James. *The Beaten Track: European Tourism, Literature, and the Ways to Culture, 1800–1918*. Clarendon Press / Oxford UP, 1993.

Campos, Álvaro de. "Lisbon Revisited (1926)." Arquivo Pessoa, http://arquivopessoa.net/textos/158.

Camus, Marcel, dir. *Black Orpheus*. Lopert Pictures, 1959.

Carandell, Josep Maria. *El Temple de la Sagrada Familia*. Triangle Postals, 1997.

Carbó, Ferran. "Els exilis de Vicent Andrés Estellés." *Caplletra*, vol. 36, 2004, pp. 93–116.

Cardoso Pires, José. *Lisboa, livro de bordo: Vozes, olhares, memoraçaões*. Cículo de Leitores, 1998.

Careri, Francesco. *Walkscapes: El andar como práctica estética – Walking as an Aesthetic Practice*. Gustavo Gili, 2002. Land & Scape Series, vol. 1.

Carner, Josep. "Advertiments de l'autor." *Auques i ventalls*, edited by Joan Ferraté, Edicions 62, 1977, pp. 119–21.

Carner, Josep. *Auques i ventalls*. Edited by Joan Ferraté. Edicions 62, 1977.

Carner, Josep. *Les bonhomies i altres proses*. Edicions 62, 1981.

Carner, Josep. *La creació d'Eva i altres contes*. Edited by Albert Manent, Editorial Laia, 1980.

Carner, Josep. *La paraula en el vent*. Fidel Giró, 1914.

Carner, Josep. *Poesia*. Editorial Selecta, 1957.

Carnero, Guillermo. "Cotidianismo y sátira en la poesía de Vicent Andrés Estellés." *Papeles de son Armadans*, no. 244, 1976, pp. 25–41.

Castells, M., J. Caraca, and G. Cardoso, editors. *Aftermath: The Cultures of the Economic Crisis*. Oxford UP, 2012.

Cavafy, C.P. "The City." *Poetry Foundation*, 2020. https://www.poetryfoundation.org/poems/51295/the-city-56d22eef2f768.

Cavallin, Jean-Christophe. "Baudelaire et 'l'homme d'Ovide.'" *Cahiers de l'Association internationale des études francaises*, vol. 58, no. 1, 2006, pp. 341–57.

Cela, Camilo José. *Viaje al Pirineo de Lérida*. Editorial Noguer, 1965.

Certeau, Michel de. *The Practice of Everyday Life*. U of California P, 1984.

Charbonnier, Georges, editor. *Entretien avec Claude Lévi-Strauss*. Union Generale d'Editions, 1961.

Chupeau, Jacques. *Un nouvel art du roman: Techniques narratives et poésie romanesque dans* Les illustres françaises *de Robert Challe*. Paradigme, 1993.

Clifford, James. *The Predicament of Culture: Twentieth-Century Ethnography, Literature, and Art*. Harvard UP, 1988.

Cócola Grant, Agustín. *El Barrio Gótico de Barcelona: Planificación del Pasado e Imagen de Marca*. Ediciones Madroño, 2011.

Comadira, Narcís. *The English Experience: The Annual Joan Gili Memorial Lecture*. Hallamshire Press / Anglo-Catalan Society, 2000.

Corbalán, Ana. "Encuentros transnacionales en el cine español: Perpetuación del sujeto femenino silenciado en *El Próximo Oriente*." *Romance Notes*, vol. 53, no. 1, 2013, pp. 105–15.

Cornejo-Parriego, Rosalía. "Espacios híbridos, iconos mestizos: Imaginando la España global." *Letras peninsulares*, vol. 15, no. 3, 2002, pp. 515–31.

Cornudella, Jordi. "Estudi introductori." *Vers i prosa*, edited by Gabriel Ferrater, L'Estel, 5, 3i4, 1988, pp. 9–47.

Cortázar, Julio. "Acerca de la situación del intelectual latinoamericano." *Último round*, vol. 2, Siglo XXI, 2014, pp. 265–80.

Cortázar, Julio. "Bajo nivel." *La Jornada Semanal*, no. 53, 10 March 1996, https://www.jornada.com.mx/1996/03/10/sem-julio.html.

Cortázar, Julio. *Cuentos Completos*. Alfaguara, 1994.

Cortázar, Julio. *Rayuela: Edición conmemorativa de la Real Academia Española (RAE) y la Asociación de Academias de la Lengua Española (ASALE)*. Editorial Alfaguara, Penguin Random House, 2019.

Cortázar, Julio, and Carol Dunlop. *Los autonautas de la cosmopista o Un viaje atemporal París-Marsella*. Muchnick Editores, 1983.

Crook, Stephen, Jan Pakulski, and Malcolm Waters. *Postmodernization: Change in Advanced Societies*. Sage, 1992.

Cunqueiro, Álvaro. *La cocina cristiana de Occidente*. Tusquets, 1981.

Cunqueiro, Álvaro. *A cociña galega*. Galaxia, 1980.

Daguerréotypes. Directed by Agnès Varda. ZDF, Ciné-Tamaris, 1975.

Dalí, Salvador. "Salvador Dalí escribe a Federico García Lorca." *Poesía*, vol. 27–8, 1987.

Dann, George. "Tourism: The Nostalgia Industry of the Future." *Global Tourism: The Next Decade*, edited by W. Theobald, Butterworth Heinemann, 1994, pp. 55–67.

Darsy, Sébastien. "La poésie du quotidien: Prévert nous parle." *L'Humanité*, 9 September 2020, https://www.humanite.fr/node/233373.

Davies, Catherine. *Spanish Women's Writing, 1849–1996*. Athlone Press, 1998.

Débord, Guy. "Introduction à une critique de la géographie urbaine." *Les lèvres nues*, no. 6, 1955, http://www.larevuedesressources.org/introduction-a-une-critique-de-la-geographie-urbaine,033.html.

Deiros Quintanilla, Ivan. "El finançament de les grans obres d'infraestructures ferroviàries: El cas de la línia 9." *Infrastructura del Transport i del Territori (ITT)*, Universitat Politècnica de Catalunya, 2012. http://upcommons.upc.edu/bitstream/handle/2099.1/14553/Tesina_Ivan_Deiros.pdf?sequence=1.

Deleuze, Gilles, and Félix Guattari. *A Thousand Plateaus: Capitalism and Schizophrenia*. U of Minnesota P, 2004.

Denil, Mark. "The Search for a Radical Cartography." *Cartographic Perspectives*, vol. 68, March 2011, pp. 7–28, doi:10.14714/CP68.6.

Despoix, Philippe. *Avant-propos, Siegfried Kracauer*: *Le voyage et la danse*. Presses universitaires de Vincennes, 1996, pp. 7–21.

Deveny, Thomas G. *Migration in Contemporary Hispanic Cinema*. Scarecrow Press, 2012.

Díaz Barrado, Mario. *La España democrática*. Sintesis, 2014.

Dictionnaire de français. https://www.larousse.fr/dictionnaires/francais-monolingue.

Dillon, Brian. "Fragments from a History of Ruin: Picking through the Wreckage." *Cabinet*, vol. 20, winter 2005/06, http://www.cabinetmagazine.org/issues/20/dillon.php.

Domènech, Ignacio. *Cocina de recursos (Deseo mi comida)*. Ediciones Trea, 2011.

Domènech, Joan de Déu. *La batalla de l'ou: De quan passàvem gana (1936–1939)*. Pòrtic, 2012.

Double Indemnity. Directed by Billy Wilder, Paramount Pictures, 1944.

Duchamp, Marcel. "Apropos of 'Readymades.'" *The Essential Marcel Duchamp*, edited by Matthew Affron, Yale UP / Philadelphia Museum of Art, 2019, p. 171.

Dylan, Bob. "Desolation Row." https://www.bobdylan.com/songs/desolation-row/.

Eagleton, Terry. "Edible Ecriture." *Times Higher Education*, 1997, www.timeshighereducation.co.uk/features/edible-ecriture/104281.article.

Eco, Umberto. *The Infinity of Lists: An Illustrated Essay*. Rizzoli, 2009.

Edwards, Louise, Stefano Occhipinti, and Simon Ryan. "Food and Immigration: The Indigestion Trope Contests the Sophistication Narrative." *Journal of Intercultural Studies*, vol. 21, no. 3, 2000, pp. 297–308.

Eliot, T.S. *Four Quartets*. An Accurate Online Text, 2000. http://www.davidgorman.com/4quartets/.

Engelke, Gerrit. *Rhythmus des neuen Europa*. Eugen Diederichs Verlag, 1921.

Espín, Manuel. *Vida cotidiana en la España de la posguerra*. Almuzara, 2022.

Espinàs, Josep M. *A peu per Andalusia: Sierra Mágina; La frontera cristiano-musulmana*. Ediciona La Campana, 2003.

Espinàs, Josep M. *A peu per Castella: Terres de Sòria*. Edicions La Campana, 1999.

Espinàs, Josep M. *A peu per la Terra Alta*. Edicions La Campana, 1989.

Espinàs, Josep M. "Pròleg." *Obra completa*, vol. 5, Edicions La Campana, 1991.

Espinàs, Josep M. *Seguint tot l'Ebre amb un primitiu Velosolex*. Edicions La Campana, 2003.

Esposito, Gilles. "Voulez-vous savoir ce qu'est une anagramme de métro?" http://www.gef.free.fr/metro.html.

Esquirol, Josep Maria. *La resistència íntima: Assaig d'una filosofia de la proximitat*. Quaderns Crema, 2015.

"Les estacions fantasmes del metro de Barcelona." https://estacionsfantasmabcn.wordpress.com.

Eugenides, Jeffrey. "Joseph Roth's Movable Cafe." *New York Times*, 2 February 2003.

Eugenides, Jeffrey. *The Virgin Suicides*. Farrar, Straus and Giroux, 1993.

Eutròfics, Els Nens. "Subterrània." *En helicòpter*, Bandcamp, 2013. https://elsnenseutrofics.bandcamp.com/track/subterr-nia.

Fabre, Jaume, and Josep Maria Huertas. *Carrers de Barcelona: Com han evolucionat els seus noms*. Edhasa, 1982.

Ferraté, Joan. "*Poesia*, de Josep Carner: Ressenya i vindicació." *Els Marges*, no. 8, 1976, pp. 15–32.

Ferrater, Gabriel. *Les dones i els dies*. Edicions 62, 1968.

Ferrater, Gabriel. "Pròleg." *Nabí*, by Josep Carner, Edicions 62, 1991, pp. 5–23.

F for Fake. Directed by Orson Welles, Planfilm / Specialty Films, 1973.

Fischler, Claude. "Food, Self and Identity." *Social Science Information*, vol. 27, 1988, pp. 275–93.

Flórez-Bosque, Xavier, and Jordi Ibáñez Puente. *Les línies de tramvies de Barcelona: 1872–1971: Catàleg de línies urbanes*. Xavier Flòrez-Bosque, DL, 2001.

Foix, J.V. *Daybook 1918: Early Fragments*. Edited and translated by Lawrence Venuti. Northwestern UP, 2019.

Foley, Malcolm, and J. John Lennon. "JFK and Dark Tourism: A Fascination with Assassination." *International Journal of Heritage Studies*, vol. 2, no. 4, 1996, pp. 198–211.

Forns, Albert. *Abans de les cinc som a casa*. Edicions 62, 2020.

Franco, Jean. "Julio Cortázar: Utopia and Everyday Life." *INTI: Revista de literatura hispánica*, vol. 10, autumn–spring 1979, https://digitalcommons.providence.edu/inti/vol1/iss10/15.

François, Corinne. *Jacques Prévert, Paroles*. Éditions Breal, 2000.

Freud, Sigmund. *The Psychopathology of Everyday Life*. W.W. Norton, 1989.

Fussell, Paul. *Abroad: British Literary Traveling between the Wars*. Oxford UP, 1980.

Fuster, Joan. "Nota – provisional i improvisada – sobre la poesia de Vicent Andrés Estellés." *Recomane tenebres*, by Vicent Andrés Estellés, *Obra completa*, vol. 1, edited by Eliseu Climent, 1972, pp. 17–36.

Fuster, Joan. "Pròleg." *Les bonhomies*, by Josep Carner. Edicions 62, 1964, pp. 7–15.

Gainsbourg, Serge. "Le poinçonneur des Lilas." *Du chant à la une!*, Philips, 1958.

Gallofré, Maria Josepa. "Josep Pla, Entre el *Viaje en autobús* (1942) i el *Viaje a pie* (1949)." *Josep Pla, Memòria i escriptura: Actes del col.loqui de l'any pla, Universitat de Girona (octubre 1997)*, edited by Glòria Granell and Xavier Pla, U of Girona, 2001, pp. 65–78.

Garcia-Soler, Jordi. "I la cançó al vent." *Serra d'Or* 190, 1975, pp. 62.

Gardiner, Michael. *Critiques of Everyday Life: An Introduction*. Routledge, 2000.

Garrett, Almeida. *Viagens na minha terra*. Porto editora, 1846.

Gavagnin, Gabriella. "Mites i objectes futuristes en la poesia de Salvat-Papasseit: Apunts de lectura comparada." *Estudis romànics*, vol. 29, 2007, pp. 193–211.

Gaziel. "Pequeña elegía urbana." *La Vanguardia*, 26 April 1929, p. 5.

Gaziel. *Tots els camins duen a Roma: Historia d'un desti (1893–1914); Memòries*. Edicions 62, 1981.

Ghirardi, Mónica, editor. *Territorios de lo cotidiano: Siglos XVI–XX; Del antiguo virreinato del Perú a la Argentina contemporánea*. Prohistoria Ediciones, 2014.

Gill, Andy. *Classic Bob Dylan, 1962–69: My Back Pages*. Carlton Books, 1999.

Gilloch, Graeme. "Impromptus of a Great City: Siegfried Kracauer's *Strassen in Berlin und anderswo*." *Tracing Modernity: Manifestations of the Modern in Architecture and the City*, edited by M. Hvattum and C. Hermansen, Routledge, 2004, pp. 291–306.

Gilloch, G., and J. Kilby. "Trauma and Memory in the City: From Auster to Austerlitz." *Urban Memory. History and Amnesia in the Modern City*, edited by M. Crinson, Routledge, 2005, pp. 1–22.

Gilmour, Michael J. *The Gospel according to Bob Dylan: The Old, Old Story of Modern Times*. Westminster John Knox Press, 2011.

Gimferrer, P. *Dietari Complet*, vol. 1. Edicions 62, 1997.

Gómez de la Serna, Ramón. *Ramonismo I: El rastro. El circo. Senos*. Galaxia Gutenberg, 1998. Vol. 3 of *Obras completas*.

Gooden, Philip, and Peter Lewis. *Idiomantics: The Weird and Wonderful World of Popular Phrases*. A&C Black Business Information and Development, 2013.

Gould Levine, Linda. *Juan Goytisolo: La destrucción creadora*. J. Mortiz, 1976.

Gouldner, Alvi. "Sociology and Everyday Life." *The Idea of Social Structure: Papers in Honor of Robert K. Merton*, edited by Lewis A. Coser, Harcourt, Brace, Jovanovich, 1975, pp. 417–32.

Goytisolo, Juan. *Reivindicación del Conde Don Julián*. Edited by Linda Gould Levine, Cátedra, 1985.

Gracia, Jordi. "L'herodòxia del moralista o la novel·la de Pla a l'Espanya feixista." *La poètica de la banalitat: Actes de la Jornada d'Estudi Cinquanta Anys d'El carrer Estret*, edited by Anna Aguiló and Xavier Pla, U of Girona, Servei de Publicacions, 2003, pp. 45–53.

Gràcia, Roger de. "Qualsevol nit pot sortir el sol." https://www.ccma.cat/tv3/alacarta/treure-del-cap-1/qualsevol-nit-pot-sortir-el-sol/video/3218811/.

Gregori, Carme. "El caminant de la terra: Els primers llibres de viatge de Josep M. Espinàs." *Caplletra: Revista Internacional de Filologia*, vol. 28, 2000, pp. 121–44.

Gubert, Carla. *Un mondo di cartone: Nascita e poetica della prosa d'arte nel Novecento*. Prefazione Corrado Donati, Metauro Edizioni, 2003.

Guerola, Joaquim. "Terradas y la construcción del túnel del Metro Transversal de Barcelona." *Quark*, no. 31, 2004, pp. 85–94.

Guiral, Antoni. *El mundo de Escobar*. Ediciones B, 2008.

Guixà, Pere. "L'escriptor que camina." *La Vanguardia*, 30 April 2016.

Gunderson, Edna. "Dylan Is Positively on Top of His Game." *USA Today*, 9 Oct. 2001.

Hallbwachs, Maurice. *La mémoire collective*. Albin Michel, 1997.

Harari, Yuval Noah. *Sapiens: A Brief History of Humankind*. Harper Collins, 2011.

Harley, J.B., and David Woodward. *Cartography in Prehistoric, Ancient, and Medieval Europe and the Mediterranean*. U of Chicago P, 1987. Vol. 1 of *The History of Cartography*.

Harootunian, Harry. *History's Disquiet: Modernity, Cultural Practice, and the Question of Everyday Life*. Columbia UP, 2002.

Hauck-Lawson, Annie S. "When Food Is the Voice: A Case Study of a Polish-American Woman." *Journal for the Study of Food and Society*, vol. 2, no. 1, 1998, pp. 21–8, doi:10.2752/152897998786690592.

Heller, Agnes. "The Marxist Theory of Revolution and the Revolution of Everyday Life." *Telos*, vol. 6, fall, 1970, pp. 212–23.

Highmore, Ben. *Everyday Life and Cultural Theory: An Introduction*. Routledge, 2002.

Highmore, Ben. *The Everyday Life Reader*. Psychology Press, 2002.

Highmore, Ben. *The Great Indoors: At Home in the Modern British House*. Profile Books, 2014.

Highmore, Ben. *Ordinary Lives: Studies in the Everyday*. Routledge, 2011.

Highmore, Ben. "Something Ordinary." *Reviews in Cultural Theory*, vol. 1, no. 1, 2010, pp. 4–6.

Hirsch, Marianne. *Family Frames: Photography, Narrative and Postmemory*. Harvard UP, 1997.

Hobsbawn, Eric. *Age of Extremes: The Short Twentieth Century, 1914–1991*. Pantheon Books, 1994.

Hoffmann, Michael. Introduction. *What I Saw: Reports from Berlin, 1920–1933*, by Joseph Roth, translated by Michael Hoffmann. W.W. Norton, 2003, pp. 11–19.

Hoggart, Richard. *Everyday Language and Everyday Life*. Transaction Publishers, 2003.

Johnson, Thomas S. "Desolation Row Revisited: Bob Dylan's Rock Poetry." *Southwest Review* vol. 62, no. 2, spring 1977, pp. 135–47.

Jouet, Jacques. "Poème de métro." https://www.oulipo.net/fr/contraintes/poeme-de-metro.

Kern, Stephen. *The Culture of Time and Space: 1880–1918*. Harvard UP, 1983.

Kittler, P.G., K.P. Sucher, and M.N. Nelms. *Food and Culture*. Wadsworth, 2012.

Kowalewski, Michael. "Introduction: The Modern Literature of Travel." *Temperamental Journeys: Essays on the Modern Literature of Travel*, edited by Michael Kowalewski, U of Georgia P, 1992, pp. 1–16.

Kracauer, Siegfried. *History: The Last Things before the Last*. Columbia UP, 2013.

Kracauer, Siegfried. "Straße ohne Erinnerung." *Schriften*, edited by I. Mülder-Bach, Suhrkamp, 1990, pp. 170–3.

Kundera, Milan. *The Art of the Novel*. Grove Press, 1986.

Lahuerta, Juan José. *Antoni Gaudí: Ornament, Fire and Ashes*. Tenov Books, 2016.

Langbaum, Robert. *The Poetry of Experience*. Norton, 1957.

Larkin, Philip. *All What Jazz*. Faber and Faber, 1985.

Larra, Mariano José de. *Artículos de costumbres*. Edited by Daniel Muñoz Sempere. Oxford UP, 2017.

Latorre, Eloi. "El nyap de la línia 9 del metro: Costos per triplicat, estacions privatitzades i anys de retard." *Crític: Periodisme d'investigació*. http://www.elcritic.cat/investigacio/el-nyap-de-la-linia-9-del-metro-costos-per-triplicat-estacions-privatizades-i-anys-de-retard-4394.

Lausberg, Heinrich. *Elementos de retórica literária*. Fundação Calouste Gulbenkian, 1967.

Leed, Eric J. *The Mind of the Traveler: From Gilgamesh to Global Tourism*. Basic Books, 1991.

Lefebvre, Henri. *Critique of Everyday Life*, vol. 1. Translated by John Moore, Verso, 1991.

Lefebvre, Henri. "The Everyday and Everydayness." *Yale French Studies*, vol. 73, 1987, pp. 7–11.
Lefebvre, Henri. *Everyday Life in the Modern World*. Harper and Row, 1971.
Lefebvre, Henri. *Fondements d'une sociologie de la quotidienneté*. L'Arche, 1961. Vol. 2 of *Critique de la vie quotidienne*.
Lefebvre, Henri. *The Production of Space*. Blackwell, 1991.
Liebersohn, Harry. *The Travelers' World: Europe to the Pacific*. Harvard UP, 2009.
Linhard Tabea, Alexa. "Between Hostility and Hospitality: Immigration in Contemporary Spain." *Modern Language Notes*, vol. 122, no. 2, 2007, pp. 400–22.
Linklater, Richard, dir. *Boyhood*. IFC Films, 2014.
Links, Christoph. *Berliner Geisterbahnhöfe: The Berlin Ghost Stations; Les gares fantômes*. Ch. Links Verlag, 1994.
"List of Metro Systems." https://en.wikipedia.org/wiki/List_of_metro_systems.
Llamazares, Julio. *La lluvia amarilla*. Seix Barral, 1988.
Llovet, Jordi. "Literatura i ciutat." *Saber*, no. 15, hivern 1987/1988, pp. 5–13.
Löfgren, Orvar. *On Holiday: A History of Vacationing*. U of California P, 1999.
Löfgren, Orvar, and Billy Ehn. *The Secret World of Doing Nothing*. U of California P, 2010.
López Guallar, Marina. *Cerdà i Barcelona: La primera metròpoli, 1853–1897*. Museu d'Història de Barcelona, Institut de Cultura, Ajuntament de Barcelona, Sociedad Estatal de Conmemoraciones Culturales, 2010.
Lotman, Iurii M. "The Poetics of Everyday Behavior in Eighteenth-Century Russian Culture." *The Semiotics of Russian Cultural History*, edited by Alexander D. Nakhimovsky and Alice Stone Nakhimovsky, Cornell UP, 1985, pp. 67–94.
Luján, Néstor. *La Barcelona dels tramvies i altres textos: Selecció d'articles, dietari i apunts*. Meteora, 2015.
Luján, Néstor. *Las recetas de Pickwick*. Editorial Taber, 1969.
Maffesoli, Michel. *La conquête du présent: Pour une sociologie de la vie quotidienne*. Presses Universitaires de France, 1979.
Maffesoli, Michel. "The Sociology of Everyday Life (Epistemological Elements)." *Current Sociology*, vol. 37, no. 1, 1989, pp. 1–16.
Maierbrugger, Arno. "Das 'historische' Zeitungs-Feuilleton: Forschungsprobleme aus der Sicht der Kommunikationsgeschichte." *Zeitungen im Wiener Fin de Siöcle: Eine Tagung der Arbeitsgemeinschaft "Wien um 1900" der österreichischen Forschungsgemeinschaft*, edited by Sigurd Paul Scheichl and Wolfgang Duchkowitsch, Verlag für Geschichte und Politik, 1997, pp. 148–56.
Maistre, Xavier de. *Voyage autour de ma chambre*. Norbert Crochet, 2011.
Mandrell, James. "Etiquette and Table Manners in Larra's 'El castellano viejo': Another Point of View." *Forum for Modern Languages Studies*, vol. 22, 2011, pp. 74–84.

Manent, Albert. *Josep Carner i el Noucentisme*. Edicions 62, 1969.

Maragall, Joan. *Obres completes: Escrits en prosa*. Gustau Gili, 1912.

Maragall, Joan. *Obres completes: Obra castellana*. Editorial Selecta, 1981.

Maragall, Joan. *Obres completes: Obra catalana*. Editorial Selecta, 1981.

March, Ausiàs. *Poesies*. Edited by Pere Bohigas and Amadeu-J. Soberanas i Noemí Espinàs, Barcino, 2000.

Marrugat, Jordi. *Narrativa catalana de la postmodernitat: Històries, formes i motius*. Publicacions i Edicions de la Universitat de Barcelona, 2014.

Martín, Sandra Stickle. *Moroccan Women and Immigration in Spanish Narrative and Film (1995–2008)*. 2010. U of Kentucky, PhD dissertation.

Martínez Expósito, Alfredo. *Cuestión de imagen: Cine y Marca España*. Editorial Academia del Hispanismo, 2015.

Martín Gaite, Carmen. *El cuarto de atrás*. Edited by José Teruel, Cátedra, 2009.

Martín Gaite, Carmen. *Pido la palabra*. Anagrama, 2002.

Massumi, Brian. "The Autonomy of Affect." *Cultural Critique*, vol. 31, autumn 1995, pp. 83–109.

Masterson-Algar, Araceli. "Digging Madrid: A Descent into Madrid's Subway Museum Andén 0." *Trains, Culture, and Mobility: Riding the Rails*, edited by B. Fraser and S. Spalding, Lexington Books, 2012, pp. 205–32.

Masterson-Algar, Araceli. *Ecuadorians in Madrid: Migrants' Place in Urban History*. Palgrave Macmillan, 2016.

Masterson-Algar, Araceli. "The Subte as Looking Machine into the City: Moebius' Trajectory through Buenos Aires." *Transfers*, vol. 4, no. 4, 2014, pp. 68–85.

Medina, Jaume. "Les Horacianes de V.A. Estellés." *Els Marges*, no. 9, 1977, pp. 105–13.

Medina Arjona, Encarnación, and Paz Gómez Moreno, editors. *Escritura y vida cotidiana de las mujeres de los siglos XVI y XVII (Contexto mediterráneo)*. Alfar, 2015.

Miguel, Amando de. *Cien años de urbanidad: Crítica de costumbres de la vida española*. Planeta, 1991.

Miguel, Amando de. *La vida cotidiana de los españoles en el siglo XX*. Planeta, 2001.

Miquel, Pujadó. "Pels intestins de la ciutat." *Frontissa (1999/2002)*, Discmedi S.A., 2008.

Molas, Joaquim. "Un poeta en temps de crisi." *Joaquim M. Bartrina: Entre les raons poètiques i les científiques*, edited by Montserrat Corretger and Xavier Ferré, Publicacions de l'Arxiu Municipal de Reus, 2002, pp. 189–200.

Moncada, Jesús. *Camí de Sirga*. La Magrana, 1995.

Monegal-Brancos, Antonio. *Luis Buñuel de la literatura al cine: Una poética del objeto*. Anthropos, 1993. Autores, textos y temas: Literatura 17.

Monga, Luigi. "Travel and Travel Writing: An Historical Overview of Hodoeporics." *Annali d'Italianistica*, vol. 14, 1996, pp. 6–54.

Montoya Ramírez, María Isabel, and Gonzalo Aguilar Escobar, editors. *La vida cotidiana a través de sus textos (ss. XVI–XX)*. U of Granada, 2009.

Mora, Gabriela. "Horacio Quiroga y Julio Cortázar: Teóricos del cuento." *Revista Canadiense de Estudios Hispánicos*, vol. 11, no. 3, 1987, pp. 559–72.
Moran, Joe. *Armchair Nation: An Intimate History of Britain in Front of the Television*. Profile Books, 2013.
Moran, Joe. *On Roads: A Hidden History*. Profile Books, 2009.
Moran, Joe. *Queuing for Beginners: The Story of Daily Life from Breakfast to Bedtime*. Profile, 2007.
Moran, Joe. *Reading the Everyday*. Routledge, 2005.
Moreno, María Paz. "Beyond the Recipes: Authorship, Text, and Context in Canonical Spanish Cookbooks." *Food, Texts, and Cultures in Latin America and Spain*, Vanderbilt UP, 2020, pp. 201–19.
Moreno, María Paz. "*La cocina española antigua* de Emilia Pardo Bazán: Dulce venganza e intencionalidad múltiple en un recetario ilustrado." *La Tribuna: Cadernos de Estudos da Casa-Museo Emilia Pardo Bazán*, vol. 4, no. 4, 2006, pp. 243–51.
Morris, Jan. *Trieste and the Meaning of Nowhere*. London: Faber and Faber, 2010.
Mülder-Bach, Inka. Introduction. *The Salaried Masses: Duty and Distraction in Weimar Germany*, by Siegfried Kracauer, Verso, 1998, pp. 3–22.
Muñiz, María de las Nieves. "Noves dades sobre les proses disperses de Josep Carner: Els articles enviats a *l'Heraldo de Madrid* des d'Itàlia (1923–1924)." *Els Marges*, no. 104, 2014, pp. 64–91.
Muñoz i Lloret, Josep M. "La identitat escindida de Jaume Sisa." *L'Avenç: Revista de història i cultura*, no. 461, 2019, pp. 20–32.
Muñoz Molina, Antonio. *Los misterios de Madrid*. Seix Barral, 1992.
Navas, Teresa. "La ciutat metropolitana (1897–1939)." *Retrat de Barcelona*, vol. 2, Centre de Cultura Contemporània – Publicacions de l'Ajuntament de Barcelona, 1995, pp. 25–55.
Nervi, Mauro. "The Kafka Project: Reise August/September 1911." http://www.kafka.org/index.php?rtbas1911.
Nora, Pierre. *Les lieux de la mémoire*. Gallimard, 1997.
Novalis. *Schriften Erster Band: Das Dichterische Werk; Herausgegeben von Paul Kluckhohn und Richard Samuel*. Verlag W. Kohlhammer, 1928.
Nuzzo, Gianfranco. "Eugenio Montale o della Classicità senza classicismo." *Aevum: Rassegna di scienze storiche linguistiche e filologiche*, vol. 78, no. 1, 2004, pp. 163–77.
Ollé, Manel. "Societat Anònima." *Avui Cultura*, 5 April 2006.
Ordine, Nuccio. *L'utilità dell'inutile: Manifesto*. Bompiani, 2013.
Orlando, Francesco. *Obsolete Objects in the Literary Imagination: Ruins, Relics, Rarities, Rubbish, Uninhabited Places, and Hidden Treasures*. Yale UP, 2006.
Orlando, Francesco. *Per una teoria freudiana della letteratura*. Einaudi, 2015.
Ors, Eugeni d'. *Obra catalana completa: Glosari 1906–1910*. Editorial Selecta, 1950.
Ortín, Marcel. *La prosa literària de Josep Carner*. Quaderns Crema, 1996.

Ortín, Marcel. "Sovint les esperances que fan d'esquer són com la bella dama del tramvia." *Reduccions revista de poesia*, no. 39, 1988, pp. 51–70, https://raco.cat/index.php/Reduccions/article/view/47017.

Paisse. "Qualsevol nit pot sortir el sol." http://paisse.blogspot.it/2009/10/qualsevol-nit-pot-sortir-el-sol.html.

Panati, Charles. *Extraordinary Origins of Everyday Things*. William Morrow, 1987.

Parcerisas, Francesc. "La quotidianitat en la poesia de Vicent Andrés Estellés." *Vicent Andrés Estellés*, edited by Ferran Carbó, Enric Balaguer, and Lluís Messeguer, Alacant, IIFV, 2004, pp. 49–64.

Pardo Bazán, Emilia. *La cocina española antigua*. Renacimiento, 1913.

Pardo Bazán, Emilia. *La cocina española moderna*. Renacimiento, 1914.

Pardo Bazán, Emilia. *De siglo a siglo (1896–1901)*. Vol. 24 of *Obras completas*, http://bdh-rd.bne.es/viewer.vm?id=0000247055&page=1.

Pardo Bazán, Emilia. "En tranvía." *Cuentos completos*, vol. 2, edited by Juan Paredes Núñez, Fundación Pedro Barrié de la Maza Conde de Fenosa, 1990, pp. 97–104.

Peñalta Catalán, Rocío. "Dos espacios multiculturales de Madrid: Lavapiés y la Puerta del Sol" *Ángulo Recto: Revista de estudios sobre la ciudad como espacio plural*, vol. 2, no. 2, 2010, pp. 111–17, http://www.ucm.es/info/angulo/volumen/Volumen02-2/varia05.htm.

Perec, Georges. *L'infra-ordinaire*. Seuil, 1989.

Perec, Georges. *Je me souviens*. Fayard, 2013.

Perec, Georges. *Penser/Classer*. Hachette, 1985.

Pérez, Gato. "La rumba de Barcelona." https://www.viasona.cat/grup/gato-perez/carabruta/la-rumba-de-barcelona.

Pérez García, Norberto. "Dos tópicos clásicos en la poesía española del último tercio del siglo XX." *Cuadernos de filología clásica: Estudios latinos*, no. 14, 1998, pp. 301–9.

Pérez Turrent, Tomás, and José de la Colina. *Buñuel por Buñuel*. Plot Ediciones, 1993.

Petrarca, Francesco. *Canzoniere*. Edited by Gianfranco Contini, with a note by Daniele Ponchiroli. Einaudi, 1975.

Petroski, Henry. *The Evolution of Useful Things*. Alfred A. Knopf, 1992.

Petroski, Henry. *The Pencil: A History of Design and Circumstance*. Alfred A. Knopf, 1989.

Picon, Gaëtan. *Panorama de la nouvelle littérature française: Introduction, illustrations, documents*. Gallimard, 1960.

Picornell, Mercè. *Continuïtats i desviacions: Debats crítics sobre la cultura ctalana en el vèrtex 1960/1970*. Lleonard Muntaner, 2013.

Pijoan, Josep. *El meu don Joan Maragall*. Llibreria Catalònia, 1927.

Pike, David. *Metropolis on the Styx: The Underworlds of Modern Urban Culture, 1800–2001*. Cornell UP, 2007.

Pike, David. *Subterranean Cities: The World beneath Paris and London, 1800–1945.* Cornell UP, 2005.
Pla, Josep. *Notes del capvesprol*. Destino, 1979. Vol. 35 of *Obres completes*.
Pla, Josep. *Viaje a pie*. Destino, 1949.
Pla, Josep. *Viaje en autobús*. Destino, 2003.
Pla, Xavier. Introducción. *Viaje en autobús*, by Josep Pla, edited by Xavier Pla, Cátedra, 2021.
Pla, Xavier. "Recepció i contradicció en les edicions de *Vida privada*." *Vida privada*, by Josep M. Sagarra, Barcelon Proa, 2007, pp. 385–409.
Polizzotti, Mark. *Bob Dylan's Highway 61 Revisited*. Bloomsbury, 2006.
Pound, Ezra. "In a Station of the Metro." *Poetry: A Magazine of Verse*,, vol. 2, no. 2, 1913, p. 12.
Poyato Sánchez, Pedro. "La transducción al cine de la novela Tristana: La forma cinematográfica buñueliana." *Signa*, vol. 23, 2014, pp. 731–52.
Pratt, Mary Louise. *Imperial Eyes: Travel Writing and Transculturation*. Routledge, 1992.
Prévert, Jacques. *Œuvres complètes*, vol. 1. Édition d'Arnaud Laster et Danièle Gasiglia-Laster. Illustrations by Jacqueline Duhême, André François, Elsa Henriquez, and Ylla. Bibliothèque de la Pléiade 388. Gallimard, 1992.
Prévert, Jacques. *Paroles*. Gallimard, 2007.
Proust, Marcel. *Du côté de chez Swann*. Gallimard, 1973. Vol. 1 of *À la recherche du temps perdu*.
El próximo Oriente. Directed by Fernando Colomo, Sogecine, Fernando Colomo P.C, 2006.
Puig i Ferreter, Joan. *Camins de Franca*. Edicions 62, 1982.
"Qualsevol nit pot sortir el sol." TV3 Videos. 18 November 2011.
Quintana i Trias, Lluís. "Didàctica dels carrers: Barcelona al segle XX." *Llegint pedres, escrivint ciutats: Unes visions literàries de la ciutat*, edited by Carles Carreras and Sergi Moreno, Pagès editors, 2009, pp. 23–35.
Quintana i Trias, Lluís. "Joan Maragall, el Pla Jaussely i la Reforma de 1908 a la ciutat de Barcelona." *Zeitschrift für Katalanistik*, no. 20, 2007, pp. 149–65.
Quintana i Trias, Lluís. "El *Viaje en autobús* de José(p) Pla ¿Una incorporación al canon?" *Revista Hispánica Moderna*, vol. 59, no. 1–2, 2006, pp. 119–40.
Ray, Krishnendu. *The Ethnic Restaurateur*. Bloomsbury Academic, 2016.
Revell, Graeme. "Interview with J.G. Ballard." http://www.researchpubs.com/products-page-2/excerpt-from-interview-with-j-g-ballard-by-graeme-revell/.
Reyes, Alex. "Gran Metropolitano de Barcelona." http://www.granmetro.es/.
Riba, Carles. "Josep Carner, *Les planetes del Verdum*." *Obres completes*. Edicions 62, 1967, p. 95.
Riera i Bertran, Joaquim. "De Barcelona a Gràcia: Viatge en tramvia." *Quadres costumistes urbans del vuit-cents*, edited by Enric Cassany, Edicions 62, 1987, pp. 171–84.

Robert, Jean. *Notre Métro*. Jean Robert, 1983.
Robert, Robert. "El passeig de Gràcia." *Un tros de paper I*, Editorial Catalana, 1920, pp. 15–22.
Rodoreda, Mercè. *In Diamond Square*. Translated by Andrew Bush, Virago Press, 2014.
Rodoreda, Mercè. *La Plaça del Diamant*. Club Editor, 1962.
Rojals, Marta. *Primavera, estiu, etcetera*. La Breu, 2011.
Rojek, Chris. *Ways of Escape: Modern Transformations in Leisure and Travel*. Macmillan, 1993.
Romo, R, and J.M. Gil. "Ethnic Identity and Dietary Habits among Hispanic Immigrants in Spain." *British Food Journal*, vol. 114, no. 2, 2012, pp. 206–23.
Rosenthal, David H. *Postwar Catalan Poetry*. Bucknell UP, 1991.
Rothman, Joshua. "What Is the Struggle in *My Struggle*?" *New Yorker*, 28 May 2014. https://www.newyorker.com/books/page-turner/what-is-the-struggle-in-my-struggle.
Rousseau, Jean-Jacques. *Les Confessions – Autres textes autobiographique*. Gallimard, 1959. Vol. 1 of *Œuvres complètes*.
Rousset, Jean. *Leurs yeux se rencontrèrent*. J. Corti, 1981.
Rusiñol, Santiago. *Coses viscudes*. *Obres Completes*, Editorial Selecta, 1956, pp. 211–43.
Sagarra, Josep M. de. *Cançons d'abril i de novembre*. La Revista, 1918.
Said, Edward. *Orientalism*. Routledge and Kegan Paul, 1978.
Salmerón i Bosch, Carles. *El metro de Barcelona: Història del ferrocarril metropolità de Barcelona*. Términus, 1992.
Salvador, Vicent. "Vicent Andrés Estellés: La difusió d'una veu poètica valenciana." Lletra, http://lletra.uoc.edu/ca/autor/vicent-andres-estelles/detall.
Salvat-Papasseit, Joan. *Epistolari de Joan Salvat-Papasseit*. Edited by Amadeu-J. Soberanas i Lleó. Edicions 62, 1984.
Salvat-Papasseit, Joan. *Obra completa: Poesia i prosa*. Cercle de lectors, 2006.
Sánchez-Llama, Íñigo. "The Representation of Gastronomy and Urbanity in the Journalistic Articles of Mariano José de Larra (1808–1837): Analysis of a Modern Perspective." *The Gastronomical Arts in Spain: Food and Etiquette*, edited by Frederick A. de Armas and James Mandrell, 2022, pp. 202–24.
Sánchez Vidal, Agustín. *Sol y sombra: De cómo los españoles se apearon de las mayúsculas de la historia dotándose de vida cotidiana*. Planeta, 1990.
Sansot, Pierre. *Poétique de la ville*. Armand Colin, 1996.
Sanz Villanueva, Santos. "Pla o ol inventario de una época." *Viaje en autobús*, by Josep Pla, Fundación Wellington – Editorial Destino, 2003, pp. 17–52.
Sapegno, Maria Serena. "Costanti, varianti, 'arbitrarietà' dell'interprete: Gli 'oggetti' di Orlando e la critica tematica." *Critica del testo*, vol. 1, no. 3, 1998, pp. 1009–34.

Schlegel, Friedrich. *Charakteristiken und Kritiken I (1796–1801). Kritische Ausgabe seiner Werke*, vol. 2, edited by Hans Eichner. Verlag Ferdinand Schoningh, 1975.

Schorske, Carl E. *Wien: Geist und Gesellschaft im Fin de siècle*. S. Fischer, 1982.

Schwandl, Robert. *Metros in Spain: The Underground Railways of Madrid, Barcelona, Valencia and Bilbao*. Capital Transport Publishing, 2001.

Seaton, A.V. "Guided by the Dark: From Thanatopsis to Thanatourism." *International Journal of Heritage Studies*, vol. 1, no. 2, 1996, pp. 234–44.

Seigworth, Gregory J. "Banality for Cultural Studies." *Cultural Studies*, vol. 14, no. 2, 2000, pp. 227–68.

Sella Montserrat, Joan. "Ignacio Doménech: El cocinero escritor." *Cocina de recursos (Deseo mi comida)*, by Ignasi Domènech, Ediciones Trea, 2011, pp. 9–24.

Sempronio. *Aquella entremaliada Barcelona*. Editorial Selecta, 1978.

Seneca, "Moral letters to Lucilius / Letter 28." https://en.wikisource.org/wiki/Moral_letters_to_Lucilius/Letter_28.

Sennett, Richard. *Together: The Rituals, Pleasures and Politics of Cooperation*. Yale UP, 2012.

Serés, Francesc. *De fems i de marbre*. Quaderns Crema, 2007.

Serés, Francesc. *La força de la gravetat*. Quaderns Crema, 2006.

Serés, Francesc. *La pell de la frontera*. Quaderns Crema, 2004.

Serés, Francesc. "Pilans i parets mestres." *El País: Quadern*, 16 June 2005, p. 2.

Serrahima, Maurici. "La prosa de Josep Carner." *Obres completes*, by Josep Carner, Editorial Selecta, 1968, pp. 807–25.

Serrallonga Joan, Manuel Santirso, and Just Casas. *Vivir en Guerra: La zona leal a la república (1936–1939)*. Servei de Publicacions de la Universitat Autònoma de Barcelona, 2013.

Shakespeare, William. "As You Like It." *Complete Works*, edited by Jonathan Bate and Eric Rasmussen, The Modern Library, 2007, pp. 472–525.

Shakespeare, William. "The Tempest." *Complete Works*, edited by Jonathan Bate and Eric Rasmussen, The Modern Library, 2007, pp. 1–51.

Sheringham, Michael. *Everyday Life: Theories and Practices from Surrealism to the Present*. Oxford UP, 2006.

Shields, Rob, "Henri, Lefebvre." *Key Thinkers on Space and Place*, edited by Phil Hubbard and Rob Kitchin, Sage Publications, 2004, pp. 279–85.

Shields, Rob, "Henri Lefebvre." *Profiles in Contemporary: Social Theory*, edited by Anthony Elliot and Bryan S. Turner, Sage Publications, 2001, pp. 226–37.

Shklovsky, Viktor. *Viktor Shklovsky: A Reader*. Edited and translated by Alexandra Berlina. Bloomsbury, 2016.

Shōnagon, Sei. *The Pillow Book*. Translated by Meredith McKinney, Penguin Books, 2006.

Shove, Elizabeth, Frank Trentmann, and Richard Wilk, editors. *Time, Consumption and Everyday Life: Practice, Materiality and Culture (Cultures of Consumption)*. Berg, 2009.

Simmel, Georg. "The Metropolis and Mental Life." *On Individuality and Social Forms: Selected Writings*, edited by Donald N. Levine, U of Chicago P, 1971, pp. 324–39.
Sinclair, Iain. *London Orbital*. Penguin Books, 2002.
Sisa, Jaume. "Qualsevol nit pot sortir el sol." https://www.viasona.cat/grup/sisa/qualsevol-nit-pot-sortir-el-sol/qualsevol-nit-pot-sortir-el-sol.
Skiveren, Tobias. "On Good Listening, Postcritique, and Ta-Nehisi Coates' Affective Testimony." *Affect Theory and Literary Critical Practice: A Feel for the Text*, edited by Stephen Ahern, Palgrave Macmillan, 2019, pp. 217–33.
Solà-Morales, Ignasi de. *Gaudí*. Edicions Polígrafa, 1983.
Soldevila i Balart, Llorenç. *La Nova Cançó (1958–1987): Balanç d'una acció cultural*. L'Aixernador Edicions, 1993.
Solé, Albert. "Rodalies: Mal servei i inversió nul·la." *Ara*, 21 March 2015, pp. 4–6.
Solnit, Rebecca. *Wanderlust: A History of Walking*. Viking, 2000.
Solsona, Ramon. *Línia Blava*. Columna, 2004.
Sontag, Susan. "Model Destinations." *Times Literary Supplement*, 22 June 1984, p. 699.
Sontag, Susan. *On Photography*. AnchorBooks, 1990.
Spang, Rebecca. *The Invention of the Restaurant: Paris and Modern Gastronomic Culture*. Harvard UP, 2001.
Spitzer, Leo. *La enumeración caótica en la poesía moderna*. Translated by Raimundo Lida, Imprenta y Casa editora "Coni," 1945. Colección de estudios estilísticos, Anejo 1, Facultad de Filosofía y Letras, Instituto de Filología.
Starobinski, Jean. "Les cheminés et les clochers." *Magazine littéraire*, no. 280, 1990, pp. 26–7.
Steinrück, Martin. "Robbe-Grillet and Hesiod: Catalogue as Anti-epic." *CentoPagine*, no. 5, 2011, pp. 1–12.
Sterne, Lawrence. *A Sentimental Journey*. Oxford UP, 2008.
Stewart, Kathleen. *Ordinary Affects*. Duke UP, 2007.
Stewart, Kathleen. "Worlding Refrains." *The Affect Theory Reader*, edited by Melissa Gregg and Gregory J. Seigworth, Duke UP, 2010, pp. 339–53.
Stiegler, Bernd. *Traveling in Place: A History of Armchair Travel*. U of Chicago P, 2013.
Stone, Philip. "A Dark Tourism Spectrum: Towards a Typology of Death and Macabre Related Tourist Sites, Attractions and Exhibitions." *Tourism*, vol. 54, no. 2, 2006, pp. 145–60.
Subirana, Jaume. "Batejar carrers, imaginar països: Raons del nomenclàtor, de Víctor Balaguer a Barcelona '92." *Journal of Iberian and Latin American Studies*, vol. 198, no. 3, 2014, pp. 1–14.
Symbioz. "Les stations oubliées." https://www.symbioz.net/index.php?id=34.
Tamen, Miguel. "A Walk about Lisbon." *Iberian Cities*, edited by Joan Ramon Resina, Routledge, 2001, pp. 33–40.
Tarlow, E.P. *Dark Tourism: The Appealing "Dark" Side of Tourism and More*. Elsevier Butterworth, 2005.
Tarpino, Antonella. *Geografie della memoria: Case, rovine, oggetti quotidiani*. Einaudi, 2008.

Tausiet, Antonio. "Los grandes inventos del TBO." http://seronoser.free.fr/tausiet/tbo/TBO.htm.

Terán Reyes, Francisco Javier. "Las cartillas de racionamiento, los fielatos y el estraperlo." *Aljaranda: Revista de estudios tarifeños*, no. 86, 2012, pp. 10–19.

Theroux, Paul. "Subway Odyssey." *New York Times*, 31 January 1962, section 6.

"This American Life." Chicago Public Media. http://www.thisamericanlife.org/about/about-our-radio-show.

Thomas, Sophie. *Romanticism and Visuality: Fragments, History, Spectacle*. Routledge, 2007.

Thompson, Carl. *The Suffering Traveller and the Romantic Imagination*. Clarendon Press / Oxford UP, 2007. Oxford English Monographs.

Thompson, Zoë. *Urban Constellations: Spaces of Cultural Regeneration in Post-Industrial Britain*, Ashgate Publishing, 2015.

Thrift, Nigel. *Non-representational Theory: Space/Politics/Affect*. Taylor and Francis, 2008.

Todó, Joan. *L'horitzó primer*. L'Avenç, 2013.

Tolliver, Joyce. "Colonialism, Collages, and Thick Description: Pardo Bazán and the Rhetoric of Detail." *Imagined Truths: Realism in Modern Spanish Literature and Culture*, edited by L.C. Mary and V. Margot, University of Toronto Press, 2019, pp. 215–35.

Torres García: Museo Nacional Centro de Arte Reina Sofía, Junio/Agosto 1991. Ministerio de Cultura, Sociedad Estatal Quinto Centenario, 1991.

Tosta, Antonio Luciano de A. "Exchanging Glances: The Streetcar, Modernity, and the Metropolis in Brazilian Literature." *Chasqui: Revista de literatura latinoamericana*, vol. 30, no. 2, 2001, pp. 35–52.

Tracy, Walter. *Letters of Credit, a View of Type Design*. Gordon Fraser, 1986.

Tren de Sarrià. *150 anys: 1863–2013*. http://www.fgc150.cat.

Trogloditas, Loquillo y Los. "Avenida de la Luz." *El Ritmo del Garaje / Donde Estabas Tu en el 77*, Warner Music Spain, 2008.

Tucholsky, Kurt. *Gesammelte Werke, 3: 1929–32*. Rowohlt, 1960.

Tuffley, David. "Commentary on Desolation Row." *The Bob Dylan Commentaries Exploring the Art of Bob Dylan*. http://www.bobdylancommentaries.com/commentary-on-desolation-row-by-david-tuffley/.

Turner, Victor. *The Ritual Process: Structure and Anti-Structure*. Aldine Publishing, 1969.

Ugarte, Michael. "Soy tú. Soy él: African Immigration and Otherness in the Spanish Collective Conscience." *Studies in Twentieth and Twenty-First Century Literature*, vol. 30, no. 1, 2006, pp. 170–89, doi:doi.org/10.4148/2334-4415.1620.

Ullman, Joan Connelly. *The Tragic Week: A Study of Anticlericalism in Spain, 1875–1912*. Harvard UP, 1968.

Urbain, Jean Didier. *Ethnologue mais pas trop*. Payot, 2003.

Uzcanga, Francisco. *La eternidad de un día: Clásicos del periodismo literario alemán (1823–1934)*. Acantilado, 2016.

Valls, Mireia. *La Barcelona subterrània*. Editorial Mediterrània, 2012.
Vaneigem, R. *The Revolution of Everyday Life* [1967]. Rebel Press, Left Bank Books, 1994.
Vázquez Montalbán, Manuel. *Carvalho gastronómico: La cocina del mestizaje; Viaje por las cazuelas de Murcia, Andalucía, Extremadura y Canarias*. Ediciones B, 2002.
Vázquez Montalbán, Manuel. *La cocina del mestizaje: Viaje por las cazuelas de Murcia, Andalucía, Extremadura y Canarias*. Ediciones B, 2002.
Vázquez Montalbán, Manuel. "De Portbou a Hendaya: La vuelta a la cazuela de España." *El País*, 2000.
Vázquez Montalbán, Manuel. *Los mares del sur*. Planeta, 1979.
Vilarós, Teresa M. *El mono del desencanto: Una crítica cultural de la transición española, 1973–1993*. Siglo veintiuno, 1998.
Villena, Luis Antonio de. *Fin de siglo (el sesgo clásico en la última poesía española)*. Visor, 1992.
Viridiana. Directed by Luis Buñuel, Unión Industrial Cinematográfica, 1961.
Virilio, Paul. *The Aesthetics of Disappearance*. Semiotext(e), 1991.
La Voie lactée. Directed by Luis Buñuel, Greenwich Film Productions (Paris) / Société de production: Medusa Produzione (Rome), 1969.
Wagner, Geoffrey. *Selected Poems of Charles Baudelaire*. Grove Press, 1974.
Walser, Robert. *The Walk*. Profile Books, 2013.
Wang, Yanning. *Reverie and Reality: Poetry on Travel by Late Imperial Chinese Women*. Lexington Books, 2014.
Weisz, Pierre. "Langage et imagerie chez Jacques Prévert." *French Review*, vol. 43, no. 1, 1970, pp. 33–43.
Williams, Rosalind. *Notes on the Underground: An Essay on Technology, Society, and the Imagination*. MIT Press, 2008.
Wood, Gareth. "Sugaring the Pill: Emilia Pardo Bazán, John Stuart Mill, and the Biblioteca de la Mujer." *Bulletin of Spanish Studies*, vol. 95, no. 6, 2018, pp. 605–31, doi:10.1080/14753820.2018.1498232.
World Happiness Report, 2020. https://worldhappiness.report/ed/2020/#read.
Wright, Benjamin. "The Weird and Wonderful Literary World of Bob Dylan." *Highbrow Magazine*, 2014.
Xalabarder, María. "La Avenida de la Luz, una calle subterránea en Barcelona." *Estudios geográficos*, vol. 60, no. 236, 1999, pp. 487–512.
Yanagi, Soetsu. *The Beauty of Everyday Things*. Penguin Modern Classics, 2019.
Yates, Alan. *Una generació sense novel·la?* Edicions 62, 1975.
Young, Liam. "On Lists and Networks: An Archaeology of Form." *Amodern 2: Network Archaeology*, http://amodern.net/article/on-lists-and-networks/#pdf.
Zhou Wu, Quan. *Gazpacho agridulce: Una autobiografía chino-andaluza*. Astiberri Ediciones, 2015.
Zhu, D., J. Wang, P. Wang, and H. Xu. "How to Frame Destination Foodscapes? A Perspective of Mixed Food Experience." *Foods*, vol. 11, no. 1706, 2022, doi: https://doi.org/10.3390/.

Index

Toronto Iberic

1 Anthony J. Cascardi, *Cervantes, Literature, and the Discourse of Politics*
2 Jessica A. Boon, *The Mystical Science of the Soul: Medieval Cognition in Bernardino de Laredo's Recollection Method*
3 Susan Byrne, *Law and History in Cervantes'* Don Quixote
4 Mary E. Barnard and Frederick A. de Armas (eds.), *Objects of Culture in the Literature of Imperial Spain*
5 Nil Santiáñez, *Topographies of Fascism: Habitus, Space, and Writing in Twentieth-Century Spain*
6 Nelson R. Orringer, *Lorca in Tune with Falla: Literary and Musical Interludes*
7 Ana M. Gómez-Bravo, *Textual Agency: Writing Culture and Social Networks in Fifteenth-Century Spain*
8 Javier Irigoyen-García, *The Spanish Arcadia: Sheep Herding, Pastoral Discourse, and Ethnicity in Early Modern Spain*
9 Stephanie Sieburth, *Survival Songs: Conchita Piquer's* Coplas *and Franco's Regime of Terror*
10 Christine Arkinstall, *Spanish Female Writers and the Freethinking Press, 1879–1926*

11 Margaret E. Boyle, *Unruly Women: Performance, Penitence, and Punishment in Early Modern Spain*
12 Evelina Gužauskytė, *Christopher Columbus's Naming in the* diarios *of the Four Voyages (1492–1504): A Discourse of Negotiation*
13 Mary E. Barnard, *Garcilaso de la Vega and the Material Culture of Renaissance Europe*
14 William Viestenz, *By the Grace of God: Francoist Spain and the Sacred Roots of Political Imagination*
15 Michael Scham, Lector Ludens*: The Representation of Games and Play in Cervantes*
16 Stephen Rupp, *Heroic Forms: Cervantes and the Literature of War*
17 Enrique Fernandez, *Anxieties of Interiority and Dissection in Early Modern Spain*
18 Susan Byrne, *Ficino in Spain*
19 Patricia M. Keller, *Ghostly Landscapes: Film, Photography, and the Aesthetics of Haunting in Contemporary Spanish Culture*
20 Carolyn A. Nadeau, *Food Matters: Alonso Quijano's Diet and the Discourse of Food in Early Modern Spain*
21 Cristian Berco, *From Body to Community: Venereal Disease and Society in Baroque Spain*
22 Elizabeth R. Wright, *The Epic of Juan Latino: Dilemmas of Race and Religion in Renaissance Spain*
23 Ryan D. Giles, *Inscribed Power: Amulets and Magic in Early Spanish Literature*
24 Jorge Pérez, *Confessional Cinema: Religion, Film, and Modernity in Spain's Development Years, 1960–1975*
25 Joan Ramon Resina, *Josep Pla: Seeing the World in the Form of Articles*
26 Javier Irigoyen-García, *"Moors Dressed as Moors": Clothing, Social Distinction, and Ethnicity in Early Modern Iberia*
27 Jean Dangler, *Edging toward Iberia*
28 Ryan D. Giles and Steven Wagschal (eds.), *Beyond Sight: Engaging the Senses in Iberian Literatures and Cultures, 1200–1750*
29 Silvia Bermúdez, *Rocking the Boat: Migration and Race in Contemporary Spanish Music*
30 Hilaire Kallendorf, *Ambiguous Antidotes: Virtue as Vaccine for Vice in Early Modern Spain*
31 Leslie J. Harkema, *Spanish Modernism and the Poetics of Youth: From Miguel de Unamuno to* La Joven Literatura
32 Benjamin Fraser, *Cognitive Disability Aesthetics: Visual Culture, Disability Representations, and the (In)Visibility of Cognitive Difference*
33 Robert Patrick Newcomb, *Iberianism and Crisis: Spain and Portugal at the Turn of the Twentieth Century*

34 Sara J. Brenneis, *Spaniards in Mauthausen: Representations of a Nazi Concentration Camp, 1940–2015*
35 Silvia Bermúdez and Roberta Johnson (eds.), *A New History of Iberian Feminisms*
36 Steven Wagschal, *Minding Animals in the Old and New Worlds: A Cognitive Historical Analysis*
37 Heather Bamford, *Cultures of the Fragment: Uses of the Iberian Manuscript, 1100–1600*
38 Enrique García Santo-Tomás (ed.), *Science on Stage in Early Modern Spain*
39 Marina S. Brownlee (ed.), *Cervantes'* Persiles *and the Travails of Romance*
40 Sarah Thomas, *Inhabiting the In-Between: Childhood and Cinema in Spain's Long Transition*
41 David A. Wacks, *Medieval Iberian Crusade Fiction and the Mediterranean World*
42 Rosilie Hernández, *Immaculate Conceptions: The Power of the Religious Imagination in Early Modern Spain*
43 Mary L. Coffey and Margot Versteeg (eds.), *Imagined Truths: Realism in Modern Spanish Literature and Culture*
44 Diana Aramburu, *Resisting Invisibility: Detecting the Female Body in Spanish Crime Fiction*
45 Samuel Amago and Matthew J. Marr (eds.), *Consequential Art: Comics Culture in Contemporary Spain*
46 Richard P. Kinkade, *Dawn of a Dynasty: The Life and Times of Infante Manuel of Castile*
47 Jill Robbins, *Poetry and Crisis: Cultural Politics and Citizenship in the Wake of the Madrid Bombings*
48 Ana María Laguna and John Beusterien (eds.), *Goodbye Eros: Recasting Forms and Norms of Love in the Age of Cervantes*
49 Sara J. Brenneis and Gina Herrmann (eds.), *Spain, the Second World War, and the Holocaust: History and Representation*
50 Francisco Fernández de Alba, *Sex, Drugs, and Fashion in 1970s Madrid*
51 Daniel Aguirre-Oteiza, *This Ghostly Poetry: History and Memory of Exiled Spanish Republican Poets*
52 Lara Anderson, *Control and Resistance: Food Discourse in Franco Spain*
53 Faith S. Harden, *Arms and Letters: Military Life Writing in Early Modern Spain*
54 Erin Alice Cowling, Tania de Miguel Magro, Mina García Jordán, and Glenda Y. Nieto-Cuebas (eds.), *Social Justice in Spanish Golden Age Theatre*
55 Paul Michael Johnson, *Affective Geographies: Cervantes, Emotion, and the Literary Mediterranean*

56 Justin Crumbaugh and Nil Santiáñez (eds.), *Spanish Fascist Writing: An Anthology*
57 Margaret E. Boyle and Sarah E. Owens (eds.), *Health and Healing in the Early Modern Iberian World: A Gendered Perspective*
58 Leticia Álvarez-Recio (ed.), *Iberian Chivalric Romance: Translations and Cultural Transmission in Early Modern England*
59 Henry Berlin, *Alone Together: Poetics of the Passions in Late Medieval Iberia*
60 Adrian Shubert, *The Sword of Luchana: Baldomero Espartero and the Making of Modern Spain, 1793–1879*
61 Jorge Pérez, *Fashioning Spanish Cinema: Costume, Identity, and Stardom*
62 Enriqueta Zafra, *Lazarillo de Tormes: A Graphic Novel*
63 Erin Alice Cowling, *Chocolate: How a New World Commodity Conquered Spanish Literature*
64 Mary E. Barnard, *A Poetry of Things: The Material Lyric in Habsburg Spain*
65 Frederick A. de Armas and James Mandrell (eds.), *The Gastronomical Arts in Spain: Food and Etiquette*
66 Catherine Infante, *The Arts of Encounter: Christians, Muslims, and the Power of Images in Early Modern Spain*
67 Robert Richmond Ellis, *Bibliophiles, Murderous Bookmen, and Mad Librarians: The Story of Books in Modern Spain*
68 Beatriz de Alba-Koch (ed.), *The Ibero-American Baroque*
69 Deborah R. Forteza, *The English Reformation in the Spanish Imagination: Rewriting Nero, Jezebel, and the Dragon*
70 Olga Sendra Ferrer, *Barcelona, City of Margins*
71 Dale Shuger, *God Made Word: An Archaeology of Mystic Discourse in Early Modern Spain*
72 Xosé M. Núñez Seixas, *The Spanish Blue Division on the Eastern Front, 1941–1945: War, Occupation, Memory*
73 Julia Domínguez, *Quixotic Memories: Cervantes and Memory in Early Modern Spain*
74 Anna Casas Aguilar, *Bilingual Legacies: Father Figures in Self-Writing from Barcelona*
75 Julia H. Chang, *Blood Novels: Gender, Caste, and Race in Spanish Realism*
76 Frederick A. de Armas, *Cervantes' Architectures: The Dangers Outside*
77 Michael Iarocci, *The Art of Witnessing: Francisco de Goya's* Disasters of War
78 Esther Fernández and Adrienne L. Martín (eds.), *Drawing the Curtain: Cervantes's Theatrical Revelations*
79 Emiro Martínez-Osorio and Mercedes Blanco (eds.), *The War Trumpet: Iberian Epic Poetry, 1543–1639*
80 Christine Arkinstall, *Women on War in Spain's Long Nineteenth Century: Virtue, Patriotism, Citizenship*

81 Ignacio Infante, *A Planetary Avant-Garde: Experimental Literature Networks and the Legacy of Iberian Colonialism*
82 Enrique Fernández, *The Image of Celestina: Illustrations, Paintings, and Advertisements*
83 Maryanne L. Leone and Shanna Lino (eds.), *Beyond Human: Decentring the Anthropocene in Spanish Ecocriticism*
84 Jennifer Nagtegaal, *Politically Animated: Non-fiction Animation from the Hispanic World*
85 Anton Pujol and Jaume Martí-Olivella (eds.), *Catalan Cinema: The Barcelona Film School and the New Avant-Garde*
86 Matthew Bailey, *Speaking Truth to Power: The Legacy of the Young Cid*
87 Hilaire Kallendorf, *Perilous Passions: Ethics and Emotion in Early Modern Spain*
88 Anita Savo, *Portraying Authorship: Juan Manuel and the Rhetoric of Authority*
89 Robin M. Bower, *In the Doorway of All Worlds: Gonzalo de Berceo's Translation of the Saints*
90 Daniel Holcombe and Frederick A. de Armas (eds.), *Bodies Beyond Labels: Finding Joy in the Shadows of Imperial Spain*
91 Susan Larson (ed.), *Comfort and Domestic Space in Modern Spain*
92 Heather Jerónimo, *Performing Parenthood: Non-Normative Fathers and Mothers in Spanish Narrative and Film*
93 Enric Bou, *Cartographies of Disappearance: Vestiges of Everyday Life in Literature*

Milton Keynes UK
Ingram Content Group UK Ltd.
UKHW020709021124
450386UK00001B/2/J